THE LETTERS OF
Benjamin Franklin &
Jane Mecom

MEMOIRS OF THE
AMERICAN PHILOSOPHICAL SOCIETY
HELD AT PHILADELPHIA
FOR PROMOTING USEFUL KNOWLEDGE

VOLUME 27

THE LETTERS OF
Benjamin Franklin &
Jane Mecom

EDITED WITH AN INTRODUCTION BY

CARL VAN DOREN

PUBLISHED FOR

THE AMERICAN PHILOSOPHICAL SOCIETY

BY PRINCETON UNIVERSITY PRESS

1950

THE DEVICE ON THE TITLE PAGE
WAS MADE FROM STENCILS ORIGINALLY PURCHASED BY FRANKLIN
IN PARIS. THESE STENCILS ARE NOW IN THE POSSESSION
OF THE AMERICAN PHILOSOPHICAL SOCIETY.

PRINTED IN THE UNITED STATES OF AMERICA BY PRINCETON
UNIVERSITY PRESS AT PRINCETON, NEW JERSEY

PREFACE

THE American Philosophical Society in 1944 acquired from Dr. A. S. W. Rosenbach a collection of letters from Benjamin Franklin to his sister Jane Mecom which had been sold in London in 1928. Many of these letters had never been published, or published in full. The Society already had numerous letters from Jane Mecom to Franklin, and plans were made for the publication of both sides of the correspondence. Investigation showed that there were elsewhere still other unpublished or uncollected letters between brother and sister. Out of this has grown the present volume, which undertakes to bring together the whole surviving correspondence between the two, with additional letters between each of them and members of the other's household; all the known letters by Jane Mecom to whomever written; and the known papers concerned with her affairs, such as her "Book of Ages" and her last will and testament, with accounts of her administration of her husband's estate and of the inventory and disposition of the property which she held when she died.

Instead of the 33 letters from Franklin to Jane Mecom in the latest collected edition of his writings, 98 are here collected, 30 of them never before published at all, and several others never published in full or with accurate texts. Besides the 37 letters from Jane Mecom to Franklin or his wife which were published in 1859, 31 more from her to her brother or to various relatives and friends are here published for the first time, with several others for the first time in full. Franklin now appears much more fully in letters to his sister than ever before, and Jane Mecom at last takes her true place in history.

The appearance of these letters in print has been slow and piecemeal. William Temple Franklin in his edition of his grandfather's *Private Correspondence* (London, 1817), from 1818 called *Volume* II of *Memoirs of the Life and Writings of Benjamin Franklin, LL.D.*, printed two letters, in part, from Franklin to Jane Mecom. William Duane, who had married the widow

v

of Benjamin Franklin Bache, in *The Works of Dr. Benjamin Franklin* (Philadelphia, 6 vols., 1808-1818) added a few others. Jared Sparks in *A Collection of Familiar Letters and Miscellaneous Papers of Benjamin Franklin now for the first time published* (Boston, 1833) included twenty letters from Franklin to his sister, along with parts of several others without mention of her name. In Sparks's *The Works of Benjamin Franklin* (Boston, 10 vols., 1836-1840) most, but not all, of the letters to Jane Mecom in *Familiar Letters* were reprinted, and some further letters were added. John Bigelow in *The Works of Benjamin Franklin* (New York, 10 vols., 1887-1888) added still further letters. Albert Henry Smyth in *The Writings of Benjamin Franklin* (New York, 10 vols., 1905-1907) omitted a few of the letters from Franklin to his sister which had been printed by Sparks and Bigelow, and added the full text of one more.

In the meantime an important series of Franklin's letters had been lost sight of, though Sparks, while he was preparing the *Familiar Letters*, had seen "about 25 original letters to Mrs Mecom" which were then in the possession of Mrs. Caleb Loring of Boston. On August 6, 1833, after the publication of the book, he explained his omission of them in a letter, now in the American Philosophical Society, to Dr. Franklin Bache, son of Benjamin Franklin Bache. The letters had been given, Sparks wrote, to Mrs. Loring "by her mother, who received them from Mrs Mecom. Under these circumstances Mrs Loring has scruples about letting them be printed, though she permitted extracts to be taken. Now I think she would give up these letters to Mrs Mecom's granddaughters, if they were to make a proper application. Will you be the medium of this application? It is desirable that the letters should be printed entire, & if the granddaughters obtain them, they would no doubt give copies for this purpose. You can write to *Caleb Loring, Esq* on the subject, who is Mrs Loring's husband. They are highly respectable people. I wish you would keep my name entirely out of the matter, as I have made unavailing efforts to get the letters.

The only objection is Mrs Loring's conscientious scruples, as to her right to part with them unless it be to the descendants of Mrs Mecom. I hope you will undertake the affair, & let me know as soon as it is decided."

Whether or not Dr. Bache made the application, the affair was not decided, and it remains something of a mystery. Mrs. Loring seems to have been Love Hawk (or Hawkes), who had been first married to William Rand in 1800 and then to Caleb Loring in 1811. Unfortunately her mother has not been identified. The Boston *Directory* for 1796 lists an Elkanah Hawkes, private schoolmaster in Hanover Street; the *Directory* for 1789 an Abigail Hawkes in North Street and a Levi Hawkes, tinplate worker, in Fish Street. All of these lived in the North End, not too far from Jane Mecom's house. The mother of Love Hawk (or Hawkes) may have done Jane Mecom some service which she acknowledged with the gift of her letters from Franklin, as in her will she acknowledged the service of Elizabeth Lathrop with the gift of the Wedgwood medallion of Franklin; but no close connection between Jane Mecom and any Mrs. Hawkes has been traced.

The only granddaughters of Jane Mecom surviving in 1833 were the daughters of Benjamin Mecom, and there is nothing to show whether or not the letters went to them. In any case, the course of the letters is obscure from the date of Sparks's appeal to Dr. Bache down to December 18, 1928, when they were sold at Sotheby's in London as the property of Robert Harcourt, Esq., to find their way back to the United States and eventually to the American Philosophical Society. Sparks, in *Familiar Letters*, printed enough excerpts from the letters then Mrs. Loring's to make it certain that they were the same as Robert Harcourt's later.

Since the letters came back to the United States several of them have been printed in the *Library Bulletin 1944* of the American Philosophical Society; Carl Van Doren, *Benjamin Franklin's Autobiographical Writings*, 1945; Nathan G. Goodman, *A Benjamin Franklin Reader*, 1945; William G. Roelker, *Benjamin Franklin and Catharine Ray Greene*, 1949.

Less attention has been paid to the letters *from* Jane Mecom than to those *to* her. In 1859 William Duane, a great-grandson of Franklin, published *Letters to Benjamin Franklin, from his Family and Friends 1751-1790* in a small edition of 10 copies quarto and 250 octavo. The 37 letters included from Jane Mecom to Benjamin or Deborah Franklin then belonged to Dr. Franklin Bache. Duane omitted from some of the letters various passages which the family preferred to withhold from the public, in particular all that dealt with the insanity of Jane Mecom's sons Benjamin and Peter. These letters are now in the American Philosophical Society.

Scattered letters from both Franklin and his sister have appeared in books or periodicals, and James Parton in his *Life and Times of Benjamin Franklin* (2 vols., 1864) made excellent use of the letters in Duane's collection. These however need not here be itemized, since the date and place of the first appearance of each of the Franklin-Mecom letters or papers, whenever or wherever printed, are given in the notes preceding individual pieces in this volume. Certain excerpts first printed by Mr. Roelker in the Franklin-Greene correspondence are not included for the reason that his volume appeared too late for changes in these notes.

The letters and papers are printed from the original manuscripts when these are known to exist; otherwise, they are printed from the best available copy or the earliest printed version. The printed text follows the manuscript as closely as possible, except that the long *ʃ* is set as *s* and the superior letters dropped to the line and the periods under them omitted. Jane Mecom's manuscript is hard to reproduce with assurance. Her capital letters are often indistinguishable from the others, and she capitalized words that she wished to emphasize, whether they began a sentence or not. The stroke she was accustomed to make at the end of a sentence, while in form clearly a comma, may have seemed to her to serve for a period. She frequently omitted words, or repeated the same word, without noticing or correcting it. Her spelling was often phonetic and was by no means consistent. But she wrote, as Franklin told her in one of his letters, "better, in my Opinion, than most American Women" of her time. The errors which appear in her writing in this volume are her own, not the printer's. Since the address pages of both her letters and her brother's are usually mere addresses, they are not here printed except when they bear additional information—some of which is incorporated in the notes when it calls for explanation.

Franklin and his sister, writing about domestic affairs, could assume a great deal of knowledge which they had in common but which later readers naturally do not have. It has seemed necessary to go into detail in the notes to the individual pieces. The major sources for these details are the various volumes of the Boston Registry Records (printed as *Report of the Record Commissioners of the City of Boston*) containing births, marriages, baptisms, deaths, town records, selectmen's minutes; the files of *The New England Historical and Genealogical Register*; contemporary newspapers, genealogies, local histories, diaries, biographies, learned journals, and probate records: all which are cited, except when they are only routine statistics, in the individual notes. No statement has been made without the support of a document believed trustworthy, and no conjecture, though here or there offered, is masked as a statement. Taken together the notes make large additions to what has hitherto been known about Franklin in relation not only to Jane Mecom but also to many members of their families and circles in Boston, Rhode Island, and Philadelphia.

Acknowledgments are due, and are gratefully made, to the following societies or libraries, besides The American Philosophical Society, which have given permission to print Franklin-Mecom papers from the manuscripts in their collections or to use information derived from them: The Library of Harvard University, The Harvard School of Business Administration, The New England Historic Genealogical Society, The Massachusetts Historical Society, The Library of The Boston Athenæum, The Society for the Preservation of New England Antiquities, The Yale University Library, The New-York Historical Society, The New York Public Library, The New Jersey Historical Society, The Princeton University Library, The Library Company of Philadelphia, The Historical Society of Pennsylvania, and the Henry E. Huntington Library, San Marino, California. Specific acknowledgments are made in the notes to individual letters in the volume.

It is a pleasure to give grateful thanks for assistance on special points to Henry Adams, Julian P. Boyd, Carl Bridenbaugh, Marjorie Lyle Crandall, Verner W. Crane, Esther Forbes, Maud H. Greene, Gertrude D. Hess, Frederic R. Kirkland, William E. Lingelbach, Elizabeth Marion, William G. Roelker, Francis S. Ronalds, Andrew Ross, Clara Shackleton, Sarah P. Stetson, John Van Doren, and Nicholas B. Wainwright; and to the friendly staff of the Rare Book Room at the New York Public Library.

Mary Barnard has indispensably assisted in transcribing the manuscripts, searching (with ingenuity and imagination) among countless sources for material in the annotations, reading the proofs, and compiling the Index.

CONTENTS

CONTENTS

CONTENTS

CONTENTS

CONTENTS

SEPTEMBER 19, 1785, TO FEBRUARY 17, 1794

CONTENTS

CONTENTS

ILLUSTRATIONS

THE LETTERS OF
Benjamin Franklin &
Jane Mecom

INTRODUCTION

THE earliest but one and the latest but one of the surviving letters of Benjamin Franklin were to his sister Jane, to whom through sixty-three years he wrote more letters than he is known to have written to any other person. "You know you were ever my peculiar favourite," he told her on his twenty-first birthday, when she was not quite fifteen but was soon to be married to Edward Mecom. She remained Franklin's favorite. He was the youngest of the ten Franklin brothers, she the youngest of the seven sisters. Outliving all the others by nearly twenty-four years, the two came to love one another "proportionably more" as they stood more and more alone. No difference in their fortunes and no distance between them could alter or diminish their affection. Their final years were their most devoted and congenial, particularly after he had returned from France, and letters could go back and forth between her in Boston and him in Philadelphia full of confidences and family news and old recollections and new assurances.

Though their correspondence throws fresh light on Franklin at many points, it does more for Jane Mecom, who rises in living colors to be the heroine of the story. The misfortunes and hardships of her youth and middle years, her griefs and losses, could never break, or long bend, her resilient spirit. While she loved to live in the sun of her brother's glory, she was herself too a person, more like him than she knew. She was the only one of the many Franklins who can be compared with him.

No identified likeness of her has been preserved. When she was fifteen, and Franklin had not seen her for nearly three years, he told her he had heard she was "grown a celebrated beauty." When she was thirty-eight he wrote their mother only that he hoped his own daughter would turn out to be "an ingenious sensible, notable, and worthy Woman, like her aunt Jenny." When Jane Mecom was forty-seven her brother teased her for being one of the "fatfolks." In her letters she never mentioned her own appearance except to write, on his eighty-fourth birthday, that though she was six years younger than he, she looked that much older.

Nor are there surviving letters from her to furnish anything like a personal account of her early life, and almost nothing of her life before she was fifty. The letters she wrote then have been lost or, it appears in some cases, suppressed or destroyed because of what they revealed about her two "unhappy sons": Peter, who was deranged and helpless from his early manhood to his death at about forty; and Benjamin, who at forty-four, on the day the Hessians arrived at Burlington, New Jersey, escaped from the restraint under which he had to be kept, wandered off, and was never heard of again. In the obscure fifty years of Jane Mecom's life she bore twelve children, and buried five of them. In spite of thoughtful assistance from her brother in Philadelphia, she was always poor and overworked, as well as harried and bereft. It is a wonder that she lived at all; it is a greater wonder that she lived on, for her last fifteen years with only one child left, ageless in spirit and curiosity.

The story of her obscure half-century has to be pieced together from deficient and not always trustworthy records, which have never before been ransacked with her as the subject of inquiry. Here a name, there a date, elsewhere a characteristic or incident: these are the main sources, and they have to be enlarged out of general knowledge of the Franklin family and of their Boston and Philadelphia, with the support, in many cases, of reasonable conjecture. Her later letters, disappointingly, seldom speak of her earlier years. She did not normally live in her past, and hers was no past to wish to live in.

She was born on March 27, 1712, the year her father bought a house at the corner of Union and Hanover Streets and supposedly the year he moved his family there from the rented house in Milk Street where he had lived, certainly since 1691, possibly since he first arrived in Boston from England in October 1683. Though the new house was bought in January and Jane born late in March, it is not certain in which of the houses she was born, but in any case she cannot have remembered the one in Milk Street. She was thinking of the other when she wrote her brother on August 16, 1787: "It was indeed a lowly dwelling we were brought up in, but we were fed plentifully, made comfortable with fire and clothing, had seldom any contention among us, but all was harmony; especially between the heads, and they were universally respected, the most of the family in good reputation. This is still happier living than multitudes enjoy."[1] In this she confirms Franklin's own recollection of his father's household. She was too young to remember the time her brother paid too much for his whistle when he was seven. She may have remembered some of the other childish incidents he made famous in his *Autobiography*, but she did not recall them in any letter. Nor is there evidence that either of the two English translations of that book from the French which were published in London in 1793 ever reached her in Boston before she died in May 1794.

She is not mentioned by name in the *Autobiography*; not a word has come down about her childhood or schooling. As the favorite of a brother who afterwards could not remember when he learned to read, she must have shared his taste for reading. In her later years she read whenever she could find time for it. When Franklin ran away from Boston in September 1723 she was only eleven. His letter of January 6, 1727, may well have been the first he ever wrote her. Their old friend Captain Isaac Freeman had met Franklin in Philadelphia and had told him that Jane was beautiful and was soon to be married. If she replied to Franklin's letter, at least it was not followed by regular correspondence between them. In the summer of 1730 he told another sister in a letter that for two years he had not received a line from any relation in Boston except his father and mother. He had heard of the death of Jane's first child, who died on May 18 of that year, "and should be mighty glad of a

---

[1] Since Jane Mecom's letters in the body of this volume often look eccentric in their original spelling and punctuation, it seems fair to her in the Introduction to modernize the text and let her appear as the direct and picturesque writer she was.

Line from her." The earliest letter she is known to have written him is the missing one of May 26, 1731, to which he replied in June. In it she told him of the birth of a second child, born two months before she wrote. Small tradesmen's sons and daughters in that age exchanged few letters. Franklin and his sister were not yet aware how fond they were of each other. He was working day and night to establish his business, and she was busy with her marriage.

Her marriage turned out to be unfortunate. Edward Mecom was eight years older than his wife, but in all other respects apparently inferior. He was colorless, made no mark, and left no name. By trade a saddler, he had his shop in a room of the house in which they lived, like most small tradesmen in Boston. On March 6, 1729, about two years after his marriage, he was sworn in as one of the clerks of the market. The next year he became a communicant of the Brattle Street Church, which he and his wife attended. Besides these mentions of him, and the papers on the administration of his intestate estate, his recorded career appears only in connection with his father's family or his wife's.

He was the son of Duncan Mecom and his second wife Mary "Hore" (Hoar). The name sounds Scottish and seems to have been pronounced *May*com. It is variously spelled, in the Boston records, Macomb, Macome, Maicum, Makcum, Maycom, Maycomb, Maycombe, Maycum, Meacam, Mecum. Jane and Edward Mecom invariably spelled it in the form now accepted.

They were married on July 27, 1727, by the Reverend William Cooper of the Brattle Street Church. On June 8, 1729, Cooper baptized the first of their children, "Josiah Maycum," born on the 4th. On May 19, 1730, the minister was at the burial of "Mr Mecum's child," which had died the day before. Then for twenty-two years the exact records of the family's history are chiefly the births of eleven children, with the deaths of two of them, as set down by Jane Mecom herself in the "Book of Ages" which she began probably in 1762 and discontinued five years later. Edward was born March 29, 1731;

Benjamin, December 29, 1732; Ebenezer, May 2, 1735; Sarah, June 28, 1737; Peter Franklin, May 13, 1739; John, March 31, 1741; another Josiah, March 26, 1743; Jane, April 12, 1745; James, July 31, 1746, died November 30; Mary, February 29, 1748; Abiah, August 1, 1751, died April 23, 1752. All of the eleven names except Edward were names of Jane Mecom's parents or brothers or sisters, though Edward Mecom also had a sister Mary and a brother Ebenezer.

Till after the death of Jane Mecom's mother, the Mecom family lived with or near her parents, whom she cared for in their old age. Josiah and Abiah Franklin's "estate" was sooner or later actually four wooden houses, "tenements" as they were then called, of which the largest, on the southeast corner of Hanover and Union Streets, was the family residence, and the smaller buildings to the south, facing west in Hanover Street, were occupied by tenants or lodgers. In one or more of these tenements Jane Mecom seems to have earned a part of the Mecom income by taking boarders.

She had begun this as early as 1742, on the evidence of Captain Hugh Ledlie's letter to Franklin of May 22, 1787, inquiring about "your Sister Mrs Jane Mecom, who formerly lived near the blue bell & afterwards near the orange tree at whose house I lodged when at Boston from the Year 1742 in your honored Mother's life time until the year 1772." Ledlie had received, he said, "many past favors & acts of kindness" from Jane Mecom, but had not been able to hear of her or her family for a dozen years.[2]

The Blue Ball (not "bell" as Ledlie called it) was the tradesman's sign for Josiah Franklin's shop. The Orange Tree was a well-known inn at the foot of Hanover Street four streets away. Franklin's letter to his sister of June 28, 1756, speaks of her having moved, since their mother's death in 1752, to a "dearer"

[2] Letters in this Introduction to Franklin from persons besides Jane Mecom are in manuscript in the American Philosophical Society. All his letters to her and all hers to him or others are in the body of the present volume. Letters from Franklin to other persons may be found, in chronological order, in Smyth, *Writings of Benjamin Franklin*.

house: that is, one with a higher rent. A letter from Jonathan Williams Sr. of August 27, 1770, after Jane Mecom's return from her long visit to Philadelphia, told her brother that "Aunt Mecom" was now "well Settled in the Old place though almost a N[ew] House"—presumably near the Blue Ball again.

These few facts sketch the outline of Jane Mecom's career as boarding-house keeper in Hanover Street. A few others indicate the character of her establishment. Captain Ledlie, officer of a Connecticut regiment, at times a police officer, a land speculator, and a promoter for a new road to be built from Hartford to Boston, was only occasional in his visits. So were the country members of the Massachusetts Assembly who boarded with her during the sessions in Boston. Too many of her boarders were needy members of her own family. After the death of her daughter Sarah, Sarah's husband William Flagg came with his four small children to live with his mother-in-law. Two of the children died in her house, and Josiah at four was lamed for life by a fall. Colonel Joseph Ingersoll, whose first wife had been a niece of Jane Mecom but was now dead, put his two daughters there. Sarah Bowles, another boarder, was the widowed stepdaughter of Jane Mecom's sister Sarah Davenport. "Poor Sarah," a dependent without a surname in the letters, was now and then well enough to wash the dishes, but much of the time in her later years could not leave her room. Jane Mecom's ailing or shiftless sons from time to time quartered themselves on their mother, and John brought his wife. There is a wistful note in something Jane wrote in December 1770 to Deborah Franklin about Captain Isaac All in Philadelphia. "I wish I had such a constant boarder to pay me three dollars a week the year round. I could then do pretty well." But for thirty years no such good fortune came her way.

That her colorless husband was long a sick man appears from her letter of September 28, 1765, to Deborah Franklin, just after his death. He had been called, the widow said, "out of this troublesome world where he had enjoyed little and suffered much by sin and sorrow." Did she mean his sin or the sin of others? Though it is not clear, she seems to have been implying some taint in the Mecom blood which was thought responsible for the early death, insanity, instability, or uncertain health of so many of their children.

But when the sons were growing up, their mother was brisk with plans to have them taught self-supporting, self-respecting trades. Edward, almost as dim as his father in the record, and also a saddler, was ailing from his youth. He was able only to get married at twenty-four, have a child at twenty-five, and die at twenty-seven. Ebenezer became a baker, like his uncle James Davenport, had a shop for a time at Cape Ann (Gloucester), did not marry, and died at twenty-seven. Peter learned his grandfather's trade of soap-boiling from his uncle John Franklin, who in his will of January 1756 left the youth a suit of clothes and a half-share of "the Utensils belonging to my Business" to come to him after the death of John Franklin's widow. But in five years Peter had grown too languid to want to do anything; and two years after that Benjamin Franklin, in a letter of November 28, 1763, to Jonathan Williams Sr., asked that the rent of a house which Franklin owned in Boston be set aside "to assist my Sister Mecom in the maintenance of her unhappy Son." Peter was then twenty-four, but he lived fifteen years longer, boarded by a woman somewhere in the country. He was "no comfort to any one nor capable of enjoying any himself," his mother wrote on February 14, 1779, after Peter's death. John Mecom, following the trade of his cousin William Homes, became a goldsmith, but he too turned out to be sickly and unstable. He left Boston for New York, was married in New Jersey at twenty-four, wandered off to the West Indies leaving his wife with Deborah Franklin in Philadelphia, returned and took his wife to his mother's house, and died in New Jersey at twenty-nine. Josiah, the second of that name born to the Mecoms, began work as a saddler, but was on a whaling vessel at twenty-seven and contemplating marriage. In May 1775 he enlisted in a Massachusetts regiment, but served only two months. By November 29 of that year his mother, as she

[9]

wrote from Philadelphia to Catharine Greene, had heard of the death of "poor Josiah since I came here, but by what means I am not informed." He had lived to be thirty-two.

Benjamin seemed the most promising of the Mecoms, and he was apprenticed at twelve or so to James Parker the printer, Franklin's partner in New York. Then began a dreary chapter that lasted for thirty years. All of Benjamin Mecom's letters to his mother and to his uncle are missing, without much doubt deliberately destroyed. The early part of the story has to be drawn almost wholly from Franklin's letters to Jane Mecom. There it appears that Benny, as mother and uncle called him, was restless from the first, as full of schemes as his uncle had been in youth, but without any of his uncle's steady judgment. In the late summer of 1752, before Benny was twenty, the uncle sent the youth to Antigua in the Leeward Islands, where a partner of Franklin had been publishing *The Antigua Gazette*. It was a hasty move. Benny was as restless under his uncle's direction as he had been under James Parker's. "I fear," Franklin wrote to his sister on November 30 when the first letters had come back from Antigua, "I have been too forward in cracking the shell, and producing the chick to the air before its time." After four years Benny wished to leave Antigua. He talked of going to London, but instead came back to Philadelphia late in 1756, and then on to Boston.

About September 1757 he married Elizabeth Ross of Elizabeth, New Jersey, whom he had met, probably, during his days as apprentice in New York. In Boston he was enterprising but injudicious. He undertook to print, for the booksellers, 30,000 copies of *The New-England Psalter* on terms so low that he made no profit from the venture. He showily wore coat, hat, wig, and gloves while working at the press. At the end of six years, in spite of much activity, he saw no further hope in Boston and removed his printing press to New York. But while in Boston he had done one notable thing, by printing in 1758 *Father Abraham's Speech*, the first separate issue of Franklin's famous preface to the year's *Poor Richard* which has since come to be known as *The Way to Wealth*. With it Benjamin Mecom included "Poor Richard's Description of his Country Wife Joan," the first known printing of Franklin's drinking song called later *My Plain Country Joan*. In the first number of *The New England Magazine*, which Benjamin initiated in August 1758, he printed Franklin's famous epitaph on his parents on the tomb "lately erected" in Boston. When Benjamin in 1760 reprinted his uncle's Canada pamphlet, *The Interest of Great Britain considered with regard to Her Colonies And the Acquisitions of Canada and Guadaloupe*, of which the authorship had been a guarded secret in London, the nephew did not hesitate to ascribe the work on the title page to "B - - - - - - n F - - - - - - n, LL.D."

In New York Benjamin was less successful than in Boston, and within a year went to New Haven, where he acted as James Parker's deputy as postmaster and revived *The Connecticut Gazette* which Parker had discontinued the year before. In New Haven Benjamin rapidly deteriorated in will and energy. He failed to clear his accounts with Parker or even to answer Parker's letters, and in February 1767 had to be dismissed from the post office. Early the following year he made a further move, with the New Haven printing press and his wife and his children, to Philadelphia.

On May 20 of that year Deborah Franklin wrote to her husband in London: "I donte know wuther you have bin told that Cosin Benney Mecome and his Lovely wife and five Dafters is come hear to live and work Jurney worke I had them to Dine and drink tee yisterday they have a little garle a servent so the Company was 8 in all you yoused to love Betsey as I did I Cold wish she had better Looke [luck] but god rules the world and I submit." And Franklin replied on December 21: "I cannot comprehend how so very sluggish a Creature as Ben. Mecom is grown, can maintain in Philadelphia so large a Family. I hope they do not hang upon you: for really as we grow old and must grow more helpless, we shall find we have nothing to spare."

A letter from William Franklin to his father, fragmentary and wanting the date but apparently of that same year, reported: "Coz. Ben Mecom is starving at Philadelphia, and would have been, I suppose, in Gaol by this Time, if it had not been for the Assistance my Mother and I have afforded him & his Family. Goddard would have given 35/ a Week to him if he would have work'd as other Journeymen do, but he insisted on coming & going just as he pleas'd, on which Goddard and he quarrel'd & parted. He has likewise been at work at some Printing Offices in Philada but cannot agree with any Body, and is I believe now without any Imploy. His Pride and Laziness are beyond any Thing I ever knew, and he seems determin'd rather to sink than to strike a Stroke to keep his Head above Water. He has had Seventeen Pounds of me, & what of my Mother I know not. He has got it in his Head that you intend to set him up again in a Printing Office on your return, & therefore seems determin'd to idle away his Time till your Arrival. In short, I look upon him to have a Tincture of Madness." (William Franklin added, about another of the Mecom sons: "I have likewise assisted his Bror John with Money, who has turn'd out as bad as Ben, & gone and quarter'd himself & wife on his Mother at Boston.")

Early in 1769 Benjamin Mecom began the publication, on Franklin's printing press brought from New Haven to Arch Street, of a small newspaper called *The Penny Post*, which appeared three times a week but seems to have run for only nine numbers. He had, on whatever terms, to go back to journeywork with William Goddard, printer of the *Pennsylvania Chronicle*. This may not have been till after September 11, 1770, when Benjamin sent a petition, by his wife, to the Mayor, Recorder, and Aldermen of Philadelphia, saying that for more than two years he had been unable to find "Constant Employment" at his own "Business" and applying for a license for his wife and himself to sell "spirituous Liquors by small Measure, at a House where we have now lived in almost a quarter, where such Sale has been continued. We are not fond of the Prospect it affords, farther than as it may contribute to support a number of young growing Children." The license was not granted. Another child, named John Ross, was born to the Mecoms on October 24, 1771, though not baptized till August 22, 1772.

About 1774 the Mecom family moved to Burlington, where William Franklin lived, and where Benjamin got employment as journeyman with Isaac Collins. This did not last long. On July 19, 1776, J. M. Lawrence and William Smith of Burlington wrote to Franklin at Philadelphia. "At the Request of Mrs Mecum, who has been an Inhabitant of this City for some time past and behav'd with Prudence and Industry, We take the Liberty to Inform you that her husband's Conduct is such, as to render her Scituation Disagreeable, and at times very Dangerous he being often Depriv'd of his Reason and likely to become very Troublesome to the Inhabitants. If a Place in the Hospital of Philada can be Procur'd or any other way of Confineing wch may be thought more Eligeable she begs your Assistance And that you wo'd be pleas'd to favor us with an Answer on the Subject of this Letter."

In the tumult of that July of the Declaration of Independence Franklin undertook the support of another deranged nephew. On December 11, when Benjamin Franklin was on his triumphant way from Nantes to Paris, and Jane Mecom with the Baches had fled to the country from threatened Philadelphia, Benjamin Mecom was on his way, whatever it may have been, to some bewildered, desperate, anonymous, unrecorded death, probably not far from Burlington.

Almost four years before, on February 14, 1773, Franklin had refused to appoint still another nephew, Josiah Davenport, to the post office in Philadelphia. "I have been hurt too much," the uncle bluntly explained, "by endeavouring to help Cousin Ben Mecom. I have no Opinion of the Punctuality of Cousins" —calling his nephews cousins in the manner of the time. Deborah Franklin had been more patient. Benjamin Mecom had written her pleasant letters from Antigua and Boston, and had named one of his daughters Deborah. At Benjamin Mecom's marriage his aunt had presented the couple with a set of silver spoons, ordered from his brother John. No doubt William Franklin was right in suspecting that his mother assisted Benjamin and his family in Philadelphia, and this may have gone on till her death in December 1774. She was kind to John Mecom and hospitable to his wife. She was concerned for the fate of Peter, and asked about him in letters to his mother.

Unfortunate in her sons, Jane Mecom was hardly more fortunate in her daughters. Abiah, the youngest of all the children, died in infancy. Sarah, married at eighteen to William Flagg, had four children in six years, and herself died at twenty-seven. Mary (Polly), the youngest Mecom child that grew up, died at nineteen, "at my Nantucket," Jane Mecom wrote in her "Book of Ages," "at the house and under the most affectionate care of my dear friend Kezia Coffin."

About Polly's death her mother was more outspoken and more eloquent than about any other of her losses. In the surviving fragment of a missing letter dated October 23, 1767, she wrote to Franklin: "Sorrows roll upon me like the waves of the sea. I am hardly allowed time to fetch my breath. I am broken with breach upon breach, and I have now, in the first flow of my grief, been almost ready to say, 'What have I more?' But God forbid that I should indulge that thought, though I have lost another child. God is sovereign, and I submit." Then on December 1 she wrote again: "Oh, my brother, she was everything to me. Every word and every action was full of duty and respect, and I never looked on her but with pleasure except when she was sick or in trouble. How to make me easy and happy was what she had most at heart, and rather than give me pain she concealed her own infirmities and did so much more than she was able that it increased her disorder and hastened her end."

After Polly's death her mother made no further entries in her "Book of Ages." Almost ten years later, on August 18, 1777, she said in a letter to Franklin her saddest words about her fate as mother. "I think there was hardly ever so unfortunate a family. I am not willing to think it is all owing to misconduct. I have had some children that seemed to be doing well till they were taken off by death."

Yet even in her dark years she could rise above them, charming and lively. John Hughes, of Philadelphia, wrote from Boston on September 19, 1769, to his friend Deborah Franklin: "Upon my arival at Boston, I Did myself the pleasure to wait upon your Sister Meacum, And Altho, I am not very forward in Saluting Ladies, Yet it was not in my power to Refrain taking the Sister of my Good friend in my Arms & Saluting her, perhaps the Good Lady, may think that as a stranger, I have been Rather Rude, And as I Expect you will have the pleasure of Seeing her this fall, before I shall, I beg you will Excuse me to the Good Lady, if any part of my Conduct has been thought to free, but at the same time I must Confess, that it wou'd be Laying a Great Constraint upon my Temper, not to Act in the same Manner, was I to meet with another Sister of Docr Franklins." Far from taking offense, Jane Mecom in a letter to Deborah Franklin of September 14 had already said she had been "in hopes to have had the company of your friend Mr. Hughes" on her trip to Philadelphia, "but he talks of not going till November, which will be so late I shall not dare to venture."

Apparently in September she set out for the first extended journey of her life, intending to stop on the way to visit her son John at New Brunswick and her nephew William Franklin at Burlington, and to see her son Benjamin and his family at Philadelphia as well as Deborah Franklin and her household, which now included her daughter Sarah and her husband Richard Bache and their infant son named Benjamin Franklin after his grandfather. On October 4 Deborah Franklin wrote to her husband in London that "Antey Macom" was expected at Burlington. On December 13 Deborah wrote that "Sister," now in Philadelphia "is verey a greeabel to me and makes everey thing very plesant to me and we air as happy as we Cold expeckte to as in your absenes."

The plight of John Mecom, sick in New Brunswick, and of

Benjamin, stranded with his family in Philadelphia, was depressing, agonizing. Jane Mecom's fall down the stone steps that led to the garden at the Franklin house in Philadelphia made her lame for months. What friends of the Franklin circle she met are named only in her letters after she returned to Boston. But those letters have more cheerful gossip than any she ever wrote. In Philadelphia, in the household of her famous brother even in his absence, she had been delighted with the kind of "conversation" she so often spoke of missing in Boston —in that crowded boarding house with its occasional transients and its persistent poor relations.

In January 1770 she said in a missing letter to her brother that she might settle in Philadelphia, and on March 15 he replied that he would be happy to have her near him. But instead she returned in the summer to Boston, and during the next four years wrote no letters that have been preserved except two to her sister-in-law and one to her brother, though he regularly mentioned letters he had received. Her letters for the period may have been merely lost, or they may have been destroyed because of their revelations. In those years however her fortunes were considerably improved through the "bounty" of her brother.

Another nephew, Samuel Hall, who was married to a daughter of her brother James and was also a printer, owed Franklin some money of which for seven years neither principal nor interest had been paid. Franklin, who rarely pressed a debtor for payment, now made an exception, for the sake of his sister, and on January 17, 1772, told her he had requested Jonathan Williams Sr. to force some action. Williams brought suit, with the legal assistance of John Adams, and on February 15, 1773, could report that "Hall or rather Halls Friends" had produced the first £100 sterling of the debt and had promised to pay the remainder within twelve months. The total, paid not quite so soon as promised, came to £152 1s. 6d. sterling (202.15.4 Massachusetts money), the largest sum Jane Mecom had ever had at one time. A "middling family" could then live in Boston on

fifty pounds a year. Moreover, Franklin in 1773 made a present
of fifty pounds to Jane Mecom's daughter Jane, on her marriage
that year to Peter Collas: the amount to be laid out "in bedding
or such other furniture as my sister shall think proper to be
given the new-married couple towards housekeeping."

Relieved in the matter of her daughter's marriage, and with
capital in hand, Jane Mecom promptly wanted "to be doing,"
as Williams reported on February 15. Through Williams she
sent Franklin fifty pounds with an invoice "of such Goods as
she Wants to make a beginning with." Franklin on July 7 replied that the trunk, of millinery materials, had been shipped.
Margaret Stevenson, his landlady in Craven Street, had under-
taken "the Purchasing them with great Readiness and Pleasure." But when they arrived in Boston they did not entirely suit
Jane Mecom, perhaps because of the difference in fashion between Boston and London. On October 17 Williams wrote to
Franklin that his sister could probably in the future "Supply
herself with every sort of Goods" from Boston merchants "on
better Terms than Can be imported from England."

Her stock of course was small, and her shop presumably a
room in her house. But she was busy and happy in this venture
till the outbreak of the Revolution drove her out of Boston in
May 1775 and obliged her to leave behind, and eventually lose,
some of her stock and much of her household goods.

During these same years 1773 to 1775 she had another cause
for satisfaction in Abigail Royall, the "poor little delicate neighbor" whom Jane Mecom mentioned in her letter of May 14,
1775, with whom, she wrote on July 14, she had lived "so
happily" for two years. Abigail Royall, daughter of William
Tailer who had been lieutenant governor of Massachusetts, was
the widow of Jacob Royall, who died in June 1773. The Royalls
had lived in a "large genteel Brick Dwelling House" in Orange
Street, which was mortgaged for more than its value when
Jacob Royall died. If Jane Mecom, who continued for the next
two years to live in Hanover Street, lived with Abigail Royall
and her family, this appears to mean that Mrs. Royall and her

companion, Elizabeth Moncrieff, boarded then with Jane Mecom, her chief if not her sole boarders. This could mean less
crowding, and more regular payment, and better conversation
—as well as the pleasure of managing the little shop.

To offset these advantages there was the disadvantage of
living in a city full of British troops put there to keep a hostile
populace in order. No writer then, or since, has given a more
graphic account of the apprehension felt by quiet citizens in
those tense months than Jane Mecom wrote to her brother on
November 3, 1774.

"At present we have a melancholy prospect for this winter
at least. The town's being so full of profligate soldiers and many
such officers, there is hardly four and twenty hours passes without some fray amongst them, and one can walk but a little way
in the street without hearing their profane language. We were
much surprised the other day upon hearing a tumult in the
street, and looking out saw a soldier, all bloody, damning his
eyes but he would kill every inhabitant he met; and pressing
into a shop opposite us, with his bayonet drawn, bursting
through the glass door, and the man of the house pushing him
out, and he, to do what mischief he could, dashing the china and
earthenware, which stood on the window, through the sashes
with the most terrible imprecations. The case, it seems, was he
perceived they sold liquor and went into the house demanding
some; but being refused he went into the closet and took out a
gun and said his commanding officer told him he might take
anything out of any house he had a mind to; upon which the
battle ensued, and the man and his servant were both very much
wounded. There were two of them (soldiers), but I saw but
one. A guard with an officer came and carried him away, and I
have heard nothing of him since. But this has made me more
timorous about what may be before winter is out."

The winter was hardly out when British soldiers in April
1775 marched to Lexington and Concord and encountered a
resistance that drove them back into Boston and began a war.
"The horror the town was in when the battle approached within

hearing, expecting they would proceed quite into town," Jane Mecom wrote to her brother on May 14; "the commotion the town was in after the battle ceased, by the parties coming in bringing their wounded men, caused such an agitation of mind I believe none had much sleep; since which we could have no quiet, as we understood our brethren without were determined to dispossess the town of the Regulars, and the General shutting up the town, not letting any pass out but through such great difficulties as were almost insupportable." But when, rising above those difficulties, she "got packed up what I expected to have liberty to carry out, intending to seek my fortune with hundred others not knowing whither," she was invited to take refuge with friends in Warwick, Rhode Island. With her granddaughter Jane Flagg and trunks and chests and millinery goods she made the anxious flight. The day she reached Providence she "had the unspeakable pleasure of hearing my dear brother was safe arrived at his own home. Blessed be God for all his mercies to me an unworthy creature!"

At Warwick she was the guest of William Greene and his wife Catharine Ray—the Caty Greene who had been Franklin's dear friend for twenty years. Some degree of cousinship bound all the refugees at the Greene house at Warwick. Catharine Greene's sister Judith Ray had married Thomas Hubbart of Boston, who was a stepson of John Franklin, brother of Jane and Benjamin. The Greenes of Warwick were close friends of the Hubbarts of Boston, and Jane Mecom had the sure affections of both families. She remained at Warwick till late in October, when Franklin, having gone to Cambridge with a committee of the Continental Congress to confer with Washington, commander in chief of the Continental Army, bought a carriage and took his sister back with him to Philadelphia.

That journey was the high point of Jane Mecom's life: as much conversation as she could desire, with the beloved brother whose conversation she valued above that of any other human being. With what absorption they talked appears from a letter to Catharine Greene written at Philadelphia on November 24.

"My seat was exceeding easy and journey very pleasant. My dear brother's conversation was more than an equivalent to all the fine weather imaginable. But I met with one mortification on the road. We had appointed to dine at Wethersfield, where Mrs. Hancock is, and had considerable talk about it; but we being engaged at that time in other conversation, the postillion drove a mile or two beyond before we discovered it, and I could not prevail with him to go back, so we did not dine till we put up for the night." They were in Philadelphia by November 15, where Franklin took up the ceaseless round of his public duties, and his sister devoted herself to sparing and protecting him, herself at ease in his household where another grandchild, Sarah, was born two days after Jane Mecom's letter. What if she had had "a bad fit of asthma" since her journey, and did not "sleep well on nights"?

For a year there was no occasion for letters between brother and sister, because they were together except during his expedition to Canada. Their friends William and Catharine Greene came to Philadelphia to visit them. Then in October 1776 Franklin left on his precarious voyage to France as commissioner from the United States, and Jane Mecom left with Sarah Bache and her child to what seemed a safer place in the country. Philadelphia was in danger as Boston had been. Once more back in Philadelphia in August 1777, Jane Mecom set out for Rhode Island again, in the company of Major Samuel Ward, fiancé of a daughter of William Greene. Major Ward went with a phaeton all the way to Philadelphia to bring Franklin's sister back. They could not go by way of New York, now occupied by the British, but had to travel at least as far north as Peekskill to cross the Hudson.

While Jane Mecom was in Philadelphia her granddaughter Jane Flagg, who had come out from Boston with the other refugees in May 1775, had been married to Elihu Greene, brother of Major General Nathanael Greene and a cousin of the William Greenes. Elihu Greene was one of several brothers who had a grist mill and forge in Potowomut, Rhode Island,

and another forge in Coventry not far away. For six years Jane Mecom spent most of her time with her granddaughter and her husband, at Coventry or Potowomut near Warwick, where the William Greenes lived. And again she lived through a chapter of misfortunes and losses and grief.

Jane Flagg, married at eighteen, had four children in six years and died at twenty-five. The first of her children, Celia, lived less than three months. The fourth, named Jane, died sixteen months old. After the death of Jane Flagg Greene, in April 1782, Jane Mecom was left with the bereaved husband and orphans and remained in charge of the household. On June 17, 1782, she wrote to Franklin: "Jenny, who died of a consumption, has left three sweet babes, one about two months old, a sorrowful husband, and a distressed grandmother. I enjoyed sweet peace in her pleasant conversation and great comfort in her dutiful and tender attention; was pleased with the hopes of the continuance of it the remainder of my life. But those comforts are vanished and a care devolved on me that I find myself unequal to: that of the children. The youngest is at nurse, but the other two require some person more lively and patient to watch over them continually. My dear child urged me earnestly not to leave them as long as I live, and though I made her no promise, I find the request to be very powerful. Her husband is desirous I should continue with him and treats me very respectfully [so] that I have no thoughts of removing at present; but circumstances may alter in time. I can't expect it to be otherways, as he is a young man." She could not give as many particulars as she would like: "my little ones are interrupting me every minute, and it is so hot I am not willing to trust them out of my sight."

Grieving and exhausted, she went to spend the winter with her daughter Jane Collas in Cambridge, then to go back in the summer of 1783 to Elihu Greene and his children, after the death of little Jane Greene in April. The following winter Jane Mecom returned to Cambridge and about January 1784 settled finally in Boston in the house Franklin owned there in Unity Street "at the North End."

Her correspondence with her brother was bound to be irregular while the war went on. Letters were lost or delayed by the action of vigilant British cruisers. On April 29, 1783, she wrote that she had had no letter from him for three years. Nor had he been able to write often. "If you do not hear from me so often as formerly," he said in his letter of April 22, 1779, "impute it to the too much Business upon my Hands and the Miscarriage of Letters, or any thing rather than a diminution of Affection."

In his missing letter of November 26, 1778, which she acknowledged on July 27, 1779, he said something which affected her more than the generous gift he had made her. "You say you wish we may spend our last days together. O my brother, if this could be accomplished it would give me more joy than anything on this side Heaven could possibly do. I feel the want of suitable conversation. I have but little here," in the household of Elihu Greene. "I think I could assume more freedom with you now and convince you of my affection for you. I have had time to reflect and see my error in that respect. I suffered my diffidence and the awe of your superiority to prevent the familiarity I might have taken with you, and ought, and your kindness to me might have convinced me would be acceptable; but it is hard overcoming a natural propensity, and diffidence is mine."

Though what she wrote after that does not show any notable increase of "freedom" on her part, she was probably less self-conscious than before. Her letters, more numerous than his, were full of her delight in every honor paid him, every good word spoken about him. When she heard the rumor that an attempt had been made on his life, and that he might not recover, she was in terror till she learned that the story was mere fabrication. All her own misfortunes and her family's could never make her feel envy of her brother's triumphs, which were hers too.

The death of her wandering son Josiah and of her distracted sons Benjamin and Peter did not end her current anxieties. There was Peter Collas, her daughter's husband. Collas had come to America from the Channel Island of Guernsey. Nothing seems to be known about him except the history of his bad luck. He was as unlucky as any Mecom. Absent on some voyage when hostilities broke out, Collas went to sea again in 1776, but was promptly captured by the British, held for months on a prison ship in New York, and exchanged in the summer of 1777. On August 15, 1778, Jane Mecom reported to her brother that Collas had "since been taken twice, once drove back in port by storm to refit." Now she supposed he had been taken again. She was right. Collas had lost his ship because he put too much confidence in his pilot, who said that a ship they encountered was an American privateer when in fact it was British. For eight days a prisoner on his native Guernsey, Collas was then removed to Southampton, and finally exchanged with Franklin's help. He set out for Boston again that summer and was once more taken by a Guernsey frigate and some property seized from him because it was of British manufacture. When he had recovered that, again with Franklin's help, Collas thought of another career that might be more profitable. He would learn how to make crown soap and carry on the Franklin trade.

Franklin wrote to Jonathan Williams Sr. with the proposal that Collas be encouraged in this undertaking. On July 29, 1779, Williams, who understood that the new business was to be partly for the benefit of Jane Mecom, replied that, while he was willing to do what he could, he had found it usually cost more to set a helpless person up in business as a means of supporting him than to support him outright. Collas went back to sea. On February 14, 1779, Jane Mecom counted four times since the beginning of the war that Collas had been taken. On October 23, 1781, after one successful voyage, he was again in the hands of the enemy in Halifax. After that he found it difficult to get a ship, was sick, lived for a time on borrowed money and his mother-in-law, took to carrying lumber along the

Nova Scotia-Maine coast, and became more and more seedy and unreliable till he faded out, as if off the edge, of the record. His wife continued to have faith in his heart if not in his head, convinced that he owed his misfortunes largely to his marrying into so unfortunate a family.

While Jane Mecom lived with the Baches and the Greenes, Franklin assumed that she was taken care of, but after her removal to Cambridge with the Collases he wrote her a missing letter which she acknowledged on April 29, 1783. In his letter he sent her the assurance of an income for the rest of her life— probably fifty pounds a year. Hereafter "I am enabled," she said, "to live at ease in my old age, after a life of care, labor, and anxiety."

Besides the money she was to have the use and occupancy of the house which had for years been rented for the support of her mad son Peter. The house had belonged to Franklin's eldest sister Elizabeth, who had inherited it from her first husband, Captain Joseph Berry, and had lived in it with her second, Captain Richard Douse, till his death and then to her own in 1759. She too had been assisted by Franklin in her old age. When she died the house had come to him, by foreclosure of a mortgage, as both she and he had understood in advance. Now it was to serve for his youngest sister. He wrote on June 17, 1784, that she might consider it her own; "and I hope you will be happy in it."

As houses then went in Boston, for any but the rich, this was a dwelling to be happy in. It was substantially built of brick, two stories with two rooms each, and smaller bedrooms in the garret. It had seven windows and faced the sun in Unity Street. "The house is pleasant for light and air," Jane Mecom wrote her brother on August 16, 1784, "having a large opening back and forward, as nobody has builded near it since you saw it." On May 29, 1786, she wrote: "I have this spring been new planking the yard, made new gate and new cedar doors, and am painting the front of the house to make it look decent that I may not be ashamed when anybody inquires for Dr. Franklin's sister in the neighborhood." On January 8, 1788, she was more detailed about her manner of life in Unity Street. "I have a good clean house to live in, my granddaughter constantly to attend me to do whatever I desire in my own way and in my own time. I go to bed early, lie warm and comfortable, rise early to a good fire, have my breakfast directly and eat it with a good appetite, and then read or work or what else I please. We live frugally, bake all our own bread, brew small beer, lay in a little cider, pork, butter, etc. and supply ourselves with plenty of other necessary provision daily at the door. We make no entertainments, but sometimes an intimate acquaintance will come in and partake with us the dinner we have provided for ourselves, and a dish of tea in the afternoon. And if a friend sits and chats a little in the evening, we eat our hasty pudding (our common supper) after they are gone."

In addition to Jane Mecom and her daughter Jane Collas, whose husband was often away, a third Jane, Benjamin Mecom's daughter, lived in the Unity Street house. Her father had wished his sister Jane to take the child when the Collases were married, in 1773, but this had not seemed possible at the time. She had come about ten years later, then about eighteen years old.

In that quiet household, with a depressed, complaining daughter and a youngish granddaughter, Jane Mecom had little suitable conversation. When she first moved from Hanover Street she was, as she said on August 16, 1784, "far from the few relations and acquaintances I have in town," but she made friends rapidly. She transferred her membership from Brattle Street to the Second (North) Church, which after the destruction of its old meeting house by the British during the occupation had merged its congregation with that of the New Brick Church in Hanover Street. The minister, John Lathrop, who lived in North Square, paid her considerate attentions. Captain Obadiah Rich, who lived in Unity Street, carried letters for her on his voyages to Philadelphia. Henry Roby, her next-door neighbor, had done the glazing for her house and took a friendly interest in it. That she was watched over by the neighborhood appears from her letter of December 17, 1786. "The snow has been so deep, and we no man in the house, that we might have been buried alive were it not for the care of some good neighbors who began to dig us out before we were up in the morning; and Cousin Williams came puffing and sweating as soon as it was possible, to see how we were and if we wanted anything, but thank God we had no want of anything necessary if we had been shut up a fortnight—except milk."

Some of the consideration shown Jane Mecom was of course in honor of her brother. Lafayette, visiting in Boston in 1784, took charge of her letter of October 21 to Franklin in Paris. The Marquis, she wrote, was "much honored and caressed among us." There is nothing to indicate that she met him, but there was always somebody to let her know if anybody in Boston was to go to Paris or Philadelphia. Whenever she received a letter from her brother some of her neighbors came at once to hear the news it might contain. Her talk was likely to be about him.

No record has come to light, for these years at Unity Street, of what she said about him. But there is a record of her conversation with Ezra Stiles at William Greene's house at Warwick on September 28, 1779. Stiles, already president of Yale but still technically pastor of the Second Congregational Church at Newport, owed his degree as doctor of divinity from the University of Edinburgh to the recommendation of Franklin, and was one of Franklin's correspondents. If Stiles and Jane Mecom talked of anything besides her brother and her family, at least there is nothing else in the notes Stiles took. She "shewed me," he wrote, Franklin's "Epitaph in his own handwrit[in]g," which Stiles said, and Jane may mistakenly have thought, was "composed 20 years ago." She told Stiles about Josiah Franklin, his coming to America, his marriage to "Mrs Abiah Foulgier," his children, the date of his death—which Jane Mecom either gave or Stiles set down wrongly as December 1, 1744. "The Doctor read his Bible at five years old,"

Stiles was pleased to note. She told of a "specimen" of the boy's "Ingenuity," that is, some verses which he wrote at seven and which were sent to his Uncle Benjamin in London; and of how the young poet received a letter "in 1713—'If the Buds are so precious what may we expect when the fruit is ripe?'." Actually, the uncle had written: "For, if the bud bear grain, what will the top?" But this had been when Jane Franklin was a year old. She told Stiles that her brother "learned Latin chiefly himself, tho' he went to the Latin School in Boston. Studied incessantly a nights when a boy. Addicted to all kinds of reading. His Brother James was a Printer in Bo[ston] with whom he lived an Apprentice: and after some political Quarrels the *Courant* was printed in Benjamins name. Upon his Br James removing his press to Newport, Benja went to Philada aet. 17." Here Jane Mecom was wrong about a date, or perhaps did not care to say that her brother Benjamin had run away at seventeen from his apprenticeship to her brother James, three years before James removed to Newport. Stiles noted that from Philadelphia Franklin "went to London & worked Journey Work about two years, and then returned & set up his Business at Philadelphia. His Uncle Benja came over also & settled in Dr Coleman's Chh in Boston, where he died a good old Man. Dr. Coleman preached his funeral sermon on '*Mark the perfect man* &c.' " Then Stiles added, as a note on his source, "Ex ore Mrs Macom the Doctors Sister now living at East Greenwich."; and a final recollection about Franklin's loyalist son: "Gov. Franklin now aet 47, ex ore Mrs. Macom his Aunt." The age here given for William Franklin made him appear to be at least a year younger than he was, and consequently to have been born something like two years after Franklin's marriage to Deborah Read. Jane Mecom may have actually been in error, or she may have been preferring to keep a family secret to herself.

The happiest years in Jane Mecom's life were those between September 1785, when Franklin returned from France, and April 1790, when he died. In that brief time she wrote him more letters that survive than in all her years before. She was easy in her circumstances at last, and at last she was in frequent and regular correspondence with her brother. Her only disappointment was that he did not settle in New England, as she had let herself hope, or even find it possible to visit Boston. Her only distress, though this was often acute, was over his painful malady, from which he insisted that she suffered more than he.

Even at a distance she was watchfully protective. She apologized when her friends or acquaintances tried through her to obtain Franklin's interest in their affairs. She thought it impertinent when members of the Franklin family looked for aid to their great relation. Her grandson Josiah Flagg, for instance, must have reminded her of her son Benjamin, in his readiness to expect patronage from Franklin. Josiah, now twenty-five, had lived with certain of his Flagg relations at Lancaster, Massachusetts, but when Franklin returned from France Josiah was at some kind of clerical work in Petersburg, Virginia. He at once applied to Franklin for help in getting a clerkship in Philadelphia. When Franklin sent a friendly reply, Josiah felt encouraged to go to Philadelphia for a visit. From there on April 17, 1786, Josiah wrote a letter to his grandmother asking her to say favorable things about him to Franklin, but not to tell him that Josiah had worked for three years at the trade of shoemaker: or as he put it, that he had "spun out three years under the patronage of St. Crispin." Franklin, as long ago as in *Poor Richard* for 1749, had said all there is to say about early poverty: "Having been poor is no shame, but being ashamed of it is"; and his letters to Jane Mecom now spoke often about the crown soap which the Boston Franklins had made and in which Franklin took a tradesman's pride. But Josiah Flagg, set on escaping from a trade into a more "genteel" occupation, was unaffected by his uncle's example. Jane Mecom wrote apologetically to Franklin and sternly to her grandson. Franklin was as kind to the young man as if Benjamin Mecom had never disappointed his mother and his uncle.

The relation between Jane Mecom and Franklin in the letters of these years was that of absolute affection on the ground of their common interests. "I rejoice in every honorable mention that is made of you," she wrote on January 6, 1786, "but I cannot find in my heart to be pleased at your accepting the government of the State [of Pennsylvania] and therefore have not congratulated you on it. I fear it will fatigue you too much." Franklin replied on the 24th in the smiling language with which he always met her disapproval. "I do not wonder at your blaming me for accepting the Government. We have all of us Wisdom enough to judge what others ought to do, or not to do in the Management of their Affairs; and 'tis possible I might blame you as much if you were to accept the Offer of a young Husband. My example may teach you not to be too confident in your own Prudence; as it teaches me not to be surpriz'd at such an Event should it really Happen."

Once he said something that hurt her. It was on May 31, 1788, when he warned her against "imagining & foreboding" misfortunes that might come to him, but also might not. "Death, however is sure to come to us all, and mine cannot now be far off, being in my 83d year; but that may be to me no misfortune, and I shall take care to make it as small a one to you, as possible." What he had in mind was his will, signed on July 17 of that year, in which he bequeathed to his sister the house in Unity Street and an annuity of £50, increased in a later codicil to £60. She at her first reading of his letter saw in it a reproach. "Is it possible my dear brother can think my concern is merely for my own support?" she asked on June 25. Then in a postscript of July 1, after reading his words several times again, she had begun to doubt that he had been angry with her. "If you were not, pray don't let this make you so, but impute it all to a weakness of mind depraved by my old age." It was difficult for her, all her life, not to take offense where none was intended, but easy to forget when from time to time he smiled at her "miffy temper."

The longest gap in their correspondence during these four years was the four months of the summer of 1787 when Franklin was sitting in the Federal Convention in Philadelphia; but the last letter he wrote before the Convention submerged him was to his sister, on May 30, as was the first he wrote, on September 20, after the Constitution had been signed and published. While in England he had more than once taken pains to give her his true reasons for conduct which the public misunderstood or misrepresented. In these later years he wrote her little about public affairs. They were always with him in his daily work. When he wrote to her he turned aside from the perpetual demands on him to confide, if only briefly, in a comfortable companion whom he had loved longer than any one else. As if to direct their correspondence a little, he asked her to try making crown soap for him, to send to his friends in France; and to tell him about their relations in New England. He knew she would be happy with something definite to do. She was delighted to be able to be of service to the brother to whom she had all her life been under so many obligations.

Though he always wrote consolingly to her about his illness, she could not help learning from others about his painful decline. She dreaded to think he might die before her. "Who that know and love you," she wrote on his eighty-fourth birthday, "can bear the thoughts of surviving you in this gloomy world?" But she did survive him. His last letter to her, three weeks before his death, said he was "quite free from pain" and remembering "what a long life of health" he had been blessed with, free from worse pains than those he suffered. Three days after his death on April 17, 1784, Richard Bache wrote to tell her of it. "And lest the news should reach you & be communicated to you in an abrupt manner & that your tender feelings might be still more wounded, I have thought it best to inclose these few lines to a friend, who I hope will first prepare you for the shock."

Then silence from her till September 6 when she wrote about her brother to Sarah Bache. "He while living," she said, "was to me every enjoyment. Whatever other pleasures were, as they mostly took their rise from him, they passed like little streams from a beautiful fountain. They remind me of two lines of a song Mr. Peters used to sing at your house.

But now they are withered
And waned all away.

"To make society agreeable there must be a similarity of circumstances and sentiments, as well as age. I have no such near me; my dear brother supplied all. Every line from him was a pleasure. If I asked questions he did not think proper to inform me on, he would sometimes give me a gentle reproof. At other times he entirely passed it over. That I knew was always fitted for the occasion, and all was pleasure.

But now they are withered
And waned all away.

"It is, however, very agreeable to me to see there is hardly a newspaper comes out in this town without honorable mention of him, and indeed it is a fund that cannot be exhausted."

After that her surviving letters were chiefly to Franklin's executors on the subject of his will, which continued his support of her to her death early in May 1794. The exact day is not certain. But on May 10 the *Columbian Centinel* of Boston published a death and funeral notice in which her name for the first time, so far as is known, appeared in print. "Mrs. Jane Mecom, widow of the late Mr. Edward Mecom, of this town, and the only sister of the late Doctor Benjamin Franklin, in the 83d year of her age. Her funeral will be this afternoon, precisely at 5 o'clock, from her late dwelling near the North Church, which her friends, and the friends of the late Dr. Franklin, are requested to attend."

Her will, made on February 17 of that year, when she was, "although weak in body, yet of sound mind and memory; well knowing that the time must arrive when I shall be called upon to resign this decaying body to its parent dust, and my spirit to GOD who gave it," left a generous legacy to her granddaughter Jane Mecom, but left the house in Unity Street to Jane Collas only in trust: no doubt to protect it from her own bad judgment or from her husband, if he was still alive.

Of Jane Mecom's sixteen descendants living at the time of

her death, Jane Collas lived till 1802, still owning the house but not occupying it. Josiah Flagg lived in Lancaster, where he married and had six children, and as town clerk for over thirty years adorned the town books with his "excellent penmanship." Of the children of Jane Flagg Greene in Rhode Island, Sarah was killed by a fall from a horse in October 1795, but Franklin lived to be married to another Greene cousin. All the rest of Jane Mecom's descendants were children, or grandchildren, of Benjamin Mecom. His daughter Jane, who had lived with her grandmother in Boston, married Simeon Kinsman in 1800, and was still alive in 1859, ninety-four years old. Abiah, another daughter, lived for some years, presumably with relatives of her mother, at Amboy, New Jersey, and then drifted back to Philadelphia. At any rate, it is supposed that she was the Abiah Mecom who, as keeper of a store or, later, of boarding houses at various addresses, was listed in Philadelphia directories as early as 1807 and as late as 1833. No later record has been found of her sisters Deborah and Sarah, and none of her brother John Ross, or of the other (name unknown) of the "five Dafters" who dined with Deborah Franklin in May 1768. Benjamin and his wife and his offspring either left no later records or were afterwards removed from those that did exist.

As for Jane Mecom herself, she survives essentially, and no doubt she would have preferred this, in her correspondence with her brother. That was her one continuing happiness, her one pride and triumph. Never suspecting that what she wrote would ever be read by strangers, she poured out her heart, which was regulated by a clear and steadfast mind. Line by line, year after year, she revealed her own character while she told her story. The story is at many points incomplete, and baffling. But it seems baffling only because it is absorbing, and rouses curiosity for more. Handicapped by domestic misfortunes as Franklin never was, Jane Mecom survived as he did, and rose above her circumstances as he did. If she had lived in circles anything like his she might have been influential and memorable in her own day, instead of waiting for a century and a half for the recognition due her. "The truth is," she wrote on April 22, 1786, "when I am in agreeable company, it raises my spirits and might then have some influence on my activity; and for the greatest part of my time, when I am sitting at home, I am apt to imagine, as Samson did when he lost his hair, that I can arise and shake myself and go forth as at other times; but on trial, like him, I am woefully disappointed and find my feet crippling and my breath short; but I am still cheerful, for that is my natural temper, and, as you advise me, thankful that I escape many grievous calamities."

Her freedom to live a full life came so late, after so much care, labor, and anxiety, that she had not much life left, nor special talents, nor special opportunities to make herself felt. She was content to make use of her particular talent, which was a kind of lyric candor about her small affairs, and of her particular opportunity, which was to be able to converse, in letters, with the most sympathetic and devoted listener she could have found in her world.

THE LETTERS OF
Benjamin Franklin &
Jane Mecom

"Excuse this freedom"

[First printed in Duane, *Works*, VI, 3, from a manuscript now missing, and here reprinted from Duane. The letter was written on Franklin's twenty-first birthday (New Style, January 17), when Jane Franklin was not yet quite fifteen but was to be married to Edward Mecom the following July. Isaac Freeman, captain of a Boston ship which had come to Philadelphia, was a friend of the Franklin family.]

Philadelphia, January 6, 1726-7

DEAR SISTER,

I am highly pleased with the account captain Freeman gives me of you. I always judged by your behaviour when a child that you would make a good, agreeable woman, and you know you were ever my peculiar favourite. I have been thinking what would be a suitable present for me to make, and for you to receive, as I hear you are grown a celebrated beauty. I had almost determined on a tea table, but when I considered that the character of a good housewife was far preferable to that of being only a pretty gentlewoman, I concluded to send you a *spinning wheel*, which I hope you will accept as a small token of my sincere love and affection.

Sister, farewell, and remember that modesty, as it makes the most homely virgin amiable and charming, so the want of it infallibly renders the most perfect beauty disagreeable and odious. But when that brightest of female virtues shines among other perfections of body and mind in the same person, it makes the woman more lovely than an angel. Excuse this freedom, and use the same with me. I am, dear Jenny, your loving brother,

B. FRANKLIN

"She was a good woman"

[First printed in Duane, *Works*, VI, 3-5, from a manuscript now missing, and here reprinted from Duane. The letter was misdated 1730 by Duane and by Sparks, *Familiar Letters*, pp. 5-7, but dated correctly 1731 in Sparks, *Works*, VII, 4-6, and by later editors. There can be no doubt that it was written in 1731. Jane Mecom's second child, Edward, was born March 29 of that year; Sarah Franklin Davenport died on May 23; the Pennsylvania Assembly convened on August 2 in 1731 but not in 1730. Franklin's sister Lydia was married in 1731 to Robert Scott. The considerate affection that Franklin felt for his sisters Sarah and Jane, and for his sister Mary Homes and his half-sister Elizabeth Douse, appears in his letter to "Sister Davenport" written probably in the summer of 1730, after the death of Jane Mecom's first child on May 18. This letter was first printed entire in Carl Van Doren, *Benjamin Franklin's Autobiographical Writings*, pp. 31-32, from the manuscript in the American Philosophical Society.]

Philadelphia, June 19, 1730 [1731]

DEAR SISTER,

Yours of May 26, I received with the melancholy news of the death of sister Deavenport, a loss, without doubt, regretted by all that knew her, for she was a good woman. Her friends ought, however, to be comforted that they have enjoyed her so long and that she has passed through the world happily, having never had an extraordinary misfortune or notable affliction, and that she is now secure in rest, in the place provided for the virtuous. I had before heard of the death of your first child, and am pleased that the loss is in some measure made up to you by the birth of a second.

We have had the small pox here lately, which raged violently while it lasted; there have been about fifty persons innoculated, who all recovered, except a child of the doctor's upon whom the small pox appeared within a day or two after the operation, and who is therefore thought to have been certainly infected before. In one family in my neighbourhood there appeared a great mortality, Mr. George Claypole, (a descendant of Oliver Cromwell) has, by industry, acquired a great estate, and being in excellent business, (a merchant) would probably have doubled it, had he lived according to the common course of years.

He died first, suddenly; within a short time died his best

negro; then one of his children; then a negro w
children more, buried at the same time; then two m
I saw two double buryings come out of the house in one
None were left in the family, but the mother and one chil
and both their lives till lately despaired of; so that all the father's wealth, which every body thought, a little while ago, had
heirs enough, and no one would have given six pence for the
reversion, was in a few weeks brought to the greatest probability
of being divided among strangers: so uncertain are all human
affairs: the dissolution of this family is generally ascribed to
an imprudent use of quick silver in the cure of the itch; Mr.
Claypole applying it as he thought proper, without consulting
a physician for fear of charges, and the small pox coming upon
them at the same time made their case desperate. But what gives
me the greatest concern, is the account you give me of my sister Home's misfortune: I know a cancer in the breast is often
thought incurable: yet we have here in town a kind of shell
made of some wood, cut at a proper time, by some man of great
skill (as they say,) which has done wonders in that disease
among us, being worn for some time on the breast. I am not apt
to be superstitiously fond of believing such things, but the instances are so well attested as sufficiently to convince the most
incredulous.

This if I have interest enough to procure, as I think I have,
I will borrow for a time and send it to you, and hope the doctors
you have will at least allow the experiment to be tried, and shall
rejoice to hear it has the accustomed effect.

You have mentioned nothing in your letter of our dear parents, but I conclude they are well because you say nothing to
the contrary. I want to hear from sister Douse, and to know
of her welfare, as also of my sister Lydia, who I hear is lately
married. I intended to have visited you this summer, but printing the paper money here has hindered me near two months,
and our assembly will sit the 2d of August next, at which time
I must not be absent, but I hope to see you this Fall.

I am, Your affectionate brother,

B. FRANKLIN

ery kindly"

cies, in Duane, *Works*, VI, 5-6; here
the American Philosophical Society.
was his *Articles of Belief and Acts of*
ript, in the Library of Congress, Novem-
to Jonathan Edwards' "late Book" was to
.]

Philada July 28. 1743

NY

onition very kindly, and was far from being
on⌐   r it. If I say any thing about it to you, 'tis only
to rectify   wrong Opinions you seem to have entertain'd of
me, and that I do only because they give you some Uneasiness,
which I am unwilling to be the Occasion of. You express yourself as if you thought I was against Worshipping of God, and
believed Good Works would merit Heaven; which are both
Fancies of your own, I think, without Foundation.—I am so far
from thinking that God is not to be worshipped, that I have
compos'd and wrote a whole Book of Devotions for my own Use:
And I imagine there are few, if any, in the World, so weake as
to imagine, that the little Good we can do here, can *merit* so
vast a Reward hereafter. There are some Things in your New
England Doctrines and Worship, which I do not agree with,
but I do not therefore condemn them, or desire to shake your
Belief or Practice of them. We may dislike things that are nevertheless right in themselves. I would only have you make me the
same Allowances, and have a better Opinion both of morality
and your Brother. Read the Pages of Mr Edward's late Book
entitled Some Thoughts concerning the present Revival of Religion in N. E. from 367 to 375; and when you judge of others,
if you can perceive the Fruit to be good, don't terrify your self
that the Tree may be evil, but be assur'd it is not so; for you
know who has said, *Men do not gather Grapes of Thorns or
Figs of Thistles.* I have not time to add but that I shall always be

Your affectionate Brother

B FRANKLIN

P.S. It was not kind in you to
imagine when your Sister commended Good
Works, she intended it a Reproach to you.
'Twas very far from her Thoughts.

"The true way to get friends"

[Printed first, from a manuscript now missing, in Sparks, *Familiar Letters*, p. 10, from which it is here reprinted. It is there undated, but it is assigned to 1743 in the Index to Sparks, *Works*. The more probable date is 1744-1745, because of Franklin's reference to his father's sickness. Josiah Franklin died January 17, 1745, and his children did not remember him ever to have had any sickness except the last. Moreover, Benjamin Mecom would have been barely eleven at the end of 1743 and would hardly have been sent away from home at that age, even with Franklin's New York partner James Parker. Though this letter, with others concerned with Benjamin Mecom, was addressed to both his father and mother, Edward Mecom seems to have been included chiefly as a matter of form. He was a saddler, but his earnings did not support his large family, and his wife had begun by 1742, if not before, to take boarders. The only trace of any other occupation Edward Mecom had is the record of his appointment on March 6, 1729, as one of the clerks of the Boston public markets. Boston Registry Records, XII (Town Records, 1729-1742), 7, where the month is mistakenly given as May. Edward Mecom became a communicant of the Brattle Street Church in 1730, at least three years after he had been married to Jane Franklin by the church's minister and a year after the baptism of the first Mecom child. The will of Josiah Franklin, made October 20, 1744, bequeathed to Jane Mecom a ninth part (or equal share with her brothers and sisters) of their father's "house and land and goods." Josiah Franklin left to his "loving wife Abiah Franklin all the incomes or rents of my whole estate and goods and the use of the two rooms we now live in allowing the Lodgers to be in as is used she allowing out of it the interest that will be due to my Creditors while she lives." As his house was actually four "tenements," and as the inventory of his estate in the Registry of Probate, Suffolk County, Massachusetts, shows him to have died possessed of a great many beds, it seems virtually certain that the houses were occupied by lodgers from whom Josiah Franklin's income was derived rather than, at his late age, from his trade of tallow chandler. And it is nearly as certain that the Edward Mecoms occupied one of the tenements, close enough for Jane Mecom to be in regular attendance upon her aged parents. The estate of Josiah Franklin was not finally administered till after the death of his widow in 1752; and John Franklin's final account, in the Registry of Probate with the date February 25,

1754, shows that then, if not in 1745, there were debts due the estate from Josiah Franklin's eldest daughter Elizabeth Douse, £6.13.4; from the son of his daughter Mary Homes, William Homes, £6.2.8; and from "Edward Malcolm," £23.8.2. This "Malcolm" is almost certainly a mistake for Mecom. Josiah Franklin's personal estate was appraised at £59.12.2¼ but at auction brought £11.5.1 more. The house was appraised at £253.6.8, but after some delay was sold on April 15, 1754, for £188.13.4 to William Homes, who in June 1757 sold it to Jonathan Dakin for £266.13.4. For these transfers see N. B. Shurtleff, *A Topographical and Historical Description of Boston*, 3d ed., 1890, p. 633-634. It is not clear what Jane Mecom received. Benjamin Franklin gave her both his share in the estate and the bond for "thirty pounds old tenure" which was due him from his father at his death.]

DEAR BROTHER AND SISTER,   Philadelphia [1745?]

If you still continue your inclination to send Benny, you may do it by the first vessel to New York. Write a line by him, directed to Mr. James Parker, Printer, on Hunter's Key, New York. I am confident he will be kindly used there, and I shall hear from him every week. You will advise him to be very cheerful, and ready to do every thing he is bid, and endeavour to oblige every body, for that is the true way to get friends.

Dear Sister, I love you tenderly for your care of our father in his sickness.

I am, in great haste, your loving brother,

B. FRANKLIN

"The nature of boys"

[Printed first, from a manuscript now missing, in Sparks, *Familiar Letters*, pp. 10-13, from which it is here reprinted. Benny Mecom, restless in his apprenticeship to James Parker, soon began to cause the trouble which appears in the letters of Franklin to Jane Mecom for several years. Jemmy (James) Franklin of Newport, son of Franklin's brother James, had been apprenticed to his uncle in Philadelphia on November 5, 1740, but had since returned to the Newport printing house of his widowed mother. Though this letter is not dated, it belongs certainly to 1748, after the "March last" when Franklin saw Benny in New York. That was in March 1848 when Franklin went with a commission to ask Governor George Clinton for cannon to be used in fortifying Philadelphia. Franklin's son William spent the winter of 1747-

1748 with his regiment in Albany. It is not known what were the letters
to "Mr. Vanhorne," nor who he was, nor where they were sent under
Franklin's cover by George Whitefield the evangelist.]

DEAR SISTER, Philadelphia [1748]

I received your letter, with one for Benny, and one for Mr.
Parker, and also two of Benny's letters of complaint, which, as
you observe, do not amount to much. I should have had a very
bad opinion of him, if he had written to you those accusations of
his master, which you mention; because, from long acquaintance
with his master, who lived some years in my house, I know him
to be a sober, pious, and conscientious man; so that Newport,
to whom you seem to have given too much credit, must have
wronged Mr. Parker very much in his accounts, and have
wronged Benny too, if he says Benny told him such things, for
I am confident he never did.

As to the bad attendance afforded him in the smallpox, I believe, if the negro woman did not do her duty, her master or
mistress would, if they had known of it, have had that matter
mended. But Mrs. Parker was herself, if I am not mistaken,
sick at that time, and her child also. And though he gives the
woman a bad character in general, all he charges her with in
particular, is, that she never brought him what he called for
directly, and sometimes not at all. He had the distemper favorably, and yet I suppose was bad enough to be, like other sick
people, a little impatient, and perhaps might think a short time
long, and sometimes call for things not proper for one in his
condition.

As to clothes, I am frequently at New York, and I never saw
him unprovided with what was good, decent, and sufficient. I
was there no longer ago than March last, and he was then well
clothed, and made no complaint to me of any kind. I heard both
his master and mistress call upon him on Sunday morning to
get ready to go to meeting, and tell him of his frequently de-
laying and shuffling till it was too late, and he made not the
least objection about clothes. I did not think it any thing extraordinary, that he should be sometimes willing to evade going

[41]

to meeting, for I believe it is the case with all boys, or almost all. I have brought up four or five myself, and have frequently observed, that if their shoes were bad, they would say nothing of a new pair till Sunday morning, just as the bell rung, when, if you asked them why they did not get ready, the answer was prepared, "I have no shoes," and so of other things, hats and the like; or if they knew of any thing that wanted mending, it was a secret till Sunday morning, and sometimes I believe they would rather tear a little, than be without the excuse.

As to going on petty errands, no boys love it, but all must do it. As soon as they become fit for better business, they naturally get rid of that, for the master's interest comes in to their relief. I make no doubt but Mr. Parker will take another apprentice, as soon as he can meet with a likely one. In the mean time I should be glad if Benny would exercise a little patience. There is a negro woman that does a great many of those errands.

I do not think his going on board the privateer arose from any difference between him and his master, or any ill usage he had received. When boys see prizes brought in, and quantities of money shared among the men, and their gay living, it fills their heads with notions, that half distract them, and put them quite out of conceit with trades, and the dull ways of getting money by working. This I suppose was Ben's case, the Catherine being just before arrived with three rich prizes; and that the glory of having taken a privateer of the enemy, for which both officers and men were highly extolled, treated, presented, &c. worked strongly upon his imagination, you will see, by his answer to my letter, is not unlikely. I send it to you enclosed. I wrote him largely on the occasion; and though he might possibly, to excuse that slip to others, complain of his place, you may see he says not a syllable of any such thing to me. My only son, before I permitted him to go to Albany, left my house unknown to us all, and got on board a privateer, from whence I fetched him. No one imagined it was hard usage at home, that made him do this. Every one, that knows me, thinks I am too indulgent a parent, as well as master.

I shall tire you, perhaps, with the length of this letter; but I am the more particular, in order, if possible, to satisfy your mind about your son's situation. His master has, by a letter this post, desired me to write to him about his staying out of nights, sometimes all night, and refusing to give an account where he spends his time, or in what company. This I had not heard of before, though I perceive you have. I do not wonder at his correcting him for that. If he was my own son, I should think his master did not do his duty by him, if he omitted it, for to be sure it is the high road to destruction. And I think the correction very light, and not likely to be very effectual, if the strokes left no marks.

His master says farther, as follows;—"I think I can't charge my conscience with being much short of my duty to him. I shall now desire you, if you have not done it already, to invite him to lay his complaints before you, that I may know how to remedy them." Thus far the words of his letter, which giving me a fair opening to inquire into the affair, I shall accordingly do it, and I hope settle every thing to all your satisfactions. In the mean time, I have laid by your letters both to Mr. Parker and Benny, and shall not send them till I hear again from you, because I think your appearing to give ear to such groundless stories may give offence, and create a greater misunderstanding, and because I think what you write to Benny, about getting him discharged, may tend to unsettle his mind, and therefore improper at this time.

I have a very good opinion of Benny in the main, and have great hopes of his becoming a worthy man, his faults being only such as are commonly incident to boys of his years, and he has many good qualities, for which I love him. I never knew an apprentice contented with the clothes allowed him by his master, let them be what they would. Jemmy Franklin, when with me, was always dissatisfied and grumbling. When I was last in Boston, his aunt bid him go to a shop and please himself, which the gentleman did, and bought a suit of clothes on my account dearer by one half, than any I ever afforded myself, one suit excepted; which I don't mention by way of complaint of Jemmy, for he and I are good friends, but only to show you the nature of boys.

The letters to Mr. Vanhorne were sent by Mr. Whitfield, under my cover.

I am, with love to brother and all yours, and duty to mother, to whom I have not time now to write, your affectionate brother,

B. FRANKLIN

"As soon as you can spare him"

[Printed first, and hitherto only, in Sparks, *Familiar Letters*, pp. 19-20, from a manuscript now missing; and here reprinted from Sparks. The Reverend Samuel Cooper was then minister of the Brattle Street Church in Boston.]

Philadelphia, 20 September, 1750

DEAR SISTER,

I received yours the 11th instant, with one enclosed for cousin Benny; but he, I suppose, is in Boston with you before this time, as he left New York fifteen days since with a fair wind for Rhode Island. I do not know how long his master gave him leave to stay; but as I hear the Assembly there is sitting, and doing business, I believe he will be wanted, and therefore would advise him to return expeditiously, as soon as you can spare him.

Mr. Cooper is not yet arrived. I shall be glad to see him; but as he has not had the smallpox, I suppose he will not come so far, for it is spreading here. As the doctors inoculate apace, they will drive it through the town, so that we may expect to be free of it before the winter is over.

My love to brother Mecom and the children, and duty to mother.

I am, dear sister,

Your affectionate brother,

B. FRANKLIN

Abiah Franklin and Jane Mecom to Benjamin and Deborah Franklin

[Printed first in Duane, *Letters to Benjamin Franklin*, pp. 9-10; here printed from the manuscript in the American Philosophical Society. The postscript is the earliest surviving written word, so far as is now known, from Jane Mecom to her brother. Though Franklin's mother did not include the year in the date of her letter, it was certainly 1751: her son had been chosen alderman of Philadelphia on October 1 of that year. Abiah Folger Franklin, born in Nantucket, had numerous "cousins" (that is, all sorts of relations) there, including the Coffins here mentioned. The "workes and Letter" about which "Cozen Kesiah" inquired have not been identified.]

LOVING SON AN DAUGHTER   Boston   Oct 14 [1751]

I did not rite to you last post but it was becase I was taken with the stomakake so bad all day that I coold not set up to rite on any acount my Cozen Kesiah Coffin was hear last week and she was sorroy that the workes and Letter was not yet printed she bid me tell you that she shoold be glad how soon you Coold do them for she wants to have a few of them very much   my Cozen Hiniry Coffin is gon to your place I am afraid he will get the smol pox thare I desire you woold advise him not to goo any whare you know or think it has bin and if you have any bis nes with him send him away as fast as you can   I am glad to hear that you are so well respected in your town for them to chuse you alderman altho I dont know what it means nor what the better you will be of it besids the honor of it   I hope you will look up to god thank him for all his good providnces to-ward you he has prosperd you much in that place and I am very thankful for it   I hope you will cary well so that you may be liked in all your posts   I am very weake and short bretht so that I Cant set to rite much al tho I slepe well anits and my Coff is better and I have a prity good stumak to my vethels   pray excuse my bat riting an inditing for all tels me that I am two old to rite letters I can hardly se and am grone so def that I can hardly hear any thing that is sed in the house   Love and sarvis to all frinds from your loving mother

ABIAH FRANKLIN

ps   mother says she ant able & so I must tell you myself that I rejoyce with you & bles god for you in all yr prosperity and doubt not but you will be grater blessings to the world as he bestows upon you grater honers

J M

"Unacquainted with the ways of your place"

[Printed first in Sparks, *Familiar Letters*, p. 21, from a manuscript now missing; and here reprinted from Sparks. William Franklin, then only twenty but since August 13, 1751, clerk of the Pennsylvania Assembly in succession to his father, had set out by sea during a recess of the Assembly to visit relatives in Boston. Franklin's "new niece" was Abiah Mecom, who was born on August 1 of that year and died April 23, 1752. The "cousin at Casco Bay" was the niece Elizabeth Davenport, married to Lieutenant-Colonel Joseph Ingersoll of Falmouth, Maine. By "brother and sister Davenport" Franklin meant James Davenport, whose wife Sarah Franklin had died in May 1731, and his third wife, Mary Walker, whom he had married in November of the same year. "Mrs. Billings" was the mother of Sarah, wife of Josiah Davenport, who was the son of James and Sarah Franklin Davenport.]

DEAR SISTER, Philadelphia, 24 October, 1751

My son waits upon you with this, whom I heartily recommend to your motherly care and advice. He is indeed a sober and discreet lad of his years, but he is young and unacquainted with the ways of your place.

My compliments to my new niece, Miss Abiah, and pray her to accept the enclosed piece of gold, to cut her teeth; it may afterwards buy nuts for them to crack.

Some time since I sent a letter to your care for our cousin at Casco Bay. Have you had an opportunity to forward it?

My love to brother Mecom and your children; and to brother and sister Davenport and children; and respects to Mrs. Billings and her daughter, and all other friends, from, dear sister, Your affectionate brother,

B. FRANKLIN

Benjamin Franklin to Abiah Franklin

[Printed first, and hitherto only, in Sparks, *Familiar Letters*, pp. 20-21, from which it is here reprinted. Sparks mistakenly gives the date as 1751. It was written after Franklin had received the letters, now missing, from his mother dated April 13 and 20; and before his own letter of May 21, 1752, to Edward and Jane Mecom. Boston had been visited early in 1752 by a severe epidemic of smallpox which killed at least five hundred victims, among them apparently Jane Mecom's youngest daughter Abiah, called "Biah" in this letter. She died on April 23, before the letter could reach her grandmother, who died on May 8. The order for six pistoles was drawn on Ellis Huske, identified in the note to the letter of May 21. A pistole was a Spanish coin then common in the English colonies and was worth about 18 shillings.]

Philadelphia, [May, 1752]

HONORED MOTHER,

We received by this post both your letters of April 13th and 20th. The account you give of poor little Biah grieves me, but I still hope the best. However, God's will must be done. I rejoice that the rest of sister's children and brother Davenport's are likely to escape so well, and Mrs. Billings's.

Enclosed I send an order for six pistoles, which I believe will be paid on sight. I beg sister to accept four of them, and you the other two.

I am your dutiful son,

B. FRANKLIN

"Our dear good mother's death"

[First printed, from a manuscript now missing, in Sparks, *Familiar Letters*, pp. 22-23, from which it is here reprinted. Abiah Franklin had died on May 8. Ellis Huske was then printer of the *Boston Post-Boy* and postmaster of Boston.]

Philadelphia, 21 May, 1752

DEAR BROTHER AND SISTER,

I received yours with the affecting news of our dear good mother's death. I thank you for your long continued care of her in her old age and sickness. Our distance made it impracticable for us to attend her, but you have supplied all. She has lived a good life, as well as a long one, and is happy.

Since I sent you the order on Mr. Huske, I have received

his account, and find he thinks he has money to receive, and, though I endeavour by this post to convince him he is mistaken, yet possibly he may not be immediately satisfied, so as to pay that order; therefore, lest the delay should be inconvenient to you, I send the six pistoles enclosed. But if the order is paid, give those to brother John, and desire him to credit my account with them.   Your affectionate brother,

B. FRANKLIN

"On the Voyage to Antigua"

[Printed first in Sparks, *Familiar Letters*, pp. 24-26, with the correct date, but wrongly dated November 14 in Sparks, *Works*, VII, 59, and by later editors. Here printed from the manuscript in the American Philosophical Society. The letter opens an episode which runs through the Franklin-Mecom correspondence for the next four or five years. In 1748 Franklin had sent Thomas Smith, a journeyman who had worked for Franklin both in New York and in Philadelphia, to Antigua in the Leeward Islands, where Smith in that year established *The Antigua Gazette*. After Smith died in the summer of 1752 Franklin somewhat hurriedly decided to send Benjamin Mecom to take Smith's place. The best account of the venture is by Wilberforce Eames, "The Antigua Press and Benjamin Mecom," *Proceedings of the American Antiquarian Society*, New Series, XXXVIII (1929), 303-348. Much of the account is based on Franklin's letters to his sister and her husband from this date to February 21, 1757.]

DEAR BROTHER & SISTER,   Philada Sept. 14. 1752. NS.

Benny sailed from hence this Day two Weeks and left our Capes the Sunday following. They are seldom above 3 Weeks on the Voyage to Antigua.

That Island is reckoned one of the healthiest in the West Indies. My late Partner there enjoy'd perfect Health for four Years, till he grew careless and got to sitting up late in Taverns, which I have caution'd Benny to avoid, and have given him all other necessary Advice I could think of relating both to his Health & Conduct, and hope for the best. He will find the Business settled to his Hand, a Newspaper establish'd, no other Printing-house to interfere with him or beat down his Prices, which are much higher than we get on the Continent. He has the Place on the same Terms with his Predecessor, who I understand cleared 5 or 600 Pistoles during the 4 Years he lived there.

I have recommended him to some Gentlemen of Note, for their Patronage & Advice.

Mr Parker, tho' he looked on Benny as one of his best Hands, readily consented to his going on the first Mention[in]g of it. I told him Benny must make him Satisfaction for his Time. He said he would leave that to be settled by me; and Benny as readily agreed with me to pay Mr Parker as much as would hire a good Journeyman in his Room. He came handsomely provided with Apparel, and I believe Mr Parker has in every respect done his Duty by him, and in this Affair, has really acted a generous Part, therefore I hope if Benny succeeds in the World he will make Mr Parker a Return beyond what he has promis'd. I suppose you will not think it amiss to write Mr & Mrs Parker a Line or two of Thanks; for notwithstanding some little Misunderstandings, they have on the whole been very kind to Benny.

We have Vessels very frequently going from this Port to Antigua. You have some too from your Port. What Letters you send this way, I'll take Care to forward.

Antigua is the Seat of Government for all the Leeward Islands, to wit, St. Christophers, Nevis, and Montserrat. Benny will have the Business of all those Islands, there being no other Printer.

After all, having taken care to do what *appears to be for the best*, we must submit to God's Providence, which orders all things *really for the best*.

While Benny was here, and since, our Assembly was sitting, which took up my Time that I could not before write you so fully.

With Love to your Children, I am, Dr Brother & Sister,

Your affectionate Brother

B FRANKLIN

[49]

"Too forward in cracking the shell"

[Printed first, and hitherto only, from a manuscript now missing, in Sparks, *Familiar Letters*, p. 27, from which it is here reprinted.]

Philadelphia,
30 November, 1752

DEAR BROTHER AND SISTER,

I congratulate you on the news of Benny's arrival, for whom I had been some time in pain.

That you may know the whole state of his mind and his affairs, and by that means be better able to advise him, I send you all the letters I have received from or concerning him. I fear I have been too forward in cracking the shell, and producing the chick to the air before its time.

We are at present all well, thanks to God, and hope you and yours are so. I am

Your affectionate brother,

B. FRANKLIN

P.S. In my opinion, if Benny can but be prevailed on to behave steadily, he may make his fortune there. And without some share of steadiness and perseverance, he can succeed no where. Please to return me the letters.

"The loss of our dear brother"

[Printed first, from a manuscript now missing, in Sparks, *Familiar Letters*, p. 38, from which it is here reprinted. John Franklin died in Boston on January 30, 1756, and Benjamin Franklin wrote, besides this letter to Jane Mecom, a famous letter to Elizabeth Hubbart, John Franklin's stepdaughter, dated February 23. John Franklin's will, of which there is a copy in the American Philosophical Society, was dated January 22, 1756, with a codicil of the 26th. It bequeathed to Jane Mecom "1 pair of Silver Canns with my arms upon Them" and an equal share with her brothers and sisters in the remainder of the "Real and Personal Estate" after the specified legacies had been paid. Provision was made for Peter Mecom, then not quite seventeen and apprenticed to his uncle, "Tallow Chandler." All the "Utensils belonging to my Business" were to go to the widow "during her Natural life," and "also the Use of my Negro named Cesar: and after her Decease I give all the same to my Kinsmen, Peter Franklin Mecom and James Barker equally between them." Barker was related to John Franklin's wife and was also an apprentice. Peter Mecom was to have a "Suit of Cloaths, but not mourning." The codicil added a further provision: "And Whereas I have given to my Wife the Use of my Negro named Cesar during her Natural Life I now give my Executors Liberty to Dispose of him if he Behaves ill, and my said Wife to have the Use of the Money and at her Death to be Devided Equally between my Kinsmen Peter Franklin Mecom James Barker and John Mecom." John Mecom, Peter's brother, was then under fifteen, and apprenticed to his cousin William Homes, who was less prosperous than John Franklin. The executors of the will were Jonathan Williams, a nephew, and Tuthill Hubbart, a stepson of John Franklin. The witnesses to the will were Joseph Edwards, Thomas Leverett, and Dudson Kilcup; and to the codicil John Perkins (presumably Dr. John Perkins), Silvester Gardiner, and Gillam Tailer. The will empowered the executors to carry out the partition of the property "Germantown so called in Braintree" on which John Franklin had agreed with the other proprietors. It left "My Brother Benjamin's Picture" (supposed to be the portrait first reproduced in the frontispiece to Sparks, *Works*, Vol. 1) to James Franklin of Newport, "the Son of my Brother James Franklin Deceased." The Inventory of John Franklin's "Real & Personal Estate" in the Registry of Probate of Suffolk County, Massachusetts, shows him to have had a well-furnished shop and house and an unusually extensive library of theology, philosophy, science, history, literature, and miscellaneous titles. There is nothing that could have been by his brother Benjamin unless it was in "Magazines 2 Vols." There was a "Stove" which may have been a "Pennsylvanian Fire-Place" or, as it has since come to be called, a Franklin stove. The whole was appraised at £302.3.9, but did not include the house, which belonged to the widow.]

Philadelphia, 12 February, 1756

DEAR SISTER,

I condole with you on the loss of our dear brother. As our number grows less, let us love one another proportionably more.

I am just returned from my military expedition, and now my time is taken up in the Assembly[.] Providence seems to require various duties of me. I know not what will be next; but I find the more I seek for leisure and retirement from business, the more I am engaged in it.

Benny, I understand, inclines to leave Antigua. He may be in the right. I have no objection.

My love to brother, and to your children. I am, dearest sister,

Your affectionate brother,

B. FRANKLIN

[51]

"A few Things that may be of some Use"

[Here first printed, from the manuscript in the American Philosophical Society. The "Negro Child" was the child of a slave belonging to Franklin. Joseph Choate was a colonel in the Massachusetts regiment raised for the expedition against Louisburg in 1745. Jane Mecom's first grandchild, whose name is not known and who died an infant, was the child of Edward Mecom Jr., married on July 22, 1755, to Ruth Whittemore. Boston Registry Records, xxx (Marriages 1752-1809), 369, gives his name as Edward Macomb.]

DEAR SISTER,   Philada June 10. 1756

We wrote to you per Capt. Morton who sailed yesterday, & sent you a few Things that may be of some Use perhaps in your Family. I hope, tho' not of much Value, they will be acceptable. Inclos'd is an Acct of Particulars, and the Captain's Receipt, with the Key of the Trunk.

Our Family is well. The Small Pox is beginning in Town by Inoculation, but has not otherwise spread as yet; those who have been inoculated not being yet in the ripe state to communicate Infection. We have only a Negro Child to have it.

Pray let me know by a Line whether you did not some Months ago receive a Pacquet from me for Col. Choate, & whether he has got it. My Respects to him, & to all Friends. With Love to Br. Mecom & your Children, I am, Dr Sister

Your affectionate

I congratulate you on   Brother
the Birth of a Grandchild   B FRANKLIN

"Unsettledness of Temper"

[Printed first in Sparks, *Familiar Letters*, pp. 40-43, and here more correctly from the manuscript in the American Philosophical Society. William Strahan was already Franklin's friend and correspondent in London.]

DEAR SISTER   New York, June 28. 1756

I received here your Letter of extravagant Thanks, which put me in mind of the Story of the Member of Parliament, who began one of his Speeches with saying, he thank'd God he was born & bred a Presbyterian; on which another took leave to observe, that the Gentleman must needs be of a most grateful Disposition, since he was thankful for such very small Matters.

You desire me to tell you what I know about Benny's Removal & the Reasons of it. Some time last Year, when I return'd from a long Journey, I found a Letter from him which had lain some time unanswered; and it was some considerable Time afterwards before I knew of an Opportunity to send an Answer.—I should first have told you, that when I set him up at Antigua, he was to have the Use of the Printing House on the same Terms with his Predecessor, Mr Smith; that is, allowing me one Third Part of the Profits. After this, finding him diligent & careful, for his Encouragement I relinquish'd that Agreement, and let him know that as you were remov'd into a dearer House, if he paid you yearly a certain Sum, I forget what it was, towards discharging your Rent, and another small Sum to me in Sugar & Rum for my Family Use, he need keep no farther Acct of the Profits, but should enjoy all the Rest to himself. I cannot remember what the whole of both Payments amounted to, but I think they did not exceed 20 £ a Year.— The Truth is, I intended from the first to give him that Printing House; but as he was very young and unexperienc'd in the World, I thought it best not to do it immediately but to keep him a little dependant for a Time, to check the flighty Unsettledness of Temper which on several Occasions he had discovered; and what I receiv'd from him I concluded to lay out in new Letters, that when I gave it to him intirely it might be worth his Acceptance.—And if I should die first, I put it in my Will, that the Letters should be all new cast for him.— This Proposal of paying you & me a certain annual Sum did not please him; and he wrote to desire I would explicitly tell him how long that annual Payment was to continue? whether on Payment of that, all prior Demands I had against him for the Arrears of our first Agreement, were likewise cancel'd? and finally insisted that I would name a certain Sum that I would take for the Printing House, & allow him to pay it off in Parts as he could, and then the yearly Payments to cease; for tho' he had a high Esteem for me, yet he lov'd Freedom, and his Spirit could not bear Dependance on any Man, tho' he were the best Man living. This was the Letter which occasionally remain'd, as I said, so long unanswered. At which he took farther Offence, and before I could answer it, I receiv'd another from him, acquainting me, that he had come to a Resolution to remove from that Island; that his Resolution was fix'd, & nothing that could be said to him should move or shake it; and propos'd another Person to me to carry on the Business in his Room. This was immediately follow'd by another & a third Letter to the same purpose, all declaring the inflexibility of his Determination to leave the Island; but without saying where he propos'd to go, or what were his Motives.—So I wrote him that I should not attempt to change his Resolution; that I made no Objection to his Quitting, but wish'd he had let me know where he was going: That as to the Person he recommended to succeed I had kept the Office there after Mr Smith's decease in hopes it might be of use to him (Benny) but since it was not agreable to him to continue in it, I did not incline to be concern'd with any other there. However, if the Person would buy it, I named the Price. If not, I directed it to be pack'd up & sent home. [*Written lengthwise in the margin*: All I desir'd of him, was to discharge what he ow'd to Mr Strahan, Bookseller in London, one of my Friends who had credited him on my Recommendation.] By this Post I receiv'd the enclos'd Letter, & understand the Things are all arrived. I shall be very glad to hear he does better in another Place, but I fear he will not for some Years be cur'd of his Fickleness, & get fix'd to any purpose. However we must hope for the best, as with this Fault he has many good Qualities & Virtues.

My Love to Brother & the Children, and to all that love you.
I am, Dear Sister,   Your affectionate Brother,

B FRANKLIN

"Perhaps all is for the best"

[Printed first, and hitherto only, in Sparks, *Familiar Letters*, pp. 43-44, and now reprinted from Sparks. The Earl of Loudoun was then commander in chief of the British forces in North America.]

DEAR SISTER, New York, 12 July, 1756

I am still here, waiting the arrival of Lord Loudoun. I received yours of the 5th instant, and shall forward the letter to Benny. I would not have you grieve about the affair; perhaps all is for the best. When I get home, I shall send you his letters for your full satisfaction.

My love to brother, and your children.

I am, dear sister,

Your loving brother,

B. FRANKLIN

"He has settled Accounts with me"

[Printed first in Sparks, *Familiar Letters*, p. 47, and here from the manuscript in the American Philosophical Society. Benjamin Mecom's settlement of his account with his uncle included a bond signed on December 27 of that year saying that the nephew owed Franklin £100 sterling but that on payment of half the amount, with interest, on December 27, 1757, the whole indebtedness would be discharged. The bond, signed by Mecom in the presence of Mary Smith and William Franklin, was never paid and is still among the Franklin papers in the American Philosophical Society. Franklin in his will of April 28, 1757, bequeathed the bond to Benjamin, which meant that the debt would be forgiven.]

DEAR BROTHER & SISTER Philada Dec. 30. 1756.

You will receive this by the Hand of your Son Benjamin, on whose safe Return from the West Indies I sincerely congratulate you.—He has settled Accounts with me, & paid the Ballance honourably. He has also clear'd the old Printing House to himself, and sent it to Boston, where he purposes to set up his Business together with Bookselling, which, considering his Industry & Frugality, I make no doubt will answer. He has good Credit & some Money in England, and I have help'd him by lending him a little more; so that he may expect a Cargo of Books and a Quantity of new Letter in the Spring; and I shall from time to time furnish him with Paper.—We all join in Love to you & yours,—I am

Your Loving Brother

B FRANKLIN

"A good deal depends on the first appearance"

[Printed first in Sparks, *Familiar Letters*, p. 48, from which it is here reprinted. By "whisk seed" Franklin meant the seed of broom-corn (*Sorghum vulgare*), then little known in the northern colonies. Samuel Cooper and James Bowdoin were already friends of Franklin, as they were to remain throughout their lives. Franklin's "cousin Sally" was actually his niece, Jane Mecom's daughter Sarah, who had been married to William Flagg on March 18, 1756. Boston Registry Records, XXX (Marriages 1752-1809), 19.]

DEAR SISTER,   Philadelphia, 21 February, 1757

I am glad to hear your son is got well home. I like your conclusion not to take a house for him till summer, and if he stays till his new letters arrive, perhaps it would not be amiss; for a good deal depends on the first appearance a man makes. As he will keep a bookseller's shop, with his printing-house, I don't know but it might be worth his while to set up at Cambridge.

I enclose you some whisk seed; it is a kind of corn, good for creatures; it must be planted in hills, like Indian corn. The tops make the best thatch in the world; and of the same are made the whisks you use for velvet. Pray try if it will grow with you. I brought it from Virginia. Give some to Mr. Cooper, some to Mr. Bowdoin.

Love to cousin Sally, and her spouse. I wish them and you much joy. Love to brother, &c.

B. FRANKLIN

"Old Folks & old Trees"

[Printed first in Sparks, *Familiar Letters*, pp. 50-51, and here printed from the manuscript in the American Philosophical Society. It is the earliest of the three surviving letters that Franklin wrote to Jane Mecom while he waited in New York for the ship that was to take him to England. At the date of this letter Elizabeth Douse, his eldest sister, was eighty and more or less dependent on her family, particularly her youngest brother Benjamin, for her support. He held a mortgage on her house in Unity Street, Boston, and her bond for sums advanced. Nine days after the date of this letter to Jane Mecom he made his will of April 28, 1757, printed in facsimile by The Franklin Institute of the State of Pennsylvania as *The Will of Benjamin Franklin 1757* (1949) with an introduction by Carl Van Doren. The second of his legacies reads: "I give to my dear Sister Jane Mecom, the Mortgage I have on my Sister Douse's House and Lot in Boston, with said Douse's Bond, and every Demand I have against my said Sister Douse's Estate. Only I will that my said Sister Douse be never disturbed in her Possession of the said House and Lot during her Life, tho' she should not be able to discharge the said Mortgage or pay the interest arising on the same. Also I give to my Sister Jane Mecom the Share of my Father's Estate, and the particular Legacy which he left me by his will, and also the Debt due to me from that Estate. Also I give to my Sister Jane Mecom, my least Silver Tankard." Jonathan Williams Sr., who was a nephew of Franklin's, not a cousin, had charge of Elizabeth Douse's house and generally of Franklin's affairs in Boston.]

DEAR SISTER   New York, April 19. 1757

    I wrote a few Lines to you yesterday, but omitted to answer yours relating to Sister Douse: As *having their own Way*, is one of the greatest Comforts of Life, to old People, I think their Friends should endeavour to accommodate them in that, as well as in any thing else.—When they have long liv'd in a House, it becomes natural to them, they are almost as closely connected with it as the Tortoise with his Shell, they die if you tear them out of it.—Old Folks & old Trees, if you remove them, tis ten to one that you kill them. So let our good old Sister be no more importun'd on that head. We are growing old fast our selves, and shall expect the same kind of Indulgencies. If we give them, we shall have a Right to receive them in our Turn.

    And as to her few fine Things, I think she is in the right not to sell them, and for the Reason she gives, that they will fetch but little. When that little is spent, they would be of no farther Use to her; but perhaps the Expectation of possessing them at her Death, may make that Person tender & careful of her, and helpful to her, to the amount of ten times their Value. If so, they are put to the best Use they possibly can be.

I hope you visit Sister as often as your Affairs will permit, and afford her what Assistance & Comfort you can, in her present Situation. *Old Age, Infirmities,* & *Poverty,* joined, are Afflictions enough; the *Neglect & Slight* of Friends & near Relations, should never be added.—People in her Circumstances are apt to suspect this sometimes without Cause; *Appearances* should therefore be attended to, in our Conduct towards them, as well as Realities.

I write by this Post to Cousin Williams, to continue his Care, which I doubt not he will do.

We expect to sail in about a Week, so that I can hardly hear from you again on this Side the Water. But let me have a Line from you now & then while I am in London. I expect to stay there at least a 12 month. Direct your Letters to be left for me at the Pensilvania Coffee House in Birchin Lane London. My Love to all, from Dr Sister,

Your affectionate Brother

B FRANKLIN

P.S. April 25. We are still here, & perhaps may be here a Week longer. Once more Adieu my dear Sister.

"We give our consent heartily"

[First printed, from a manuscript now missing, in Sparks, *Familiar Letters*, pp. 52-53, from which it is here reprinted. While Franklin waited impatiently in New York his wife came from Philadelphia and joined him at the house of his partner, James Parker, at Woodbridge, New Jersey. Franklin had furnished Benjamin Mecom with a horse, presumably for the trip from Philadelphia to Boston, to be sold there. "Miss Betsey," whom Benny was to marry, was known to the Franklins, who thought highly of her. Her surname, not hitherto identified, was almost certainly Ross. The record of her marriage seems to have been lost along with the other records of the First Presbyterian Church of Elizabeth during the Revolution, possibly in the fire which destroyed the building on January 25, 1780. Elizabeth Ross appears to have lived in Elizabeth (then commonly called Elizabethtown to distinguish it from Elizabethport), for Franklin in a letter of November 22, 1757, to his wife wrote from London: "I am glad you went to Elizabethtown, and that Ben has got that good girl." Her only son was John Ross Mecom, born in Philadelphia on October 24, 1771, and baptized on August 22, 1772, by the Reverend James Sproutt of the Second Presbyterian Church, of which the records are in the Historical Society of Pennsylvania. This name of the son points to a presumable grandfather in John Ross, former mayor of Elizabeth, who had died in 1754. His will, proved September 9 of that year, left his estate to his wife and children, among them John, Mary Baldwin (wife of Matthias Baldwin), Elizabeth, and Joanna. A letter in the American Philosophical Society from Benjamin Mecom to Deborah Franklin dated January 30, 1758, asked her in a postscript in behalf of his wife to "frank the inclosed Letter to her Brother Baldwin"—which would mean Betsey Mecom's brother-in-law. A letter from Jane Parker, daughter of James Parker, to Deborah Franklin, dated September 16, 1771, and in the American Philosophical Society, said that Joanna could not go to Philadelphia to nurse Mrs. Mecom in her expected lying-in, which would have been the birth of John Ross Mecom. It seems difficult to believe that Betsey, who certainly had a brother-in-law named Baldwin and a son named John Ross, and who almost certainly lived in Elizabeth and had a sister named Joanna, was not the daughter of John Ross, who had daughters named Elizabeth and Joanna and a son-in-law named Baldwin, and who himself lived in Elizabeth.]

Woodbridge, New Jersey, 21 May, 1757

DEAR SISTER,

I received your kind letter of the 9th instant, in which you acquainted me with some of your late troubles. These are troublesome times to us all; but perhaps you have had more than you should. I am glad to hear that Peter is at a place where he has full employ. A trade is a valuable thing; but, unless a habit of industry be acquired with it, it turns out of little use; if he gets *that* in his new place, it will be a happy exchange, and the occasion not an unfortunate one.

It is very agreeable to me to hear so good an account of your other children; in such a number to have no bad ones is a great happiness.

The horse sold very low indeed. If I wanted one to-morrow, knowing his goodness, old as he is, I should freely give more than twice the money for him; but you did the best you could, and I will take of Benny no more than he produced.

I don't doubt but Benny will do very well when he gets to work; but I fear his things from England may be so long a coming, as to occasion the loss of the rent. Would it not be better for you to move into the house? Perhaps not, if he is near being married. I know nothing of that affair, but what you write me, except that I think Miss Betsey a very agreeable, sweet-tempered, good girl, who has had a housewifely education, and will make, to a good husband, a very good wife. Your sister and I have a great esteem for her, and if she will be kind enough to accept of our nephew, we think it will be his own fault, if he is not as happy as the married state can make him. The family is a respectable one, but whether there be any fortune I know not; and as you do not inquire about this particular, I suppose you think with me, that where every thing else desirable is to be met with, that is not very material. If she does not *bring* a fortune she will help to *make* one. Industry, frugality, and prudent economy in a wife, are to a tradesman, in their effects, a fortune; and a fortune sufficient for Benjamin, if his expectations are reasonable. We can only add, that, if the young lady and her friends are willing, we give our consent heartily, and our blessing. My love to brother and the children.

Your affectionate brother,

B. FRANKLIN

P.S. If Benny will promise to be one of the tenderest husbands in the world, I give my consent. He knows already what I think of Miss Betsey. I am his loving aunt,

DEBORAH FRANKLIN

William Franklin to Jane Mecom

[Printed first in Duane, *Works*, VI, 17, from which it is here reprinted. William Franklin, who was to accompany his father to England, had been waiting with him in New York.]

DEAR AND HONOURED AUNT, New York, May 26, 1757.

To find ourselves affectionately remembered by those for whom we have the highest esteem, is of all things most agreeable: this pleasure was afforded me in the greatest degree, when I received your favour of the 9th instant. The many kind wishes it contains for my welfare, lays me under the greatest obligations. I hope my conduct will ever be such as to merit a continuance of your regard.

Being just on the point of embarkation, prevents my adding more than my best respects to Mr. Mecom, cousin Benny, &c. and to desire you will believe me to be,

Your affectionate

And dutiful nephew

WM. FRANKLIN.

"No soapboiler in the king's dominions"

[Printed first, from a manuscript now missing, in Sparks, *Familiar Letters*, pp. 54-57, from which it is here reprinted. Parts of this letter are obscure because the correspondence is one-sided. Of Jane's sons, Edward, a saddler like his father, was then twenty-six, and apparently tubercular. Ebenezer, a baker, was twenty-two, and John, apprenticed to a goldsmith, was sixteen. Peter, eighteen, had learned the family trade of soapboiler from his uncle John, and now, since his uncle's death, hoped to go on making the soap, stamped with a crown, for which John Franklin had had a reputation. Franklin's objection to putting the Franklin arms on the soap recalls a little known letter from Josiah Franklin, the father, to his son Benjamin in Philadelphia dated May 26, 1739, and printed in Duane, *Works*, I, 4n. "Your uncle Benjamin made inquiry of one skilled in heraldry, who told him there is two coats of armour, one belonging to the Franklins of the north, and one to the Franklins of the west. However our circumstances have been such that it hath hardly been worth while to concern ourselves much about these things, any farther than to tickle the fancy a little." As to Benjamin Mecom, it seems clear that he desired an appointment from Franklin to a place in the post office. This seems to have led to a conflict between the Mecoms and the family of John Franklin, who had been postmaster of Boston at the time of his death and had been succeeded by his stepson, Tuthill Hubbart. Evidently Benjamin Mecom and his family believed that a nephew of Franklin ought to be preferred to a stepnephew. Franklin here refused to take sides in that remote family quarrel of the

Boston Franklins. The passage about the aunt and the hammer seems to mean that Peter had made some use of a hammer belonging to his aunt Elizabeth, widow of John Franklin, without her permission, and that she was suspected of having written to Franklin in complaint, when in fact she had not. The aunt in Philadelphia who might sell Peter's soap there was Deborah Franklin. If the youngest of the Mecom sons, Josiah, was not here mentioned, that was no doubt because he was then only fourteen and was already working at the saddler's trade under the direction of his father.]

DEAR SISTER,   New York, 30 May, 1757

I have before me yours of the 9th and 16th instant. I am glad you have resolved to visit sister Douse oftener; it will be a great comfort to her, to find she is not neglected by you, and your example may, perhaps, be followed by some others of her relations.

As Neddy is yet a young man, I hope he may get over the disorder he complains of, and in time wear it out. My love to him and his wife, and the rest of your children. It gives me pleasure to hear, that Eben is likely to get into business at his trade. If he will be industrious and frugal, 'tis ten to one but he gets rich, for he seems to have spirit and activity.

I am glad that Peter is acquainted with the crown-soap business, so as to make what is good of the kind. I hope he will always take care to make it faithfully, and never slight the manufacture, or attempt to deceive by appearances. Then he may boldly put his name and mark, and in a little time it will acquire as good a character, as that made by his late uncle, or any other person whatever. I believe his aunt at Philadelphia can help him to sell a good deal of it; and I doubt not of her doing every thing in her power to promote his interest in that way. Let a box be sent her (but not unless it be right good), and she will immediately return the ready money for it. It was beginning once to be in vogue in Philadelphia, but brother John sent me one box, an ordinary sort, which checked its progress. I would not have him put the Franklin arms on it; but the soapboilers' arms he has a right to use, if he thinks fit. The other would look too much like an attempt to counterfeit. In his advertisements, he may value himself on serving his time with the original maker, but put his own mark or device on the papers, or any thing he may be advised to as proper; only on the soap, as it is called by the name of crown-soap, it seems necessary to use a stamp of that sort, and perhaps no soapboiler in the king's dominions has a better right to the crown than himself.

Nobody has wrote a syllable to me concerning his making use of the hammer, or made the least complaint of him or you. I am sorry, however, that he took it without leave. It was irregular, and if you had not approved of his doing it, I should have thought it indiscreet. *Leave*, they say, *is light*, and it seems to me a piece of respect, that was due to his aunt, to ask it, and I can scarce think she would have refused him the favor.

I am glad to hear Johnny is so good and diligent a workman. If he ever sets up at the goldsmith's business, he must remember, that there is one accomplishment without which he cannot possibly thrive in that trade, i.e. *perfect honesty*. It is a business, that, though ever so uprightly managed, is always liable to suspicion; and if a man is once detected in the smallest fraud, it soon becomes public, and every one is put upon his guard against him; no one will venture to try his wares, or trust him to make up his plate; so at once he is ruined. I hope my nephew will, therefore, establish a character as an *honest* and faithful, as well as *skilful* workman, and then he need not fear for employment.

And now, as to what you propose for Benny, I believe he may be, as you say, well enough qualified for it, and when he appears to be settled, if a vacancy should happen, it is very probable he may be thought of to supply it; but it is a rule with me not to remove any officer, that behaves well, keeps regular accounts, and pays duly; and I think the rule is founded on reason and justice. I have not shown any backwardness to assist Benny, where it could be done without injuring another. But if my friends require of me to gratify not only their inclinations, but their resentments, they expect too much of me. Above all things I dislike family quarrels, and when they happen among my relations, nothing gives me more pain. If I were to set myself up as a judge of those subsisting between you and brother's widow and children, how unqualified must I be, at this distance, to determine rightly, especially having heard but one side. They always treated me with friendly and affectionate regard; you have done the same. What can I say between you, but that I wish you were reconciled, and that I will love that side best, that is most ready to forgive and oblige the other? You will be angry with me here, for putting you and them too much upon a footing; but I shall nevertheless be,

Dear Sister,

Your truly affectionate brother,

B. FRANKLIN

Jane Mecom to Deborah Franklin

[Printed first in Duane, *Letters to Benjamin Franklin*, p. 183, and here printed from the manuscript in the American Philosophical Society. Preposterous news had come to America that Franklin had been made a baronet and appointed governor of Pennsylvania. Jane Mecom, hastening to write to Deborah Franklin in Philadelphia, explained how the news had got to the Mecom household, where Sarah, servant or dependent, was sick. Thomas Flucker, a Boston merchant and justice of the peace who was later to be the last royal secretary of Massachusetts, had told Jonathan Williams Sr., who had told Dr. John Perkins, who had told Jane Mecom's son Edward, from whom the news reached his mother. The words in square brackets were on a small piece torn from the manuscript, but are almost certainly as here supplied. Edward Mecom Jr., who had had "a nother relaps into Raising Blood," died intestate on December 7 of that year. The inventory of his estate, in the Registry of Probate of Suffolk County, Massachusetts, shows that his possessions were small, lists only a "Parcle Sadlers Tools" of nominal value, and indicates that he must have kept a miscellaneous shop in which he, or perhaps his wife, sold flour, sugar, coarse earthenware, quills, cowskins, spurs, spice, crown soap, mustard seed, raisins, butter, needles, thread, garters, beeswax, silk handkerchiefs, hog's-fat, tobacco, short pipes, New England and West India rum, etc. The signature "E Mecom," one of the bondsmen for the administration of the will, seems to be the only surviving first-hand record of Edward Mecom Sr. The total estate, including the stock of the store, was appraised at £45.3.5 lawful money.]

[64]

DEAR SISTER   Boston Janr 29 1758

for so I must call you come what will & If I dont Express
my self proper you must Excuse it seeing I have not been
acostomed to Pay my Complements to Governer & Baronets
Ladys   I am in the midst of a grate wash & Sarah still sick, &
would gladly been Excused writing this Post but my husband
says I must write & Give you Joy which we [sin]searly Joyn in;
I sopose it will [not be?] news to you, but I will tell you how
I [came] by it, Mr Fluker Tould Cousen willams & he Docter
Perkins who Brought it to my Poor Son nedey who has a nother
relaps into Raising Blood & has not Done won stroke of work
this month but was Just a going to begin when he was again
taken Ill pray Pardon my Bad writing & confused composure &
acept it as coming from your Ladyships affectionat Sister & most
obedent
                                       Humble Servant

                                     JANE MECOM

"An acrostick on her name"

[Printed first, from a manuscript now missing, in Duane, *Works*, VI,
39-42, from which it is here reprinted. Sparks, *Works*, VII, 182-185,
omitted the passage between "filthy rags" and "So much by way of
commentary" without indicating the omission. The letter "containing
an account" of the travels of Franklin and his son William in the summer of 1758 was to Deborah Franklin from London, September 6 of
that year.]

DEAR SISTER,   London, September 16, 1758

I received your favour of June 17.   I wonder you have had
no letter from me since my being in England, I have wrote you
at least two, and I think a third before this, and what was next
to waiting on you in person, sent you my picture. In June last
I sent Benny a trunk of books, and wrote to him; I hope they
are come to hand, and that he meets with encouragement in his
business. I congratulate you on the conquest of Cape Breton,
and hope as your people took it by praying, the first time, you

will now pray that it may never be given up again, which you then forgot. Billy is well, but in the country. I left him at Tunbridge Wells, where we spent a fortnight, and he is now gone with some company to see Portsmouth. We have been together over a great part of England this summer, and among other places, visited the town our father was born in, and found some relations in that part of the country still living.

Our cousin Jane Franklin, daughter of our uncle John, died about a year ago; we saw her husband, Robert Page, who gave us some old letters to his wife, from uncle Benjamin. In one of them, dated Boston, July 4, 1723, he writes your uncle Josiah has a daughter Jane, about 12 years old, a good humoured child. So keep up to your character, and don't be angry when you have no letters. In a little book he sent her called "None but Christ," he wrote an acrostick on her name, which for namesakes sake, as well as the good advice it contains, I transcribe and send you, viz.

> Illuminated from on high,
> And shining brightly in your sphere,
> Ne'er feint, but keep a steady eye,
> Expecting endless pleasures there.
>
> Flee vice as you'd a serpent flee:
> Raise *faith* and *hope* three stories higher,
> And let Christ's endless love to thee
> Ne'er cease to make thy love aspire:
> Kindness of heart by words express,
> Let your obedience be sincere,
> In prayer and praise your God address,
> Nor cease, till he can cease to hear.

After professing truly that I had great esteem and veneration for the pious author, permit me a little to play the commentator and critic on these lines. The meaning of *three stories higher*, seems somewhat obscure. You are to understand then that faith, hope, and charity have been called the three steps of Jacob's ladder, reaching from earth to heaven; our author calls them *stories*, likening religion to a building, and these are the three stories of the christian edifice. Thus improvement in religion is called *building up* and *edification*. *Faith* is then the ground floor, *hope* is up one pair of stairs. My dear beloved Jenny, don't delight so much to dwell in those lower rooms, but get as fast as you can into the garret, for in truth the best room in the house is *charity*. For my part, I wish the house was turned upside down; 'tis so difficult (when one is fat) to go upstairs; and not only so, but I imagine *hope* and *faith* may be more firmly built upon *charity*, than *charity* upon *faith* and *hope*. However that may be, I think it the better reading to say—

Raise faith and hope one story higher.

Correct it boldly, and I'll support the alteration; for when you are up two stories already, if you raise your building three stories higher you will make five in all, which is two more than there should be, you expose your upper rooms more to the winds and storms; and, besides, I am afraid the foundation will hardly bear them, unless indeed you build with such light stuff as straw and stubble, and that you know won't stand fire.

Again, where the author says: "Kindness of heart by words express." Strike out *words* and put in *deeds*. The world is too full of compliments already. They are the rank growth of every soil, and choak the good plants of benevolence, and beneficence; nor do I pretend to be the first in this comparison of words and actions to plants; you may remember an antient poet, whose works we have all studied and copied at school long ago.

A man of words and not of deeds
Is like a garden full of weeds.

'Tis pity that good works, among some sorts of people, are so little valued, and good words admired in their stead: I mean seemingly pious discourses, instead of humane benevolent actions. Those they almost put out of countenance, by calling morality *rotten morality*—righteousness *ragged righteousness*, and even filthy rags—and when you mention virtue, pucker up their noses as if they smelt a stink; at the same time that they eagerly snuff up an empty canting harangue, as if it was a posey of the choicest flowers: so they have inverted the good old verse, and say now

A man of deeds and not of words
Is like a garden full of

I have forgot the rhyme, but remember 'tis something the very reverse of perfume. So much by way of commentary. My wife will let you see my letter, containing an account of our travels, which I would have you to read to sister Douse, and give my love to her. I have no thoughts of returning till next year, and then may possibly have the pleasure of seeing you and yours —take Boston in my way home.

My love to brother and all your children, concludes at this time from,

Dear Jenny,

Your affectionate brother,

B. FRANKLIN

"Our Grandfather Peter Foulger"

[Printed first in Goodman, *A Benjamin Franklin Reader*, pp. 751-752, and here more correctly from the manuscript in the American Philosophical Society. Attleborough is in Norfolk, not in Suffolk, and near Norwich, from which Peter Folger came to Massachusetts about 1635. The "Germantown Affair" was a plan to manufacture glass with the aid of imported German glassblowers at a point in Boston Harbor in what is now Quincy. John Franklin was one of the proprietors in the company, and Peter Franklin, though not a proprietor, seems to have been interested in it. Benjamin Franklin had built two "tenements," small wooden houses, there, which he had bequeathed, in his will of April 28, 1757, to his nephew James Franklin of Newport. For an account of the undertaking, and its failure, see William S. Pattee, *A History of Old Braintree and Quincy* (Quincy, 1878), pp. 473-483. Franklin had read in Cotton Mather's *Magnalia Christi Americana* of William Laud, archbishop of Canterbury, and of Thomas Mayhew, patentee and first governor of Martha's Vineyard and missionary to the Indians there. Abisha Folger of Nantucket was a grandnephew of Franklin's mother.]

DEAR SISTER   London Nov. 11, 1758

I wrote you a long Letter of Sept. 26. & again I wrote to you
Oct. 2. since which I have receiv'd your Favour of Augt 15.
You mention its being sent by the Son of our good Friend Dr
Perkins. I have not seen him yet, but shall endeavour to find
him out. I hope my Health is now pretty well established by
the frequent Journies I have made this Summer, and that I
shall be able to go pretty well thro' another Winter. In our last
Journey, stopping at a Place call'd Attleborough, I think it was
in Suffolk, we found in the Church Yard the following Inscription on a large handsome Stone

*"In Memory of Thomas Foulger, late of Illington Hall, who
"died Dec. 23d 1754, aged 51 Years.*

As I have never in my Life met with or heard of any Foulgers
but those of our Family, I made Billy copy it, intending to
enquire after them when we return'd, but we came another
Way. Pray ask Cousin Abisha Foulger if he or any in Nantucket
can tell what Part of England our Grandfather Peter Foulger
came from. I think I have heard our Mother say he came out
of Suffolk, but am not certain. In Dr Mather's Magnalia, I find
that in Bishop Laud's Time a great many eminent Ministers
with Numbers of their Friends and Hearers went out of Suffolk, Norfolk, & Lincolnshire, to New England, flying from the
Persecution then on foot against the Puritans. It is possible he
might be among them. The Dr mentions him in Page 54 of
Book VI. in the terms of "an able and godly Englishman, well
learn'd in the Scriptures," who about the year 1647 was employ'd as an Assistant to Mr Mayhew, the same that converted
the Indians of Marthas Vineyard. I never expected much from
the Germantown Affair, so am not disappointed. I took Lots and
built there in Complaisance to my Brothers, but the Expence
was not great. I wish the Glasshouse you mention may have all
the Success the Undertakers can desire.

Mr Strahan has sent a very large Cargo to Benny wch I hope
will turn out to his Advantage. I have also order'd him a Cargo

of Stationery which will go per the next Ship. I am glad to hear he is industrious and frugal, and that you like his Wife: I make no doubt, that with those Qualities, & the Advantage of so discreet a Partner, he will do well in the World, which will give me great Pleasure.

Billy presents his Duty to you & Brother, & joins with me in Love to you all. He last Week put on the Gown as a Lawyer, being call'd to the Bar in Westminster Hall. He was enter'd of the Middle Temple some Years before we came over. I am, my dear Sister,

Your affectionate Brother

B FRANKLIN

"The four American Shares"

[Here first printed from the manuscript in the American Philosophical Society. The "Cousin Fisher" mentioned was Mary Fisher, daughter of Josiah Franklin's eldest brother Thomas. Benjamin Franklin had met both her and her husband, Richard Fisher, at Wellingborough in Northamptonshire in the summer of 1758. "Cousin Samuel Franklin" was the son of Franklin's Uncle Benjamin and lived in Boston.]

London, July 14. 1759

DEAR SISTER,

I received your kind Letter of Jany 31. You are very good in not resenting some Part of my Letter of September 16. which I confess was a little rude; but you fatfolks can't bear Malice.

Our Cousin Fisher & her Husband are both dead since I saw them. She surviv'd him but a few Days. What she had in her Disposal was but little; and it was divided into 7 equal Shares, among seven of us who were her Relations in equal Degree, viz. three here in England 1. Mrs Ann Farrow Daughter of our Uncle John Franklin; 2 Mrs Eleanor Morris, Daughter of our Aunt Hannah: 3. My self.—And four in America, 1. Cousin Samuel Franklin. 2 Sister Dowse. 3. Brother Peter. 4. Yourself.—Each Share was just £11.8.4 Sterling. I divided what came to me equally between Mrs Farrow & Mrs Morris, the two Cousins here, they being ancient Women &

[70]

poor. The four American Shares are paid into my Hands for the Parties, and I desire you would let me know what will be most agreable to have it sent in. I would have you also visit Sister Dowse, and read her this Letter, & help her to contrive what I shall send hers in. I can now only add, that I am,

Your ever Affectionate Brother

B FRANKLIN

"There now remains but three"

[Excerpts from this letter were printed in Sparks, *Familiar Letters*, p. 9n., as "to a relative," and p. 63n., as "to a sister in America"; it was first printed entire in Goodman, *A Benjamin Franklin Reader*, pp. 753-754. It is here printed more correctly from the manuscript in the American Philosophical Society. Elizabeth Franklin Douse had died about the 1st of October 1759, and the three surviving Franklins were Jane, Peter, and Benjamin. Jacob Bailey, who carried this letter to Jane Mecom, dined in London with Franklin on March 5 and 25. William S. Bartlett, *The Frontier Missionary: A Memoir of the Life of the Rev. Jacob Bailey, A.M.* (New York, 1853), pp. 63, 66.]

DEAR SISTER,   London, Jan. 9. 1760

I received a Letter or two from you, in which I perceive you have misunderstood and taken unkindly something I said to you in a former jocular one of mine concerning Charity. I forget what it was exactly, but I am sure I neither exprest nor meant any personal Censure on you or any body. If any thing, it was a general Reflection on our Sect; we zealous Presbyterians being too apt to think ourselves alone in the right, and that besides all the Heathens, Mahometans and Papists, whom we give to Satan in a Lump, other Sects of Christian Protestants that do not agree with us, will hardly escape Perdition. And I might recommend it to you to be more charitable in that respect than many others are; not aiming at any Reproof, as you term it; for if I were dispos'd to reprove you, it should be for your only Fault, that of supposing and spying Affronts, and catching at them where they are not. But as you seem sensible of this your

[71]

self, I need not mention it; and as it is a Fault that carries with it its own sufficient Punishment, by the Uneasiness and Fretting it produces, I shall not add Weight to it. Besides, I am sure your own good Sense, join'd to your natural good Humour will in time get the better of it.

I am glad that Cousin Benny could advance you the Legacy, since it suited you best to receive it immediately. Your Resolution to forbear buying the Cloak you wanted, was a prudent one; —but when I read it, I concluded you should not however be without one, and so desired a Friend to buy one for you. The Cloth ones, it seems, are quite out of Fashion here, and so will probably soon be out with you; I have therefore got you a very decent one of another kind, which I shall send you by the next convenient Opportunity.

It is remarkable that so many Breaches should be made by Death in our Family in so short a Space. Out of Seventeen Children that our Father had, thirteen liv'd to grow up and settle in the World. I remember these thirteen (some of us then very young) all at one Table, when an Entertainment was made in our House on Occasion of the Return of our Brother Josiah, who had been absent in the East Indies, and unheard of for nine Years. Of these thirteen, there now remains but three. As our Number diminishes, let our Affection to each other rather increase: for besides its being our Duty, tis our Interest; since the more affectionate Relations are to one another, the more they are respected by the rest of the World.

My Love to Brother Mecom and your Children. I shall hardly have time to write to Benny by this Conveyance. Acquaint him that I received his Letter of Sept. 10. and am glad to hear he is in so prosperous a Way, as not to regret his leaving Antigua. I am, my dear Sister,

Your ever affectionate Brother

B. FRANKLIN

March 26. The above was wrote at the time it is dated; but on reading it over, I apprehended that something I had said in it about Presbyterians, and Affronts, might possibly give more Offence, and so I threw it by, concluding not to send it. However, Mr. Bailey calling on me, and having no other Letter ready nor time at present to write one, I venture to send it, and beg you will excuse what you find amiss in it. I send also by Mr Bailey the Cloak mention'd in it, and also a Piece of Linnen, which I beg you to accept of from

Your loving Brother

BF.

I recd your Letter, & Benny's & Peter's by Mr Bailey, which I shall answer per next Opportunity.

Jane Mecom to Deborah Franklin

[Here first printed from the manuscript in the American Philosophical Society. In the *Pennsylvania Gazette* for March 6, 1760, William Dunlap, a cousin of Deborah Franklin, advertised for sale *A Letter to the People of Pennsylvania: occasioned by the Assembly's passing that important Act for constituting the Judges of the Supreme Court and Common Pleas, during Good Behaviour.* "Cousen Holmes" was William Homes, son of Jane Mecom's dead sister Mary Homes. "Beney & Betsey" were Benjamin Mecom and his wife Elizabeth. They then had at least one daughter, named Sarah, who had been baptized on October 1, 1758. *The Manifesto Church. Records of the Church in Brattle Square Boston 1699-1872*, Boston, 1902, p. 178, which gives the name of the mother as Elizabeth Mecom but does not mention the father. On February 9, 1761, Benjamin Mecom wrote his aunt Deborah Franklin that he had another daughter, Deborah, baptized five weeks before. There was a third, Abiah, whose name does not appear among Boston baptisms and who may have been born after the family left for New York. A fourth, Jane, seems to have been born about 1765. Duane, *Letters to Benjamin Franklin*, p. 4. And by May 20, 1768, there was a fifth, whose name is not known but who was presumably among the "five Dafters" mentioned by Deborah Franklin in a letter of that date to her husband. "Litle Ben," who had apparently been mentioned in a letter from Deborah Franklin, has not been identified. "Jeney Mecom," who seemed to be "going the same way of her father & sister," is a mystery. If "Beney & Betsey . . . with all there famely" were well, this could not have been a daughter of theirs. Nor does it seem possible that the reference could have been to Jane Mecom's

[73]

daughter Jane, who was then within a month of being fifteen and would not have spent so much time in her cradle. The best guess seems to be that "Poor Litle Jeney Mecom" was a child of Edward Mecom Jr. and his wife Ruth Whittemore. Franklin had congratulated Jane Mecom on having a grandchild in his letter of June 10, 1756. That child seems to have died, and its father died in January 1758. "Litle Jeney" might seem to be following her father and her sister—if the elder child was a girl. Ruth Whittemore Mecom, as will appear in a later note, married Thomas Foot on November 20, 1760.]

DEAR SISTER

I have recd yrs with the Adishonal satisfaction of my Brothers, Informing of his Good Helth but not a word of his coming Home, I cannot Return his Leter this Post because I shant have time to shew it to Cousen Holmes as you Desiered. mean while I have a favour to Ask which is that you would send me won of them Leters to the People of Pensylvania Advertised in yr Paper to be sould by Mr Dunlap.

Beney & Betsey are well with all there famely & our Relations in General Exept Poor Litle Jeney Mecom who seems to be going the same way of her father & sister, she Pines a way Looses her Apetite but withall her Bowels swells Prodidgusly so that with a Litle slip out of a Chare she bust her self, She seems often to have somthing choaking in her throat & dont Incline to stir but mostly keeps in her cradle her mother has but Ill helth, but why should I Enumerate trobles it is an unpleasing subject.

Letle Ben has expearanced what is the comon fate of all children at some time or other but the Litle Rogues all want to be Pityed by them that Loves them & I sopose to Recve that comfort he would be brought to you to Kiss the Dear Lip after it was Hurt, if you Pleas you may add to the number on my acount who would have taken Pleasure in an opertunity to do it my self, dos he Look Like his Unkle. Remember my Love to Saley & to all friends & Exept the same from yr affectionat sister

JANE MECOM

Boston   march 17, 1760

"Excuse the shortness of this"

[Here first printed from the manuscript in the American Philosophical Society. "Cousin Benjn" was Benny Mecom. William Franklin, appointed royal governor of New Jersey, had not accompanied his father home.]

DEAR SISTER,   Philada Nov. 11. 1762.

I received your kind Letter of the 1st Instant. It was on that Day I had the great Happiness of finding my Family well at my own House after so long an Absence.—I am well except a little Touch of the Gout, which my Friends say is no Disease.— Cousin Benjn has been to see me as you supposed, & yesterday he return'd homewards.—My Love to Brother Mecom & your Children. Excuse the shortness of this, as my Time is much taken up at present. I am, my dear Sister,

Your affectionate Brother

B FRANKLIN

Billy stays in England
a little longer
My Wife can't write now
but sends her Love

"The Promotion & Marriage"

[Here first printed from the manuscript in the American Philosophical Society. William Franklin, now promoted to his governorship, had been married to Elizabeth Downes of Barbados in London on September 4.]

DEAR SISTER,   Philada Nov. 25. 1762

I thank you for your obliging Letter of the 12th Instant. — My Wife says she will write to you largely by next Post, being at present short of Time. — As to the Promotion & Marriage you mention, I shall now only say that the Lady is of so amiable a Character, that the latter gives me more Pleasure than the former, tho' I have no doubt but that he will make as good a Governor as Husband: for he has good Principles & good Dispositions, & I think is not deficient in good Understanding. I am as ever

Your affectionate Brother

B FRANKLIN

Our love to Brother &
your Children.

"Bachelor's Hall"

[Here first printed from the manuscript in the American Philosophical Society. By "your Sister" he meant his wife. He seems not to have kept house in Boston.]

DEAR SISTER   Philada Feb. 21. 1763

I have now the Pleasure of acquainting you that my Son & Daughter are safely arriv'd at my House, and both very well. They present their Duty to Brother Mecom & you. He sets out for his Government on Wednesday.

I am greatly to blame for not sending the enclos'd sooner. It was wrote by your Sister several Weeks since, & given to me to be forwarded. I thought it was done, or rather did not think of it at all till this Morning, when I found it on my Desk cover'd with some Papers. Excuse me, if you can.

Tell me how you do, & where you live, and what you would advise me to concerning Lodging when I come to Boston. As I think I shall stay two or three Months, I have half a mind to keep House that is, Bachelor's Hall, in that which was Sister Douse's.— Cannot one hire Furniture for a Quarter or Half a Year? In London one may very easily. — I hope to see you in May or June.

My Love to all. I am as ever

Your affectionate Brother

B FRANKLIN

"The Pleasure of seeing you"

[Here first printed from the manuscript in the American Philosophical Society. John Foxcroft and Franklin each had the title of Joint Deputy

B. FRANKLIN, L.L.D. F.R.S.

Born at Boston in New England, Jan 17.th 1706.

NON SORDIDUS AUCTOR NATURÆ VERIQUE.

New York, June 19. 1763

Dear Sister,

We are thus far on our Way to Boston, and hope to be there in about three Weeks. — I purpose to lodge at your House if you can conveniently receive me. Sally is now with her Brother at Amboy, and will be here in a few Days. If I can well do it, I shall bring her with me; and if you cannot accommodate us both, one of us may lodge at Cousin Williams's, — on second Thoughts, it will be best that she should be there, as there is a Harpsichord; & I would not have her lose her Practice: — and then I shall be more with my dear Sister. — I have seen Cousins Benny & Johny here, and they are both well, & the Children; I purpose to go again this Afternoon, to see Betsey, who was not at home when I was there. — My Love to Brother, &c. I am, Dear Jenny,

Your ever loving Brother

B Franklin

Benjamin Franklin to Jane Mecom, June 19, 1763

Postmaster General and Manager of the Posts in North America, Foxcroft concerned particularly with the service in Virginia and southward.]

DEAR SISTER   Philada May 20. 1763

I am just return'd from Virginia, & find your Favour of April 11. I purpose setting out with my Colleague Mr Foxcroft for New England, the Beginning of next Month, & hope soon for the Pleasure of seeing you; but have no Expectation of bringing my Dame to undertake such a Journey; and have not yet ask'd her Opinion of Sally going.— My Love to Brother & your Children.   I am,

Your affectionate Brother

B FRANKLIN

"I purpose to lodge at your House"

[Here first printed from the manuscript in the American Philosophical Society. "Cousin Williams," Jonathan Williams Sr., was married to Franklin's niece Grace Harris, daughter of Anne Franklin Harris. Benjamin Mecom had then failed in Boston and had set up in New York at "The Modern Printing-Office on Rotten Row." John Mecom was in New York with his brother. Sally's "Brother at Amboy" was Governor William Franklin, and Betsey was Elizabeth, wife of Benjamin Mecom. The *Boston Evening-Post* for July 25 announced the arrival of Franklin and Foxcroft on the afternoon of the 20th.]

DEAR SISTER,   New York, June 19. 1763

We are thus far on our Way to Boston, and hope to be there in about three Weeks.— I purpose to lodge at your House if you can conveniently receive me. Sally is now with her Brother at Amboy, and will be here in a few Days. If I can well do it, I shall bring her with me; and if you cannot accommodate us both, one of us may lodge at Cousin Williams's; — on second Thoughts, it will be best that she should be there, as there is a Harpsichord; & I would not have her lose her Practice:— and then I shall be more with my dear Sister.— I have seen Cousins Benny & Johny here, and they are both well, & the Children;

I purpose to go again this Afternoon, to see Betsey, who was not at home when I was there.— My Love to Brother, &c. I am, Dear Jenny,   Your ever loving Brother

B FRANKLIN

"Safe home on Saturday Night"

[Printed first in Carl Van Doren, *Benjamin Franklin's Autobiographical Writings*, pp. 143-144; and here printed again from the manuscript in the American Philosophical Society. The letter furnishes the only detailed itinerary of one of Franklin's many journeys from Boston to Philadelphia. His friend Dr. Joshua Babcock lived at Westerly, Rhode Island, where he was postmaster. In the letters of the years 1761-1763 neither Franklin nor his sister mentions her son Peter, whose mind was evidently failing. On February 9, 1761, Benjamin Mecom wrote from Boston to Deborah Franklin: "Brother Peter Franklin Mecom is returned from the Camp," which may mean that Peter had enlisted or tried to enlist in the Massachusetts forces raised in 1760 for the attack on Canada. His name however does not appear in any list of soldiers. "Though he was unwel when he first came to Town," Benjamin Mecom went on, "he is now quite recovered and thinks seriously of settling to Business for Nothing prevents his really doing so but *Want*"— that is, wanting to. "We are unwilling to disturb you with our Uneasiness, hoping hereafter to be able to send you better News." This letter was printed in Duane, *Letters to Benjamin Franklin*, pp. 184-185, but it is here quoted from the manuscript in the American Philosophical Society. Franklin's visit to Boston in 1763 made him aware, if he had not known it before, that Peter Mecom was insane. Writing from Philadelphia on November 28, 1763, Franklin instructed Jonathan Williams Sr. to have the house, formerly Elizabeth Douse's, in Unity Street "near Dr Cutler's Church," repaired and let "to as good a Tenant and for as good a Rent as you can well get. . . . It is farther my Desire & Direction, that the Rent of the House be applied to assist my Sister Mecom in the Maintenance of her unhappy Son, and I request you to pay it for that purpose as it arises." Elizabeth Douse, dying intestate, left a "Mansion House & Land" valued at £150 in the Inventory in the Registry of Probate of Suffolk County, Massachusetts, and personal property worth about £40. Her indebtedness to her brother Benjamin was £251.17.11 1/5, and he was obliged to spend £148.4.8 on repairs to make it rentable, as appears from his manuscript accounts with Jonathan Williams Sr. in the American Philosophical Society. The accounts show that when one tenant, James Reilly, "proved unable to pay and at last was Oblig'd to quit the House by a Writ of Ejectment, the Rent was regularly paid to Mrs. Mecom." The balance thus provided by Williams up to September 1768 amounted to £18.8.5, but it does not appear what the normal rent was, or whether there was difficulty with other tenants. Fifteen pounds a year, a probable rent, would then have paid for boarding Peter with a woman in the country.]

DEAR SISTER   Philada Nov. 7. 1763

We stopt one Day at Mrs Green's, and got to Newport the Saturday Evening after we left you, staid there till Tuesday Afternoon, got to Dr Babcock's on Wednesday, staid there till Friday, then went to New London, where we staid among our Friends till Tuesday, then set out for Newhaven, where we arriv'd on Thursday Morning, set out from thence on Friday Afternoon & got to New York on Monday following, and after staying one Day there, one at Woodbridge with Mr Parker, & one at Burlington with Billy who met us 20 Miles on the Road, we got safe home on Saturday Night the 5th Instant, having had a most pleasant Journey without the least ill Accident, and found all well: Thanks to God.

Sally joins in Love to all Friends, and will write if she is not too much interrupted by visiting Friends. I am

Your affectionate Brother

B FRANKLIN

"Very happy in being at home"

[An excerpt from this letter was printed in Sparks, *Familiar Letters*, p. 88n, as "to another friend." The whole was printed first in Goodman, *A Benjamin Franklin Reader*, pp. 754-755. It is here more correctly printed from the manuscript in the American Philosophical Society. At Portsmouth, New Hampshire, Franklin had fallen from his horse and dislocated a shoulder which was slow in healing. Sarah Bowles, who lodged with Jane Mecom, was a stepdaughter of Sarah Franklin Davenport, whose husband had first married Grace Tileston of Dorchester. Sarah, daughter of James and Grace Davenport, was the widow of Samuel Bowls (or Bowles) of Dorchester, an apothecary, and in 1763 was forty-four. Boston Registry Records, XXVIII (Marriages 1700-1751), 94, 141; *New England Historical and Genealogical Register*, XXXIII, 31-32.]

DEAR SISTER   Philada Dec. 15. 1763

I thank you for your kind Congratulations on my safe Return. Brother Peter is with me, & very well, except being touch'd a little in his Head with something of *the Doctor*, of which I hope to cure him.— For my own Part, I find my self at present quite clear of Pain, & so have at length left off the cold Bath; there is however still some Weakness in my Shoulder, though much stronger than when I left Boston, & Mending. I am otherwise very happy in being at home, where I am allow'd to know when I have eat enough & drank enough, am warm enough, and sit in a Place that I like, &c. and no body pretends to know what I feel better than I do my self. Don't imagine that I am a whit the less sensible of the Kindness I experienc'd among my Friends in New England, I am very thankful for it, & shall always retain a grateful Remembrance of it. Remember me affectionately to all that enquire after

Dear Sister,

My Compliments to good   Your loving Brother
Mrs Bowles.—Sally   B FRANKLIN
writes.

"The Death of your Daughter"

[Here first printed from the manuscript in the Yale University Library. Sarah Mecom Flagg had died on June 12 of that year. Peter Franklin had gone from Newport to be postmaster in Philadelphia.]

DEAR SISTER   Philada July 10. 1764

We all condole with you most sincerely on the Death of your Daughter. She always appear'd to me of a sweet and amiable Temper, and to have many other good Qualities that must make the Loss of her more grievous for Brother & you to bear. Our only Comfort under such Afflictions is, that God knows what is best for us, and can bring Good out of what appears Evil. She is doubtless happy:—which none of us are while in this Life.

Brother Peter & Sister are well. Their Maid which they brought with them, and a young Girl, have been both inoculated & have got finely over the small Pox. They join with Mrs Franklin Sally & my self in Love to you & yours: But do not write; as no Letters can now go free in America but mine, Mr Foxcroft's & our Secretary's:—the latter only Business of the Office. The Act of Parliament forbidding.—I am

Your ever affectionate Brother

B Franklin

"To attempt it would hazard my Place"

[Here first printed from the manuscript in the American Philosophical Society. Jane Mecom's "late Loss" was the death of her daughter Sarah Flagg on June 12 of that year. The "Mr Flag" who must pay for letters to him is less likely to have been her surviving husband, whom Franklin would naturally have called Cousin Flagg, than some elder Flagg, perhaps William Flagg's father or uncle.]

Dear Sister   Philada July 24. 1764

It is not in my power to dispense with an Act of Parliament.—To attempt it would hazard my Place.—The Privilege of Franking my own Letters is indulg'd to me by the Act;—but I have been given to understand that 'tis a Trust, which tis expected I will not violate by covering the Letters of others. Mr Flag must therefore pay for the Letters you send him; & I think he should also pay the Letters he sends to you.—Your Sister has just now paid 2/6 for a Letter to herself from New York.—She would have wrote to condole with you on your late Loss, & so would Brother Peter; but that they would not put you to Charge.—We all join in Love to you & yours.

Your affectionate Brother

B Franklin

Jane Mecom to Deborah Franklin

[Here first printed from the manuscript in the American Philosophical Society. The child that had died was Mary (Polly) Flagg, about the beginning of March according to Jane Mecom's "Book of Ages." The other child was Josiah Flagg, born November 12, 1760, lamed for life by a fall in his fifth year. Still another Flagg child, Sarah, had died on November 9, 1764, "aged 17 months." The father, William Flagg, had apparently hurt his arm in some accident. The ailing dependent elsewhere called "Poor Sarah" was the "my Sarah" here mentioned. By "cousin Sally" Jane Mecom meant her niece Sarah Franklin. The Polly who held "beter but far from well" was Mary Mecom, then seventeen.]

DEAR SISTER   Apr 6—1765

I have yrs of March 5th & Recd the magizeen for which I thank you, I have brewed the spruce Bear twice & have Reason to think it is Good in the case you were so Good as to care for, Polly holds beter but far from well.   the sick child I mentioned to you in my Last Died the next Day, & the other childs Knee grows worce, the fathers Arm Grows beter but is so weak He cant Lift it to His Head nor Do the Least thing & my Sarah has keept her bed Ever since Ecxep 2 or 3 Days she has sat up in a chare about 2 Hours so that my mind is keept in a contineual Agitation that I Dont know how to write.
we have Grat Joy with you at the News of our Brothers arival in England tho we know it no other way than by that smal line in the News Paper there is two Ships Arived hear from London since & not a word of Him.
Pray Remember my Love to cousin Sally & Brother Peter & wife, & Exept the same yr self from yr Loving sister

JANE MECOM

"The Use of my Arm"

[Here first printed from the manuscript in the American Philosophical Society. Edward Mecom, to whom Franklin sent his love, died on September 11, 1765, before this letter could reach his widow.]

London, Augt 29. 1765.

DEAR SISTER,

It pains me that I have so long omitted writing to you;—and I do not complain that it is so long since I have been favour'd with a Line from you: for being so bad a Correspondent my self, I have no right to complain of others.—Indeed I have so many and such long Letters to write, which I cannot dispense with, that I am forc'd to trespass on the Goodness of such Friends as I trust will be kind enough to make some Allowance for me; as my writing Work really grows heavy on me, & hurts my Health by confining me too much, & preventing my taking proper Exercise.

How have you done since I last heard from you, & how is it with your Family?—I have pretty well recover'd the Use of my Arm, and think it may in time be as strong as ever. Give my Love to Brother Mecom & your Children. I can now only add, that I am, as ever,

Your affectionate Brother

I purpose writing to my
Cousin Williams & other   B FRANKLIN
Boston Friends shortly

Jane Mecom to Deborah Franklin

[Here first printed from the manuscript in the American Philosophical Society. The "Grat Pope" was Alexander Pope, whose work Jane Mecom more than once mentioned in her letters. The "four Near & Dear Relations" whom Jane Mecom had lost in "fiveteen months" were her daughter Sarah Flagg, on June 12, 1764; Sarah's two daughters, Sarah on November 9, 1764, and Mary early in March 1765; and now Edward, Jane Mecom's husband, September 11. It was the Reverend Samuel Cooper of the Brattle Street Church who preached a special sermon for his bereaved parishioner and comforted her with the thought that even "Pall" (St. Paul) had suffered many afflictions.]

Boston Sept 28 1765

DEAR SISTER

Nothing but troble can you hear from me but I do my Endevour to adopt the Grat Popes Doctrin with Regard to the Providence of God what Ever is is Right in fiveteen months I have been bereved of four Near & Dear Relations, in a few Days after I wrote my Last to you it Pleased God to Call my Husband out of this Troblesom world where he had Injoyed Litle & suffered much by Sin & Sorrow. He is Gone to a world of Spirits from whence none has Ever Returned to give us an acount of what is there transacted, but it has Pleased God to favour us with a Revealation in which we are asured the Godly shall Injoy a Perfect Happyness in His Presence for Ever,

Mr Cooper the first sabath I went to meeting after a Long confinement with my sick family comforted me with a Sermon from the fourth chapr of 2d of Corenthans 17 vs for our Light Afflictions which is but for a moment worketh for us a far more Exeding and Eternal weight of Glory. He shew in How many Respects Afflictions workd thus to a belever, & only to them; for to the wicked worldly sorrow worked Death, & that it was Pall that could say this that had meet with such a Large Portion of affliction Ever since He had Profesed Christ. to me the Sermon was a master Peec of the kind & several others I heard Speak of it were of my mind, but I am not Good at Repeeting or Remembring tho I hope I Retain so much of the Sence as in some measure to Enable me with the asistance of Gods Spirit to Influenc my conduct Hear in this world & throw the merits of Christ Give me Hopes of a Gloryous Eternity.

I am Dear Sister yr affectionat Sister

JANE MECOM

Remember my Love to
Cousen Sally & to brother
when you write to Him

Edward Mecom: Intestate

[Edward Mecom, "Sadler," died intestate on September 11, 1765. The Registry of the Court of Probate of Suffolk County, Massachusetts, shows that on October 25 Jane Mecom, Jonathan Williams Sr., and Josiah Mecom, Saddlemaker, gave bond in the amount of £1000 lawful money of the province, which would be due at the end of one calendar year unless Jane Mecom had by January 25, 1766, presented a "true and perfect Inventory of all and singular the Goods, Chattels, Rights and Credits of the said Deceased, which have or shall come to the Hands, Possession or Knowledge of her the said Administratrix or into the Hands or Possession of any other Person or Persons," to the Register of the Court. On October 30, 1765, Timothy Newell and Moses Deshon, appraisers, completed the inventory, which Jane Mecom presented to Thomas Hutchinson, judge of probate, on December 19. She asked to be allowed £4 12s for "Funeral Charges," £5 "for what I am to pay the Dr for last Sickness," 10s for the cost of executing the administratrix's bond, and other small expenses amounting to £10 13s. Hutchinson allowed these charges and also £30 13s 4d "for necessary Implements and her trouble as Administratrix." The inventory put the value of Edward Mecom's property "in the Shop" at £2 19s: including "3 Shop Windows, a parcell old Sadlers Tools, 8 doz White Setts, 10 p[airs] Bridle Bills, 1 piece Girth Webb, 2 Girths, 4 old Saddle Trees, 2 old Bills, 6 Blocks, old Iron cup, old iron Kettle, a Bench, 1 Close Hawse [clothes horse?], 1 old Lamp"—this last item valued at 2 shillings. His "wearing Apparell," was "1 Thick Sett Coat 1/16/0, 2 old Coats &c 5s, 1 Beaver Hat £1, 1 old hat 2 old Wiggs 2s 8d." Besides these things particularly his, all the household goods were listed as his assets: in the lower room, which was presumably on the ground floor behind the shop, in the kitchen, and in the chambers. His clothes and the rest of the household goods were valued at a total of £38 5s 4d. The nine chairs and the table in the lower room seem to indicate that the family and the lodgers used it for a dining room. That this was a boarding house appears from the list of five beds, "3 Straw Beds 3 old Bedsteads," a "Servants Bed & Bed[din]g, 2 old Bedsteads," though with them went a surprisingly small amount of bedding, and no pillows listed. The house seems to have been, on the whole, adequately though not expensively equipped. There were "3 Large 9 Tea Spoons, Tea Tongs," presumably silver, valued at £2 12s 6d, but the rest of the tableware listed was "Old Pewter Plates, Dishes &c" valued at £2 4s 4d. There were "21 Pictures 20/" and a pair of "Dogs," presumably china. The Josiah Mecom associated in the administration was Jane Mecom's son, then twenty-two, who had chosen his father's trade.]

"The best of Brothers"

[Here first printed from the manuscript in the American Philosophical Society. Jane Mecom's household in Hanover Street included her daughters Jane (Jenny) and Mary (Polly), her son-in-law William Flagg, whose wife Sarah had died the year before, and two small Flagg children, Jane and Josiah. Two others, Sarah and Mary, had died in Jane Mecom's house since their mother's death. Flagg worked at manual labor, and could pay little for the keep of his family. The other boarders were Colonel Joseph Ingersoll's two orphaned young daughters; Sarah Bowles, identified in an earlier note as a widowed stepdaughter of Sarah Davenport; and the dependent "Old Sarah." The Flaggs and Ingersolls and Sarah Bowles were all needy relations, whom Jane Mecom kept "at a Low Rate" which barely enabled her to meet her indispensable expenses. In the midst of these troubles Jane Mecom had been further disturbed by the news that her brother had nominated his friend John Hughes to the office of stamp collector in Philadelphia; and horrified by the actions of the Boston mob which in August 1765 had destroyed Lieutenant Governor Thomas Hutchinson's house. Hutchinson had been kind to her "in the capasety of a Judg," as probate judge, an office he had held since 1752. Hutchinson did not in fact go to London that winter, or take Jane's letter; and he was eventually indemnified for his losses at the hands of the mob. A few illegible words in the manuscript are indicated with questions in square brackets [?], but on the whole the letter was written no worse than others, though Jane Mecom apologized for it.]

DEAR BROTHER   Boston, Dec. 30, 1765

I have alredy wrote you two Leters won about four months ago by Capt. Freeman, the other about a month Past by Capt. Logee, since which I recved won from you which came by way of Nantucket which was Extreemly comforting to me, as I was almost Tempted to think you had forgot me, but I check those thoughts with the consideration of the dificulties you must labour under in the station you are in in those dificult times I never can forgit that you have not only been the best of Brothers but as a Tender Father to me & mine. So I allways have a pleader in my own bossom that finds an Excuse for all unkind apearances there has never any thing given me so grate a shock on your account as to see yr Friend Huges Apointed Stamp master. I feared His apointment was by your means, but Even this I concluded you must have some good Reasons for, which others could not see into. the confusion & distres those Opresive Actts have thrown us Poor Americans into is un Discribable by me, but you see the Newspapers full of them, but they have fallen very short I am Tould of a [tragic?] Discription of The Leftanant Gouverners (Hutchinson) sufferings which all surcumstances considered was never Equeled in any Nation, Our

Savours only Exepted & Like Him I am Tould He bore it; Praying for His Enemies at the Instant they were Persecuteing Him. & our Obdurete Harts will Do nothing to make up His Lose.

He is now going from us, the Gratest ornement of our Country, & the most Indefateguable Patrioat. He Does me the Honr to be the barer of this & has shewn me the Gratest Clemency in the capasety of a Judg, may God Protect & Preserve Him still for the Good of mankind & confer on Him the Honour He Deserves, my writing so much of the Gouvner at this time Looks as tho [?] influenced by His Goodnes to me in perticular, but I asure you my opinyon of the Gentileman was the same before I had any Busness with Him & my concern at the unjust treetment He met with that for some Days it overpowered all my other trobles (which were then very Grate.) I think you & His Honr. may compare notes & console won an other.

My famely is now in a beter state of Helth than they have been for two years Past old Sarah Lives yet & is got Down stars again. I have son Flagg boards with me & cousen Ingersols two Daughters, Mrs. Bowls is also Returned after a twelve months absence, but I have them all at a Low Rate because I can Do no beter, so that my Income suplys us with vitles fiering candles & Rent but more it cannot with all the Prudence I am mistres of, but thus I must Rub along till Spring when I must strive after some other way but what at Present I cant tell Haveing no means for any thing I know my Dear Brother is allways Redey to asist the Indegent & I now Intreet yr advice & Direction [if?] you think it Proper to aford me it at this time [?] Endevour it shall not be thrown away. I feel now as if I could carey on some Biusnes if I was in it but at other times I fear my years are two far advancd to do any thing but jog on in the old track but my two Daughters if they have there Helth are capeble & willing to Do there Part towards giting a Living & son flagg is dutifull & Kind & takes much care of my minde but He has two children to maintain & is in no way but his own hard labour.

[87]

I have wrote & spelt this very badly but as it is to won who I am shure will make all Reasonable allowances for me and not let any won Els see it I shall venter to send it & subscrib my self yr Ever affectionat Sister

JANE MECOM

When I read this over I see so many buts I am ashamed   Place them to the old accompt

This was wrote some time ago but His Honour is still uncertain when He shall go & there is some things in this I want you should know I send it by this opertunity

J M

Jane Mecom to Deborah Franklin

[Printed first in Duane, *Letters to Benjamin Franklin*, pp. 186-188. The manuscript, in the American Philosophical Society, is now in bad condition, probably worse than it was when printed by Duane. The letter is here printed from the manuscript so far as possible, with illegible words supplied in square brackets from the Duane text, which itself is corrected from the legible parts of the manuscript. Deborah Franklin's letter acknowledged by Jane Mecom had been brought to Boston by Josiah Franklin Davenport, Jane Mecom's nephew. He and his wife Sarah Billings had gone to Philadelphia, where he was at first a baker, in September 1749. Of Jane Mecom's two daughters, it was Mary who had suffered from a "Painfull Deseas" and Jane from a "Languishing." Deborah Franklin's old friend Mrs. Smith died on March 22, 1766. Duane, *Letters to Benjamin Franklin*, p. 28. The threat to Franklin's house is told in a letter from Deborah Franklin to her husband, dated September 22, 1765, printed in part in Duane, pp. 16-18. "Cousen Griffith," whose child had died in Boston, was the daughter of Sarah Franklin Davenport and the wife of John Griffith. "Cousen Holmes are all well" referred to the family of William ("Billey") Homes, whose wife had a small child. "Cousen Willames," who looked as if she might have two children, was the wife of Jonathan Williams Sr., and Jane Mecom's niece. "Cousen Sally," to whom Jane Mecom sent her love, was Sarah Franklin.]

DEAR SISTER Feb. 27, 1766.

Yr kind Leter I recd by Post the same week [cousin Daven]-port came to Town & acknolidg yr Goodness with the Sinsearest Gratitude. I sent the Leter to Cousen williams [to] Read & He

[88]

came Emediatly Himself & ofered me Eaght Dolars I Exepted it (as I was still in want of won [very necessary] thing which I Layed it out on) notwith[standing] my Dear brother & yr Dear Husband had Just [sent me a consider]able Present of Cloathing [from England by Capt. Free]man who arived hear just [before I] recd yr Leter & Present we are now suplied with not only nesesary but credable cloathing for Brother has sent us Each of us a Printed coten Gownd a quilted coat a bonit Each of the Garls a cap & some Ribons mine is very suteable for me to were now being black & a Purple coten but the Garls are Light colared.   I hope God will Bless You boath for the Good you do not only to me but to others as you see ocation, I understand yuo still Continou to visit the sick & comfort the [affl]icted cosen Davenport tells me you used to visit Him Every Day when He was sick & bring Him Goodies   o How comfortable is such a Neibour in a time of sickness   I hope I shall all ways Gratfully Remember I had sev[eral] such while my famely were sick & be Inabled Properly to Improve the Helth & comforts we now Injoy I have at Present a compitency & will not fear but it shall allways be so, if I should now Repine or Distrust Provedenc I should be most ungratfull of all His Cretures for I have been aboundantly suplied beyond what I could Rationaly Expect & [have] my two Daughters in Helth whom I [had] Grate Reason to fear Incureable won of a Painfull Deseas the other falling in to a Languishing   Bless the Lord o my Soul who not only grantest these but contineuest the Day & meens of Grace that if it is not our own faults we may be Happy [here]after

I [am] Greved to hear Poor Mrs Smith has Got [the] numb Palsey   Pleas to Present my love & best wishes to her.

I am amaizd beyond measure at what cousen Davenport tells me that yr House was thretned [in the tumult]   I thought there had bene none among you would [proceed] to such a Length to Persecute a man merely for being of the best of charecters & Really Deserving good from the hand & tougue of all His felow cretures, I knew there was a Party that did not

[89]

Aprove His Prosecuting the busness he is gone to England upon, & that some had used Him with scurillous Language in some Printed Papers [but] I was in Hopes it had so far subsided as not [to] give you any Disturbance, when I [think what you] must Have suffered at the time [how I] pity you; but I think yr Indignation must [have] Exeded yr fear, what a wretched world would [this] be if the vile of mankind had no Laws to [re]strain them!

my famely all thank you for yr kind remembrance of them the children Desier the[ir] Duty, & Mrs Bowls her compliments, Cousen Griffeth can asign no cause for the Death of her child Exept it was fright She Recved won Evening her Husband being absent when some men in Liquer next Dore got to fighting & there was screeming murther. Cousen Holmes are all well billeys wife has calld in to see me with Her son which is a fine won, Cousen willames Looks soon to Lyin she is so big [I tell] Her she will Have two, Poor Sarah has been beter so as to wash the Dishes but she is now wors again her age as you say is not a time to Expect a cure for old Disorders & the Docr says there is no Hopes for her but she will Dwindle away, she is a Good Creture & Paitent It would Greve you to hear what a Cough she has that Repels all medicens but she is Hardly Ever Heard to complain.

Remember my Love to Cousen sally & Primit me again to thank you for [yr] Pres[ent and] subscribe my self yr affectionat & obliged

Sister

JANE MECOM

1766
Boston feb 27

"Hosanna to day, and tomorrow, Crucify him"

[An excerpt from this letter was printed in Sparks, *Familiar Letters*, pp. 98-99n. It is here first printed in full from the manuscript in the American Philosophical Society. The "Cards" Franklin mentioned in his postscript bore copies of his famous symbolical plate called "Magna

Britania her Colonies Reduc'd." Franklin in this letter was just to Governor Francis Bernard and Lieutenant Governor Thomas Hutchinson, with whom he was later to be in emphatic disagreement on other points of conflict.]

DEAR SISTER   London, March 1. 1766

I acknowledge the Receipt of your kind Letters of Nov. 12. & Dec. 20. The latter per Mr Williams. I condole with you on the Death of your Husband, who was I believe a truly affectionate one to you, and fully sensible of your Merit.——It is not true that I have bought any Estate here. I have indeed had some Thoughts of re-purchasing the little one in Northamptonshire that was our Grandfather's, & had been many Generations in the Family but was sold by our Uncle Thomas's only [eldest Daughter only: *struck out*] Child Mrs Fisher, the same that left you the Legacy. However I shall not do it unless I determine to remain in England, what I have not yet done.

As to the Reports you mention that are spread to my Disadvantage, I give myself as little Concern about them as possible. I have often met with such Treatment from People that I was all the while endeavouring to serve. At other times I have been extoll'd extravagantly where I have had little or no Merit. These are the Operations of Nature. It sometimes is cloudy, it rains, it hails;——again 'tis clear & pleasant, and the Sun shines on us. Take one thing with another, and the World is a pretty good sort of a World;——and 'tis our Duty to make the best of it and be thankful. One's true Happiness depends more upon one's own Judgement of one's self, on a Consciousness of Rectitude in Action and Intention and in the Approbation of those few who judge impartially than upon the Applause of the unthinking undiscerning Multitude, who are apt to cry Hosanna to day, and tomorrow, Crucify him.——I see in the Papers that your Governor, Mr Barnard, has been hardly thought of, and a little unkindly treated, as if he was a favourer of the Stamp Act: Yet it appears by his Letters to Government here, which have been read in Parliament, that he has wrote warmly in favour of the Province and against that Act, both before it pass'd and since; and so did your Lieutenant Governor to my certain Knowledge, tho' the Mob have pulled down his House. Surely the N. England People, when they are rightly inform'd, will do Justice to those Gentlemen, and think of them as they deserve.

Pray remember me kindly to Cousin Williams, and let him know that I am very sensible of his Kindness to you, and that I am not forgetful of any thing that may concern his Interest or his Pleasure, tho' I have not yet wrote to him.—I shall endeavour to make that Omission up to him as soon as possible.

I sent you some things by your Friend Capt. Freeman, which I shall be glad to hear came safe to hand, and that they were acceptable from

Your affectionate Brother

B FRANKLIN

My Love to your }
Children— }

P.S.   I congratulate you & my Countrymen on the Repeal of the Stamp Act. I send you a few of the Cards on which I wrote my messages during the Time it was debated here whether it might not be proper to reduce the Colonies to Obedience by Force of Arms:—The Moral is, that the Colonies may be ruined, but that Britain would thereby be maimed.

"You & I only are now Left"

[Printed first in Duane, *Letters to Benjamin Franklin*, pp. 29-31, and here printed from the manuscript in the American Philosophical Society. Peter Franklin had died July 1 of that year. *The Examination of Doctor Benjamin Franklin*, before the House of Commons in February 1766, had been promptly reprinted in Boston, as elsewhere in America, and his sister had read it. The "vile Pretended Leter" was possibly *An Essay, Towards discovering the Authors and Promoters of the memorable Stamp Act, In a Letter from a Gentleman in London, to his friend in Philadelphia*, which had appeared anonymously in the *Pennsylvania Journal*, Supplement, September 18, 1766, at Philadelphia, and accused Franklin of supporting the Act. The "six good Honist old Souls" were evidently members of the General Court (Assembly) of Massachusetts

My dear Sister,   Philad Jan. 1. 1786.

Our good God has brought us old Folks,
the last Survivors of 17 Brothers & Sisters,
to the Beginning of a new Year.   The
Measure of Health & Strength we enjoy at
so advanc'd an Age, now near Fourscore,
is a great Blessing.   Let us be chearful
& thankful. —

I received in their time your kind Letters
of Nov 7. & 30.   I am sorry our Cousin W.
troubles himself with chemical Experiments
for which he does not seem to have had the
proper previous Instruction, to prevent their
being dangerous to his Health.   You do not
explain to me what the Difficulties are that distress his Mind, and which I wish to know.
I am glad to hear he is better, that your
Daughter is mended, & your Son-in-law has
good Prospects. —

Young Oliver's Fine was remitted before my Arrival, but he lay in Goal for his

Fees. He is now, as then Discharged, thro' the good Office of Mr. Master.
&c. on the Name of the Shirt you Cousin, that I may Direct my
Letter so as not to give Cousin W. any Trouble. — My Love to him & his
Family, and to your, from your affectionate Brother
                                                        B Franklin
His Family join in Love &c

Dear Sister   Apr 6 · 1765

I have yrs of march 5th & Recd the magezeen
for which I thank you, I have brewed the Spruce
Beer twice & have Reason to think it is Good
in the cafe you were so Good ys to care for, Sally
holds beter but far from well. the Sick child Is
mentioned to you in my Last Died the next Day,
& the other childs Knee grows worce, the fathers
Arm Grows beter but is so weak He cant Lift it
to His Head nor Do the Least thing & my Sarah has
keept her bed Euer Since Except 2 or 3 Days She has
Sat ups in a Chare about 2 Hours So that my
mind is keept in a Continual Agitation that I
Dont know how to write.
we have Great Joy with you at the News of our
Brothers arival in England tho we know it no
other way than by that Small line in the News
Paper there is two Ships Arived hear from
London Since & not a word of Him.

Pray Remember my Love to cozen Sally
& Brother Peter & wife, & Except the same
yr self from yr Louing Sister

        Jane mecom

Jane Mecom to Deborah Franklin, April 6, 1765

who had come to Boston to attend the current session and boarded with Jane Mecom in Hanover Street. "Mrs. Steevenson" was Margaret Stevenson, Franklin's landlady in Craven Street, London. "Lining" was Jane Mecom's spelling of linen. By "old tenor" Jane Mecom meant the earlier Massachusetts paper money, now depreciated in value but still in circulation. What Jane Mecom called "good old unkle Benjamins memorandoms" were probably in her Uncle Benjamin Franklin's manuscript treatise "Dyeing and Coloring" since printed in *Publications of the Colonial Society of Massachusetts*, X (1907), 206-225.]

Nov. 8; 1766

you wonce told me my Dear Brother that as our Numbers of Bretheren & Sisters Lessened the Affections of those of us that Remain should Increes to Each other. you & I only are now Left. my Affection for you has all ways been so grate I see no Room for Increec, & you have manifested yrs to mee in such Large measure that I have no Reason to suspect Itts strength & therefore know it will be agreable to you to hear that my self & the childrin I have the care of are in no wors situation than when I Last wrot you, & should Rejoyce to hear the same of you since I understand by Sister you were in an Ill state of Helth & thought Proper to travel for the Recovery of it. I hope in god you have Recovered it & will Live Long to make yr Inemies ashamed, yr Ansurs to the Parlement are thought by the best Judges to Exeed all that has been wrot on the subject & being given in the maner they were are a Proof they Proceeded from Prinsiple & suficent to stop the mouths of all gain-sayers. the vile Pretended Leter which no Doubt you have seen gave me some uneaseyness when I heard of it before I could git a sight of it, as considering when a grat Deal of Durt is flung some is apt to stick but when I Read it I see it was filld with such bare faced falshoods as confuted them selves. theyre treetment of you among other things makes the World Apear a miserable world to me not withstanding yr good opinyon of it. for would you think it our General Court has sett allmost a Fortnight cheaffly on the subject of Indemnifieing the sufferers by the Late mobs & cant yet git a Vote for it tho they sitt Late in the Evening & the friends to it strive hard to git it acomplishd. I have six good Honist old Souls who come groneing Home Day by Day at the Stupidety of there Bretheren I cant help Interesting my self in the case & feel in mere Panicks till they have Brought the matter to a conclution.

I writ this in hopes you will be in England when this gits there & that you will find time to writ me a few Lines by the barer Capt freeman when he Returns.

& I have a small Request to ask tho it is too trifeling a thing for you to take care of Mrs Steevenson I Dont Doubt will be so good as to do it if you will give her the meterals it is to Procure me some fine old Lining or cambrick (as a very old shirt or cambrick hankercheifs) Dyed into bright colors such as red & green a Litle blew but cheafly Red for with all my own art & good old unkle Benjamins memorandoms I cant make them good colors. & my Daughter Jeney with a litle of my asistance has taken to makeing Flowers for the Ladyes Heads & Boosomes with Prity good acceptance. & If I can Procure them coulars I am In hopes we shall git somthing by it worth our Pains if we live till Spring. it is no mater how old the Lining is I am afraid you never have any bad a nouf

Present my compliments to Mrs Steevenson & Excuse my Presuming to give her this troble.

I have had a Respectfull Letter from Gouvr Franklin this sumer with a Present of six Barrils of flower amounting to sixty odd Pounds old tenor which was a grat help to me & his notice of me a grat satisfaction, all our Relations & friends hear are well as useal my Daughters Desire there Duty to you I am Dear Brother yr Ever affectionat Sister

JANE MECOM

Boston Novr 8 1766

Jane Mecom to Deborah Franklin

[Here first printed from the manuscript in the American Philosophical Society. Governor William Franklin and his wife had both been sick in New Jersey, and Deborah and Sarah Franklin had gone to assist them. "Cousen Huseys Son" was Albert, son of Christopher Hussey of

Nantucket, who had sent the youth to Philadelphia to be inoculated against smallpox. Letters to Deborah Franklin from Christopher Hussey, of the Nantucket Franklin-Folger connection, announced on August 27, 1766, that the boy was being sent and on December 2 that he had returned. These letters are in the American Philosophical Society. The "young man" mentioned but not named by Jane Mecom was Ephraim Brown, adopted son of Peter and Mary Franklin. Peter Franklin had died July 1 of that year, and his wife the following month. A letter from Brown to Franklin, dated August 25 and now in the American Philosophical Society, said that Mary Franklin had left no will and few possessions. Brown expected to go to England, where he hoped with Franklin's help he would find employment as a printer. The maid with whom he had traveled to Providence was presumably the one mentioned by Franklin in his letter to Jane Mecom of July 10, 1764. Jane Mecom believed that Brown and the maid had got away with more of Mary Franklin's possessions than they were willing to admit or than Deborah Franklin had realized. A letter from Deborah Franklin to her husband, dated October 19, 1767, and now in the American Philosophical Society, indicates that she had kept some of her sister-in-law's clothing and had recently sent it to Boston, along with some of Franklin's own clothes for "poor Petter" Mecom. *The Ladies Library*, published by Richard Steele, had appeared in three volumes in London in 1714. Deborah Franklin had never been in Boston, and Jane Mecom was thinking of Sarah when she said: "hear when you were." The "she" who had been in Boston when Sarah was there must have been the wife of Christopher Hussey and the mother of the boy who had been sent to Philadelphia. Franklin had been in Germany in the summer of 1766, and Jane Mecom did not yet know that he had "Returned to England."]

DEAR SISTER   Nov 24, 1766.

I have recd yrs which Informes me of my Brothers Helth which I was very Anxious about, Blessed be God for his mercy to us all on that acount. I have recd no Leter from Him since that Cousen Davenport saw nor could hear any thing of Him by any Bodey but what came from you. & now can't understand whither He is Returned to England. I Rejoyce also to hear the Governer is Recovered I heard it was sickly at that Place but not that He was sick. I hope my Dear Cousen Sallys troble & Fetigue will not be two hard for her. I am Glad you went to viset & comfort them in there troble I shall be Impatient till I hear there Helth is confirmed.

I think it was very good in you to take the care of Cousen Huseys Son if He had been bad it would have been a grat troble but as it is all is well. I Remember she was hear when you were, & so was cousen Kezia Coffin, she has been in town this fall & Desiered me to Remember Her to you when I wrot

I recd the Box with the Gownds & books in good order, as you sent the cotten gound of yr own acord I could wish you had sent the Riding hood in the Reom of it, as you say it has met with a mischance which has spoild it for a cloak it would have made me a hansom winter Gownd which I am in some want of & cant well afford to git as boath my Daught[ers] must have won I think first as being Rather more nesesary.

you say you have heard nothing of the young man since he came from yr Place but that he Intends for England. I heard that two. & that he came to Provedence with the maid & his Sister & Left the maid to come to Boston with the careyr He & His Sister coming the Day before in a Chase to go to concord to viset His Relations & that the mades own Sister tould at Provedenc that He & His sister was to wait for her at Boston & that she was to be mareyed to him   I heard also that she gave the careyer a Dolar Extroydnary to bring her & half a Dolar to takle his shase to bring her to my House & that the careyer should say she had a Litle trunk almost full of Dolars & I am shure she had a Purple Chins Gownd on vastly finer than any Gownd I have in the world. my thought is they two Pilfered all of all kinds that they thought you could not Detect them in. for I am shure my Brother & Sister would not have Left them selves so bare as it seemes. She allways keept her self full of good Living & I heard won say that saw her Just before she Left Rhoad Island that she had very good shifts then by her that she had before she was mareyed & a boundance of good aprons & hankerches & Laced caps for they sayed she never wore a Plane won, but Prehaps these things are Past Recovery, as they two had all at there comand when Sister was first taken & she not sensable, as the maid tould me she was not I askd her how then could she give you so many things, She said it was in there Helth they said she should have them   I said it was very odd they should give their own bed from under them in there Helth when they did not know but you might Die before them. but after all there combineations I fancy He thinks Himself two much of a Gentileman to marry her so she is wise so far as that wisdom Reaches to keep her Dolars to her self, He Disopointed her with Regard to waiting for her in Boston, for they say he was gone when she got hear & she obliged to Return with the careyer as she came. I have fill'd the Paper with such trumpry you will be vexd to give yr self the troble of Reading it but as I hant time to writ a nother must send it you have not wrot me if you have recd the necklace & how you like it   Pray be so good as to Let me know by next opertunity, there is also a Book of mine among my Brothers   the second volum of the Ladys Libriary, wrot in a blank Leaf borowed of Sister Mecom, if you have a convenant opertunity I shuld be glad you would send it as it breaks the sett

I am with Love to all friends

Dear Sister yr Loving Sister

JANE MECOM

Boston Novr 24—1766

Jane Mecom to Margaret Stevenson

[Here first printed from the manuscript in the American Philosophical Society. Margaret Stevenson, Franklin's landlady in Craven Street, London, had bought millinery goods, paid for by Franklin, to be sent to Jane Mecom in response to her request in her letter of November 8, 1766.]

Boston May 9—1767

I am Extreemly Obliged to you Dear madam for so Readily complying with the Request I presumed to make, & the Pains you have taken to Furnish us with what the best of Brothers Bounty has bestowed on us, They apear to me to be Extroydnary good of the kind; & tho the fashons are new to most of us I make now Doubt they will Obtain by Degrees when our Top

Ladys sett the Example. as they are Just come on Shore I have had no Opertuni[t]y yet to know what Incuridgment we are Like to have, but could not Let this opertunity slip of Informing you that we have Recd them in Good Order, & shall not fail to Accept yr kind offer to Procure us more when we have Ability to send for them.

In the mean Time if opertunity Presents & any new Fashon comes out of Caps, or Hankerchifs, Ruffels, Aprons, Cloaks, hatts, shaids or Bonetts, & you will be kind anouf to send me Paterns cut in Paper with Directions how to make them, & how they are worn, it will Add still Grater obligations & shall be Gratfully Acknolidged by your

Humble Servant

my Daughters send there
complments & thanks 〕 JANE MECOM

the colors are Good we shall be
glad of som when we send again.
To Mrs Stevenson 〕 I send a Line Inclosed to my Brother
London which Pleas to send back to Him if He
is come away J M

"She was Every thing to me"

[Here first printed from the manuscript in the American Philosophical Society. Jane's daughter Mary had died in September at the house of her mother's friend Kezia Coffin in Nantucket. A few sentences from the letter written "some time ago," October 23, and now missing, were printed in Sparks, *Works*, VII, 515n. "Sorrows roll upon me like the waves of the sea. I am hardly allowed time to fetch my breath. I am broken with breach upon breach, and I have now, in the first flow of my grief, been almost ready to say, 'What have I more?' But God forbid, that I should indulge that thought, though I have lost another child. God is sovereign, and I submit." Franklin's daughter Sarah had married Richard Bache at Philadelphia in October. John Winthrop, professor of astronomy and natural history at Harvard, was one of Franklin's regular correspondents on scientific matters. The words "to were our old cloaths over again" echo the final reply in Franklin's *Examination* before the House of Commons.]

My Dear & only Brother   Boston Decr 1—1767

I wrot to you some time ago & Informed you of the Death of my Child & of the Helth of the Rest of the Famely I have now a Twofold Benifit to Acknolidg & thank you for The Recipt of what you mention in yr Last to me by Mr Barrett. Mr Winthrop came & Paid me five Giuenys. & yr Advancing so much for me when Capt Freeman came. I am not unsensable of the oblegation you contineually Lay me under but Realy my Spirits are so much Broken with this Last Hevey Stroak of Provedenc that I am not capeble of Expresing my self as I ought.

Oh my Brother she was Every thing to me, Every word & Every Action was full of Duty & Respect, & I never Lookd on Her but with Pleasur Exept when she was sick or in troble. How to make me Easey & Happy was what she had most at Heart, & Rather than Give me Pain she concealed her own Infirmities & Did so much more than she was Able that it Increased Her Disorder & Hastened Her End.

but why should I Entertain you with this meloncholy Subject when you are calld to Rejoyce at the settling in marage of yr Belovd Daughter to a worthy Gentleman whom She Loves & the only won that can make her Happy. I congratulate you on it & wish it may Give you a Lasting Pleasure. I am uterly at a Lose to Expres the sence I have of Mrs Steevensons Goodnes in takeing such Pains to serve me & must beg of you to do it for me & Pray the contineuance of Her favour for yr sake for I am not capeble of makeing any sutable Returns

I send all the mony I can git but it Proves a Litle unlucky for me that our People have taken it in there Heads to be so Exsesive Frugal at this Time as you will see by the Newspapers our Blusterers must keep themselves Imployed & If they Do no wors than Perswade us to were our old cloaths over again I cant Disaprove of that in my Hart tho I should Like to have those that do bye & can afford it should bye what Litle I have to sell & Imploy us to make it up.

I think I Desiered you to send me all the Pamphlets & Papers

[99]

that have been Printed of yr writing. do Gratifie me & I will
contineu to be as Ever yr affectionat & most obliged Sister

JANE MECOM

My Daughter
Desiers her Duty

Jane Mecom: "Book of Ages"

[Printed first in *New England Historical and Genealogical Register*,
XXVII (1873), 253, and here printed from the manuscript in the New
England Historic Genealogical Society. The original "Book," in Jane
Mecom's hand with some tentative and inaccurate additions (here disregarded) by Josiah Flagg, is in a small memorandum book which after
her death was in the possession of that grandson. The "Book" seems to
have been written at various times; the entry for "Janeuary the 18
1762" is the earliest that was certainly made on the day of record. She
seems not to have known, or to have forgotten, her husband's birthday,
which was December 15. She here gives the date of her father's death
as January 17, 1745, but the *Boston News-Letter* in an item dated
January 17 of that year says he died "last night"—possibly, however,
after midnight.]

Edward Mecom Senr Born in December 1704
Jane Franklin Born on March 27-1712
Edward Mecom Marryed to Jane Franklin the 27th of July
1727
Josiah Mecom their first Born on Wednesday June the 4: 1729
and Died May the 18-1730
Edward Mecom Born on Munday the 29 March 1731
Benjamin Mecom Born on Fryday the 29 of December 1732
Ebenezer Mecom Born on May the 2 1735 on friday
Sarah Mecom Born on Tuesday ye 28 June 1737
Peter franklin Mecom Born on ye Lords Day May the 13.1739
John Mecom Born on Tuesday March ye 31.1741
Josiah Mecom Born on friday March ye 26.1743
Jane Mecom Born on Saturday April the 12.1745
James Mecom Born on July 31.1746
Died november ye 30 1746
Mary Mecom Born febr'y ye 29 1747/8
Abiah mecom born augst 1st 1751 died april ye 23 1752

Father Franklin Died Jany 17 1744
my Dear mother Died May 8 1752
my Eldest son Ed mecom Died Decr 7-1758
Janeuary the 18 1762 this morning Died a worthy & Dutifull
Son Ebenezer mecom
June the 12-1764 Died a Beloved & Deservedly Lamented
Daughter Sarah Flagg. She has Left four Children. Jane. Mary
Josiah & Sarah:
Novr 9-1764 Died under my Care my Daughter flaggs young-
est Child aged 17 months.
March 1765 begining Died my Daughter Flagg Second Daugh-
ter Polly a sober Plesant Child
Sepr 11-1765 God sees meet to follow me with Repeeted cor-
rections this morning 3 oclock Died my husband in a Stedy hope
of a happy hear after
September 19-1767 at my Nantuckett at the House and under
the most Affectionat care of my Dear Friend Kezia Coffin Died
my Dear & Beloved Daughter Polly Mecom.
The Lord Giveth & the Lord taketh away oh may I never be so
Rebelious as to Refuse Acquesing & & saying from my hart
Blessed be the Name of the Lord.

"Time proves our best Comforter"

[An excerpt from this letter was printed in Sparks, *Familiar Letters*,
22n. It was first printed entire in Goodman, *A Benjamin Franklin
Reader*, pp. 761-762. It is here printed again from the manuscript in the
American Philosophical Society. Franklin's paper *On Smuggling*, published in the *London Chronicle* on November 24, 1767, had been written at the country house, at Richmond in Surrey, of Grey Cooper, then
secretary of the treasury.]

London, Dec. 24. 1767

DEAR SISTER

I have received yours of Oct. 23. and condole with you most
affectionately in the Affliction you must have suffered by the
Loss of so valuable and so amiable a Child. The longer we live
we are expos'd to more of these strokes of Providence: but tho'
we consider them as such, and know it is our Duty to submit to
the Divine Will, yet when it comes to our Turn to bear what so

many Millions before us have borne, and so many Millions after us must bear, we are apt to think our Case particularly hard, Consolations however kindly administred seldom afford us any Relief, Natural Affections will have their Course, and Time proves our best Comforter.—This I have experienc'd myself. And as I know your good Sense has suggested to you long before this time, every Argument, Motive & Circumstance that can tend in any degree to relieve your Grief, I will not by repeating them renew it.—I am pleas'd to find that in your Troubles you do not overlook the Mercies of God, and that you consider as such the Children that are still spar'd to you. This is a right Temper of Mind, & must be acceptable to that beneficent Being, who is in various Ways continually showring down his Blessings upon many, that receive them as things of course, and feel no grateful Sentiments arising in their Hearts on the Enjoyment of them—

You desire me to send you all the political Pieces I have been the Author of. I have never kept them. They were most of them written occasionally for transient Purposes, and having done their Business, they die and are forgotten. I could as easily make a Collection for you of all the past Parings of my Nails.—But I will send you what I write hereafter, and I now enclose you the last Piece of mine that is printed. I wrote it at a Friend's House in the Country who is of the Treasury, if possible to do some Service to the Treasury, by putting a little out of Countenance the Practice of encouraging Smugglers in buying their Commodities. But I suppose it did very little.

Probably the Gentleman has call'd on you with the small Sum I mention'd; if not, I would not that you should call upon him for it; and therefore do not give you his Name.

Mrs Stevenson is glad to learn that the Things she sent you were suitable and pleas'd. You mention that you should write for more per Capt. Freeman. We suppose you did not then know, that your People would resolve to wear no more Millenery.—He is not yet arriv'd. Pray are those Resolutions like to be steadily stuck to?

My Love to Jenny, & all our Relations & Friends, and believe me ever

Your affectionate Brother

B FRANKLIN

"The Business you are fallen into"

[Here first printed from the manuscript in the American Philosophical Society. As it appears from Jane Mecom's letter of November 18, 1767, she and her daughter Jane had begun to make artificial flowers for the Boston "Ladyes Heads & Boosomes," but had found the public in a mood of economy.]

MY DEAR SISTER,   London, Feb. 21. 1768

I received your kind Letter of Dec. 1. I condole with you affectionately once more on the grievous Affliction you have met with, praying God to make the rest of your Life more comfortable & happy.

I thank you for your Congratulations on my Daughter's Marriage. She has pleas'd herself and her Mother, and I hope she will do well: but I think they should have seen some better Prospect than they have, before they married, how the Family was to be maintain'd.

It is a little unlucky that the Business you are fallen into, happens at present to be in disgrace with your Town Meeting: perhaps you may think of some other less exceptionable if their Resolutions continue and are regarded by the Ladies.

My Love to your Daughter, and believe me ever

Your affectionate

Brother

B FRANKLIN

"The Article of Boarders"

[Here first printed from the manuscript in the American Philosophical Society. Some of the out-of-town members of the Massachusetts Assembly boarded during the sessions in Boston with Jane Mecom. The

[103]

"Mezzotinto Print" which Franklin sent was the engraving by Edward Fisher from the portrait of Franklin painted by Mason Chamberlin in 1762.]

London, Sept. 20. 1768

DEAR SISTER,

The last Letter I have received from you is dated May 11. I hope you continue well, tho' 'tis so long since I have heard from you. As your good Friend Capt. Freeman has not been here this Summer, I am afraid his Sickness that you mention proved fatal to him, which I shall be sorry to hear, as I had conceiv'd a great Esteem for him. I suppose the Dissolution of your Assembly will affect you a little in the Article of Boarders; but do not be discouraged. Your Debt to Mrs Stevenson is paid, and she presents her kind Respects to you, and desires you will freely command her Service at any time. I cannot always conveniently send you the Pieces I write in the Papers here, for several Reasons; but will do it when I can.—I send the Mezzotinto Print herewith. My Love to Cousin Jenny & all enquiring Friends, from

Your affectionate Brother

B FRANKLIN

"A Sketch of the Table and Company"

[Printed first, from a manuscript in the American Philosophical Society, in Carl Van Doren, *Benjamin Franklin's Autobiographical Writings*, pp. 181-183. Franklin dined on October 1, 1768, with King Christian VII of Denmark, then visiting in London. The following week Franklin wrote an account of the dinner in a letter to his son which is now missing. A part of the letter, copied in another hand, was sent to Jane Mecom, with a "Sketch of the Table and Company" which is herewith reproduced. The names, from the King counter-clockwise round the table, are Admiral (George Brydges) Rodney, Dr. Matthew Matty (actually Maty), Baron Bulow, Baron Schimmelman, Count Behrnstorff, Gen[eral] Edward Harvey (not Hervey), Count Holeke, Count Moleke, Baron Diede, Secretary Schumacker, M. de Passon, Mr. (John) Duning (actually Dunning), Count Ahlefeldtz, Officer on Gu[ar]d, B. Franklin, Lord Moreton (James Douglas, 14th Earl of Morton).]

The King of Denmark at present engrosses all the Conversation. That young Monarch gains daily on the Affections of this Nation by his great Affability & Condescension, and the Pleasure he appears to take in every thing he sees, and in every Amusement & Entertainment contrived for him here. I had seen him at the Ridotto and had no Expectation of seeing him again; but on Friday last I receiv'd a very polite Card from Baron Diede his Minister here expressing that the Prince of Travendahl (the King's travelling Name) desired much to make an Acquaintance with me, and had ordered him to invite me to his Table for Saturday at St. James's. I went accordingly, and was most graciously receiv'd. He was pleased to say that he had long desired to see and converse with me. The Questions he ask'd were such as shew'd an inquisitive mind and a good Understanding. I was placed near him at Table, only Lord Moreton being between us, who was so good as to be my Interpreter, I not chusing to speak in French, a Language that I do not speak well. The King had been at Greenwich that day by Land to see the Hospital &c. Lord Moreton as President of the Royal Society, and Dr. Matty the Secretary, met him there to shew him the Royal Observatory. Admiral Rodney brought him back by Water in the Admiralty Barge, to shew him the Shipping in the River. These with the Officer on Guard and myself, were all the English at Table. The rest were the Officers of the Danish Court. I inclose a Sketch of the Table and Company, with their Names and Situations as well as I can remember. After Dinner the King went into another room, and Lord Moreton and my self were shewn in after him, where he again asked me several Questions, & discours'd with me some time. Count Holeke came in too, and talk'd with me a little in English, which he takes pains to learn and has made a considerable Progress. The King was pleas'd to add, just as we came away, that he purposed to see me again before he left England, and I am told he will do me the very great Honour of a Visit in Craven Street. Abundance of People, during the second course, were admitted to pass thro' the Room, and see the King

[105]

at Dinner. This is only for you and Betsy to read, with your Mother and Sister. For it will not be decent in us to talk of these kind of Things.

"Politices & Riligous Contryverces"

[Here first printed from the manuscript in the American Philosophical Society. It was from "Capt. Foulger" (Captain Timothy Folger of Nantucket) that Franklin learned about the course of the Gulf Stream, concerning which he wrote his famous letter of October 29, 1769, to Anthony Todd. Governor William Franklin had gone to meet with Sir William Johnson, superintendent for the Crown of the affairs of the Six Nations of the Iroquois, at the treaty of Fort Stanwix. Both William Franklin and his father were interested in the formation of the western colony later called Vandalia. The meeting at Fort Stanwix was to determine the Indian boundary. A letter from William Franklin to his father, with the date missing but evidently written late in 1768 and now in the American Philosophical Society, informed Franklin that John Mecom had turned out as bad as Benjamin, "& gone and quarter'd himself & his Wife on his Mother at Boston." John had married Catherine Ouke (variously spelled Auke, Oakee, Oakey) of New Brunswick, New Jersey, on September 11, 1765. A letter from his wife to Deborah Franklin, dated April 13, 1767, and now in the American Philosophical Society, indicates that John Mecom had gone to the West Indies leaving Catherine with his aunt Deborah Franklin, and expecting his wife to follow him there, possibly to St. Eustatius. It does not appear why he had gone or whether she went. Richard and Sarah Bache, "cousen Beach & His wife," had visited Boston in the summer of 1768. A letter from Sarah to her mother, dated August 14 and in the American Philosophical Society, said: "I dined at Aunt Mecom's to day where I now am She desires me not to forget her love to you."]

MY DEAR BROTHER   Boston Novr 7 1768

I cannot neglect writing to you by my Neibour Capt Freeman tho it be no more to yr satisfaction than to Inform you that I am well and that my Famely are as useal.
The whol conversation of this Place turns upon Politices & Riligous contryverces. Boath managed with two much Biterness as you will see by the News Papers If you give yr self the Troble to Read them, But they will not Infalably Informe you of the Truth; for Every thing that any Designing Person has a mind

to Propagate Is stufed into them, & it is Dificult to know whither Either Party are in the Right. for my Part I wish we had Let alone strife before it was medled with & folowed things that make for Peace.

I wrote to you & Mrs Steevenson by Capt Foulger & then sent some mony which I hope came saif to hand. but I can send none now tho I hear you are not coming Home, by a kind Leter from yr sons wife which I Recd by Last Post Her Husband being absent to meet the Indians at Sr Willam Jonsons I have Heard from sister & cousen Beach & His wife since they got Home there all well.

I hope yr Endevours for the Good of the Nation & the Col-onies will be blessd with Suckses & we shall at Last be favoured with Quietness at Least. My son John & wife are Hear & send there Duty as Does my Daughter Jeney Pleas to Present my best Respects to Mrs Steevenson & Acept the sinsearest Afec-tion from

yr Most obliged Sister

JANE MECOM

"Just now very busy"

[Here first printed from the manuscript in the American Philosophical Society. Franklin's account with Mrs. Stevenson, in the American Philosophical Society, "for Sundries Purchased for & sent to Mrs Jane Mecom of Boston" show that from October 18, 1765, to November 17, 1768, Mrs. Stevenson bought and sent goods to the value of £41.19.10 above what Jane Mecom had sent her, £24.14.1½. Franklin paid the dif-ference.]

DEAR SISTER, London, Nov. 20. 1768

By this Ship, (Capt. Scot,) Mrs Stevenson sends you half a Piece of Muslin, Apron width, which cost Four Guineas.—She hopes it will please, & presents her Compliments and best Wishes. I am in very good Health, Thanks to God:—but just now very busy. So can only add, that I am, as ever,

Your affectionate Brother

B FRANKLIN

Mrs Stevenson receiv'd the 32 Dollars,
3 Crowns & one Guinea, per Coz. Folger.
You will write for any thing else you want

"*Your Squabbles about a Bishop*"

[The second paragraph of this letter was printed in Sparks, *Familiar Letters*, 119-120n., as "to a friend in America"; and in Sparks, *Works*, VII, 437-438n., as "to his sister." It is here first printed in full from the manuscript in the American Philosophical Society. "Mr Leadly" was Hugh Ledlie, who lodged with Jane Mecom from 1742 to 1772, according to a letter from Ledlie to Franklin, dated May 22, 1787, and now in the American Philosophical Society. Major John Small, then with the British forces stationed in Boston, was a brother of Alexander Small, a British Army surgeon who was a friend and correspondent of Franklin in London. The "philosophical Papers" of which Franklin sent his sister six copies to be delivered to various persons was the 1769 edition of his *Experiments and Observations on Electricity. . . . To which are added, Letters and Papers on Philosophical Subjects.* Jane Mecom's own copy, now defective but with her signature on the half-title, is in the possession of the present editor. To John Winthrop, professor of mathematics and natural philosophy at Harvard College, Franklin on March 11, 1769, wrote: "By a late Ship, I sent your College a Copy of the new Edition of my Philosophical Papers; and others, I think, for yourself and for Mr. Bowdoin." These three copies may have been among the six sent to Jane Mecom to "have delivered as directed" or may have been in addition to them.]

DEAR SISTER,   London, Feb. 23. 1769

I have received your kind Letters of Sept. 26. Oct. & Nov. 7.—That of Sept. 26. is directed to my Wife, but she sent it to me, I suppose that I might see your Opinion of Mr Bache: I am glad you approve the Choice they have made. I write a few Lines to Mr Leadly: I cannot say much on the Subject till I see Mr Foxcroft, whom I now expect daily. I am glad Major Small call'd on you. He is a Man I much esteem, as I do his Brother with whom I am intimately acquainted here.—My best Respects to him.

Your Political Disputes I have no Objection to if they are carried on with tolerable Decency, & do not become outrageously abusive. They make People acquainted with their Rights

You guess'd right upon the Similitude with Mrs Blount's Letter. But hold your Tongue.

Love to your Children, from

Your affectionate Brother

B FRANKLIN

Jane Mecom to Deborah Franklin

[Here first printed from the manuscript in the American Philosophical Society. It is not certain just when Jane Mecom set out for Philadelphia, but letters from Deborah Franklin to her husband, and now in the Society's collections, indicate that the sister from Boston had not arrived in Philadelphia on November 2, 1769, but was there on December 13 and being "verey a greabel" to Deborah and Sally. "Mr Hewhs" was John Hughes. Benjamin Mecom was then in Philadelphia and John Mecom had gone to Brunswick (New Brunswick), New Jersey, where by the following year at least he had set up as a jeweler. Jane Mecom's stop at Burlington would be with Governor William Franklin.]

Boston Sept 14 1769

DEAR SISTER

I have no leter from you nor my son since I wrot you I was Going to Philadelphia, but Still Persist in my Intent & Porpose to sit out in about a fortnight, but shall Stop a Litle [at] Brunswick & at Burlington & make them a longer viset at my Return. I was In Hopes to have had the Company of yr Friend Mr Hewhs but He Talks not of Going till November which will be so Late I shall not Dare to venture.

all other maters & things I shall Leave to Discours on when I shall Have the Pleasure to convers with you by yr own Fier side & only ad my Love to all

from yr Affectionat

SISTER JANE MECOM

Jeney Presents her Duty
& Love to Cousens Beach & Litle Benjamin Franklin

[111]

"A good sensible Instinct"

[Printed first, not quite correctly, in Goodman, *A Benjamin Franklin Reader*, pp. 762-763. Here again printed from the manuscript in the American Philosophical Society. The sermon which Jane Mecom supposed to be by her brother has not been identified. Since her letter of June 13 is missing, it is impossible to tell what was the weight which had lain so heavily upon her.]

London, Sept. 29. 1769

DEAR SISTER.

When I returned lately from France, I found among other Letters for me that had been here sometime, yours of June 13.

It pleases me to hear you are at present relieved from the Weight, which lately lay so heavy on you that "all the Assistance of Reason and Religion were scarce sufficient to keep your Spirits up."—It is well you had such Aids. Our Reason would still be of more Use to us, if it could enable us to *prevent* the Evils it can hardly enable us to *bear*.—But in that it is so deficient, and in other things so often misleads us, that I have sometimes been almost tempted to wish we had been furnished with a good sensible Instinct instead of it.

The Sermon which you call mine, I know nothing of. I have only heard of it: I never saw it. It was wrong to give me as the Author of it. Whether it be good or bad, I have no Right to the Reputation or the Censures it may deserve.

Mrs Stevenson scarce ever can prevail on herself to write a Letter to anyone; but she acknowledges the Receipt of yours, presents her best Respects, and holds herself always ready to serve you.

My Love to Jenny, & believe me ever

Your affectionate Brother

B FRANKLIN

"A pleasure to me to have you near me"

[Printed first, and hitherto only, from a manuscript now missing, in Sparks, *Familiar Letters*, pp. 123-124, from which it is here reprinted.]

London, 15 March, 1770

DEAR SISTER,

I received your kind little letter of January 3d from Philadelphia. I am glad your visit thither proves agreeable to you. Since your family is so much reduced, I do not see why you might not as well continue there, if you like the place equally with Boston. It would be a pleasure to me to have you near me; but your own discretion must govern you. I propose, God willing, to return this summer.

With true regard, I am ever

Your affectionate brother,

B. FRANKLIN

Jane Mecom to Deborah Franklin

[Here first printed from the faded and defaced manuscript in the American Philosophical Society. The missing words are most of them accounted for by pieces torn off the top of the letter and from a lower corner. These, and some words merely illegible, are indicated by dots. James Parker had died at Burlington, New Jersey, on July 2 of that year. Richard Bache had gone to visit his mother in England and to look for a possible government post with the aid of Franklin. "King Bird" was what Deborah Franklin called her grandson Benjamin Franklin Bache. Jane Mecom had not yet recovered from her fall down the stone steps into the garden at the Franklin house in Philadelphia. Jane Flagg, then thirteen, could not live with her grandmother because her father had been married again, to a woman with children of her own. Josiah Mecom had apparently given up his trade as saddler and gone to sea. The "comly well behaved" young woman whom he thought of marrying and who worked for her "Liveing" was probably a servant: there was little other paid work for Boston girls in that age. John Mecom died at New Brunswick on September 30, 1770. *Documents Relating to the Colonial History of the State of New Jersey*, Series 1, Vol. 27, *Newspaper Extracts*, p. 285.]

Boston Aug[?] 1770

DEAR SISTER

I Recved your kind Leter of June 25 some time ago but as I had Just wrot to you (& Inclosed it to Mr Parker who I Percived by the Papers was Dead before that could Reach Him

yet I hope you have got it) & was in a Hurry a mooving I Did
not take the [time] to Ansur yr Leter as I ought to have Done
& won opertunity has slipt away after a nother but you must
forgive me as you are sensable it can not be for want of Affection to you & your Children who are all very Dear to me, but a
veriety of accedents happening to hinder me I am sorry for the
Death of yr F[riend] Mr Parker I think that comunity has
Lost a Usefull member. . . . . . must be much felt by His
Famely. I sopose my Cousen Bache has Left you & Especially
wish Him Pro . . . . . . it was only a Pretenc to be ofend[ed]
that I Did not send my Love to Him He could not but observe
He was the first Person I mentioned in my Leter & affectionatly
two, tho not in the same [words?] I mentioned others.   your
King Bird I Long to see I have watched Every child to find
some Resemblanc but have seen but won & that was only in
Good Natuer & Sweet Smell. Polly Jervis is not Brought to
bed yet but has been Ill this is the third Day Lingering but not
very bad. my Lamenes continus yet that it is with Grat Pain
I walk as far as [to] Dr Coopers meeting, my Daughter Jeney
has been at home with [me] about a fortnight she is well &
sends her Duty, I cannot git Jenny Flagg to Live with me
Again tho she . . . . . . come Her Father keeps her . . . . . . to
tend His Wifes children Her . . . . . . to see me sinc I came
Home . . . . . . been Let to come but Just Run . . . . . . sent on an
Erand Exept won & then He[r]. . . . . . was so Full she could
hardly Speak till . . . . . . time for her to go away. My Son
Josiah is not mareyed He is at sea Whaleing I saw the woman
she is as comly well behaved a Person as any you shall see in
her Station, she works for her Liveing & if they Dont make
them selves Poorer [by] mareying I have no Objection for I
am convinced Poverty is Intailed on my Famely Prehaps for
wise Ends & I Indvour to be content. Johney has been sick Ever
since His wife wrot me to Philadelphia, has a Bad cough, & a
chilly fitt & Fevour Every Day has not been Able to Do any
work nor so much as write. His wife writs me He is Pined to
Skin & Bons. How it is with my son Ben & Famely I should be

Glad to know I have not recd but won Leter since I came home I Inclose won for them which Please to send

Present my Respects to Every Inquiering Friend & Beleve me to be as Ever

yr affectionat Sister

JANE MECOM

Since I wrot the above I have recd yrs of Sept 29 wherin you tell me our [dear] child has been sick thank God he has Recovered I dont Doubt they are all very happy at yr sons my Love to them when they come home yr Leter was Brought me by a Negro who Did not know the man that gave it Him so I Dont know . . . . . . the Bonitt as to the coat of . . . . . . osed of it as I was sorry . . . . . . as soon as my Leter was Gone

Loving Sister

JANE MECOM

"*With much fear about yr wellfare*"

[Here first printed from a defective manuscript in the American Philosophical Society. The missing words or letters, along the margins of the original, are either supplied in this text from fairly certain conjecture or else indicated by question marks. Jane Mecom's date does not give the year, and the "Sep 25. 1770" is in another hand. The correction was made, presumably, because Franklin in his letter of July 17, 1771, gave the date as September 25, though his sister plainly wrote "Sepr 22." The grounds of her anxiety over Franklin appear in his reply of November 7, 1770. The "well Respected & much Esteemed Kinsmen" by whom she sent her letter were her grandnephews Josiah and Jonathan Williams, sons of Jonathan Williams Sr. Josiah's "Sceme" was to study music with Franklin's friend John Stanley, the blind organist of the Inner Temple.]

Boston Sepr 22 [1770]
Sep 25. 1770

I have trobled my Ever Dear Brother [with] Several Leters since I have had the Pl[easure of] won from Him but cannot omit Ading won [more] by my well Respected & much Esteemed Kinsmen whome wee all Part from with Regrett not withstanding we hope There Future Benifit & Saif Ret[urn] will be occasion of Joy to all there Friends

Josiah says He fears nothing He shall ha[ve] to Incounter so much as your Disaprobatio[n] of His Sceme, He Expects you will advise Him to Return in the [first] Ship, yet He cant conqu[er] His Inclineation. I tell Him you have seen s[o] much of the Follies of Human Nature & so L[ittle] Els in the comon Run of man kind, that you will know Beter how to Pitty & Advice Him

[?] a Rumer Hear that you have mett with some [?] Treetment & I cant Help being conserned about [?] forbad me, I Fansey by this time you have [found there?] are more wicked folks in the world than [you thou]ght there was; & that thay are capeble of Doing [?]rt, I Pray God to Preserve yr Usefull Life among them & that Every Good man may not be Distroyed from of the Face of the Earth.

I am Desiered by a Lady of my Acquaintanc to send for the Pamphlit Discribed by this note & says if I will send for two she will make me a Present of won, she is won I should be Glad to oblige & think it may be Agreable to me to have won. [?] beg the favour of you to send a cople if to be had

Cousin Josiah will be Able to Inform you Every thing that conserns me that will be Agreable to you to know [so?] that I need not make my Leter more Lengthy & only add that I am with much fear about yr wellfare

Yr Ever Affectionat Sister

J[ANE MECOM]

"I am obnoxious enough here already"

[Here first printed from the manuscript in the American Philosophical Society. George Whitefield had died in Newburyport, Massachusetts, on September 30 of that year. The letter Franklin had written to Philadelphia may have been that to the Committee of Merchants in that town, dated July 9, 1769, which was first printed in Sparks, *Works*, VII, 445-446, and reprinted in Smyth, *Writings*, V, 220-221.]

London, Nov. 7. 1770

DEAR SISTER,

I received your kind Letter of July 6. and was glad to hear (since you chose to return) that you were got so well home. I hope the Hurt you receiv'd will be attended with no bad Consequences. My Arm, that had given me no Uneasiness for several Years, had lately begun again to pain me, from a slight Strain, and I am now afraid will continue to do so as long as I live, since it has not mended for some Months past. But as I grow old, being now near 65, it is a Comfort that nothing can pain me long. You had not, I hope, any Offence in Philadelphia, that induc'd you to leave it so soon. I must stay here this Winter, but hope to be in that dear Place pretty early in the next Summer, being quite uneasy under so long a Banishment from my Country & my Family. I have been for a great part of my Day engag'd abroad in the Bustle of Publick Business: It is time now that I should return home, spend the Evening with my Friends, and be ready to go chearfully to Bed. My Respects to Dr. Cooper, Love to Cousin Jenny, & believe me ever

Your affectionate Brother

B FRANKLIN

I condole with you on the loss of my
dear old Friend Mr. Whitefield which I have
just heard of.

Nov. 9—70

Since writing the above I have received yours of Sept. 29. by our Kinsmen, who are safe arrived, & lodge with Mrs. Stevenson. We shall endeavour to make their Residence here as agreable to them as possible. Be in no Concern about any Abuses I receive here in the Newspapers. 'Tis the Fashion to roast one another, and I sometimes take a little of that Diversion myself. I enclose you a Newspaper or two which you may show to Dr. Cooper, but if you think you see any thing of mine there, don't let it be publish'd as such; for I am obnoxious enough here already on Acct. of some Letter I wrote to Philada. I will en-

[117]

deavour to get the Books you desire, but suppose it will be difficult.

Jane Mecom to Deborah Franklin

[Printed first, and hitherto only, in Duane, *Letters to Benjamin Franklin*, pp. 192-195, with some misreadings and with the question whether Sarah Franklin was "Like to have another child" modestly omitted; here printed from the manuscript in the American Philosophical Society. The queried date is in another hand, and is plainly wrong: from its contents the letter cannot have been written before December in answer to the missing letter from Deborah Franklin of what must have been the 15th of that month. Captain Sparks (not "Franks" as in Duane) sailed between Philadelphia and London and was a friend of the Franklins. Josiah and Jonathan Williams had left for London with their "Unkle the Inspector," John Williams, after the date of Jane Mecom's letter of September 22 to her brother. Elizabeth Hubbart, now Mrs. Partridge ("Pateridge"), Susannah ("Suckey") Hubbart, and Tuthill Hubbart were stepchildren of John Franklin, Jane Mecom's deceased brother. "Cousen Ingorsol" was Colonel Joseph Ingersoll. Governor John Wentworth of New Hampshire, who had succeeded his uncle Benning Wentworth in that post in June 1767, had been married in November 1769. His uncle had died on October 14, 1770, without issue. It is not clear which Governor Wentworth Deborah Franklin had asked about. The Reverend William Gordon, subsequently author of *The History of the Rise, Progress, and Establishment of the Independence of the United States* (4 vols., 1788), had arrived from England, with his family, in Philadelphia on November 1, 1770. The following year he settled at Roxbury, Massachusetts, and became minister of the Third Congregational Church of that town. The many friends whom Jane Mecom had made in Philadelphia, and about whom she asked, included Dr. Thomas Bond (one of the original members of the American Philosophical Society), Thomas Yorke (formerly a fellow member with Franklin in the Pennsylvania Assembly), Dr. John Shippen (who had died on November 26), Captain Isaac All ("Cousen All," a relation of Deborah Franklin's who often appears in the Franklin correspondence), and the Reverend Jacob Duché ("Dushay," the popular preacher whom Jane Mecom had heard at Christ Church, attended by Deborah Franklin and the Baches). William Goddard, then publisher of the *Pennsylvania Chronicle* with the assistance of his sister Mary Katherine Goddard, was Benjamin Mecom's employer in Philadelphia. The "Duke of Wharton, Marquis of Rockingham" was Samuel Wharton, who was associated with Franklin in the plans for the Vandalia colony, and it was rumored he might become governor of it: that is, get "His Goverment," as Jane Mecom put it. Deborah Franklin's "Nibour Hadock" was probably

Rebecca Haydock, whom Franklin called "your young Neighbour Haddock" in a letter to his wife dated January 28, 1772; though the neighbor may have been an Eden Haydock with whose estate Franklin had an account according to a letter to him from Edward Garrigues dated February 20, 1787, and now in the American Philosophical Society. John Foxcroft had been married to Judith Osgood in London in August 1770 and had brought his wife home to Philadelphia. His brother Thomas ("Tomey") was postmaster there. The child's "old maid" was Benjamin Franklin Bache's nurse, Mrs. Ashmead. "Georg, bob & [Jack?]" were servants in or about the Franklin-Bache household. "Aunt wood" was a relation of the Boston Williamses. "Mrs Leegay," "Mrs Smiths Daughter," "Townly," and "Mrs Kepley" (spelled Keppele by Duane) have not been identified. "Deby" (Deborah) was presumably a child of Josiah Franklin Davenport. The "Catey" mentioned in the postscript was Catherine, widow of Jane Mecom's son John.]

DEAR SISTER   Before Aug. 1770?

I recd yrs of 15 Inst & you cant think how much Pleasure it gave me to hear so Perticulary about the Litle Grandson, I cant find won since I came home as Looks a bit Like him. I am Glad you hear so often from my Brother I all most Dispaired when I wrot you Last of Ever haveing a nother Leter from Him. but soon After Recd won that by some means or other was four or five months a coming, several Gentilemen arrived hear from London says as yr Capt Sparks does that He Looks Extreemly well & is in good Helth. cosen williames sons went with ther Unkle the Inspector won in hopes of Recieving some Benifit, the other to Purchase Goods to sett Him self up Hear but we hear His uncle has Pro[cur]ed him a Clarks Birth to the East Indies which He accepts & has only sent some Goods to His Aunt wood & Josiah is coming Home without Him.

I have never yet Recovered my fall & can not walk near so well as you can, that if it was not nece[sary] to me to fill up my time other ways I shuld take much Pleasure in conversing with you in this way & as I have now so Good an opertunity I will Endevour to Ansure all yr Inquieries.

In the first Place I have never seen Mrs Pateridge sinc I came Home but wonce in the Street   I have not Heared whither she is Like to have another child. The Nabours say she

Lay a bed afore with her Hare Poudered & a Grat Plum in it. Suckey is not mareyed she wons calld to see me of an Evening. I beleve Tuthill Has no Thoughts of matreymony. Cousen Ingorsol has the same wife He had when Cousen Bache was Hear I beleve they are well, there Daughter was not like to have a nother child when I saw her Last. I now forgit who the controlors Lady was that went from Boston, I have never Heard whither Govr wintworth has a child, I see so few Intilegent People that I know the Least News of any won in the world. I am a Grat Deal a Lone Exept some young persons coming back on Erands, for as I cant go a broad People Dont come to see me & Jeney is a good Deal out. I have Heared nothing of Mr Gordon & His Famely was he to have setled in Boston & now I have filld won side with Ansuring yr Qustions, Give me Leve to Desier you to Do the same by me. Even now before you forgit it you will find some opertunity to send it, when do you Expect cousen Bache Home? is His wife Like to have a nother child? How Does Mrs Smiths Daughter & Famely do if you will beleve me I cannot now think of her Name How is Dr Bond & Famely Do you Ever see my obliging Mr York. Did Mrs Leegay go to the West Indieas, is it that Dr Shipin that is Dead whose child made the Speach at yr House, How goes on Godard & his sister & Townly Did they Ever Pay my son the mony they owed Him, or Did you Ever git yr Rent. how Does yr Good Nibour Hadock, Duke of Wharton, Marquis of Rockingham has he got His Goverment. how do you Like Mr Foxcrofts Lady is Tomey mareyed. Is Cousen All Turned Marchant & stay at home constantly I have never seen Him Entered or cleared in the Papers. I wish I had such a constant Border to Pay me 3 Dolars a week the year Round I could then do Prity well. I am Glad the child Has his old maid tell Her I all ways think of her with Respect she was so good to me when I hurt my self Does Georg, bob & [Jack?] Do any beter, & how Does the Litle molato Behave to his master. Does Mr Dushay Preach as well as Ever? I should Admire to come & see & hear all about Every thing there wonc a year & stay a fortnight   I fancy so short a Time would Affect my my Helth with change of Climate, I Percive Deby Davenport has got a Litle of her mothers Flatring Disposition but obligeing Actions are more substantial than words tho they are not Disagreable if they come from the Hart,

I wish Mrs Kepley very happy in her New Habitation   Present my Respectfull complements to Her & Every won that Inquier After me, Cousin Bache knows she is a Leter in my Dept & I will not Excuse her Exept she is in sircumstances & very sick, so you must tell me that & Every other thing that you know I shall Like to hear, if you send it to my son He will find a vesel to send it by & Pleas to tell them [*interlined*: my son & his wife] that I shall Expect a Long Leter from Each of them for I have heard nothing of them this whol winter I beleve by this time you are hartyly tiered with this trumprey that in compashon to you I conclud

yr affectionat Sister

JANE MECOM

Dear Sister if Catey should send a Leter to you for me Do be so Good as git it sent to me by water

"That Christian virtue of resignation"

[Printed first in Sparks, *Works*, VII, 495-498, from which it is here reprinted. Smyth, *Writings*, V, 288-292, credits his text to a manuscript in the British Museum, but the Keeper of Manuscripts of the Museum reported on December 30, 1948, that no such manuscript could be found; and the Smyth text varies from that of Sparks only in the substitution of capital letters and the occasional use of " 'd" for "ed" through the first three paragraphs and a part of the fourth. The two books for which Jane Mecom had asked in her letter of September 22 (not 25 as Franklin mistakenly says), and which he now sent her have not been identified. The printer's widow whom Franklin had known during his first visit to England, 1724-1726, was Elizabeth Ilive, who died in 1733. Her son was Jacob Ilive. His "solemn discourse," or Oration, was delivered, according to the article on him in the *Dictionary of National Biography*, at Brewers' Hall and at Joyners' Hall on September 10 and September 23 respectively, the year of his mother's death.]

London, 30 December, 1770

DEAR SISTER,

This ship, staying longer than was expected, gives me an opportunity of writing to you, which I thought I must have missed when I desired cousin Williams to excuse me to you. I received your kind letter of September 25th, by the young gentlemen, who, by their discreet behaviour have recommended themselves very much to me and many of my acquaintance. Josiah has attained his heart's desire, of being under the tuition of Mr. Stanley, who, though he had long left off teaching, kindly undertook, at my request, to instruct him, and is much pleased with his quickness of apprehension and the progress he makes; and Jonathan appears a very valuable young man, sober, regular, and inclined to industry and frugality, which are promising signs of success in business. I am very happy in their company.

As to the rumor you mention, (which was, as Josiah tells me, that I had been deprived of my place in the postoffice on account of a letter I wrote to Philadelphia,) it might have this foundation, that some of the ministry had been displeased on my writing such letters, and there were really some thoughts among them of showing that displeasure in that manner. But I had some friends, too, who, unrequested by me, advised the contrary. And my enemies were forced to content themselves with abusing me plentifully in the newspapers, and endeavouring to provoke me to resign. In this they are not likely to succeed, I being deficient in that Christian virtue of resignation. If they would have my office, they must take it.

I have heard of some great man, whose rule it was, with regard to offices, *never to ask for them, and never to refuse them*; to which I have always added, in my own practice, *never to resign them*. As I told my friends, I rose to that office through a long course of service in the inferior degrees of it. Before my time, through bad management, it never produced the salary annexed to it; and, when I received it, no salary was to be allowed, if the office did not produce it. During the first four years it was so far from defraying itself, that it became nine hundred and fifty pounds sterling in debt to me and my colleague. I had been chiefly instrumental in bringing it to its present flourishing state, and therefore thought I had some kind of right to it. I had hitherto executed the duties of it faithfully, and to the perfect satisfaction of my superiors, which I thought was all that should be expected of me on that account. As to the letters complained of, it was true I did write them, and they were written in compliance with another duty, that to my country; a duty quite distinct from that of postmaster.

My conduct in this respect was exactly similar to that I held on a similar occasion but a few years ago, when the then ministry were ready to hug me for the assistance I afforded them in repealing a former revenue act. My sentiments were still the same, that no such acts should be made here for America; or, if made, should as soon as possible be repealed; and I thought it should not be expected of me to change my political opinions every time his Majesty thought fit to change his ministers. This was my language on the occasion; and I have lately heard, that, though I was thought much to blame, it being understood that every man who holds an office should act with the ministry, whether agreeable or not to his own judgment, yet, in consideration of the goodness of my private character (as they were pleased to compliment me), the office was not to be taken from me.

Possibly they may still change their minds, and remove me; but no apprehension of that sort will, I trust, make the least alteration in my political conduct. My rule, in which I have always found satisfaction, is, never to turn aside in public affairs through views of private interest; but to go straight forward in doing what appears to me right at the time, leaving the consequences with Providence. What in my younger days enabled me more easily to walk upright, was, that I had a trade, and that I knew I could live upon little; and thence (never having had views of making a fortune) I was free from avarice, and contented with the plentiful supplies my business afforded me. And now it is still more easy for me to preserve my freedom and integrity, when I consider that I am almost at the end of my journey, and therefore need less to complete the expense of it; and that what I now possess, through the blessing of God, may, with tolerable economy, be sufficient for me (great misfortunes excepted), though I should add nothing more to it by any office or employment whatsoever.

I send you by this opportunity the two books you wrote for. They cost three shillings apiece. When I was first in London, about forty-five years since, I knew a person, who had an opinion something like your author's. Her name was Ilive, a printer's widow. She died soon after I left England, and by her *will* obliged her son to deliver publicly, in Salters' Hall, a solemn discourse, the purport of which was to prove, that this world is the true Hell, or place of punishment for the spirits, who had transgressed in a better state, and were sent here to suffer for their sins in animals of all sorts. It is long since I saw the discourse, which was printed. I think a good deal of Scripture was cited in it, and that the supposition was, that, though we now remembered nothing of such a preëxistent state, yet after death we might recollect it, and remember the punishments we had suffered, so as to be the better for them; and others, who had not yet offended, might now behold and be warned by our sufferings.

In fact, we see here, that every lower animal has its enemy, with proper inclinations, faculties, and weapons, to terrify, wound, and destroy it; and that men, who are uppermost, are devils to one another; so that, on the established doctrine of the goodness and justice of the great Creator, this apparent state of general and systematical mischief seemed to demand some such supposition as Mrs. Ilive's, to account for it consistently with the honor of the Deity. But our reasoning powers, when employed about what may have been before our existence here, or shall be after it, cannot go far, for want of history and facts. Revelation only can give us the necessary information, and that, in the first of these points especially, has been very sparingly afforded us.

I hope you continue to correspond with your friends at Philadelphia. My love to your children; and believe me ever your affectionate brother,

B. FRANKLIN

[124]

"Disposed to like the World as I find it"

[An excerpt from this letter was first printed in Sparks, *Familiar Letters*, pp. 22-23, with no indication of the recipient; and another excerpt in the same book, p. 133n., as "to one of his family connexions in America," and also in Sparks, *Works*, VII, 380n., as "to his sister." The letter, except for the genealogical chart, was printed in Goodman, *The Ingenious Dr. Franklin* (1931), pp. 50-53, from the manuscript then in the possession of A. S. W. Rosenbach. The manuscript is now in the American Philosophical Society, and the letter is printed entire from it. Since Jane Mecom's letter of May 10 is missing, it does not appear what she had wrongly suspected her brother of.]

DEAR SISTER,   London, July 17. 1771

I have received your kind Letter of May 10. You seem so sensible of your Error in so hastily suspecting me, that I am now in my turn sorry I took Notice of it. Let us then suppose that Accompt ballanced and settled, and think no more of it.

In some former Letter I believe I mention'd the Price of the Books, which I have now forgotten: But I think it was 3s each.—To be sure there are Objections to the Doctrine of Preexistence. But it seems to have been invented with a good Intention, to save the Honour of the Deity, which was thought to be injured by the Supposition of his bringing Creatures into the World to be miserable, without any previous misbehaviour of theirs to deserve it.—This, however, is perhaps an officious Supporting of the Ark, without being call'd to such Service. When he has thought fit to draw a Veil, our Attempting to remove it may be deem'd at least an offensive Impertinence. And we shall probably succeed little better in such an Adventure to gain forbidden Knowledge, than our first Parents did when they ate the Apple.

I meant no more by saying Mankind were Devils to one another, than that being in general superior to the Malice of the other Creatures, they were not so much tormented by them as by themselves. Upon the whole I am much disposed to like the World as I find it, & to doubt my own Judgment as to what would mend it. I see so much Wisdom in what I understand of its Creation and Government, that I suspect equal Wisdom may be in what I do not understand: And thence have perhaps as much Trust in God as the most pious Christian.

I am very happy that a good Understanding continues between you and the Philadelphia Folks. Our Father, who was a very wise Man, us'd to say, nothing was more common than for those who lov'd one another at a distance, to find many Causes of Dislike when they came together; and therefore he did not approve of Visits to Relations in distant Places, which could not well be short enough for them to part good Friends.—I saw a Proof of it, in the Disgusts between him and his Brother Benjamin; and tho' I was a Child I still remember how affectionate their Correspondence was while they were separated, and the Disputes and Misunderstandings they had when they came to live sometime together in the same House.—But you have been more prudent, and restrain'd that "Aptness" you say you have "to interfere in other People's oeconomical Affairs by putting in a Word now and then unasked." And so all's well that ends well.

I thought you had mentioned in one of your Letters a Desire to have Spectacles of some sort sent you; but I cannot now find such a Letter. However I send you a Pair of every Size of Glasses from 1 to 13. To suit yourself, take out a pair at a time, and hold one of the Glasses first against one Eye, and then against the other, looking on some small Print.—If the first Pair suits neither Eye, put them up again before you open a second. Thus you will keep them from mixing. By trying and comparing at your Leisure, you may find those that are best for you, which you cannot well do in a Shop, where for want of Time and Care, People often take such as strain their Eyes and hurt them. I advise your trying each of your Eyes separately, because few Peoples Eyes are Fellows, and almost every body in reading or working uses one Eye principally, the other being dimmer or perhaps fitter for distant Objects, and thence it happens that the Spectacles whose Glasses are Fellows suit

sometimes that Eye which before was not used tho' they do not
suit the other.—When you have suited yourself, keep the
higher numbers for future Use as your Eyes may grow older;
and oblige your Friends with the others.

I was lately at Sheffield and Birmingham, where I bought a
few plated Things which I send you as Tokens, viz. A Pair of
Sauceboats, a Pair of flat Candlesticks, and a Saucepan, lined
with Silver. Please to accept of them. I have had one of the
latter in constant use 12 Years, and the Silver still holds. But
Tinning is soon gone.

Mrs Stevenson and Mrs Hewson present their Compliments.
The latter has a fine Son. Sally Franklin sends her Duty to
you. I wonder you have not heard of her till lately. She has
lived with me these 5 Years, a very good Girl, now near 16.
She is Great Grandaughter of our Father's Brother John, who
was a Dyer at Banbury in Oxfordshire, where our Father
learnt that Trade of him, and where our Grandfather Thomas
lies buried: I saw his Gravestone. Sally's Father, John's Grandson, is now living at Lutterworth in Leicestershire, where he
follows the same Business, his Father too being bred a Dyer,
as was our Uncle Benjamin. He is a Widower, & Sally his only
Child. These two are the only Descendants of our Grandfather
Thomas now remaining in England that retain the Name of
Franklin. The Walkers are descended of John by a Daughter
that I have seen, lately deceased. Sally and Cousin Williams's
Children, & Henry Walker who now attends Josiah are Relations in the same degree to one another and to your & my Grandchildren, viz

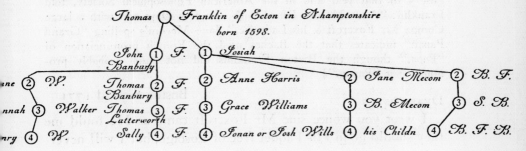

What is this Relation called? Is it third Cousins? Having mentioned so many Dyers in our Family, I will now it's in my Mind request of you a full & particular Receipt for Dying Worsted of that beautiful Red, which you learnt of our Mother.—And also a Receipt for making Crown Soap. Let it be very exact in the smallest Particulars. Enclos'd I send you a Receipt for making soft Soap in the Sun.

I have never seen any young Men from America that acquir'd by their Behaviour here more general Esteem than those you recommended to me. Josiah has stuck close to his musical Studies, and still continues them. Jonathan has been diligent in Business for his Friends as well as himself, obliging to every body, tender of his Brother, not fond of the expensive Amusements of the Place, regular in his Hours, and spending what Leisure Hours he had in the Study of Mathematics. He goes home to settle in Business, and I think there is great Probability of his doing well.

With best Wishes for you & all yours, I am ever,

Your affectionate Brother

B FRANKLIN

I have mislaid the Soap Receipt ⎱
but will send it when I find it. ⎰

Jane Mecom to Deborah Franklin

[Here first printed from the manuscript in the American Philosophical Society. John Foxcroft, with his wife, was then in Boston on affairs of the post office. Jonathan Williams, in an unpublished letter dated August 5 of that year and in the American Philosophical Society, told Franklin: "Aunt Mecom Dined with us a few Days ago with a large Compa Mr Foxcroft & his Lady &c." Jane Mecom's spelling "Grand Papah" indicates that the Baches used the French pronunciation of "Papa," though the Boston Franklins did not—and probably pronounced it "Pappy."]

DEAR SISTER   Boston Sep 2d 1771

I wrot you wonce sinc Mr Foxcroft came as He tould me they should go in His Paquet free of Postage, but I will nevertheless take this Opertunity to Inform you that I am well, have got so far over my Lamenes as to be Able to walk much about as well as I could before I fell, but you know that was but Poorly, as you could out walk me by a Grat Deal, we shall Nither of us now I beleve Atain to what my Brother writs me of Himself that He has Lately walkd ten miles without Resting, & is in fine Helth which I am shure you & I Joyn in Blessing God for. Mrs Foxcroft & my self have often Pleasd ourselves with Talking of Litle King Bird she Agrees with us that He is an Extroydnary Fine child God Bless Him, may He live to be a Blessing to Grand Papah & all the Rest, I Love Every won I had any Acquaintanc with at Philadelphia, so as far as my Respects or complements will be Acceptable Pray Present them from

yr affectionat Sister

JANE MECOM

turn over [*to postscript on other side of sheet*]
you wrot me you had a Pare of Buter Boats of chineis of yr own manifactor to send me but wanted an opertunity I beg you would not forgit them, I should be very fond of them, if you give them to any master of a vesel that traids there Directed to Cousen williams & a Leter with them I Dont Doubt they will take care to Diliver to me & then I shall git them. Jeney sends her Duty

J M

"For Makeing Crown Soap"

[Here first printed from the manuscript in the American Philosophical Society. Franklin asked for this recipe in his letter of July 17, 1771, and on January 13, 1772, thanked his sister for it. On October 27, 1785, he told her it had been lost, and asked her for another copy. With her letter of January 6, 1786, she sent the copy, which is very defective but of which the surviving fragment is printed with that letter. The present version has only now been identified as by Jane Mecom. The drawings at the end appear to be by Franklin and the words "hand Gauge" are almost certainly written by him. It is not clear what the notation "72—4" under Jane Mecom's title means, but the "72" presumably refers to the year he received or acknowledged it.]

[129]

For Makeing Crown Soap
72—4

Sett a Leach or Leaches that will contane Eighteen Bushels of Ashes and won Bushel of Stone Lime two hogsheds will do they must be very tite made clean a hole bored in the botom Near the chine but not close, nor Near a seam in the head, with a Large tap-borer, fitt a Pine Plug to prevent its Leaking. let your Leach be set high anouf to set a tub under and with a very small Decent to wards the tap, suround the hole Inside with Bricks Leaving a Pasage betwen for the lye to Run and lay more bricks over or a flat stone on Part of a barrill head to Prevent the ashes pressing & some Light sticks around also a handfull of hay that will cover the boton but thickest about the tap to keep the Lye clear as Posable

Let your Ashes be lade on a clean Place make a Large hole in the midle Put your Lime in & Slack it Gently with water covering it with some of the Ashes to keep in the Steeme till it is all slackd then let it be mixd as masons do there morter & fill your Hogsheads Leve the Edg a litle above & let the Ashes Lay with a small decent to wards the midle then fill with water till the water stands on the top and let them stand ten or twelve days.

Draw of yr first run of Lye & fix yr copper over night see that your Lye is strong anouf to bare an Egg   Put a few Pails full in to yr copper haveing reddy thirty pounds of clean hard Tallow and fiveteen Pounds of the Pureist baberry wax of a Lively green colar if you can git it broak in to small Peeces Add this by Litle & Litle over a Gentle Fier and now and then a Pail or two of Lye keeping it stiring till all is Desolved still Adding Lye till it Incorporates filling it with Lye as it Runs till the whol Amounts to About two Barrils in this Proces you may Leve it all Night with a moderate Heat under it. when you have got so much In and the Soap is come to a Good consistence you may make it Boil hard and Proceed to Sepperation which is done by sprinkling salt to the Quantity of about

[a] Peck in about the space of a quarter of an hour keeping it constantly stiring from the Botom & freaquently holding up the stick to observe the Drops that fall from it which when the seperation has taken Place will as the soap cools on it be as clear as medarah wine as soon as you find that Put in no more salt (the consequence would be makeing Britle) but Proceed to boil it off as fast as you can takeing care that it does not Boil over which it will in that state be very much Inclined to do but may be keept down by flirting the froith with a scimer the harder it Boils the sooner it will Boil down that Froith which must be all boiled in not Puting any more Lye in to the copper after it is seperated with the salt till it is done (but keeping some water by you to throw under the copper to slaken your fier if it is two fierce) when the froith is all Boiled in the Soap will lay on the top of the salt lye then clear away your fier cool under yr copper with a litle water & put won Pail full of Lye in to it to help the Soap to Rise the quicker then Leave it still till next morning when the soap will be all coold on top in a hard cake which must be cut out & if any Soil adhears to the under side it must be wiped of. the salt lye thron away the coper washd clean & sett over the fier again Puting in all the soap with the same Quantity of Lye as was in the Day be fore if you have it Run if not you must keep a slow fier till you have (the weak Lye that Runs after the first Boiling Ansures for this) when you have got your Quantity Proceed to Boiling as fast as you will Seperating it with salt as the Day before. when all the froath is Boild in Put in a Pail of cold Lye and take away yr fier as before & let it stand about half an Hour and it will be fitt to take off.

you must have your mould Reddy to Recive it which is Planks of 12 Inches wide as long as you chuse Keyd to gather that may be taken to Peaces when the Soap is cold it must be Lined with a Lining Cloath not too coars takd down at the corners & made Smoth all Round & tackd on the Edges then let won take of the soap cautiously with a litle Lye as Posable puting it in to the frame while another keeps it stiring with a small crutch made on Purpose to m[ould] it & keep it smoth on the top take care to let your Frame stand on a Level let care be taken when it is in that it Is not Jogd nor any thing fall in it to Brake the Surface, in the morning it will be cool anouf to cut up if it should stand too long it will be Dificult & also if you cut it too warm it will not be Smoth apt to warp & crack, when you are going to cut it take out the taks un Key your frame & take it of. Peal down the Lining quite to the boton Plank and mark it all Round the thickness of Each cake with a Marker made on Purpose with spears in it when you have Leveled the top mark it a long Exactly in midle or a crose the size of the cakes, & if you have a [*word cut off margin*] stamp stamp it, then Proceed to cut of the whole slab with a small wier fixed to a round stick at Each End to Pull by, then hold it up on Edg and cut it throw Length ways Laying won half at a time in a gage made on Purpose Just the thicknes of the cake with the stamp Downwards and Smoth it to a Level then lay it on a table to be cut in to Seperat cakes & Proceed to do the other in like manner.

If for sale as Each cake ought to be of Equal weight we have a small gage to Put Each in & Pare it fitt

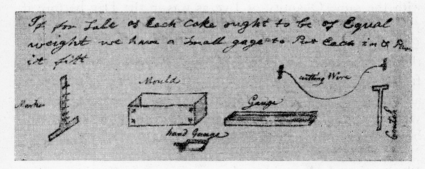

"The idea of my Son Franky"

[Printed first in Sparks, *Familiar Letters*, pp. 145-147, from which it is here reprinted. With it is printed a fragment of the draft which Franklin kept and which is now in the American Philosophical Society. The "pleasant companion" with whom Franklin had recently traveled was

Richard Jackson. "Brasiletto" was a species of dyewood then imported to the northern colonies from Jamaica. The debt due Franklin for seven years was from Samuel Hall, a printer who had become a partner of Ann Franklin, widow of the elder James Franklin, in Newport shortly before her death in 1763. Hall continued to publish *The Newport Mercury*, founded by her son James Franklin in 1758, till 1768, when he founded *The Essex Gazette*, the first newspaper printed in Salem. Married to a daughter of Ann and James Franklin, Hall was Benjamin Franklin's nephew by marriage. It is not certain what his debt to Franklin was for, but it presumably had something to do with paper or printing. Franklin's famous saying about principle and interest had appeared in *Poor Richard* for 1753: " 'T is against some Mens Principle to pay interest, and seems against others Interest to pay the principal." The grandson who brought to mind Franklin's son Francis, who had died in 1736 at the age of four, was Benjamin Franklin Bache, born August 12, 1769.]

My Dear Sister,   London, 13 January, 1772

I received your kind letters of September 12th, and November 9th. I have now been some weeks returned from my journey through Wales, Ireland, Scotland, and the North of England, which, besides being an agreeable tour with a pleasant companion, has contributed to the establishment of my health; and this is the first ship I have heard of, by which I could write to you.

I thank you for the receipts; they are as full and particular as one could wish; but they can easily be practised only in America, no bay-berry wax, nor any Brasiletto, being here to be had, at least to my knowledge. I am glad, however, that those useful arts, which have so long been in our family, are now put down in writing. Some future branch may be the better for it.

It gives me pleasure, that those little things sent by Jonathan proved agreeable to you. I write now to cousin Williams to press the payment of the bond. There has been forbearance enough on my part; seven years or more, without receiving any principal or interest. It seems as if the debtor was like a whimsical man in Pennsylvania, of whom it was said that, it being against his principle to pay interest, and against his interest to pay the principal, he paid neither one nor the other.

I doubt you have taken too old a pair of glasses, being tempted by their magnifying greatly. But people in choosing should only aim at remedying the defect. The glasses that enable them to see *as well*, at the *same distance* they used to hold their book or work, while their eyes were good, are those they should choose; not such as make them see *better*, for such contribute to hasten the time when still older glasses will become necessary.

All, who have seen my grandson, agree with you in their accounts of his being an uncommonly fine boy, which brings often afresh to my mind the idea of my son Franky, though now dead thirty-six years, whom I have seldom since seen equalled in every thing, and whom to this day I cannot think of without a sigh. Mr. Bache is here; I found him at Preston, in Lancashire, with his mother and sisters, very agreeable people, and I brought him to London with me. I very much like his behaviour. He returns in the next ship to Philadelphia. The gentleman, who brought your last letter, Mr. Fox, stayed but a few minutes with me, and has not since called, as I desired him to do.

I shall endeavour to get the arms you desire for cousin Coffin. Having many letters to write, I can now only add my love to cousin Jenny, and that I am, as ever,

Your affectionate brother,

B. FRANKLIN

P.S. Sally Franklin presents her duty. Mrs. Stevenson desires to be affectionately remembered. No arms of the Folgers are to be found in the Herald's Office. I am persuaded it was originally a Flemish family, which came over with many others from that country in Queen Elizabeth's time, flying from the persecution then raging there.

[*variant fragment of the draft*]
have seen my Grandson agreed in their Accounts of his being an uncommonly fine Boy, which brings often fresh to my Mind the Idea of my Son Franky, tho' now dead 36 Years, whom I

have seldom since seen equal'd in every thing, and whom to this Day I cannot think of without a Sigh. Mr Bache is here. I found him at Preston in Lancashire with his Mother and Sisters, very agreable People, and I brought him to London with me. I very much like his Behaviour. He returns in the next Ship to Philadelphia. The Gentlemen who brought your last Letter, Mr Fox, stay'd but a few Minutes with me, & has not since call'd as I desired him to do. I shall endeavour to get the Arms you desire for Cousin Coffin. Having many Letters to write, I can now only add my Love to Cousin Jenny, & that I am as ever

Your affectionate Brother

B F

Sally Franklin presents her Duty
Mrs Stevenson desires to be affectionately
remember'd   S. Franklin

"I shall recommend her among my Friends"

[Here first printed from the manuscript in the American Philosophical Society. Patience Wright, already noted in America for her portrait models in wax, had just arrived with her three children in London to begin her still more notable European career. The "Mr Fox" who had brought Jane Mecom's letter to Franklin was perhaps from Philadelphia, but has not been positively identified.]

DEAR SISTER,   London, March 30. 1772

I have this Day receiv'd your kind Letter by Mrs Wright. She has shown me some of her Work which appears extraordinary.—I shall recommend her among my Friends if she chuses to work here.

I will enquire for the Books Jenny desires, and send them if I can get them.

As you are so curious to know something of Mr Fox, I will see if I can find him out in St. James's Street. He never call'd after he left your Letter; tho' I requested he would, & told him I should be very glad to see him.

Mr Bache is gone; and I hope near home by this time. I hope

Josiah, who is on the point of going, will get safe & well to his Friends. I send this Line by him just to let you know that I continue well, and that I am ever

Your affectionate Brother

B FRANKLIN

"1773 is my Period for visiting Boston"

[Here first printed from the manuscript in the American Philosophical Society. The expression "sailed in Asworth" meant sailed in the ship commanded by Captain Asworth.]

DEAR SISTER, London, April 13. 1772

I received your kind Letter by Mrs Wright, and shall do her all the Service in my Power. I think I wrote to you by Cousin Josiah, who sailed in Asworth last Week, and I hope will get safe home to his Friends. I continue well, and purpose returning this Summer, God willing, and then may hope next year for the Pleasure of seeing you, as 1773 is my Period for visiting Boston, having left it in 1723, and visited it in 1733, 43, 53, & 63.—My Love to your Daughter, and best Wishes of Health and Happiness to you and all you love, from

Your affectionate Brother

B FRANKLIN

Deborah Franklin to Jane Mecom

[Here first printed from a manuscript in the American Philosophical Society. The questioned date is in another hand, but cannot be far wrong. Franklin had urged Richard Bache not to seek a government post and had given him £200 with which to open a store in Philadelphia. Deborah Franklin had received a letter from Jane Mecom with a "bundel" for her son Benjamin, whose wife ("Cusin Betsey") had brought her child, probably the baby named John Ross, to dinner. The "Governor and his ladey" were William Franklin and his wife. "Brother Davenporte" was James Davenport in Boston. "Polley" was probably the former maid who had left Philadelphia with Ephraim Brown. Peter was Jane Mecom's distracted son Peter Franklin. "Mrs Defeld" was Mrs. Edward Duffield.]

[136]

MY DEAR SISTER   May 1772?

I did reseve yours by Capt Roger with a bundel for Mr. Macum which I reseved and sente with your letter to him and by Mr Prockter with one in Closed for Mrs Macum which I all so sente to him senes that Cusin Betsey come with the Child and dined with us as shee dus some times I advised that they shold write to you

you will see that Mr Bache is safe arived thank god he has opned store he is well as is Salley and our Kingbird. I supose Mr Bache or Salley will write to you as I am not a bel to write nor am I abel to write agreeabel letters as ones I yous to doe for I have not so good matter to worke on as I yous to write on or to make letters on but I will say all the good I can my one famely is well as to the reste I hear not quite so well but I expeckte the Governer and his ladey to town aboute two or three week and then I beleve thay will write to you

give my love to all that Loves me tell me hough Brother Davenportes children is tell me aney thing of poor Polley that did live hear I seme much Consernd for her let me know hough is Peter I have not heard a boute him a long while I ofen think of him now I have indevered to make as good a letter as I cold I donte let aney bodey see my letter as I write so bad my love to Jenney and the other Jenney [*interlined*: flag] and to Cusin Kisiah and her Dafter Mrs Replay is very well and her son who is well Mrs Defeld and famely and maney of your friend they ofen aske a boute you and send love to you

My Dear Sister I wrote I had but one only other thing I wold writ if I had but one thing I wold write to you but I have not anything that wold give you aney pleshuer

"The greater Pleasure of seeing you"

[Printed first in the *Century Magazine*, XXXII (June 1886), 263-264, by John Bigelow, and included in Bigelow, *Works*, v, 110-111, from the manuscript in the Library of Congress; printed in Smyth, *Writings*, VI, 21, with unwarranted dependence on the Bigelow text; here printed more correctly from the manuscript. Captain Jenkins was one of the

Nantucket-Rhode Island connections of the Franklins, but has not been further identified. Franklin had been in Boston, "Brother John then living" and after their father's death, in 1753 and in the winter of 1754-1755. The manuscript "State of the Acct between Doctor Benjamin Franklin and Jonathan Williams Senr as it should properly stand" for the years 1763 to 1774, now in the American Philosophical Society, shows that the first installment of "Hall's Money" had been £100 sterling (133.6.6 lawful money of Massachusetts) and had been paid in January 1773. The remainder in four installments brought the total amount received to £152.1.6 (lawful money 202.15.4). The same "Acct" shows a payment of £5.0.6 to John Adams for bringing suit against Hall for the recovery of the money. In the Adams Papers the law dockets of John Adams list "Benjamin Franklin vs Samuel Hall" as of "July Court 1772." An unpublished letter from Jonathan Williams Sr., dated February 15, 1773 and in the American Philosophical Society, informed Franklin that the settlement had been brought about by "a proposal made by Hall or rather Halls friends."]

DEAR SISTER   London, March 9. 1773

I received your kind Letter of Dec. 30. & rejoice to find you were well. I may possibly hav[e] the greater Pleasure of seeing you before the Year is ou[t.] I have desired Cousin Williams to give you the Money he may recover from Hall. I would only mention to you, that when I was in Boston in 175 [*torn off*] Brother John then living, an old Man whose Name I have forgotten, apply'd to me with a Bond of our Father's of about 15 or 17 Pound if I remember right, desiring I would pay it, which I declin'd with this Answer, that as I had never receiv'd any thing from the Estate, I did not think myself oblig'd to pay any of the Debts. But I had another Reason, which was that I thought the Care of those Matters belong'd more properly to my Brother. If you know that Person, I wish you would now out of Hall's Money pay that Debt: for I remember his Mildness on the Occasion, with some Regard.

My Love to Jenny. I am ever,

Your affectionate Brother

B FRANKLIN

I have not yet seen
Capt. Jenkins, but
will enquire him out
when I next go to the
City

"A little Affectation in your Apology"

[Printed first in Bigelow, *Works*, v, 190-191, from the manuscript now in the Library of Congress; reprinted largely from Bigelow in Smyth, *Writings*, vi, 93-94; here printed more correctly from the manuscript. The Paddock to whom Franklin referred was probably Captain Seth Paddock (or Paddack) from whom there are letters to Franklin in the American Philosophical Society which make it appear that Paddock was one of the Nantucket kinsmen. "Young Hubbard" was Samuel Hubbart, son of Thomas and Judith Ray Hubbart. There is some mystery about the date July 7 for this letter. On July 6 Franklin wrote to his wife from West Wycombe on his way to Oxford, where he remained a week. The explanation seems to be that he wrote the letter to Jane Mecom, and others also dated the 7th, before he left, to be sent as of that date; or that he actually wrote all the letters of the 7th at West Wycombe, at the house of his friend Baron Le Despencer, but dated them at London which was a permanent address. Lord Le Despencer was one of Franklin's British chiefs in the post office. It is no wonder that this letter to Jane Mecom seems hastily written, for on that same date Franklin wrote two long letters on Massachusetts affairs to Thomas Cushing, and one partly political to Samuel Cooper; with briefer letters to Samuel Mather, son of Cotton Mather, and to two cousins, Samuel Franklin and Jonathan Williams Sr.]

DEAR SISTER,   London, July 7. 1773

I believe it is long since I have written any Letters to you. I hope you will excuse it. I am oppress'd with too much Writing, and am apt to postpone when I presume upon some Indulgence.

I received duly yours of Jan. 19., Apr. 20., May 5 and May 15.

Our Relations Jenkins & Paddock came to see me. They seem to be clever sensible Men.

Is there not a little Affectation in your Apology for the Incorrectness of your Writing? Perhaps it is rather fishing for

Commendation. You write better, in my Opinion, than most American Women. Here indeed the Ladies write generally with more Elegance than the Gentlemen.

By Capt. Hatch went a Trunk containing the Goods you wrote for. I hope they will come safe to hand and please. Mrs Stevenson undertook the Purchasing them with great Readiness and Pleasure. Teasdale, whom you mention as selling cheap, is broke & gone. Perhaps he sold too cheap. But she did her best.

I congratulate you on the marriage of your Daughter. My Love to them. I am oblig'd to good Dr Cooper for his Prayers.

Your Shortness of Breath might perhaps be reliev'd by eating Honey with your Bread instead of Butter, at Breakfast.

Young Hubbard seems a sensible Boy, & fit, I should think for a better Business than the Sea. I am concern'd to hear of the Illness of his good Mother.

If Brother John had paid that Bond, there was no Occasion to recal it for you to pay it; for I suppose he might have had Effects of our Fathers to pay it with. I never heard how it was managed.

Mrs Stevenson presents her Respects, and I am ever

Your affectionate Brother

B FRANKLIN

Jane Collas to Benjamin Franklin

[Here first printed from the manuscript in the American Philosophical Society. Franklin, hearing that his sister's daughter Jane was to be married, had requested Jonathan Williams Sr. on November 3, 1772, to "lay out the sum of fifty pounds, lawful money, in bedding or such other furniture as my sister shall think proper to be given the new-married couple towards housekeeping, with my best wishes; and charge that sum to my account." The records of the Brattle Street Church show that Samuel Cooper married Peter "Collis" (Collas) and Jane Mecom on March 23, 1773.]

My DEAR AND HONOURD UNCLE Boston July 9th 1773

My Heart, has ever been susceptible of the warmest greati-
tude for your frequent Benefactions to the whole of our Family,
but your last *kind*, unexpected as well as undiserved *Noble*
present in particular to me, calls for a particular acknoledge-
ment from me. Except then dearest Sir, my most sincear and
hearty thanks, with a promise that your kindness Shall ever be
greatefully rememberd, and your donation be made the best
use of: as it will be laid out by my Mamma and the good Mrs.
Williams, who is allways, ready with Mr Williams, to give
their friendly advice, and asistance on every ocasion, few are
blessed, with such friends as we are; how then can we be unhappy; I am not nor would I change conditions with one person
living were I sure of fullfilling my most *ardent* wish, that every
action of my life, may be a credit to my Uncle, my constant
endeavours and earnest prayers, shall not be wanting. When
dear sir, shall I have the happiness, of thanking you in person,
for all your kindness; god send it may be soon: till then, please
to except this incorrect Scrawl and permit me to Subscribe myself, your sincearly affectionate forever obliged, and ever Dutifull Neice,

JENNY MECOM

PS the Man, who will Share your goodness with me desires
his most dutifull respects and Sincear thanks.

J M

"A Paper of mine printed here"

[Here first printed from the manuscript in the American Philosophical
Society. With this letter Franklin sent his *Rules for reducing a Great
Empire to a Small one*, which had appeared in the *Public Advertiser*
for September 11, 1773, and had been followed by *An Edict of the
King of Prussia* on September 22.]

DEAR SISTER, London, Oct. 9. 1773

I have not heard from you since your Goods arriv'd. I hope
they got safe to hand, and that they please.—

I write this Line just to let you know I am well, Thanks to God, and to cover a Paper of mine printed here, which I send because you desired I would send you what I published from time to time, and I am willing to oblige you; but often they are things out of your way so much that I omit sending them, and sometimes I forget it, and sometimes I cannot get a Copy to send, which was the Case of a Piece since this now enclos'd, viz. *An Edict of the King of Prussia,* all that were printed being gone in a few Hours.

I hope you & Jenny & her Husband continue well which to hear will always be a Pleasure to

Your affectionate Brother

B FRANKLIN

"I have been saucy"

[Reproduced in facsimile in the *Library Bulletin 1944* of the American Philosophical Society, from the manuscript in the Society; and first printed in Carl Van Doren, *Benjamin Franklin's Autobiographical Writings,* pp. 297-298. The next-to-the-last paragraph was printed in Sparks, *Familiar Letters,* p. 120n., with no indication of the person to whom the observation was addressed. "Coz. Jenny's" (that is, Jane Mecom's daughter Jane's) verses are missing. The news of the death of Jane Mecom's "Neighbor Hall" had been, it appears, reported in her missing letter of June 28. The *Massachusetts Gazette* for June 14 to June 21 of that year announced the death of "Hugh Hall, Esq; aged 80." Hugh Hall, graduate of Harvard, slave trader, and owner of a good deal of Boston real estate, had formerly lived near the Orange Tree Inn, which would have made him a neighbor of Jane Mecom, though it does not appear just where he lived when he died. *Sibley's Harvard Graduates,* VI, 11-18. By referring to him as "Neighbor Hall" Franklin was clearly distinguishing Hugh Hall from the tardy Samuel Hall who had lately settled his account with Franklin to the benefit of his sister.]

DEAR SISTER, London, Nov. 1. 1773

I received your kind Letter of June 28. with great Pleasure, as it inform'd me of your Welfare.

I thank you for your good Wishes, that I may be a means of restoring Harmony between the two Countries. It would make me very happy to see it, whoever was the Instrument. I had

us'd all the smooth Words I could muster, and I grew tired
of Meekness when I saw it without Effect. Of late therefore I
have been saucy, and in two Papers, *Rules for reducing a great
Empire to a Small one*, and, *An Edict of the King of Prussia*,
I have held up a Looking-Glass in which some Ministers may
see their ugly Faces, & the Nation its Injustice. These Papers
have been much taken Notice of, many are pleas'd with them,
and a few very angry, who I am told will make me feel their
Resentment, which I must bear as well as I can, and shall bear
the better if any publick Good is done, whatever the Consequence to myself. In my own private Concerns with Mankind,
I have observ'd that to kick a little when under Imposition, has
a good Effect. A little Sturdiness when Superiors are much in
the Wrong, sometimes occasions Consideration. And there is
truth in the Old Saying, That *if you make yourself a Sheep, the
Wolves will eat you*. [*Written lengthwise in the margin of this
paragraph*:] This to yourself.

I communicated Coz. Jenny's Verses to my little Circle of
Female Friends who made the *Bouts Rimes*, and they were
pleas'd to praise them. I hope she is got well home from her
Visit to Nantucket. My Love to her.

Your Neighbor Hall must have been pretty well advanc'd
in Years when he dy'd. I remember him a young Man when I
was a very young Boy. In looking back how short the Time
seems! I suppose that all the Passages of our Lives that we
have forgotten, being so many Links taken out of the Chain,
give the more distant Parts Leave as it were to come apparently
nearer together.

I was glad to hear of the Ship's Arrival in which I sent your
Things. I hope they will prove agreable & advantageous to you.
If you possibly can, try to increase your Capital, by adding the
Profits.—Consuming all the Profits and some of the Principal,
will soon reduce it to nothing.

I am ever, my dear Sister,

Your very affectionate Brother

B FRANKLIN

[143]

"Enough in our Pockets to pay the Post Chaises"

[Here first printed from the manuscript in the Historical Society of Pennsylvania. Franklin had been dismissed from his place in the Post Office on January 30.]

London, Feb. 17. 1774

DEAR SISTER

I received your kind Letter of Dec. 11. and rejoice to hear of your Welfare & easy Situation.

You will hear before this comes to hand, that I am depriv'd of my Office. Don't let this give you any Uneasiness. You and I have almost finished the Journey of Life; we are now but a little way from home, and have enough in our Pockets to pay the Post Chaises.

Intending to disgrace me, they have rather done me Honour. No Failure of Duty in my Office is alledg'd against me; such a Fault I should have been asham'd of. But I am too much attach'd to the Interests of America, and an Opposer of the Measures of Administration.—The Displacing me therefore is a Testimony of my being uncorrupted.

Thanks to God I continue in good Health, and am ever,

Your affectionate Brother

B FRANKLIN

My best Respects to good Dr Cooper }
I shall write to him soon ⎰

"A violent Cold"

[Here first printed from the manuscript in the American Philosophical Society.]

London, March 23. 1774

DEAR SISTER,

A violent Cold which affects my Head and Eyesight, makes it inconvenient to me to write much; yet I would not miss the Opportunity of giving you this Line just to let you know that I am otherwise as usual.—I hope you and yours are well, and am ever

Your affectionate Brother

B FRANKLIN

"An infamous Falshood, as you supposed"

[Printed first from the manuscript in the American Philosophical Society, in Carl Van Doren, *Benjamin Franklin's Autobiographical Writings*, pp. 338-339. Franklin's salary from the post office had been £300 a year; his fees from Pennsylvania, New Jersey, and Massachusetts as their agent in London amounted to £1000 a year. In mentioning that figure he disregarded the £100 due from Georgia at first, and later £200, because he seems never to have been paid by that colony. The pamphlets he sent with this letter to his sister are missing, but those he is known to have "encouraged" that year are Arthur Lee's *An Appeal to the Justice and Interest of the People of Great Britain, in the present Disputes with America* and *A True State of the Proceedings in the Parliament of Great Britain, and in the Province of Massachusetts Bay* . . . ; Joseph Priestley's *An Address to the Protestant Dissenters of all Denominations, on the approaching Election of Members of Parliament* . . . ; and Jonathan Shipley's *A Speech intended to have been spoken on the Bill for altering the Charters of the Colony of Massachusetts Bay*.]

London July 28. 1774

DEAR SISTER

I received your kind Letters of May the 1st & 18th.—I rejoice to hear that you and yours continue in Health, as I do, Thanks to God.

The Report you mention that I offer'd to desert my Constituents, and banish myself if I might continue in Place, is an infamous Falshood, as you supposed.—And as ridiculous as false, since it implies that I have not Arithmetic enough to calculate the Difference between 300 & 1000.—They are every now & then reporting here, that I am using Means to get again into Office. Perhaps they wish I would.—But they may expect it till Doomsday. For God knows my Heart, I would not accept the best Office the King has to bestow, while such Tyrannic Measures are taking against my Country.—Be assured I shall do nothing that will prejudice me in your Opinion, or be inconsistent with the honest Public Character I have hitherto maintained. I kept my former Post indeed till it was taken from me, because I did not receive it as a Favour from Government, but rose to it in the Course of Office from Seniority join'd with Merit; I therefore thought I had a right to it, and I did not chuse to compliment them with a Resignation, rather liking that they should take upon themselves the Shame of depriving me. They have done me honour by turning me out, and I will take care they shall not disgrace me by putting me in again.

All this to yourself.—To the World such Declarations might seem incredible, & a meer puffing of ones own Character: therefore, my dear Sister, show this to no body: I write it meerly for your Satisfaction; and that you may not be disturb'd by such Idle Reports.
I am ever,

Your affectionate Brother

B FRANKLIN

The Inclos'd Pamphlets were encourag'd by me, being written by Friends of mine, and printed at my Expense.

"I shall stay here another Winter"

[Here first printed from the manuscript in the American Philosophical Society.]

London, Sept. 3. 1774

DEAR SISTER,

Hearing just now of this Opportunity, I write a Line to acquaint you that I am well and hearty, Thanks to God, as I hope you are.

It seems likely now that I shall stay here another Winter; you will therefore be kind in continuing to write to me—

My Love to Jenney &c. I am ever

Your affectionate Brother

B FRANKLIN

"I am anxious to preserve your good Opinion"

[A part of this letter was first printed in Sparks, *Familiar Letters*, pp. 150-151, as "To a Friend in America"; and again in Sparks, *Works*, VIII, 136-137, as to Jane Mecom. It was first printed in full in Carl Van Doren, *Benjamin Franklin's Autobiographical Writings*, pp. 341-

342, and is here printed again from the manuscript in the American Philosophical Society. Mary (Polly) Stevenson, daughter of Franklin's landlady in Craven Street, had been married in 1770 to William Hewson. The aunt from whom she had inherited a fortune was a Mrs. Tickell.]

DEAR SISTER, 	London, Sept. 26. 1774

I have had no Line from you since those you favour'd me with by Cousin Jonathan Williams. I hope you continue in health, as I do, Thanks to God. But I wish to know how you fare in the present Distress of our dear Country. I am apprehensive that the Letters between us, tho' very innocent ones, are intercepted. They might restore me yours at least, after reading them; especially as I never complain of broken patch'd-up Seals, (of late very common) because I know not whom to fix the Fact on.

I see in a Boston Paper of Aug. 18. an Article expressing "that it is now generally believed Dr Franklin has received a Promise of being restored to the royal Favour, and promoted to an Office superior to that which he resigned."—I have made no public Answer to any of the Abuses I have received in the Papers here, nor shall I to this. But as I am anxious to preserve your good Opinion, and as I know your Sentiments, and that you must be much afflicted your self, and even despise me, if you thought me capable of accepting any Office from this Government while it is acting with so much Hostility towards my native Country, I cannot miss this first Opportunity of assuring you that there is not the least Foundation for such Report; that so far from having any Promise of royal Favour, I hear of nothing but royal and ministerial Displeasure, which indeed, as things at present stand, I consider as an Honour.—I have seen no Minister since January, nor had the least Communication with them. The generous and noble Friends of America in both Houses do indeed favour me with their Notice and Regard, but they are in Disgrace at Court as well as myself.—Be satisfied, my dear Sister, that I shall do nothing to lessen my-self in your Esteem or my own: I shall not with the least Concurrence with the present Measures merit any Court Favour, nor accept of any if it were offered me, which however is not at all likely to happen.

Mrs Stevenson presents her Respects to you. Her Daughter Mrs Hewson, who lost her Husband in May, has lately got a third Child, a Girl, born 5 Months after its Father's Death: A melancholy Circumstance!—But her Aunt, a Sister of Mrs Stevenson, dying lately, and leaving her Fortune to Mrs Hewson, which was considerable, puts her into easy Circumstances, and will enable her to bring up her Children decently.

As those here who most interest themselves in behalf of America, conceive that my being present at the Arrival of the Proceedings of the Congress & the Meeting of Parliament, may be of Use, I submit to their Judgment, and think it now likely that I shall not return till Spring.

Jonathan joins me in Love to you and yours. My love to his Family, & to Dr Cooper.—I am ever,

My dear Sister,

Your affectionate Brother

B FRANKLIN

"*My only comfort is God Reigns*"

[Here first printed from the manuscript in the American Philosophical Society. Franklin had sent his sister the pamphlet *Of the Stilling of Waves by means of Oil* published that year. The Reverend Charles Chauncy was minister of the First Church of Boston. John Mecom's widow Catherine had been married at New York on June 19, 1774, to Thomas Turner. *Documents Relating to the Colonial History of the State of New Jersey. Newspaper Extracts*, x, 410. Turner, of the British 47th (or Lancashire) Regiment, had been commissioned adjutant on May 28, 1768, ensign on December 17, 1772. He became lieutenant November 22, 1775. W. C. Ford, *British Officers serving in the American Revolution, 1774-1783* (1897). A letter from Catherine Turner to Franklin, dated Leigh, Lancashire, April 7, 1783, said that Lieutenant Turner had been wounded at "Lexenton and at Bunkers hill," had never recovered from his wounds, and had died in Lancashire in June 1782. Her letter, hinting at possible help but not asking outright for it, is in the American Philosophical Society. The Bishop to whom Jane Mecom referred was Franklin's friend Jonathan Shipley, Bishop of St. Asaph. Deborah Franklin, at the time of this letter, was near her death, which occurred on December 19 of that year. The "Hored lie tould & Published about yr son" was that William Franklin sided with the British ministry in its conflict with the American colonies —which turned out to be the truth. William Hyslop, who had three sons but only one daughter and who seems to have attended the Brattle Street Church as Jane Mecom then did, was presumably the messenger who had failed to call for her letter.]

MY EVER DEAR BROTHER   Boston Novr 3 1774

I have Just recd yrs of August 18 wonder to see you complain of not recveing leters from Boston I think what ever they omited they would not neglect that, but it is like they have been Intercepted, I wrot abt a month ago to go by Mr Hyslop but He liveing out of town & leaveing His only Daughter very sick I beleve made Him forgit to call for it but I got it in to the bag with won I wrote to cousen Jonathan, I wish you may have recd them. I thank you for the Pamphlits you then sent & another I have Just recved [interlined: Novem 18 I had begon this leter at the date above] concerning the stilling the wavs with oyl. I think it is not Profanity to compare you to our Blesed Saviour who Enploued much of His time while hear on Earth in doing Good to the body as well as souls of men & I am shure I think the compareson Just ofton when I hear the calumny Invented & thrown out aganst you while you are Improveing all yr Powers for the Salvation of them very Persons, oh my Dear Brother may you & I Imitate Him also in Holynes & in that way trust in Him for Eternal Happines, I am well Asured that you as well as my self are convinced that it must ever be imperfect Hear, I speak not that I have met with any thing New for I am as Happy as the Present state of affairs will Premit owing to yr Bounty without which I must have been distrest as much as many others, Docter Chauncy says we have allredy had miricles wrought in our favour won of which is the Uniteing of the Colonies in such a maner, another the Extroydnary fruitfull seasons & Bounty of our friends & looks

[149]

on it as a token of Gods Design to deliver us out of all our trobles, but at Present we have a maloncholy Prospect for this winter at Least the towns being so full of Proflegate soulders & many such Officers there is hardly four & twenty hours Pases without some fray amongst them & won can walk but a litle way in the street without hearing there Profane language, we were much surprised the other day upon hearing a Tumult in the street & looking out saw a soulder al Bloody damning His Eyes but He would kill Every Inhabatant He mett & Pressing into a shop oposite us with His Bayonet drawn bursting throw the Glas Dore & the man of the house pushing Him out & he to do what mischeif He could Dashing the chiney & Earthen were which stood on the window threw the sashes with the most terrable Imprecations, the case it seems was He Percved they sould liquer & went into the House Demanding some but being refused He went into the closet & took out a gon & said His comanding officer tould Him he might take any thing out of any house He had a mind to upon which the batle Ensued & the man & His servant were boath very much wounded there were to of them [*interlined*: soulders] but I saw but won, a Gaurd with an officer came & careyed Him away & I have heard nothing of Him since but this has made me more Timerous about what may be before winter is out my only comfort is God Reigns.

My Son Johns widow that was, has mareyed an officer & come hear among them His name is Turner she sayes He is an Adjutant & Insign but whither he is Payd in Boath capasetys I know not He takes a good deal of Pains to convince us he is a friend to the country haveing been hear formerly & kindly treeted.

My Daughter Collas has been in the Country most of the sumer & Purposes to spend the winter there as she Expects her Husband will be most of the time at sea she has not curidge to stay in town & they have there Board so cheap find it les Expensive, she hapened to be hear when I recd yr last & desiered her Duty to you the man where she Boards is the majr of the Rigement & is a moderate whig but cant be convinced that we ought not to Pay for the Tea I sent Him up yr two boks & he was mightyle Pleasd with them they are much Esteemd by all good Judges & I hope have done much to wards Instructing the People of England what sort [of] Parlement men they ought to choes & may God defend [*word torn off margin*] there harts from all Bribery & coruption. I think our Congress Adress to the People of England is a Grand Performance & does them Honour & shews there was Realy the wisdom among them that the Colonies Endevoured to colect which Joynd with yrs & the Bishops will I hope work som Glorious Effect you have millions of Prayers going up to Heaven for it Dayly Private & Publick.

I have had no leter from Philadelphia a long time tho I have wrote several times the last I wrote I heard my sister Put under her cushing I sopose in order to Read at more Leasure & Prehaps never thought of it more & won of the children git it & tore it up, as we know my sister is very forgitfull, I now & then hear from them by travelers that they are well & that Gives me Pleasure, I think it is Presumeing on yr Patience but I must Just mention the Hored lie tould & Publishd hear about yr son & with such Plausabelity of what you had wrote concerning it that at first it struck with a fear that it might be trew & I cant Expres to you the Pain it gave me on yr acount but a litle consideration convinced me it was Imposable & I soon had the Pleasure of hearing it contredicted. I shall ad no more at this time but my respects to Mrs Stevenson my love to cousen Jonathan & yr self & beg you would forgive my sending you such very bad writing which will be very difficult to find out but as the vesal is so near sailing this or none must go from yr

Ever Affectionat & obliged

SISTER JANE MECOM

Novr 21—1774

"Bad Weather *does not last always in any Country*"

[Reproduced in facsimile in the *Library Bulletin 1944* of the American Philosophical Society, from the manuscript in the Society, and first printed in Carl Van Doren, *Benjamin Franklin's Autobiographical Writings*, p. 346. The "Head they make here and sell at the China Shops" was presumably the Wedgwood portrait medallion of Franklin of 1775.]

London, Feb. 26. 1775

DEAR SISTER,

I hope you continue well, as I do, Thanks to God.—Be of good Courage. *Bad Weather* does not last always in any Country.—Supposing it may be agreable to you, I send you a Head they make here and sell at the China Shops. My Love to your Children, & to Cousin Williams and Family. I am ever

Your Affectionate Brother

B FRANKLIN

"*God Apeard for us & drove them back*"

[Here first printed in full from the manuscript in the Yale University Library. Franklin, accompanied by William Temple Franklin, son of William Franklin, had arrived in Philadelphia on May 5. His letter to his sister of February 26 had been sent by Josiah Quincy Jr., "Poor Quensey" in her spelling, who had died on April 26 on his voyage home. In the turmoil after Lexington and Concord Jane Mecom, with her granddaughter Jane Flagg, had been invited to take refuge with the William Greenes at Warwick, Rhode Island, where the house was crowded with relatives from Boston. Catharine Greene's sister, Judith Ray, had been married to Thomas Hubbart of Boston, whose mother after her first husband's death had married John Franklin, Jane Mecom's brother. Though Judith Ray Hubbart had died on March 8 of that year, the general family relationship had not been affected. Thomas Hubbart had not come to Warwick, but his sister Susannah ("Suckey") Hubbart was expected; and so was another sister, Elizabeth Hubbart Partridge ("Patridg," "Pateridg"). "Old Mr Gough & wife" were Captain James Gooch, who was a half-brother of Elizabeth Gooch (Hubbart) Franklin, and his third wife, Elizabeth Craister, who was not the mother of his son William Gooch. The younger Gooch had been married to Deborah Hubbart, a daughter of Judith Ray Hubbart, on May 31, 1770. His wife had come to Warwick, and he too was expected. The daughter of Elizabeth Partridge was actually her stepdaughter, Rebecca, born to Captain Samuel Partridge by an earlier marriage. Thomas Leverett, a Boston bookseller, was a more distant connection of the Greenes and Hubbarts. Mrs. Russell Hastings, "Some Franklin Memorabilia Emerge in Los Angeles," *Antiques*, November 1939, furnishes interesting details, with numerous illustrations, of the Franklin-Hubbart-Greene relationships. "My Poor litle litle Delicat nabour Mrs Royall" was Abigail Tailer Royall, daughter of William Tailer, former lieutenant governor of Massachusetts, and widow of Jacob Royall, who had died June 5, 1773. *New England Historical and Genealogical Register*, XXXIX, 353, and LXXXIV, 364. The Jacob Royalls had lived in a "large genteel Brick Dwelling House" in Orange Street, which was mortgaged for more than its value at Royall's death and was advertised for sale in the *Boston Gazette* for August 9, 1773. Mrs. Royall's "Famely" included Elizabeth Moncrieff, who had lived with the Royalls for several years and remained with the widow after her husband's death. Abigail Royall was sixty-eight in 1775 and died four years later. The "old Mrs Downs" who had been invited to Warwick but had not come was Anna Hill Downe (Down, Downe, Downes), mother-in-law of James Hubbart, another son of Elizabeth Gooch (Hubbart) Franklin. Henry Marchant, by whom "favors" had come from Benjamin Franklin to the Greenes, was attorney general of Rhode Island. The postscript by Catharine Greene to Jane Mecom's letter follows it on its third page. The address page of the letter is endorsed by Franklin "Sister Mecom May 14, 1775"; and bears the notation "Forwarded by Yr most obedt hum Servt Eben Hazard New York May 29th 1775." Ebenezer Hazard had been authorized on May 1 to organize the New York postal service. He served under Franklin as surveyor general of the United States post office, and in 1782 succeeded Richard Bache as postmaster general. There is a woodcut of the William Greene house, as it was about a hundred years after this letter, in Oliver Payson Fuller, *The History of Warwick, Rhode Island* (Providence, 1875), p. 157.]

Warrick 14 May 1775

My Ever Dear & much Hond Brother

God be Praised for bring you saif back to America & soporting you throw such fatuges as I know you have sufered while the minestry have been distresing Poor New England in such a cruil maner. yr last by Poor Quensey Advises me to: keep up my curidg & that faul wither does not last all ways in any country. but I beleve you did not then Imagin the Storm would have Arisen so high as for the Generl to have sent out a party to creep out in the night & Slauter our Dear Brethren for Endevering to defend our own Property, but God Apeard for us

& drove them back with much Grater Lose than they are willing
to own, there countenances as well as confeshon of many of
them shew they were much mistaken in the people they had to
Deal with, but the distress it has ocationed is Past my discription. the Horror the Town was in when the Batle Aprochd
within Hearing Expecting they would Proceed quite in to town,
the comotion the Town was in after the batle ceasd by the Parties coming in bringing in there wounded men causd such an
Agetation of minde I beleve none had much sleep, since which
we could have no quiet, as we under stood our Bretheren without were determined to Disposes the Town of the Regelors, &
the Generol shuting up the town not Leting any Pass out but
throw such Grate Dificulties as were allmost insoportable, but
throw the Goodnes of God I am at last Got Saif Hear & kindly
Recved by Mr Green & His wife (who to my grate comfort
when I had got Pact up what I Expected to have liberty to
carey out intending to seek my fourtune with hundred others
not knowing whither) sent me an Invitation in a leter to Mrs
Patridg of which I gladly acepted an the day I arived at Provedence had the unspeakable Pleasure of hearing my Dear Brother
was saif arived at His own home, Blessed be God for all His
mercys to me an unworthy creature, these People seem formed
for Hospetality Apear to be Pleasd with the vast Adition
to there famely which consists of old Mr Gough & wife,
there sons wife & negro boy, Mr Thomas Leverett's wife 2
children & a made, my self an Grand Daughter who I could not
leve if I had it would have been her Death, & they Expect this
Day 3 more of Mr Leveretts chilen young Mr Gouge, Suckey
& Mrs Pateridg & Daughter. & seem as tho there harts were
open to all the world   they sent for old Mrs Downs but dont
know if she designs to come as it is so Extreemly difecult to git
a line to pass to Each other, Mrs Leveritt is trying to git a
house to keep house by her self. My Poor litle litle Delicat
nabour Mrs Royall & Famely came out with me not knowing
where she should find a Place   I left them at Cambridg in a
most shocking Disagreable Place but since hear she is gone to

wooster, my own Daughter had been at Board at Roxbury almost a year before but she with the famely were obliged to fly
in to the woods & tho they Returnd again they think them selves
very unsaif & she was in grate concern what cours to take when
the day before I left her she Recd a leter from her husband
that He was saif Arived at Bedford in Dartmouth not Dareing
to venture in to salem from whence they saild, this also was a
grat Ease to my mind as she might now soon Expect her husband to take the care of her,

I am Still under grate concern for cousen williams   He was
out of Town at the time of the batle & was Advised to keep out &
His Poor wife slaved her self almost to Death to Pack up &
Secure what She could & sent away her two Daughters Intending to go to Him & behold in comes he in to town the day before
I came out Imagining (as I was told for I did not see him) that
was the saifest Place I can hear nothing of Him since,

you will have seen the Generl leter to conettacut & be able
to Judge of the truth of His Insineuations by his fidelity to us
Poor bostonians.

I have wrot a grat number of leters to you the winter & Spring
Past but cannot Prercive by yr self or cousen Jonathan that you
have recved any of them I sent won about a month ago but as
you are Returnd it is no mater if you never git it.

Present my love to my cousens Beaches' & the Dear children
& Exept the same from yr Ever

Affectionat Sister

JANE MECOM

Is Jonan come with you if he is remember my love to Him

Dear Brother I am tould you will be joynd to the Congress
& that they will Remove to conetecut will you Premit me to
come & see you there Mrs Green says she will go with me

[Postscript in Catharine Greene's hand]

MY DEAR DEAR FRIEND

Welcom a Hundred times Welcom to our once happy Land.
Are you in Health and allow me to ask you the old question

over again if you are the Same good good old Soul you used to
be your arrival gives New Spring to all have heard mention
it   When Shall We See you here   do let it be as Soon as the
Congress is adjournd or dont know but your good Sister and
Self Shall mount our old Naggs and Come and See you Mr
Greene would Send Plenty of love if at home we are all well
hope you found all that is Dear to you So. We Receivd your
favors by Mr Marchant many thanks to you for them this is but
the fore runner of a longer letter

from your affectionate

Real Friend

CATY GREENE

"*The Repose I wish'd for*"

[First printed in Sparks, *Works*, VIII, 154, from a copy sent to Sparks
by Benjamin Franklin Stickney of Vistula, Michigan Territory, on April
29, 1833. Vistula, later incorporated as a part of Toledo, lay in a district
that in 1833 was claimed by Michigan, but was assigned by Congress to
Ohio in June 1836. Stickney, considering the original of the letter in
his possession "of too great value to intrust to the mail," sent only a copy,
but he copied it with unusual accuracy. Sparks, who seems to have had
no other source, altered the copy in several respects and omitted the
postscript altogether. The letter is here printed from Stickney's copy,
now in the Harvard University Library. It was more probably from John
than from Samuel Adams that Franklin had heard his sister was at
Warwick. Stickney's copy notes that the letter had been postmarked both
Cambridge and Newport, and that it bore a note reading: "This Letter
has been three weeks at Newport post office Forwarded to Mrs. Mecom
by her Hble Servt A. Maxwell Wedny 10 O'Clk at [ante] M."]

Philada May 26 1775

DEAR SISTER

I have just now heard by Mr Adams, that you are come out
of Boston, and are at Warwick in Rhodeisland Government:
Suppose it must be at good Mr & Mrs Greens, to whom present
my affectionate Respects. I write this Line just to let you know
I am return'd well from England; that I found my Family
well; but have not found the Repose I wish'd for; being the

next Morning after my Arrival delegated to the Cong[ress] by our Assembly. I wish to hear from you, and to know how you have left your Affairs in Boston; and whether it will be inconvenient for you to come hither, or you wish rather that I should come to see you, if the Business I am engag'd in will permit. Let me know if you want any Assistance; and what is become of Cousin Williams & Family, and other Friends. Jonathan was at Paris when I left England, but to return in a Week or two. I am ever, my dear Sister

Your very loving Brother

B Franklin

Send me what News you can
    that is true
Sally presents her duty to you
    & Love to Mr and Mrs Green

"I sympathise most sincerely with you"

[Printed first in Carl Van Doren, *Benjamin Franklin's Autobiographical Writings*, pp. 404-405, from the manuscript in the American Philosophical Society. "Cousin Williams," Jonathan Williams Sr. whose son Jonathan had remained in France, had left Boston for Worcester, Massachusetts, where he lived for a time in the house of the loyalist James Putnam, who had moved into Boston to the Williams house. The "Infant Hercules" was Franklin's grandson William Bache, now two years old. The grandson from England was William Temple, illegitimate son of Governor William Franklin.]

My dear Sister,   Philada June 17. 1775

I wrote to you some time since, having heard from one of the Delegates that you were at Warwick, and I supposed it must be with that good Family, so I directed my Letter to you there; I hope you receiv'd it.—I have since received your kind Letter of May 14. with one from dear Mrs Green. I sympathise most sincerely with you and the People of my native Town & Country. Your Account of the Distresses attending their Removal affects me greatly. I desired you to let me know if you wanted any thing, but have not since heard from you. I think so many People must be a great Burthen to that hospitable House; and I wish you to be other wise provided for as soon as possible, and I wish for the Pleasure of your Company, but I know not how long we may be allowed to continue in Quiet here if I stay here, nor how soon I may be ordered from hence; nor how convenient or inconvenient it may be for you to come hither, leaving your Goods as I suppose you have in Boston. My son tells me he has invited you to Amboy: Perhaps that may be a Retreat less liable to Disturbance than this: God only knows, but you must judge. Let me know however if I can render you any Service; and in what way. You know it will give me Pleasure. I hear the [that] Cousin Williams is at last got out with his Family:—I shall be glad to hear from them, and would write if I knew where they were. I receiv'd the other Day here, a Letter I wrote to you from London the 20th of February. It had been to New England, and I suppose your being not found there, occasion'd its being forwarded to me. I am, Thanks to God, very hearty and well, as is this whole Family. The youngest Boy is the strongest and stoutest Child of his Age that I have seen: He seems an Infant Hercules. I brought over a Grandson with me, a fine Lad of about 15. His Father has taken him to Amboy. You will be pleas'd with him when you see him. Jonathan Williams was in France when I left London. Since I have been here I receiv'd a Letter he sent me there: I enclose it for your Amusement; and to show to his Father & Mother, as it may be some Satisfaction to them, if they have not lately heard from him.

I am ever, my dear Sister,

Your affectionate Brother

B FRANKLIN

"Dont go, pray Dont go"

[Printed first, and hitherto only, in Duane, *Letters to Benjamin Franklin*, pp. 62-66, and here printed from the manuscript in the American Philosophical Society. The bottom of each of the three pages of the letter is mutilated, and the missing words are here indicated by dots. Some words supplied by Duane are disregarded as not indisputably the correct ones. The "Daughter foot" who had gone to Dunstable "in a bad stat of helth" was Ruth, the widow of Edward Mecom Jr. She had been married to Thomas Foot, a joiner (cabinetmaker), on November 20, 1760, about two years after the death of her first husband. Boston Registry Records, xxx (Marriages 1752-1809), 37, 372. William Flagg, whose wife Sarah Mecom had died in 1764, had since been married again and had died in Boston in June 1775. The "cousen Coffen" who had invited Jane Mecom to Nantucket was Kezia Coffin. By "ben franklin" Jane Mecom meant Benjamin Franklin Bache. The notes from William and Catharine Greene fill the whole of the third page of the manuscript, but they are really postscripts.]

Warwick July 14—1775

The Concern I knew—my Ever Dear Brother would be in to know what was become of me made me take the first opertunity to write to him & twice since, but did not recve a line from you till the day befor yesterday when I recd yrs of the 17 June & this Day I have recd the first you wrot, it had been Returnd from Cambridg & had lane 3 weeks in Newport office,

your care for me at this time Added to the Innumerable Instances of yr Goodnes to me gives me grat comfort under the Dificulties I feel with others but not in a grater Degree for I am in want of nothing haveing mony suficent to soport me some time if I should go to board (which however Mrs Green will not consent to) & I have with me most of the things I had to sell & now & then sell som small mater. I thought I had tould you I Brought out what I could Pack up in trunks & chists & I so contrived to Pack em in our wereing Aparil Lining & Beding that they Pasd Examination, without discovery, this was not an unlawfull smugling which you would have reproved for they were not owed for, nor any won cheated of Duties, I wish I could have brought all my Effects in the same maner but the whol of my Houshold furniture [*interlined*: some wood, soap, &c—&c—&c] Exept a few small maters I put into my trunk I left behind, secured Indeed in the house with locks & bars but those who value not to Deprive us of our lives will find a way to brake throw them if they are premitted . . . . . . My Daughters Goods are there two for tho She Board[ed in] the country some time before the Town was . . . . . . She din not . . . . . . [re]move her furniture, what . . . . . . of there . . . . . . Cousen Williams got out . . . . . . but hear . . . . . . Estates with . . . . . . man at . . . . . . there to Liv . . . . . . Leter Pleased me much, shall convey it to them first opertunity, My Daughter foot Gone to Dunstable she in a bad stat of helth, left there Goods in Boston my son John's widow who mareyed Mr Turner an Officer left them in Boston how it has faired with them can not hear tho I wish them saif for He realy apeared a Good sort of man o how horrable is our situation that Relations seek the Destruction of Each other.

por Flagg tho He has used me very Ill I Deplore His Fate the more as there is two of my Daughters Children left I know not how they will be Provided for, His storey is two long & two full of shocking sircumstances to troble you with, shall only tell you that in the winter He was taken in a fitt which terminated in Distraction & confined Him some time, but got so much beter as to go about His Bus[iness] & sent out His wife & children Intending to folow them but was soon After taken in the same maner as in winter & Died in a few days. my Good Mrs Royal & famely that I lived so happyley with 2 year is Gone to worcester. I have not recved the Invitation you say yr [son] was so good as to send me nor a Line from Him a long time tho I have wrot several by such hands as I know he must have recved, cousen Coffen has Invited me to nantuckett which was sent to Boston & Returnd before the Resolves of the Congress, I dont know if it would be [prudent?] for me to go now, I cannot Determin what . . . . . . take at Present. I wish you could Advise me, I . . . . . . at being an Incumbrance to this good Famely as my . . . . . . is for me, but I strive all in my Power . . . . . . as light as I can, when Mrs. [Greene] . . . . . . In a jocoos . . . . . . our mounting our . . . . . . & see you . . . . . . Remember . . . . . . should . . . . . . I am rejoyced that yr children & famelys are well I have before heard of yr young Hercules, my Neice was so good as to write me won long leter about the children, & ben franklin won for Himself of which I wrot you to England, you say nothing about *him* he apeard to me to be an Extrodnary child, I ansured His leter but He does not contineu the corispondenc.

I could have wishd you had been left to yr own Option to have assisted in Publick Affairs so as not to fatigue you two much but as yr Talents are superour to most other men I cant help desiering yr country should Injoy the benifit of them while you live, but cant bare the thought of yr going to England again as has been sugested hear & won sentance in yr leter seemes to favour, you Positively must not go, you have served the Publick in that way beyond what any other man can Boast till you are now come to a good old Age & some younger man must now take that Painfull service upon them. Dont go, pray Dont go, you certainly may do as much good hear as surcumstances are at present & posable the Congress may not think it proper to send since those late transactions of the Armey I am so much at a lose to know whether the News I hear be trew or no that prehaps I had beter leve it to other hands, but my Daughter wrot me last week from Roxbury that on our Army's fiering canon that reachd into the fortification & killd six men Genl Gage sent out word we had beter not proceed to Extremeties for the King had sent for two of the men of war home. I left my Daughter in so much fear that she could not sleep on nights but she now writs me (from the same place) that she hopes all things, & fears nothing, the Reason she Imagins because she sees all about her in the same disposition.

the Famely . . . . . . well & almost as numerous, Mrs Greene says she will . . . . . . I only add my love to all yr Children & grand children . . . . . . I am as Ever yr most

Affectionat Sister

JAN. . .

[*From William Greene, written at the top of his wife's note. Long, Deer, and "Petteck's" (Pettick's, Pedick's, Peddock's) were islands in Boston Harbor.*]

our men have taken [three?] yslan and brought of Eaght hundred Sheep and Catle of one an Other five hundred Sheep & Catle of the other. & a man awar barge with fore men. Col Robenson has taken long Ysland and brought of two hundred sheep & some Catle and Eaght Men and One young Lade with out the loss of a Man two of the Yslands was taken last week and the Other this week—July th18—Sickly in Boston the Solders and Ynhabatants Die fast. the Names of the other Yslands Deer Ysland & Petlecks—

[Note from Catharine Greene enclosed in Jane Mecom's letter. Catharine Greene, hoping Franklin would "Stay at home," meant remain in Philadelphia; but by "going home again" she meant going to England, which Americans had long called "home." The signature and the words and letters in square brackets in the farewell line are supplied from Duane, who may have seen the manuscript in better condition than the present.]

My Dear Friend your letter which had the Pleasure of Receiving gave me great Pleasure as it gave me a fresh Proff of your own Dear Self, & being once more on the Same Land with us, your Dear Good Sister Grew Very impatient till she heard from you and began to fear you was not come. She was kind enough to Shew me her letter and you are fear full She will be trouble Some but be assured that her Company Richly Pays as She goes along and we are Very happy together and shall not Consent to Spare her to any body but her Dear Brother was he to Stay at home and Be Positive but if you are to Journey we must have her for She is my mama and friend and I tell her we are Rich that we have a lot here and another there and have 3 or 4 of them and we Divert one another Charmingly do Come and See us Certain! dont think of going home again Do Set Down and injoy the Remainder of your Days in Peace have Just been enguaged in something that Prevents my writing as I designd to have done I hope . . . . . . I write to be more my . . . . . . kind love to . . . . . . Mrs Beach and the D . . . . . . hope your . . . . . . Sympathiss with you . . . . . . up in them . . . . . .

girl So is mine . . . . . . of each other . . . . . . love to . . . . . .
him Nancy . . . . . . [affec]tionate friend [as long as life]

[CATY GREENE]

"God bless those two good ones!"

[Printed first in Roelker, *Benjamin Franklin and Catharine Ray Greene*,
pp. 56-57, and here printed again from the manuscript in the American
Philosophical Society. Samuel Ward (1725-1776), former governor of
Rhode Island, married to Catharine Greene's sister Anne, had been
serving with Franklin in the Second Continental Congress.]

Philada Aug. 2. 1775
MY DEAR SISTER

Last Night I received with great Pleasure your kind Letter
of July 14. with the most agreable Additions from Mr & Mrs
Green. God bless those two good ones!

The Congress has adjourned this morning to the 5th of September. I have now upon my Hands the Settling a new General
Post Office, and a Treaty to be held with the Indians on the
Ohio, besides smaller Businesses, all to be transacted by the time
the Congress meets again. Govr Ward is just setting out, and
I cannot send this by him if I enlarge. My Love to your Friends,
from

Your affectionate Brother

B FRANKLIN

Sally & Mr Bache send their Love
and Duty
 I think you had best come
 hither as soon as the Heats
 are over, i.e. sometime in
 September, but more of this
 in my next.

"In order to take you home with me"

[Printed first in Carl Van Doren, *Benjamin Franklin's Autobiographical Writings*, p. 412, from the manuscript in the American Philosophical

Society. Franklin had come from Congress to Washington's Headquarters with Benjamin Harrison of Virginia and Thomas Lynch of South Carolina. While in Cambridge he met John Adams's wife Abigail and General Nathanael Greene.]

Head Quarters, Camp
at Cambridge. Oct. 16.
1775.

MY DEAR DEAR SISTER

I arrived here last Night with two other Delegates of the Congress. I suppose we may stay here about a Week.—In order to take you home with me, I purpose quitting their Company, purchasing a Carriage and Horses, and calling for you at good Mrs Greene's. But let me hear from you in the mean time, and acquaint me with any thing you would have me do or get towards the Convenience of our Journey. My Love to that hospitable Family, whom I hope soon to have the Pleasure of seeing. I am ever

Your affectionate Brother

B FRANKLIN

Jane Mecom to Catharine Greene

[Printed first in Roelker, *Benjamin Franklin and Catharine Ray Greene*, pp. 61-63, and here printed again from a copy in the American Philosophical Society. Catharine Ray, though only twenty years younger than Jane Mecom, affectionately called herself the daughter of a woman she liked and admired so much. Jane Mecom's "distracted" sons were Benjamin and Peter. Her son Josiah had enlisted in Captain Charles Furbush's company of Colonel Ebenezer Bridge's Massachusetts regiment on May 29, 1775, and served two months and eight days. *Massachusetts Soldiers and Sailors of the Revolution*, x, 591. The cause and circumstances of his death have not come to light. Catharine Greene's son Ray, then ten years old, had accompanied Jane Mecom and Franklin to Philadelphia to enter the Academy there. On the way they had stopped at the "magnificient" house of Governor William Franklin at Perth Amboy. If Jane Mecom was aware of the breach between father and son, at least she did not mention it in this letter. The "young Gentleman" who set Ray a "compleat Example of good maners" was probably William Temple Franklin, then a student at the College, which was another name for the Academy. The "Mr Mumford" whom Jane Mecom had not seen has not been identified. Since the letter from Catharine Greene here answered is missing, it does not appear what was the "crine" to which she had smilingly confessed. "C - - l - - - k" was "colick." The Jenny who would have to go without her silk gown was Jane Flagg, then with the Greenes and to be married on December 5 to their cousin Elihu Greene. The "fine Garl" born to Sarah Bache on December 1 was named Sarah.]

M[y] DEAR MRS GREENE   Philadelphia Novr 24 1775

Asure yr [se]lf the Epethet of Daughter which you seem to like to use cannot be Disagreable to me would to God I had such a won all the Alurements of this Place my Brother Exepted should not seperate me from her, I write not this in Disparagement of my own Daughter for She is a good woman but Providence does not Premit us to be to gather & as to Sons I have nothing but misery in those that are left Boath of them Distracted & I have heard of the Death of Poor Josiah since I came hear but by what means I am not Informed. God grant I may make a proper Use of all His Dealings with me.

I thank you for yr very kind and perticular leter of the 12 of this month you know it will be allways agreable to me, I am sorry you were so Afflected in yr Juorny to westerly my seat was Exeding Easey & Jurney very Pleasant my Dear Brothers conversation was more than an Equivelent to all the fine wether Emaginable but I mett with won mortification on the Rhoad we had Apointed to Dine at wethersfeald where Mrs Hancock is & had conciderable talk about it but we being Engaged at that time in other conversation the Postilion Drove a mile or two beyond before we discovered it & I could not prevale with him to go back so we did not Dine till we put up for the Night, I Expect[ed] Master Ray would have Given [yo]u som Discription of [wh]at he saw on the Jurny Espeshaly at Governer Franklins house which was very magnificient & we shew him [it] all over but I percive he did not in his last & He now thinks it not proper as the Small Pox is out on him tho I dont beleve He could Infect any body he has so litle we cant number more than ten that I am afraid he will not have won pit for a Recipt he has had no Illnes but won Day a litle Shivery & feverish so much as to say he was in no hurry for His coffe, we thought it not

proper to make his cloaths till we saw how it would fare with
him but now shall have them made with all Expedition he is
very tractable & hear is a young Gent[le]man who setts him
a compleat Example of good maners that is politenes. & my
Brother will give Proper Dire[ction]s about his Scooling He
will write him self as soon as he thinks it saif. I have not seen
Mr Mumford tho I Desiered yr Brother ward to Ask him to
come but I am a going out to look for him & shall finish my
leter when I come back.

Since the Above I have recd yrs of the 21 & am Glad to find
there is won in the world so free from Giult. yr crine was un-
noticed that you might have keept yr own secrit & absolved
yr self. Ill be Ansurable for yr Husband that He shall not Beet
you, Ray Behaves well as can be Expected, Inded very well.
& he will now be able to Injoy himself without fear. I shall
have no Use for my Gownd this winter & I dont give my self
the least concern about it. I Dont know that I got cold with
my Jurny but I have had a bad fit of Astme, am now as well
as Usal have not had the C - - l - - - k but do not Sleep well on
nights, Mrs Bache is not yet abed She is as well as can be
Expected, I am so happy as to have my Choice of places of
worship so near that the wether need not hinder me from going.
Remember my kind love to Mr Greene to Dear litle Samey to
Mr & Mrs Gouch & yr mother, & respect to al[l] Inquiering
friends & beleve me to be be yr most faithfull & obliged frind

JANE MECOM

Saterday Decr 2 I h[ave] not seen Mr Mum[ford] sopose He
is Gone so Jenny m[ust be] without her silk till a nother opertunity, Ray is abroad & [well?] & harty, Mrs Beach was Last
night Deld of a fine Garl, my Brother Remembers his love to
you.

Jane Mecom to Catharine Greene

[Printed first in Roelker, *Benjamin Franklin and Catharine Ray Greene*,
pp. 71-72; and here printed again from a copy in the American Philo-

sophical Society. Nicholas Cooke was then governor of Rhode Island. Governor Samuel Ward had died of smallpox in Philadelphia on March 26. Catharine Greene in her reply of June 21 declared that the house which had been used as a shop by Thomas Leverett was "so far out of town and from all your acquaintance that I should by no means Consent to your going there"; and Jane Mecom's scheme was dropped. Her account of the action in the Delaware against the British *Roebuck*, 44 guns, on the day this letter was written, is on the whole accurate so far as that day was concerned. The next day the *Roebuck* got off the shoal on which she had been grounded and with the *Liverpool*, 28 guns, left the river.]

MY DEAR FRIEND   Philadelphia 8th may 1776

you cant Imagin the Anxiety I have been in sinse I recved yr last, hearing then of yr famely being so sick & not a word sinse maks me fear Every thing, you cant surely sopose I should think any thing of paying postage on any Extroydenary ocation I sent won large paquet to Governer Cook without a word of Apolegy you must make it for me for it was by yr order, & I had not time to write a word. I have sent a nother by yr Brother Wards servant which I hope you will git saif & soon, ansure me quick I besech you by the post, but prehaps I may meet it for there has been a Alaram hear to Day which Almost Determins me to sett out for New England Directly & if I should I shall take Ray with me for He would Brake His hart if I should Leave Him & I have promised I will not, I cannot hear whither my Daughters Goods are Gone as well as mine but Expect they are, & I think there is but very litle chance for her Husband to Escape being taken, She looks on her self alredy as a Disconsolat widdow Intreets me to promis her I will Return that we may live to gather, what if I should go & take that House Mr Leverett had near Provedence do you think we could get a liveing in the way they began   I am afraid Boston is not sufficently fortified yet. I thought not to tell you the circumstanc of the Alarm as you may hear it as quick & more perfict in the News Papers but I will Just tell you that two Ships the Roebuck & a nother came up the River I forgit how many mils Distant from the City when a number of armed Gondelos & fier ships went down to Ingage them there was Grat fiering all Day till five oclock & there is an Expres come brings News they have shatered them boath much & Drove the Roebuck on shore the same that was Ashore on Sunday week but go off again it is Expected she will be Taken, Ray desiers me to Remember His Duty love & Respects where it is Due & Pleas to do the same for your Affectionat friend

JANE MECOM

"The Respect with which I am receiv'd and treated"

[Reproduced in facsimile in the *Library Bulletin 1944* of the American Philosophical Society, from the manuscript in the Society; and first printed in Carl Van Doren, *Benjamin Franklin's Autobiographical Writings*, 424-425.]

DEAR SISTER   Nantes, in France, Dec. 8. 1776.

I arrived here safe after a Passage of 30 Days, somewhat fatigued and weakned by the Voyage, which was a rough one; but I recover my Strength fast since my Landing, and shall be able I hope in a few days to undertake the Journey to Paris of about 250 Miles. If the PostChaises here were as easy as the English, such a Journey would be no Difficulty.—I hope you continue well and happy. Remember me affectionately to Cousin Jenney, & to Mr & Mrs Greene. I am ever

Your affectionate Brother

B FRANKLIN

You can have no Conception of the Respect with which I am receiv'd and treated here by the first People, in my private Character: for as yet I have assumed no public One—

"We thought it necessary to Retire to this place"

[Here first printed from the manuscript in the American Philosophical Society. At the approach of the British Army, before the Battle of Trenton, Jane Mecom left Philadelphia with Sarah Bache and her children for refuge at Goshen, twenty-four miles from the city. They had, according to a letter from Sally to her father written the following February 23, "two comfortable rooms" at a farm house—or as she put it, at "the next plantation to where Mr. Ashbridge used to live." The "Will" who wanted to go to France was William Bache, now three and a half. Temple Franklin and Benjamin Franklin Bache had accompanied their grandfather. The Captain "Faulkner" who had recommended Peter Collas to the command of a ship in the new United States merchant marine was Franklin's friend Nathaniel Falconer, who in January 1776 had been appointed one of the commissioners of naval stores. Collas appears to have been captured on this first voyage and taken to New York, where he was for some months prisoner on a British prison ship. On June 3, 1777, he was ordered sent to Providence to be exchanged for Captain Richard Saint Hill. On September 12, 1777, Collas appears to have been assigned as lieutenant to the brigantine *Starks*, Captain John Allen Hallet. *Massachusetts Soldiers and Sailors in the Revolutionary War*, III, 503.]

Decr 15 1776
Goshen Chester County
in Pensilveny

MY EVER DEAR BROTHER

I was distresd at yr leveing us but as affairs have turned out I have blesd God you were absent, & we have Reason to hope you are saif arived at your Port, on hearing the Enemy were advancing to wards us we thought it nesesary to Retire to this place where we hope we are saif & are very comfortable   I have another mercy to be thankfull for which has given grate ease to my mind, the Return of my Son in Law Collas, who has by the Recomendation of cousen Williams, & Capt Faulkner, (who happened to be then in Boston) obtained the comand of a Contenental Ship. Expects to go to France, & is the barer of this, I hope He will aquit Himself properly in His station, I know nothing of His abilities but that He has allwas borne a good charecter. Our Famely are all well, Will as Harty & as lovely as ever Says He wants to go to france to Grandpapa & He must send a Boat for Him, we shall be very Happy to hear from you, from Temple & Benny Remember my love to them, I sopose yr son & Daughter will write & Inform of all nesesary   I only add that I am as Ever

Your Affectionat Sister

JANE MECOM

[169]

"Hardly Ever so unfourtunate a Famely"

[Printed first, and hitherto only, in *Pennsylvania Magazine of History and Biography*, LXXII (1948), 265-266, from the manuscript in the Historical Society of Pennsylvania; and here printed again from the manuscript. Elizabeth Downes, wife of Governor William Franklin, had died in New York on July 28 of that year, while her husband was still interned in Connecticut. The "very Just charecter given her in the Philadelphia Paper" appeared in the *Pennsylvania Gazette* for August 13, but there is no indication of the author, who may have been Francis Hopkinson as Jane Mecom had heard. The notice, in the form of a mortuary inscription, reads: "Last week died at New-York/Mrs. ELIZABETH FRANKLIN/ The Wife of WILLIAM FRANKLIN, ESQ;/ She was a Lady distinguished by a/ Refined Education,/ A peculiar sweetness of Manners,/ And dear to her friends/ For the VIRTUES of her HEART:/ She filled her Station in Life/ With a dignity that commanded Respect,/ And an affability that engaged the LOVE of ALL./ Her circumstances were affluent,/ Her life exemplary,/ Her death unfortunate./ A sincere Friend/Pays this small tribute to her Worth,/And embalms her Memory with/A TEAR./"]

MY DEAR BROTHER   Philadelphia 18th Augt 1777

I have several times mentioned to you my son in law being taken & in my last that there was a master of a vesel gone to Exchange for Him. He is since got Home, & has the Prospect of a nother vesel for France, & desiers a Leter to you I am willing to gratifie him tho I wrot but last week & have nothing more new to write which I was in hopes I shuld by this time, however we are all well & you will no doubt hear from us in a more Direct way when any change happens. when I wrot last I had not heard of Dear Mrs Franklins Death but as Mr Bache had, I sopose he Informed you of it, I have heard no perticulars but sincearly Greve for her. She must have suffeered much in her mind how atentive so ever those about her might have been to do all that was nesesary for her, She has I think a very Just charecter given her in the Philadelphia Paper Said to be writen by Mr Hopkinson, among my other concerns she is seldom out of my mind. I loved her gratly, Temple will mourn for her much, we have never had a scrape of a pen from Him, nor have I recd more than won leter from you which was from

Nants. I do not sopose Mr Collas will see you if he gits saif there but he thinks the mention of his wifes being a Relation of yrs was the means of her giting her Petion ansured in sending a person to Exchange for Him, & prehaps He thinks the Apearance of yr name may befriend him on some other ocation. I can hardly say I hope but I wish for his suckses, I think there was hardly Ever so unfourtunate a Famely   I am not willing to think it is all oing to misconduct   I have had some children that seemed to be doing well till they were taken off by Death.

that the Blesing of God may atend you in Boath your Publick & private Affairs is the Prayer of yr Affectionat Sister

JANE MECOM

"A fine airy House upon a Hill"

[Printed first, and hitherto only, in Carl Van Doren, *Benjamin Franklin's Autobiographical Writings*, pp. 430-431, and here printed again from the manuscript in the American Philosophical Society. The Howes who in Paris were wrongly supposed to have gone to Boston were Admiral Richard, Earl Howe, and General Sir William Howe, the British commanders in North America who at the time Franklin wrote were completing the capture of Philadelphia. Peter Collas had not reached Passy when Franklin wrote, and could not have brought Jane Mecom's letter.]

DEAR SISTER,   Passy, near Paris, Oct. 5. 1777

I suppose some of your kind Letters to me have miscarried, as I have received but one since my Arrival in France. I hope nevertheless that you continue well, and that you are still with my Children, especially as it is supposed that the Howes are gone to Boston, where you must have been again disturb'd if you had return'd thither.

I enjoy here an exceeding good State of Health.—I live in a fine airy House upon a Hill, which has a large Garden with fine Walks in it, about ½ an hours Drive from the City of Paris. I walk a little every Day in the Garden, have a good Appetite & sleep well.—I think the French Cookery agrees with me better than the English;—I suppose because there is little or no Butter in their Sauces: for I have never once had the Heartburn since my being here tho' I eat heartily, which shows that my Digestion is good. I have got into a good Neighborhood, of very agreable People who appear very fond of me; at least they are pleasingly civil: so that upon the whole I live as comfortably as a Man can well do so far from his Home & his Family.

I was glad to learn by yours (which was dated December 16. 76. that your Son Calas was returned, and engaged in the Service of the Publick. I hear he was in France lately, I suppose he brought your Letter as you mention sending it by him; but he did not come in to Paris, and so I did not see him.—I wish him Success in his new Employment.

My Grandchildren here are a Comfort and Pleasure to me. I long to see little bold Will. Kiss him for me. In short I long to see & be with you all: But God only knows whether I shall ever be so happy again.

I am, as ever, my dear Sister,

Your affectionate

Brother

B FRANKLIN

Jane Collas to Benjamin Franklin

[Here first printed from the manuscript in the American Philosophical Society. The much-enduring Peter Collas, with whom this letter went to Franklin, sailed from Boston on January 14, 1778, on the *Triton*; but he put too much faith in his pilot, who told Collas that a British ship they sighted was an American privateer, was captured and taken for eight days to Guernsey, and then to Southampton, from which he wrote, on March 27, an account of his misfortunes in a letter to Jonathan Williams Jr., then at Nantes. The letter is in the American Philosophical Society. Exchanged with the help of Franklin, Collas went to France, and to Passy, where he conferred with John Adams on October 8. Adams, *Works*, III, 184. On January 9, 1779, Collas was still in France, at Nantes, but, as he wrote to Franklin that day, he had written to Jane Mecom to inquire about the making of crown soap.]

Boston
January 9th 1778

MY DEAR AND EVER HONORD UNCLE

Forgive me for dareing to incroch on one of you precious moments by obliging you to read a trifeling litter from me, but as a number of letters will by Gods permition be handed to you by the Same person who brings this I cant help letting you know that this person is my Husband, whom I tenderly love and in whome all my hopes of happiness in this life are Senterd, permit me to recommend him to your notice as prudent and industerous, and one whos Heart never knew Deceit, he has been unfortunat Extreemly so, not through any Misconduct all who knows him will own, and I can give no other reason but his being conected with one of the most unhappy familyes that I ever knew.

Will you Sir add one more obligation to the enumerable, by giveing him your advice and any assistance he may need in his beausiness if he should be so happy as to see you. I feel guilty while I am asking the favor, tho thousands perhaps who are all most strangers to you ar reaping those bennifits unasked from your benevolent disposition,

I have had the pleasure of seeing my dear Mamma since her return to Coventry, I hope if my dear Collas returns safe I shall be enable'd to keep house, and be bless'd in her company, at present I am obliged to leave all my friends and retier to country lodgings to save expences, a person must have a good income to be able to live in Town every thing is so very dear but I am lengthing out my Epissel and hindering you to no purpos I will again beg pardon for this intrusion and hasten to subcribe myself with the greatest respect your very affectionate and ever

duityfull Neice JANE COLLAS

Jane Mecom to Jane Collas

[Here first printed from a copy in N.E. Historic Genealogical Society. The note at the end is in the copyist's hand, and there in square brackets. Jane Collas had visited her mother at the Potowomut house of Jane

Mecom's granddaughter Jenny, Jane Flagg Greene, and had apparently hinted that Jenny and her husband, Elihu Greene, ought to take her brother Josiah and "put him in a way to get a genteel living," when in fact the Elihu Greenes were themselves in straitened circumstances. Jane Collas had been boarding in the country during her husband's absence. Jane Greene's first child, Celia, was born January 27, 1777, and died March 26 of that same year. This letter was written from Coventry, Rhode Island, where Elihu Greene and his brothers had a forge. The William referred to in the second paragraph was Elihu Greene's bachelor brother who also lived in the Greene house at Coventry.]

Coventry, April 1778

MY DEAR CHILD,

That I always did love you I think I have all along in life given manufest proof, tho' my circumstances did not admit shewing it in the manner you wished, and that I do still love you my own heart as well as my late conduct is a sufficient witness to myself, for I can't think that a sincere affection will suffer great mistakes to pass without endeavouring a reformation. If my reproof has effected that, the end is answered and I shall with as much satisfaction spend the remainder of my days with you as you would to have me. I am far from desiring you to perform all you profess to be willing to do, but some alteration in the disposition I observed in you when here, there must be, or I should not be happy. I see your fondness for a great deal of company is not at all abated, and that is exceeding disagreeable to me. Your aspiring so much to gentility, without means to support it, must appear as ridiculous in every prudent person's eye as it does in mine, tho' it does not concern them to let you know it, and your lying abed in a morning was always a trouble to me on many accounts, your health one of the principal. You wrote me from Wells you had tried the experiment of rising early and found your health much improved, but I found by your own relation of Mrs. Gray's maid's coming in and making your breakfast before you were up, you have relapsed into the same practice. It has often so fretted me to wait for you to come to breakfast that I could not get over it in some hours. Those are some of the reasons why I appeared indifferent about going to live with you, from which little vexatious incidents would so often accrue that it would keep my mind perpetually uneasy. My natural temper is none of the patientest, and tho' by age and experience I am brought in some measure to check the appearance of resentment, I don't know but I am as much inwardly galled as ever, therefore think it prudent to avoid such occasions as much as may be. But, after all, whenever I hear you are settled in any place that you can entertain me, you may depend on my coming to make a trial, still retaining the resolution which I suppose gave you offence, not because it gave you offence, that I must spend the remainder of my life where I can enjoy most ease and happiness. I have gone through trouble sufficient for the time. It is natural to wish for ease and quiet at my years.

You must have been very inadvertent to what fell from your pen in a part of three of your letters not to perceive strong reflections on me as well as on Jenny in them, but as you desire, [I] will pass them over and do forgive them and everything else that has appeared disagreeable to me, but still wish that you would try to correct that inadvertence. You mistook me about the word Genteel; what you wrote on that head was that Jenny ought to take her brother and put him in a way to get a genteel living. Now I thought it would be a hard injunction on him, her husband, who was obliged to do the meanest drudgery himself, by reason help is not to be had, and their frequent losses will put it still further out of his power, (not to say hers, for I don't think a woman has a right to do so great a thing). They have this morning received intelligence of two more of their vessels' being taken; one of them had been to port and would have made a fine voyage, had she come safe. William says this is nine vessels taken this war in which they had property, and that it will make them little folks. That was his expression.

As to her, poor woman, she deserves more your pity than your resentment. It is true her reception of you at Warwick appeared reproachable, and I did not fail to speak my mind, but when we consider the distress she was in about her husband, that she came into the room with her eyes full of tears and her heart ready to burst, you ought not to have insisted on it every time you wrote. Her fears and distress at that time, we have reason to think, has been one means of the death of her child, who from its birth started at every the least noise till it was taken with confulsion fits which ended its days at two months old. It was, however, a thriving and forward child a part of the time (till the fits seized it) and gave us hopes of much pleasure. Herself has not had many well days since you left her. She had first a violent cough and cold which has gone through the family, and then an ague in her head very severe, which lasted a long time, and since she has been brought to bed she has been initiated into all the exercises of a lying-in, no one incident excepted that I can think on, that kept her so weak she has been but a few days down stairs and never out before yesterday, when her husband took her on a horse a little way in the middle of the day.

I thank you for the care you have taken about my goods. I suppose you informed of what was left and you recovered if I put them into the list; I forget whether I did or no. I wish not to make a charge of what we have in possession

* * * *

[The remainder of this letter is lost]

"A report of yr Death"

[Printed first, and hitherto only, in *Pennsylvania Magazine of History and Biography*, LXXII (1948), 267-270, and here printed again from the manuscript in the Historical Society of Pennsylvania. Jane Mecom had returned from her stay with the Baches at or near Philadelphia and was living with her granddaughter Jane Greene and her husband in Warwick, Rhode Island, not far from the house of Catharine Greene. During 1777 the report of Franklin's assassination in Paris had reached London, or had at least been announced there, and disturbed his relatives and friends in the United States. His missing letters to which his sister referred in this letter had reassured her. This letter of hers to him was forwarded by Tuthill Hubbart, who on May 14 wrote to tell Franklin of the comfort his American friends took from the news that he was not, as reported, in a languishing condition after the attempt on his life. Hubbart's letter is in the American Philosophical Society. The British

evacuated Philadelphia at the end of May 1778, and in July Richard
Bache, though not yet his wife and children, returned to the Franklin
house in Philadelphia in which Captain (later Major) John André had
been billeted during the occupation. Bache's account of the condition in
which the house had been left is in Duane, *Letters to Benjamin Franklin*,
pp. 77-80. William Greene, who for two years had been first associate
justice of the superior court of Rhode Island, was elected governor in
May 1778, as Jane Mecom expected. Major Samuel Ward (1756-
1832) had been married to Phebe Greene on March 8, 1778. The
house from which Jane Mecom wrote this letter was actually at Potowomut, but as it was in the township of Warwick she gave that as an
address.]

MY EVER DEAR BROTHER   warwick May 5th 1778

I can not Expres to you the Joy your two Leters of Dcr 22
& febr 28 which boath came to hand at won time has given me,
& the News that Accompanied them to Every friend of America, a report of yr Death, & the seeming Delays of France had
made many a Hart to tremble, but thank God I hope now we
may be restored to Peace on our own Ecqutable terms of Established Independance, I rejoyce to hear Temple & Benny are
well & give you so much pleasure   Remember my love to them,
I have been very unfourtunet in haveing my leters miscarry tho
I am shure you did not suspect I had neglected to write yet as I
from time to time gave you Information of Every thing I
thought you would Expect from me & was desierous of Informing you, I am sorry they were lost & more so for the lose of
those you wrote me, but if I could flatter my self I should Ever
see you again all would be made up. yr poor Children have
been drove about as well as myself   the Last Leter I recved
from them was Dated Janr 19 at Manheim where they had
been about a fourtnit all well & not out of hopes of Returning
to Philadelphia again God send it soon but I cant help regreting
the severe lose I fear you have mett with in many of yr Instruments & valeuables which I sopose they could not Remove as
mr Bache tells me thay made much such a nother remove as we
did to Goshon   it may not be in your power to repare yr lose
which will be a grat draw back on yr Amusements if you should
be premited to take any repose as we boath wish.

[177]

you understood by mrs Greene I was with my Daugther more Properly my Daughter with me at that time, on her Husbands Arival in boston in 76 they went to house keeping & he was put in to a contenental ship to go to France but was taken in His pasage & carried in to New york & keept a priesner many months (the leter I wrot to go by him being two late went by some other hand) He was at last Exchanged Returned to Boston & went second on bord a privetere mett with hard storms in which if I remember right they were obliged to thro over some of there Guns & after meeting the Enemie of far grater force who Chasd them till all on board it is said but Him self went below to shift there Cloaths Expecting to be taken He keept the Helm six hours & got clear of them but they were so weakned they were obliged to return in to port without taking any thing, He then had an offer of an other Contenental Ship for France which he accepted, & houskeeping being so Expensive in Boston they gave up there house & on his sailing She came hear to see me staid with me about 3 weeks & Returned to board in the Country where her husband had made provision for her. I have hitherto been with my Gran-Son-in-Law (Exept a visit to our frind Greene) who sent a Pheaaton for me to Philadelphia by Majr Ward but as he had married my Grandaughter very poor & you have Generously bestowed on me where withall to provide for my self I did not let Him be at any other Expence the Majr went all the way from Pekes Kill on porpose a lone but took his servant as we came back home with us & I payd a third of the whol Expence which with a few trifels I brought to use on the Rhoad cost me about seventy Dolars the rest of the monny I had I have put to Intrest which is about four hundred Dolars & is what I have to depend on I am at no Expence at present Injoying Helth peace & competnce in my Gransons Famely who is a very Good sort of man of plain Sense & sound Judgment whose conversation is a greable when he talks but that is but litle my child makes Him a frugal Industrious & discreet wife & they are very happy She has had a fine child but has lost it I am determined to make what I have ansure my Prupose by waring my old Cloaths over agane & purchasing nothing but what is absolutly nesasery such as shoes which won cant do without but are now at such a Price in this Place that I have purchased seven Pare in Boston when I lived there for what won pare costs hear of the same sort.

these are my circumstances at present but if my Daughters husband shuld still meet with bad suckses I beleve I must try to go in to some busnes with her   She is a wery Inferm woman was sick all the first winter after you left us   She is very desirous of haveing me with her. won of my frormer leters consisted chefly in the Requests of our good friend Mrs Duffeild concerning her Son   I have never heard what became of him. in a nother I Informed you how very kind & obliging Majr Ward was to me on my Jurny   He is since married to our good friend Greene's Daughter Pheby, a good tempered sensable young Lady but there happienes is Inturupted by his being obliged to leve her and return to camp   Mrs Greene remembers her love to you thanks you for yr leter designs to write but as I have an opertunity to send this to Boston now I do not wait for hers the Judg is gone to provedence to Election   I am in Expectation he will come back Governer but she charges me not to tell you so as it is very disagreable to her. I am as Ever Dear Brother

your affectionat Sister

JANE MECOM

Jane Mecom to Jane Collas

[The original manuscript of this letter was sold from the library of Roderick Terry at the sale of the American Art Association on November 7-8, 1934, but has not been available for use in this collection. The letter is here first printed from a corrected copy in N.E. Historic Genealogical Society. Jane Mecom wrote it from the house of Catharine Greene. Elihu Greene and his brothers had a grist mill and forge at Potowomut ("Potawam" in Jane Mecom's spelling) and another forge at Coventry, both in Rhode Island. The Elihu Greenes lived sometimes at one and sometimes at the other. The "Governor's lady and the Ambassador's sister" who had made shirts for soldiers were Catharine Greene and Jane Mecom. Sarah Bache and Jane Flagg Greene had been

[179]

willing "to exchange works with the country people," as Jane Collas might do. Captain "Collings" and Mrs. Sayre have not been identified.]

MY DEAR CHILD   Warwick, May 16, 1778

Since I wrote you last I have received a long letter from you. You desire to know if I wrote two letters to go to my Brother by Mr. Collas. The one that my Brother received could not be that which he carried, as the date of his, my Brother's, was before your Husband sailed this time. I remember there was an opportunity to send directly from there, I sent it and wrote another and I hope he has that also and that you have had some certain news before now

You say you will endeavour to correct all your faults. It is not among the least that you suffer yourself to look always on the dark side of God's Providence towards you. Recollect the extent of that expression, You have a long time experienced every distress this miserable world could inflict on you, and you will find yourself mistaken; but were it so, the world has it not in his power to affect us so much as we may receive by God's immediate hand. I never informed you of half I met with, but you know enough to see a vast disproportion between what I have had to undergo and what you have met with. If the loss of near and dear relations is an affliction, I have buried the best of parents, all my sisters and brethren except one, how many of my children and in what circumstances you know, and some small remembrance of my difficulties before your father's death and after, you must have, which, if I had done as you do, might have sunk me into despair, but I always have tried to recollect the mercies afforded me and the blessings I still enjoy and endeavour to be thankful, which is a method you must take, if you mean to make the best improvement of your sufferings, for it cannot be acceptable to the Divine Being to have us always repining and take no notice of his mercies when we receive so many more than we deserve. Let us submit to His will and be cheerful. This you may assure yourself, if it is any comfort to you, that in all your afflictions I am afflicted, and, were it in my

power, would alleviate them all, and had I a sufficient income
to support us together, you should not be liable to the imposi-
tions of such complaisant folks as make extravagant demands
while they pretend to oblige you (but I hope it will not be long
before your husband comes home and then all will be well
again.) I have never yet seen it possible for us to live together,
unless we could be willing to spend all we had in a year and
have nothing to depend on, as we could not have stock sufficient
to go into any business that would support us these times, and
what little I have would soon run out were I to pay for my
board, therefore we must look on all as an overruling Providence, which may turn out for the best at last. We shall see how
little is to be expected from fair appearances and be better enabled to act with caution and prudence. I am apt to think you
might have been as happy in some plain country farmer's house
and at much less expense than where you are, and then it might
not have been thought improper for you to have done some
work, both for profit and amusement, and if you had been near
enough to have seen it, had the example of the Governor's
lady and the Ambassador's sister making ruffled shirts and
stockings for the soldiers, who were in great want and could
not get hands enough to supply them. All the families in this
place assisted and were paid for it, as they knew not who they
should give it to if they did not. Another thing, I believe, I
recommended to you once before, which was to exchange works
with the country people; you might get yourself spinning and
weaving done and at the same time keep yourself constantly
employed, which would contribute greatly to a composed mind;
I find I cannot live without it. Mrs. Bache got a great deal
done so, and so has Jenny since I put her in the way of it, and
you can not only do plain work, but make bonnets, cloaks, caps
and any thing. You ought to see, it is only in your imagination
that I am more severe to your mistakes than to others: You
know it was always my judgment and practice, if I thought I
had occasion to reprove any one to do it to themselves. Perhaps
I am too severe with every one, and I am told with myself too.

I am still at my good friend Greene's. She says she will write, but is not at home and may not have time, for she always lives just as you saw her when here. The Judge is chosen Governor, so you will know how to direct your letters for the future to be left here and not to Coventry, for Elihu is about moving to Potawam, but they are so long concluding I don't know if it will ever be. I am your sincerely affectionate mother

JANE MECOM

I was not displeased about the Massachusetts money, but thought it might buy him some trifle, and it does not pass here.

Mrs. Greene says she did send your Galoshes by Captain Collings to Mr. Gouch's. I am sorry for poor Mrs. Sayre. Send me word all about the family. I never writ a superscription myself to go to my brother, without expecting it to be enclosed if Mr. Williams sent one by your husband, and I must have sent it him when Mr. Collas was on the Privateering voyage, or should have sent it directly to you.

Mrs. Jane Collas
To the Care of Mr. William Gooch

"In constant Jeperdie since the spring"

[Printed first, and hitherto only, in Duane, *Letters to Benjamin Franklin*, pp. 81-84, without the passages on the insanity of Benjamin and Peter Mecom; here printed entire from the manuscript in the American Philosophical Society. The British held Newport from December 1776 to October 1779, and the whole of Rhode Island was in danger. John Hancock commanded the Massachusetts forces sent against the British in 1778, and Nathanael Greene and his brothers were engaged in the effort. Jane Mecom was then living with her granddaughter Jane Greene. The two brothers "Dean" were Silas and Simeon Deane. "Mr Williams" was Jonathan Williams Sr., here for some reason not called "Cousin Williams." Jane Mecom probably thought Peter Collas responsible for the loss of more letters to France than he was. Ray Greene was at Dummer Academy at Byfield, Massachusetts, of which the Reverend Samuel Moody was the first master. The "Mr Hubbard" mentioned in this letter has not been certainly identified. In this letter Jane Mecom said that her son Benjamin had strayed away "soon affter the batle at Trenton" (December 26, 1776); in her letter of February 14,

1779, she said he was "wandering about till the Hessians took possession of Burlington" (December 11 of that year). This is a discrepancy made more confusing by the fact that the Hessians did not actually take Burlington, but only entered it for a day and withdrew after being fired upon by American armed boats on the Delaware. This, however, seems the more likely time for Benjamin to have made his escape, if he was at Burlington when the town was in turmoil. Thirteen days after the date of this letter Jane Mecom had a conversation with Ezra Stiles which he recorded in his diary. *Literary Diary of Ezra Stiles* (1901), II, 375-376. He noted that she was then living at East Greenwich, which was the town nearest Potowomut.]

DEAR BROTHER   Warwick August 15 1778

I wrot you concerning the Enemie's being in posesion of Philadelphia I now congratulate you on there Evacuation of it, & that they have done so Litle Damage to the Real Estates in the city, as I hear from a Transient person for I have had no Leter from yr children yet to Inform me of particulars; no doute you have sofferd much in moveables but since they have got rid of them I hope never more to Return that will be the Easeier to be borne, what suckses we shall have hear in Expelling them from Rhoad Island is uncertain they have Fortified themselves strongly & it is said burnt & sunk all there shiping since the French Fleet came in which looks as if they Intended to fite as they have no way to Escape our Armie is gone on, what number I dont hear, but there is many volinters, my Grand-son & two of His Brothers are of that number, there Brother the Genl is also there. Mr Hancock Heads an Indepandant Company from Boston of which it is said there is not a man among them worth les than ten Thousand pounds Sterling; I hope they will have there desiered suckses for the sake of the whol comunitie & a litle for my own for I have lived in constant Jeperdie since the spring when my children removed from Coventry to this place where we are much Exposed & have been under constant Aprehensions, I have been Part of the time at the Governers but it was full as bad there for they offered a reward for Takeing him, you will acknolidg this is Rather wors than being harrised about by wons Friends, yet I doubt not but that is Troblesom to you who are so desierous of

Retierment, I fear you will never be soffered to Injoy it. I had a hint from Mr williams at the time we recvd yr Leters by Mr Dean that gave me hopes of yr Return but it is all blown over now, I was in hopes of a leter by the other Brother but sopose There was none or Mr Bache would have sent it Ere now, I do not wonder if you are discuridged from writing to me for I Fear you have never recved any of my leters but the won you mention that was to have gone by my son Collas & I think I have sent seven, I all-ways sent them threw the hands of Mr Beach, or Mr Williams, but two of them hapened to go by my son Collas & we sopose he is Taken again he has had nothing but misfourtun & the sicknes but it is very disagreable to me to write trobles & Dificulties & I have in other leters Informed you of His being a prisner at New york a long time has since been twice taken wonce drove back in port by storm to refit which was the means of his haveing two of my leters to you I had wrot many things about yr children & there children which I knew you would be glad to hear I cannot now so much as say they are well. I wrot you of our Friend Greene's being Governer, that Ray was at Mr Moodys scool & comes on bravely with His Larning, that ther Eldest Daughter was married to Majr Ward.

what I had to write concerning [myself *crossed out; inserted*: I have Injoyed many blessings] my own Perticular Famely has been as was comon to me all my life mostly distressing   poor Benjamin strayed a way soon affter the batle at Trenton & has never been heard of since, I can hear nothing of His Famely tho I have wrot several times to Inquier, but what now distresses me much now is that the woman that keeps my son peter in the Country Demands five Dolars a week for takeing care of him to comence Sepr 1777 or she would send him to boston   I wrot to Mr Williams to git Him Put in to the Alms house there but he says there is no provision for such persons there I have sent a second Leter to Urge it but have had no Ansure, I write this with grat Reluctance but as you desiered me to Inform you of my circumstances as well as helth & situation it will not be confideing in you as Such a Friend as you have all ways been

to me & prehaps the only disintrested won I have in the world
to keep it back, I did some time ago writ you that my expences
from Philadelphia had cost me seventy dolars that the Price
of won pare of shoes hear was as much as I could by Seven pr
for of the same sort when I was in boston but I then wrot a
mistake for they askd me Six dolars for a pr such as I used to bye
for half a dolar a pr by the doz in Boston but I bye as litle as
posable I also wrot you that what mony I had a mounting to
four hundrid Dolars I had put to Intrest only reserving for
nesesary Use that I Live comfortable with my Grand children
& have my Helth but no Income but what that litle mony Produces which however I should do very well with were it not for
this dredfull affair of Peter which you see will take the most I
have if I am forced to pay it & if Mr williams cant git Him in
to the Alms House God only knows what I shall do with him
in future I think you cant disaprove of my Endevouring it I
was in hopes to have bee able to Informed you it was done but
haveing opertunity to send this to Mr Williams by Mr Hubard
I would not Neglect it.

I Intended to have said a grat deal to you about many other
things but my spirets feel so deprest & I have such horrid pens
& paper I shall only add my love to yr grand sons from yr
affectionat sister

JANE MECOM

If we have the good fortune to Drive the
Enemie from Newport I hope to be able to
be won of yr first Informers & write in
a nother maner
Prehaps Mr williams may prevail with the
overseers to take in poor Peter paying
the Rent of the House you used to alow me
which I know you will have no objection
to I had forgot to mention that to Him
but shall now   J M

"Much troble & many mercys"

[Here first printed in full from the manuscript in the American Philosophical Society. Wanton Casey, who carried this letter, was the son of William Greene's neighbor, Silas Casey, mentioned though not named in Jane Mecom's letter of June 23, 1779. The notation "Answd April 22" is in Franklin's hand.]

Answd April 22

MY DEAR BROTHER   Warwick 4 Jany 1779

I wrot you about a month past but haveing an opertunity by a young Gentilman of this Nabour hood who is going directly to France & desiers to be Introduced so far to yr Notice if he goes to Paris, as to Advice him to a good scool where he may Larn the Language & perfect himself in merchants acoumpts, I would not miss it hopeing some of the many leters I write may reach yr hand I believe I have hither to been very unsuccesfull boath ways as I cant perswade my self but you have writen divers to me since Mr Simeion Dean came which was the last I recved, & I have heard of several of mine to you has fell in to the hands of the Enemie when shall we be at peace that we may at least have the comfort of Each others leters which to me is grat. I do not pretend to say any thing about publick Affairs & as to my self I have mett with much troble & many mercys, I Injoy much helth & the Same Friendly Entertainment from the Governer & wife while I am hear, & the same at my Grand childs which are blesings, there famelies are boath well & our friend Caty desiers to be remembred to you, her Husband is not at home. I write among so much noise & confusion that if I had any thing of consequence I could not Recolect it & will not atemt any more but that

I am as Ever yr affectionat sister

JANE MECOM

My love to Temple & Benny
I expect Mr Wanton Casey
who is to be the barer of this
to send for it as he is to sett
of for Boston in the morning
therefore have no other time to write

Jane Mecom to Sarah Bache

[Here first printed from a corrected copy, in another hand, in the Yale University Library. The copyist wrote "Wood" in mistake for Ward; Jane Mecom had traveled from Philadelphia to Rhode Island in the company of Major Samuel Ward. She could not help thinking that if her granddaughter Jane Flagg Greene had had so good a nurse as Sarah Bache's, Mrs. Ashmead, the "poor child" might not have had so long an illness. The greetings to "brave Will" and "dear little Sally" were to Sarah Bache's children. They had not returned to Philadelphia from the country till the past October.]

DEAR MRS BACHE.   Warwick, January 17, 1779

I have so often written to you, and had no answers. I inquired of every one that I have seen from Philadelphia concerning you, and can hear nothing about you and the little ones. I begin to conclude you are not returned to the City. I have frequently heard of Mr. Bache being there, whose business might call him, but none could say they had seen his wife. I am so anxious to hear how you all are, and in what condition you found your house &c. after the enemy left it; also, what you hear from your father and son; that I cannot neglect this favorable opportunity by my friend and fellow traveller Major Wood [Ward], to beg you to write a long letter, and tell me all about every thing you know I wish to hear concerning your own family, and your acquaintances whom you know I loved when there; they are too numerous for me to particularize, in the haste I am obliged to write and the weather so very cold. I don't doubt but you may write under more favorable circumstances, a good fire, a warm room and nobody to interrupt you: a good fire I have, but it is not sufficient to keep my old hands warm when writing.

I have the pleasure of hearing of my brother's health and fine spirits; but I have no letter since Mr Simeon Deane came; and I don't know that he has ever received but one of a great many letters I wrote him. Remember me respectfully to all who inquire after me, not forgetting good Mrs. Ashmead. I wish I had her for my grand-daughter: if she could be happy, she should do just as she pleased. I have often thought of your description of nurses and other necessary bodies in the country, since I came here. My poor child kept her chamber eight weeks, she herself thinks owing to bad management: it will be well if we can prevent it now with all our resolution: My poor daughter has been, almost all the time since I came, in trouble: her husband is now in captivity the fourth time since the war began, and she a poor low-spirited creature when any thing befals her. Remember my love to brave Will, and give dear little Sally twenty kisses for

Your affectionate aunt

JANE MECOM

Mrs Bache

"Father, Husband, Brother, & children"

[Printed first, and hitherto only, in Duane, *Letters to Benjamin Franklin*, pp. 94-96, with the passages about Benjamin and Peter Mecom omitted for the most part. Here printed entire from the manuscript in the American Philosophical Society. "Mr Williams" was Jonathan Williams Sr. and "Cousen Jonathan Williams" was his son.]

Warwick feb 14 1779

MY DEAR DEAR BROTHER
My Self & children have all ways been a heavey tax upon you, but your grat and uncoman goodness has carried you cheerfully on under it, & we have all along Injoyed many of the comforts of life throw your Bounty we must otherwise have done without, it has pleasd God to diminish us fast & thereby your Expence & care of us you I doubt not Remember you had Ingaged for the soport of poor Benjamin in His deplorable state, He never could be kept in the place you Expected, but was wandering about till the Hessians took possession of Burlington, when he disappeared & has never been heard of since, this I informed you of soon after, but yr never mentioning it to me in Ither of the few leters I recved from you, I think it did not Reach you, it has now pleasd God to take poor Peter

& by that has Releved me from great distress for tho I still Retained for him the Affection of a Parent, the grat Dificulties of the times, & the Extreem Demands of the woman where he boarded contineualy Incresing, & my Inability to satisfie them, & not being able to procure him any other Place of Residence by any means, keept me in Perpetual anxiety, & you know he has been no comfort to any won nor capable of Injoying any Himself for many years, His mouth was opened Just before His Death to comit himself to the mercy of God & wish a blesing on those about him & sunk in to Eternity without a Groan. Mr Williams has kindly & faithfully taken the care of Every thing concerning him in my absence I now thank you & him, what could I have done without Ither of you, you have suplied the means, he has taken the care. may God Reward you & make you happy in your own posterity. I wrot you about six weeks ago by a Neibour of Governer Greens Mr Wanton Casey, I hope you will recve some of the many I write & that I shall not all ways be deprived of the pleasure of yours to me which has been so long obstructed, the last I recd was by Mr Simeon Dean. Cousen Jonathan Williams was so good as to write me you were well & in good spirits which I had the good fortune to recve tho unfortunate in loosing a present of Tea he had sent me which was much agrevated by my poor Retched son in-law being the barer, who was taken the forth time since the comencement of the War. I fear his poor lonely wife has given her self up to Dispare as she is apt to sink under troble & I can no other-ways acount for her long silence to me   She used to write often & I have not had a line from her since the 27th Septr may God preserve her from the faite of her Brothers. Pardon my writing you these aprehentions I do not take pleasure in giveing you an uneasy thought but it gives some Releif to unbousom wons self to a dear friend as you have been & are to me, Father, Husband, Brother, & children may I not live to be deprived of all in you but you live to see the happines of yr childrens children confermed & a hapy peace in America Prays yr affectionate sister

JANE MECOM

febr 27

Since I wrot the above I have recd a leter from my son collas from Nants says he has seen you that you are well I have also recd won from his wife who has been sick but now prety well has recved some things her husband sent her

J M

"Too much Business upon my Hands"

[First printed in Carl Van Doren, *Benjamin Franklin's Autobiographical Writings*, pp. 467-468, and now printed again from the manuscript in the American Philosophical Society.]

Passy April 22. 1779.

DEAR SISTER,

I received your kind Letter of Jan. 4 which gave me the Satisfaction of knowing that you were well, and comfortably situated among your Friends. You mention other Letters you have written, but they are not come to hand. Don't however be discouraged from writing as often as you can; for I am uneasy when long without hearing from you; and the Chance is greater that one Letter out of many should arrive, than one out of a few. I have written to Mr Williams to assist you from time to time, as you may have occasion: and I confide in his readiness to do every thing necessary for you, as I know he Esteems you, and I have always reimbursed him. If you do not hear from me so often as formerly, impute it to the too much Business upon my Hands and the Miscarriage of Letters, or any thing rather than a diminution of Affection. I have seen nothing of Mr Casey, whom you mention as the Bearer of your Letter. I suppose he did not come to Paris.

As to myself, I continue to enjoy, Thanks to God, a greater Share of Health and Strength than falls to the Lot of many at my Age. I have indeed sometimes moderate Fits of the Gout; but I think it is not settled among the Physicians whether that is a Disease or a Remedy. I live about two Miles out of the City, in a great Garden, that has pleasant Walks in which I can take Exercise in a good Air, the Situation being high and dry. The Village has many good Houses & good Families, with whom I live in Friendship, and pass a Leisure Hour, when I have one, with pleasure. The French in general are an amiable People, and I have the good Fortune to enjoy as much of the Esteem and Affection of all Ranks, as I have any Pretensions to. Temple continues with me; but I have last week sent Benny to Geneva, where there are as good Schools as here, & where he will be educated a Republican and a Protestant, which could not be so conveniently done at the Schools in France. My Love to all that love you, and believe me ever, my Dear Sister,

Your affectionate Brother

B FRANKLIN

"Since you have rubd off the Mechanic Rust"

[Printed first, and hitherto only, in Duane, *Letters to Benjamin Franklin*, pp. 96-98. Here printed from the manuscript in the American Philosophical Society. Elkanah Watson, who carried this letter, wrote in some detail in his *Men and Times of the American Revolution* (1856) about his relations with Franklin in France. "Corl" is Jane Mecom's spelling of "Colonel." The *New Hampshire Gazette* for December 22, 1778, and other American newspapers of other dates at about the same time, had repeated a (without doubt) fictitious anecdote published in the *London Chronicle* for July 4 to 7, 1778. The *Gazette* text ran: "A gentleman just returned from Paris informs us that Dr. Franklin has shaken off entirely the mechanical rust, and commenced the complete courtier. Being lately in the gardens of Versailles, showing the Queen some electrical experiment, she asked him, in a fit of raillery, if he did not dread the fate of Prometheus, who was so severely served for stealing fire from Heaven? 'Yes, please your Majesty,' (replied old Franklin with infinite gallantry,) 'if I did not behold a pair of eyes this moment which have stolen infinitely more fire from Jove than ever I did, pass unpunished, though they do more mischief in a week than I have done in all my experiments.' " The article on Watson in the *Dictionary of American Biography* mistakenly says that he was apprenticed to John Brown (1744-1780). In fact it was to John Brown (1736-1803), who laid the cornerstone of the first building of Brown University in 1770. The "Exhibition made on the Aneversary of the French Trety" took place at the winter quarters of Washington's artillery, Pluckemin, New Jersey, on February 18, 1779. Each of the triumphal arches behind which the fireworks were set off displayed an "illuminated painting" (on transparent cloth). The 8th arch had a picture of "The American philosopher and ambassador extracting lightning from the clouds." An account of this was widely published, and Jane Mecom may have read it in almost any newspaper she saw. There are accounts of the exhibition in Benson J. Lossing, *The Pictorial Field-Book of the Revolution*, I, 334-335n., and in Frank Moore, *Diary of the American Revolution*, II, 130-134.]

DEAR BROTHER   Warwick   June 23d 1779

as I would not omit writing you by an opertunity which I Expect espeshal care will be taken to Deliver, I have complied with a Request made me by Mr Casey whose son I wrot by last fall, in favour of a Mr Elkanah Wattson, Corl Wattson's Son of Plimoth   I have given him to understand I will Inform you what he says of the young Gentileman (which is that he served an AprentisShip with Mr John Brown of provedence who gives him a very good charrecter & that His Father is a man of a plentifull Estate) & I tell him if he has merritt He may be able to Recomend Himself.

I have wrot you many Leters (some of which I hope you have recd) Informing you of Every thing concerning me worthy yr atention, I have not yet recd a line from you since that by Mr Simeon Dean, but bless God I now & then hear of yr helth & Glorious Achievments in the political way, as well as in the favour of the Ladys ("Since you have rubd off the Mechanic Rust and commenced compleat courtier") who Jonathan Williams writes me clame from you the Tribute of an Embrace & it seemes you do not complane of the Tax as a very grat penance.

We have Just heard that the Fleet of Transports from France are arived at Baltimore where I hope my Poor unfourtunate son in law Collas is so far saif among them, & as I heard Jonathan Williams was coming with them hope for leters from you by Him, we have grat News of the Defeat of the Britons at Carolina; which we hop is trew but have had no printed acount of it yet.

God grant this may put a final Stop to there Ravages, my Grandson whome I am with lives where we have frequent alarmes they have come & taken of the stock about 3 quarters of a mile distant & burnt houses a few miles from us, but hitherto we are preserved.

[192]

I have as much helth as can be Expected in comon for won
of my years & live in a very Pleasant place tho not Grand as I
sopose yrs is it gives me grat delight the Famely is kind &
courtious; my Grandson is a man of sound sense, & solid Judgment, & I take much Pleasure in his conversation tho he talks
but litl, they have won child which they call Sally. Govr Greene
& famely are well I had wrot you there Eldest Daughter was
married to Govr Wards son they have now a fine son. Ray is
still at Mr Moody's Scool a promising youth.

I see few persons hear of yr acquaintance which deprives me
of much pleasure I used to have in conversing about you but I
now & then see something in the paper which pleases me in
perticular there Placeing you a lone in won of the Arches at the
Exhibition made on the Aneversary of the French Trety.
Mr Casey calls for the Leter & that puts all Els I designed to
write out of my mind only to beg to hear perticularly about
Temple & Ben & that I am Ever

your affectionat Sister

JANE MECOM

the Inclosed coppy comes
to my hand which I send
least you should not have
recved the other

"I feel the want of suitable conversation"

[Printed first, and hitherto only, in Duane, *Letters to Benjamin Franklin,* pp. 99-101, and here printed from the manuscript in the American
Philosophical Society. Although Franklin's letter of November 26, 1778,
is missing, it is evident that he had arranged for the payment of money
to his sister, probably through Jonathan Williams, had proposed that the
Collases undertake to make crown soap like that of the earlier Franklins,
and had expressed the hope that someday he and his sister might live
together.]

Warwick 27 — July 1779

DEAR BROTHER

I have after a long year recved yr kind leter of Nov 26—
1778 wherin you like yr self do all for me that the most Affec-

tionat Brother can be desiered or Expected to do, & tho I feel my self full of gratitude for yr Generousity, the conclution of yr leter Affectes me more; where you say you wish we may spend our last days together o my Dear Brother if this could be Accomplished it would give me more Joy than any thing on this side Heaven could posally do; I feel the want of suitable conversation I have but litle hear, I think I could Asume more freedom with you now & convence you of my affection for you I have had time to Reflect & see my Error in that Respect, I Suffered my defidence & the Awe of yr Superiority to prevent the femiliarity I might have taken with you & ought, & yr kindnes to me might have convenced me would be acceptable; but it is hard over comeing a natural propensity, & Difedence is mine.

I was in a few months after I wrote you the leter to which yrs is the ansure Relived of my Distres as I have since Informed you, that if any of my leters to you must be lost I wishd it might be that as I knew it must give you pain, but as you have recd that I am not out of hope the rest or at least some of them have since come to yr hand tho those I have wrote by perticular persons who have desiered to be Introduced to yr Notice I have wrot in a hurry & comonly Just after a long won containing all the perticulars I wishd to Inform you of, that it is likely the most Insignificant have reached you & the others are lost.

I recd a Leter from Mr Beach Latly he says they have had no leter from you or there son above a year the last from Temple & that was dated in November his was June 22 they were all well then Jonathan Williams Expected but not Arived.

It is a very hapy circumstance that you Injoy yr helth so perfectly it is a Blesing vouchsaifed to me also Exept some trifeling Interuption & that but sildom which I a good deal atribute to my observation of yr former Admonitions respecting fresh Air & diet for whatever you may think, Every hint of yrs apeared of two much consequence to me to be neglected or forgoten. as I all ways knew Everything you said had a meaning.

the few friends I have hear flock about me when I recve a

leter & are much disapointed that they contain no Politicks, I tell them you Dare not trust a woman Politicks, & prehaps that is the truth but if there is any thing we could not posable misconstru or do mischief by knowing from you, it will Gratifie us mightly if you add a litle to yr future kind leters.

Mr Collas met a man in the street & sent my leter I have had no line from or His wife so do not know his Inclineation concerning the crown soap but shall as soon as posable make some to send to you but fear whether that can be till the new wax comes in for I have tryd Shops & aquaintance hear & can not procure any, the country people put it in to there sumer candles, I have desiered cousen Williams to try to pick up a litle in the Shops there, & shall try at provedence, I am sorry to be deprived of the pleasure of gratifieing you, but my power was allways small tho my will is good. yr Friends Greene are well & He gives Satisfaction in His Office, they have boath writen to you since the date of yrs to me. they are happy to hear of your helth & suckses, my Grandson & Daughter send there Duty to you—they are a happy cople have won child calld Sally, he is a sensable & very Industrous man & she a very good wife, boath treet me very kindly, & I beleve I am as happy as it is common for a human being, what is otherways may proceed from my own Impatience

that God may Grant what you hope for in the conclution of yr leter is the prayer

of yr affectionat Sister

JANE MECOM

"No won Els can make the trew soap"

[Printed first, and hitherto only, in Duane, *Letters to Benjamin Franklin*, pp. 102-104; here printed from the manuscript in the American Philosophical Society. A corner of the manuscript is now torn off, and the words in square brackets are supplied from Duane, who may have had the letter entire in 1859 or may have only conjectured the missing words. "Sall Hatch Corl Hatch's Sister who went of with the Britons" was Sarah Hatch, sister of Colonel Estes Hatch of Dorchester. He was dead and could not support her, and she had apparently left Boston for Halifax with the loyalist refugees of 1776. Franklin's letter of November 26, 1778, had been brought to Jane Mecom in Rhode Island by Peter Collas himself on his return from France where he had seen Franklin the preceding October. A letter to Franklin from Catharine Greene on September 19, 1779, said that the visit of Collas and his wife had given Jane Mecom "a good deal of Pleasure. He gave us an agreeable history of Doctr Franklin." Roelker, *Benjamin Franklin and Catharine Ray Greene*, p. 98.]

DEAR BROTHER   Warwick Sept 12—1779

I have now before me yrs of Nov 26 1778 Brought me by my unfortunate Son Collas & won of Apr 22 '79 the first I ansured some time ago but as you may not recve it I now Renew my thanks for it & the Benifits there bestowed & confermed in the other, Mr Williams writs me He is redy to comply with your Desier, but as Mr Collas does not see any other way to Settle on Shore it does not Apear to me it will in any measure do to soport a famely, it would be a grat help when we could convince people they have been decved by a miserable Imitation, & that no won Els can make the trew soap; but that would be a work of time & there will be no wax to be had till affter Frost comes. I did by laying out Every way procure a Small cake & make a litle but not of the very best Posable as you desiered owing to some unavoidable Impedements, but Sent it notwithstanding as it will Answer for your own Use, & Temples, but would wish you not to make any presents of it; as I had not convenancy to make but half the meterals I procured I hope the other will ansure your wish. & Shall make it & Send it by the first opertunity, I desiered Collas to mark it No 1—that you might know which it is if boath come to hand.

Your very affectionat & tender care of me all along in life Exites my warmest gratitude which I cannot Even think on without Tears, what manyfold blessings I injoy beyond many of my worthy Acquantance who have ben driven from there home, Lost there Intrest, & some have the Adion of Lost health, & won the Grevous torment of a Cancer & no kind Brother to Soport her* while I am kindly treeted by all about me & ample provition made for me when Ever I have ocation.

* Sall Hatch Corl Hatch's Sister who went of with the Britons.

you could not have recd Information of the Death of my son peter when you wrot the last I have recd as I had it not my self till 20 days after the date of myne which you then recved, I hope some others I wrot afterwards are come to yr hand, I can not but take grat pleasure in hearing you Injoy so much Helth & could wish you had no ocation for the Remedy of those fitts of the Gout you are some times Exercised with, I fear you feel Pane anouf when under them to consider it as a disease, or as we some times say wors—The Respect & Friendship of all Sensable people where Ever you go I am shure you can not fale of but it is a grat satisfaction to have a number of them so near you that you may take your own time to go to them. I have not the privilige of won Neibour near than two miles but we have many agreable people come to visit us & I am all ways contented at home, & pleasd to go abroad when sent for, otherways I can-not go for our people have no carrage & I hant courage to ride a hors.

you say Temple is Still with you & I hope the same Dutyfull & Affectionat child & agreable companyon remember my love to him, but poor Ben how will he soport the Lose of you boath, was he willing to go. I Lately had a Leter from Mrs Bache She maks no mention of it but I sopose they will chearfully Acquese in what you think for the best. our friends hear are well & desier to be Dutyfully Remembred to you, I heard the Gov-erners wife say she would write, when shall I have any founda-tion for the hope that we shall again meet & spend our last Days to gether, America knows yr consequence two well to premit yr Return if they can posable prevent it, & yr care for the Pub-lick good will not suffer you to Desert them till Peace is Estab-lished, & the Dismal Sound of fiveteen year from the comenc-ment of the war Dwells on my mind which I wonce heard you say it might Last, if it does it is not Likely I shall Last that long, but that you may contineu in Health & Usefullnes is the constant Prayer of yr Affectionat Sister

JANE MECOM

[I] have no Instruments
[to stamp] the Soap but hope
that will not depretiate is valeu

"After so long and stormy a Day"

[Parts of this letter were published in Sparks, *Familiar Letters*, pp. 171-172, as "To a Relation in America." It was first printed in its entirety in Carl Van Doren, *Benjamin Franklin's Autobiographical Writings*, pp. 471-473, and is here again printed from the manuscript, apparently in Temple Franklin's hand, in the American Philosophical Society.]

DEAR SISTER,   Passy Oct. 25. 1779.

I received your kind Letter of Feb. 14. the Contents of which gave me a kind of melancholy Satisfaction. The greater Ease you will now enjoy makes some Compensation in my Mind for the uncomfortable Circumstance that brought it about. I hope you will have no more Afflictions of that kind, and that after so long and stormy a Day your Evening may be serene & pleasant.

Yours of June 23d by Mr Watson is also come safe to hand. The Description you give of your present Situation is pleasing. I rejoice to hear you have so much Comfort in your Grandaughter and her good Husband. Give my Love to them.

The Account you had from Jona Williams of the Vogue I am in here, has some Truth in it. Perhaps few Strangers in France have had the good Fortune to be so universally Popular: But the Story you allude to, which was in the News Papers, mentioning "mechanic Rust." &ca is totally without Foundation. The English Papers frequently take those Liberties with me. I remember to have once counted seven Paragraphs relating to me that came by one Post, all of which were Lies except one that only mentioned my living in the same House with Mr Deane.— This Popularity has occasioned so many Paintings, Bustós, Medals & Prints to be made of me, and distributed throughout the Kingdom, that my Face is now almost as well known as that of the Moon. But one is not to expect being always in Fashion. I hope however to preserve, while I stay, the Regard you mention of the French Ladies, for their Society and Conversation when I have time to enjoy it, is extreamly agreable.

The Enemy have been very near you indeed. When only at

the Distance of a Mile you must have been much alarm'd. We have given them a little Taste of this Disturbance upon their own Coasts this Summer: And tho' we have burnt none of their Towns, we have occasioned a good deal of Terror & Bustle in many of them, as they imagined our Commodore Jones had 4000. Troops with him for Descent. He has however taken and destroyed upwards of twenty Sail of their Merchantmen or Colliers, with two Men of War, and is arrived safe in Holland with 400. Prisoners. Had not contrary Winds and Accidents prevented it, the intended Invasion of England with the combined Fleet and a great Army might have taken Place, and have made the English feel a little more of that kind of Distress they have so wantonly caused in America.

I come now to your last of July 27. I am glad to learn by it that my dear Sister continued in good Health and good Spirits; and that she had learnt not to be afraid of her Friend Fresh Air.

You will do me a great deal of Pleasure in sending me as you propose, some Crown Soap, the very best that can be made. I shall have an Opportunity of obliging some Friends with it, who very much admire the little Specimens I have been able to give them. With the tenderest Affection I am ever, my Dear Sister,

Your very loving Brother.

B FRANKLIN

My Love to Mr & Mrs Greene & to my young Friend Ray. Temple desires me to present you his Affectionate Respects.

"You can never want friends"

[Here first printed from the manuscript in the American Philosophical Society. The likeness of Franklin to which his sister referred was the engraved portrait in the *Œuvres de M. Franklin* (Paris, 1773). Franklin, in a letter to his wife, September 1, 1773, called it "a Print of me, which, tho' a Copy of that by Chamberlin, has got so French a Countenance, that you would take me for one of that lively Nation." John Adams had taken the crown soap to Franklin.]

DEAR BROTHER   Warwick 27 March 1780

I have rcd yrs of Octr 25 & rejoyce you continue in helth & have so many Comforts about you the Agreable Situation of yr Dwelling, Beautifull Gardens, & yr choice of the best of company I often form to my self an Idea of; & wish you could Injoy them hear with the Same Benifit to yr Native country. you are happy in that you can never want friends go where you will, & as far as it is posable for any created being will Remain in Fashion but if the Artists that have taken yr Face have varied as much from each other as that affixed to yr Philosophacal Papers done in France some years ago from the coppy, it will apear as changeable as the moon, however if it is calld Dr Franklin it will be revered, in my last leter I wrote to beg a couple of those Prints, or Bustos, Ither which is thought most Like you & that can be Easest or saifest conveyd, I seldom meet with any thing in the Newspapers but what is to yr honour, that of the mechanice Rust served only to make me Laugh.

I understand your Commodore Jones has been ordred to Depart out of Holland with his Effects & Fleet I hope he got off saif. Since the Enemie have Evacuated Newport we have Injoyd peace & quietnes as to them, but the depreciation of our curency makes grat Difeculties & it seemes they cannot be Remedied while the war Lasts

I have sent in the French Friggett that Mr Adams went in a small box of Soap containing but 2 Doz I thought I could have made a litle more beter but I dont think I have suckceded   I have however sent another small box down to Mr williams which I intend this Leter to go with you will be a Judg which is best when you git them if Ither will be fitt to make presents of, I hope however to make another tryal when the wether groes warm the Second box contains 2 Doz & seven.

I think I am fortunate that you have rec'd so many of my Leters I hope the Soap is also got saif to you Shall be glad to know what you think on it when you have tried it I was obliged to manage it in some Perticulars different from Useal method for want of convenencies   Shall Rejoyce if it ansures the End you wishd to have it for. be it as it will let me know. Remember my Love to Temple & to Benny when you write to him

I am Ever yr very affectionate

and obliged Sister

JANE MECOM

Jane Mecom to Sarah Bache

[Here first printed from the manuscript in the Princeton University Library. The letter is undated, but it evidently was written after Jane Mecom received Sarah Bache's letter of August 18, and before she herself wrote to Franklin on December 29, 1780. Louis Bache had been born in October 1779. The ladies of Philadelphia had raised money for the soldiers of the Continental Army in the summer of 1780. Sarah Bache and four others had supervised the collection in the district between Market and Chestnut Streets. Sarah Bache had contributed 300 Continental dollars, then much depreciated, and another 100 in the name of "Miss Bache," that is, Elizabeth, aged three. The subscription lists are printed in W. B. Reed, *The Life and Correspondence of Joseph Reed* (1847), II, 428-449. The "Infamous Fellow" who had traduced Franklin was Ralph Izard, who returned with "Lea," Arthur Lee, in the summer of 1780 to continue in America their campaign of animosity against their former colleague in Paris. The great-grandchildren Jane spoke of were the daughter and son of her granddaughter Jane Greene, with whom she was then living in Rhode Island. "Daughter Mecom" was Benjamin Mecom's widow, then in Philadelphia, and "Jenny" was her daughter, Jane Mecom, a child being cared for in or near Boston. The somewhat involved passage at the end of the third paragraph means, put simply, that Governor William Greene had been obliged to accept depreciated paper money in payment for debts owed him, but had had to pay a Newport creditor in silver for a debt contracted in paper. There is an incomplete copy of this letter in the Yale University Library.]

DEAR NEICE   [October 1780]

Your favour of August 18th gave me much Pleasure to hear you & your Famely were well & that such a friendly Intercours is keept up betwen you & that very worthy Famely Mr Deffealds, & I should have been Proud to have seen the Gentielman you would have Introduced to me & have shewn Him all the civillities in my Power, but the Leters were brought to me by an accedental hand with His Name ras'd on the outside & no message or Intemation where He might be found; Prehaps He came no farther than Newport.

but tho I am Pleas'd with this it does not give the Satisfaction I wish such Near Relation as you and I should write more constant and circumstantially I want to know a Thousand litle Perticulars about your self yr Husband & the children such as your mother used to write me & tho I readily Excuse yr not writing more at this time I cannot so Easely Excuse yr long Silence who have it allways in yr Power to send sure without Expence or troble, it would be Next to Seeing the litle things to hear some of there Prattle (Speaches If you Pleas) & have you Describe there persons & actions tell me who they Look like &c—&c— I Sopose by this time Betsy gives you grat Entertainment & Louis as much as He can, He I say for the first Idea I had when I Saw the Name was that it was given in Respect to the French King, but I am Since tould that Louis is a proper Name for a woman so am at a lose to know wither yr Last is a Son or Daughter.

I have as you Sopose heard of yr Ladies Noble & generous Subscription for the Army and honour them for it & if a harty good will in me would Effect it we would follow your Example but I fear what my Infleuence would procure would be so Deminuitive we should be ashamed to offer it, I Live in an obscure place have but Litle Acquaintance & those not very Rich, but you may [say?] a mite has been Accepted & may be again but that was a time when there was more Relidgon & less Pride. I Realy beleve our Friend mrs Greene would be forward to Sett the Example hear as any the first of yr laidies was it in her Power but they have suffered Extreemly in there Fourtune by the Depreciation Several of there Farmes were Lett on Lease & had the paper mony Tendered to them & could not help them selves Grat Part of there Intrest Lay at Block Island where they could git nothing as the posesor has proved Dishonest & poor, & a Dept He had contracted in papper money the cridetor liveing on Newport where He could not git at Him to Discharge it & now since the Britons have left it Insists on Silver & the Govr has Paid it I forgit whither it was four thousand pounds or four thousand Dolars but Ither is a grat Sumn in Silver at this Day.

I am gratly Disopointed in not hearing from my Brother in this Fleet that is come I had a short Line Dated the 5th of march Informing me he was well & would writ more Largely by the Aliance which would Sail in a few Days but after all Sumer waiting the Aliance brings me no Leter & there has been (an Infamous Fellow I will call Him) hear Endevering to tra-duce yr fathers charecter in all companies, & we hear he did the Same in all the Taverns as he went along, I sopose you have had him there for he pretended to go full freight with Accuseations to Congress against Dr Franklin with very strong Vouchers, it was won Izard Brother in law to Lea who came in the Aliance, & it is not Imposable Bribed the men on board to Run off with the Ship without my brothers Dispatches Expecting they might not be to His Honour, it all apears misterious I wish you would clear it up to me. you may think when you have got thus far it is time to close but I must tell you that I have a grat-grand Daughter Eighteen months old that will Equill any won of yrs for understanding & prity Deverting actions at Least I think so, & we have now a fine Lusty Fellow we have Named Franklin five weeks old who bids fair to Equill Will in bulk however it may be with His Intellects, His mother Fattns Him two fast to be very Strong her self but has been much beter this time than usal owing we think to her haveing more skillful help at first, She Desiers her love to you,

I have omitted Ansuring yr leter somthing the longer to have time to write to my Daughter Mecom with it but realy can not now you cant Imagen how busey I am I writ this by candle light be so good as to tell her if yo see her or Ither of the children that I have been to Boston & to see Jenny found her grown a woman well & harty & well contented she came to town & stad a day & a night with me Said she should soon writ well anouf to writ to me & her mother which I was to convey throw Mr

Baches hands who I know would faveour me so much but I have wrot to her since I came home & had no Ansure which was won Reason of my Delay but I know she is well or Cousen Williams would have Informed me.

present Respects & Complements to all who Inquier affter your

Affectionat Aunt

JANE MECOM

"So difficult to hear from Each other"

[Here first printed from the manuscript in the American Philosophical Society. Ralph Izard suspected Franklin of trying to further the fortunes of his grandnephew Jonathan Williams Jr. Jonathan Williams Sr. took care of the house in Unity Street, belonging to Franklin, of which the rent had been set aside for the support of Peter Mecom and now since his death went to his mother. The "Inventor" of crown soap was apparently her brother John Franklin. Benjamin Mecom's daughter Jane, having been for a time with strangers, was now with Jane Collas in Cambridge.]

DEAR BROTHER   Warwick Dcr 29—1780

I have many Lonely Hours to bewail the Distance betwen us which makes it so difficult to hear from Each other, it is now seven months since I recved a line from you & that was very short, Just Informing me of yr Helth & that you had recd a Small Parsel of Soap, it was Dated March 5th but that you would write more largly by the Aliance which would Sail in a few Days, but I recd none in her nor since, I some times hear by the Publick you are well for which I thank God & Pray for the coninueance of boath Life & Helth, I profess to Govern my Life & action by the Rules laid down in the scripture, & that I find, full of Prayer as well as Praise for our selves and others, with grat confiedence that God will hear & do whatsoever is best for His Cretures & most for His own Glory, & Every Christian Prays with that submishion & a dependance on His Spirit to Direct there Prayrs aright; I Long much for yr Return to your Native Country while I live to Enjoy yr company, but

have often Expearanced that Gods time has been the best time,
& tho for the present it has seemed to cross my desier it has beene
much more for my comfort that the gratification was delaied

as I hear from good Athority that you are well & do well, I
am the less concerned at the Endevours of some to Defame your
charecter, but not Perfectly Easey about it for I fear there is two
much truth in that comon saying, where much Dirt is thrown
some will Stik, tho I Percive none at Present in this case, won
Izeard was wery Laboreous at Newport to make People beleve
you had done something criminal in mony maters Respting the
men belonging to the Aliance, Pretending he had strong
Vouchers He was carrieing with him to Congres, He was askd
what he thought was yr motive, He could give no other than
that you had a Nephue there you wanted to Asist in makeing
a Fortune, General Greenes Wife was in his company when he
run on so & she advised him not to Speak Disrespectfull of you
on the Rhoad for the people would have a bad opinyon of him,
but she heard affterwards by a Gentileman that came from
Camp he said a Lady at Newport Advised him not to tell those
stories of Dr Franklin but that he had made it his busnes at
Every Stage & intended to do so till he got to Congres. I have
heard nothing of him since & it is some months ago, I fancy by
the time he got there he sunk in to oblivion.

I have not heard from Mr Beache & famely a long time it is
Trew, I do not write often my Time seemes to be filld up as
the Famely I am in Increaces fast, my Grandaughter has had
two children in Seventeen monthes the Eldest is a Daughter,
Sally, the other a son Franklin, not because we could forgit your
Name but that we love to hear it, we left out the Benjamin that
he might not be calld ben; He was as lusty, Helthy, & as fine a
child as you Ever see till about a month ago, he had a severe
Humer came in His forehead about his Eyes & spread it self
almost over his face & Ears & head & in a small Degree his whol
body which has been very Grevous to him, & troblesome to us
all, we have constantly washed it with Lead-water which I remember you used when you came from Canady & had a breaking

out on yr skin, & the child is now much beter, the Parents Desire there Duty may be Remembred to you.

I was at Boston several weeks in summer & treeted very kindly by cousen Williams & famely as Useal, He continues to take care of the House & get what Rent from time to time that He thinks Reasonable, for my Part things runs so wild & I am so out of the world, I am no Judg of what is Right.

My Daughter & her Husband Hitch along in the world as well as they can as far as I know, She is often sick, She Boards in the country comonly while he is at Sea He makes a Shift to Pay for that when he comes home, & they are now at House keeping at cambridg as he could not git a house at Boston to suite them . She has now with her a Daughter of Son Benjamins who he Desiered we would take when she was first married but we have been obliged to Leve her to the care of Strangers.

Ever since those troblesome times, they have been very kind to her & taught her good Housewifery & she is a clever Girl Mr Collas Generally gits Busnes Prety soon after he gits home he has now the care of a ship a Building at Portsmouth Piscataiw[a] & is to sail in her but where I have not heard. I had many thoughts of Instructing him in the makeing Crown Soap after your Generous offer of Setting him up in it but found so many objections in my own mind that I did not Atempt it, the Difference betwen the trew Soap & counterfitt seems to be litle known at Present   It haveing been so long out of use that it would take a long time & consequently a large stock before people would be convinced of its valeu, it is true a man of Pecular Genius that way as was the Inventor might have acomplished it but that was not he the Labour is Grate, & the operation critical, the Exact knolidg not to be atained without Expearance, my Brother Him self tould me it workd some times not to his mind in a way he could not acount for, so that all things considered I thought Collas must take His Chance for a liveing in the way He was Used to & hope they will still git along as they have no Children, but He is so unlucky he never sails but I Expect to hear he is taken or cast away,

I wrote to you when I was at Boston but have heard of no opertunity since till the ship was Gone, this Goes from Provedenc in a vesel owened by Quakers so I sopose no Guns to Defend them, I hope houever it may git saif to you, & that I shall be fortunit anouf to recve some from you, which is all ways a grate pleasure to your affectionat Sister

JANE MECOM

My love to Temple & to Benny when you
write to him, do write me somthing about
them or Preswade Temple to Spend a
Hower in gratifieing his old Aunt

"That we might End our Days to gather"

[Here first printed from the manuscript in the American Philosophical Society.]

DEAR BROTHER   Warwick March 3 1781
    you will forgive the Incorectnes of my Leter when I tell you I most comonly write on very short Notice of an opertunity as it happens now, General Greene's Wife being hear offers to send it by a saif conveyance, & I gladly Embrace it, as I am Aprehencive but few of those I writ git saif to your hand; the last I wrot went from Provedence in a New Vesel owned by *Friends there*, charls Jenkens master, without Guns; & we had a rumer she was taken soon after she sailed but as it was some time ago & there has been no confermation we have some hopes of her Escape. I wrot a Sheet full on Every thing concerning my self that I thought you would wish to know but have no coppy & can now Recolect but litle of it & Shall not have time to Repeet that Litle. I am grown Impatient to hear from you as it is now within two Days of a year since the Last Line I have recved from you was Dated.

    I am still in tolarable Helth & Ever way as comfortable

[207]

Exepting that as I grow older I wish for more Quiet & our Famely is more Incumbred we have had three children Born since I came & tho they give grat Pleasure in comon yet the Noise of them is some times troblesome, I have often heard you wish for liberty to Live more Retired but it is what nither of us have much grounds to hope for, I often contemplate the Happines it would afford me to have you settled in a Country Seat in New England & I have premition to Reside with you that we might End our Days to gather Retired from all but a few choice wons that would give & Recive Mutual Injoyment & make us forgit any litle disagreable Incidents that would Unavoidably happen while we Remane in the boddy I hope you hear oftner from your Children than I do or I know it must give you Pain for it is sildom I can hear any thing about them   I had a short Leter from my Neice Last Summer which was the Last I have heard of any of them   I hope Benny Equals yr wishes, & that Temple is still with you, whose Example & precept I know he has good sense enough to Profitt by.

I must not omit to Inform you our youngest child is a son & named Franklin a fine thriveing boy with an uncomon manly countanance & we hope with (as I sopose) all others that have named after you that he will Inherrit some of yr vertues, the Parents Desier there Duty to you & Joyn in wishing the continueance of yr Helth & Happines

with your

affectionat Sister

JANE MECOM

"Parson Odell"

[Here first printed from the manuscript in the American Philosophical Society. The Reverend Jonathan Odell, loyalist clergyman of Burlington, New Jersey, had in 1776 written *Inscription for a Curious Chamber-Stove, in the Form of an Urn, so contrived as to make the Flame descend, instead of rise, from the Fire: Invented by Doctor Franklin.* The lines, in which Odell praised Franklin as a scientist but condemned him as a politician, had been printed in various places but had only recently come to Jane Mecom's attention. She may have met Odell in Burlington before he left it to join the British in New York. She had inquired about the "Peece of the Whig Sermon" of three clergymen in Boston: Samuel Cooper, John Lathrop, and Samuel Stillman. "Crasey Harry Badcock" was Henry Babcock, son of Joshua Babcock of Westerly, Rhode Island. Henry Babcock had served as colonel of the 2nd Rhode Island Regiment, but had been dismissed in May 1776 on grounds of mental unfitness.]

MY DEAR BROTHER   Warwick June 13—1781

I saw an article in our last paper under the London head, that Dr Franklin had Paid of all his tradsmans Bills & was prepareing to Leave Parris to Embark on Board won of the Ships at Brest for America, but as I have heard no such thing any other way I think it may be Rather what they wish, & what I should hartyly wish if it is consistant with your Honour as well as comfort I am Determined to write by this opertunity by which if it comes quick to yr hands you may have a Ready & Saif conveayance to me without the Roundabout ways by Post from Philadelphia or Boston

It is so long since I have had a line from you that if I had not had a former Reprouf from you I should be almost Redy to conclud on the Last of the six chances you then Discribed to me as Reasons for my not Recveing leters; that you were tiered of corisponding with me & Resolved to write no more, it is a year the 16th of last march since the last I received from you was Dated & that was about Eight months coming to hand   I thing I can Recolect Seven I have wrot in the time won by the same Vesel this is to go in Charls Jenkens master From Provedence who made so quick a Return   Prehaps you had not recd it time anough to write by him but I think you must have got that at least I wrot since by some French Gentleman who said he knows you, to whome Genll Greene's wife conveyed it for I did not see him & I cannot Remember Names, I had no rembrance how I came by the Peece of the whig Sermon I inquiered of all I thot Like to have such a thing but found we are no Sermonizers in this Part of the country I then sent it to Cousen Williams to serch the Printers Shops but he says it was not to be found & he carried it home & left it with His wife or Daughters & they have

[209]

Lost it which I do not so much wonder at in the bustle of mar-
rieing won of the young Ladys for such a circumstance Jeneraly
taks the atention of all the famely. but I am sorry, for I sent to
desier them to try Dr Cooper, Mr Lathorp & Mr Stillman & if
I was there I Dont Doubt I could find it by what I remember
of it, but not corect anouf to write. I have heard nothing of my
Neace or her famely at Philadelphia a long time, & know but
litle how the world goes Except seeing a Newspaper some times
which contains Enough to give Pain but litle Satisfaction while
we are in Armes aganst Each other

Parson Odell has been Exersiseing His Poetical Talant on
yr Invention of the Chamber Fireplace   it came to me throw
the hands of Crasey Harry Badcock & I have half a mind to send
it to you as I think it would make you Laugh but if you should
be coming home it will serve to Divert you hear, I contineu very
Easey and happy hear have no more to trroble me than what
is Incident to human Nature & cant be avoided in any Place, I
write now in my own litle chamber the window opening on won
of the Pleasantest prospects in the country the Birds singing
about me & nobod up in the house near me to Desturb me

you will Readiely conclud from these circumstances I might
have Performd beter, but I have lost my faculty if Ever I had
any and my Dear Brother will except Sencerity in lieu of it from
his Ever affectionat Sister

JANE MECOM

My Grandson & Daughter have desiered me to present there
Duty, I want very much to hear all about Temple & benny Pray
present my love to them

"A coletcion of all your works"

[Printed first, and hitherto only, in Duane, *Letters to Benjamin Frank-
lin*, pp. 115-116, and here printed from the manuscript in the American
Philosophical Society. The "coletcion of all your works" which Jane
Mecom had in mind was the *Political, Miscellaneous, and Philosophical
Pieces* edited by Benjamin Vaughan in 1779. John Thayer, taking this
letter to Franklin, had another from Jane Collas, dated Cambridge,
June 6, introducing Thayer: her letter is in the American Philosophical

Society. Jonathan Williams Sr. declined to give Thayer a letter of introduction, and later gave his reasons in a letter to Franklin of June 12,
1785, now in the American Philosophical Society.]

DEAR BROTHER   Cambridge 23 oct 1781

I am now hear on a Visit to my Daughter who lives in this
Town, and have Accidentally mett a young Gentleman who is to
Sail for France in a few Days, I know it will be agreable to you
to hear I am well & my Daughter in much beter Health than
usiual,—but her Husband after makeing won Successfull Voige
is again in the hands of the Enemy at Halifax She Desiers
her Duty to you.

Mr John Thayer the Gentleman by whom this goes has had
a liberal Education and has served in this comon welth with
acceptance but now chuses to go abroad with a view of seeing the
world & makeing his fortune, I have no personal Acquaintance
with Him but hear He is much Esteemed in Boston, I take the
Liberty to Introduce Him to my Dear Brother in hopes this
won at Least of Seven Leters I have wrot him since the Date
of his last to me, that I have recved, will Reach his hand; if I
should be so lucky & all the rest have been lost, I shall try to
Recolect the contents of some of them (for I keep no coppies)
which I wish you to know, & send by some other opertunity I
am this Day going to Boston in Pursuit of a coletcion of all your
works which I hear is lately come from Europe. some of which
I have been in posesion of & have lost, you will say then I dont
Deserve to have them again, but may be not if you knew all the
circumstances, however there is many things I never had and I
can hardly help Envieng any won that Pleasure without my
Pertakeing.

I left my Grand Children & grat Grandchildren well where
I comonly Reside & Expect to Return in about a fortnight.
Governer Greene's wife tould me as I came a long she had
Lately wrote you, there famely all well then, from yr affec-
tionat   Sister

                                          JANE MECOM

"The Glorious News"

[Printed first, and hitherto only, in Duane, *Letters to Benjamin Franklin*, pp. 116-117, and now printed from the manuscript in the American Philosophical Society. The "Glorious News we have now recd from the Southard" was the news of Cornwallis's surrender at Yorktown, which had been printed, on the Monday this letter was written, in the *Boston Gazette*. Word had been brought to Providence by the schooner *Adventure*, Captain Lovett, and from Providence to Boston by an express rider who had arrived on "Friday morning last." The sermon which Jane Mecom sent to her brother was *A Sermon preached before the Honorable Council, and the Honorable House of Representatives of the State of Massachusetts-Bay, in New England, at Boston, May 26, 1779. Being the Anniversary of the Honorable Council. By Samuel Stillman, A. M.* Boston, 1779.]

MY DEAR BROTHER   Boston Oct 29 1781

I See you do not forgit me tho I have so Long mourned the want of a line from your own hand to convince me of it. March-79 being the date of the Last I have recd from you, but I have Just now recvd a large Package from cousen Jonathan Williams by your order of considerable Valeu but have not yet time to know Exactly, they are things much saught for by our Dressing Ladies which will procure monny tho I thank God, & you, I have not wanted any Good thing, I live very comfortable with my Grand Children for good liveing in the Famely; & your Bounty suplies me with all I ought to wish besides yr good company   The Glorious News we have now recd from the Southard makes us Flater our selves you may Return to us soon, & Mr Williams Says live & Injoy helth & happynes twenty years yet; I have no such Expectation for my self, but I wish those a Blessing I may leve behind. I have at length found the Sermon you were desierous to see among Mr Stillmans & now send it; I hope it will git saif to hand & procure you some Pleasure to find such Worthys among us. I wrote from Cambridg where my Daughter Lives by a young man who I Expected was to Sail the next Day I am afraid you will think me two Presuming to Introduce to you Persons I know nothing of but by hearsay, but I am two apt to give wey to there Soliseta-

tions & by that means have been troblesom to you, tho I hope
yr long Expearance will Enable you to git rid of them if they
Prove so.

I mentioned my being coming to Boston in Serch of a Book containing all yr Publick writings but I cannot yet find it the Person in whose hands I heard it was is gone out of town I have
only Time to subscribe

    yr most obliged Gratfull & affectionat Sister

JANE MECOM

    Pray write me
the Perticulars of the News
they send from hear in a hand bill

"*My litle wons are Interupting me*"

[Here first printed from the manuscript in the American Philosophical
Society. The "grat present" Jane Mecom had received from Franklin
through Jonathan Williams Jr. was, according to a letter from him to
Franklin dated March 2, 1782, and in the American Philosophical Society, "Silk for Cloaks, &c. Gauze, Lace, Ribbon, Linnen, & Cambrick"—evidently to be sold by her in the informal trading she carried
on in Rhode Island. Jane Flagg Greene had died on April 6 of that year.
The prisoner of war for whom William Greene asked aid was Ezekiel
Durfey, "a small officer on board of the Ship Tracy," as Greene wrote
to Franklin on June 25. Catharine Greene on October 7, 1781, had
written to tell Franklin that his brother James's son, Isaac Allen of the
Morning Star, was a prisoner in England; and on May 8, 1782, that
her sister Judith Ray Hubbart's youngest son Samuel, "a Lad of about
13 years old," was a prisoner in Ireland. A letter from Samuel Hubbart
of February 12, 1781, to Franklin told of the boy's having been brought
from Ireland to Plymouth.]

Warwick 17 June—1782

MY EVER DEAR BROTHER:

  I wrot to you in october or Novr Last from Boston to thank
you for the grat present I then recd throw the hands of young
cousen Jonathan Williams, with wich I had no Leter from my
Dear Brother nor have I recved any of a Later Date than two
years ago Last march, Since my Return home my time & atention has been fill'd with Sickness & Deaths in the Famely in

perticular that of my Dear Grandaughter Jenny who Died of
a consumption has left three sweat babes won about two months
old, a sorrofull Husband & a Distrest Grandmother   I Injoyd
Sweat Peace in her Pleasant conversation & grat comfort in her
Dutifull & tender atention was Pleased with the hopes of the
continuance of it the Remainder of my Life but those comforts
are Vanishd & a care Devouled on me that I find my Self
unequel to that of the children the youngist is at nurs but the
other too Require some person more lively & Paitient to watch
over them continuealy, my Dear Child urged me Earnestly not
to Leave them as long as I Live & tho I made her no promis I
find the Request to be very Powerfull her Husband is Desierous
I should continue with Him & treats me very Respectfully that
I have no thoughts of Removeing at Present but circumstances
may alter in Time   I can't Expect it to be other ways as he is a
young man but my stay in the world may be much shorter, &
Life becomes Less Desierable Except I could find a capasety to
be more Usefull which growing Infermities & low Spirits Prevent, my Friend Greene Tould me she wrot you soon affter my
child Died & I dont doubt she was more Perticuler than I can
be at Presant for my litle wons are Interupting me Every miniut
& it is so hot I am not willing to trust them out of my Sight,
Should not have wrot in such a hurry but at the Request of
Goverr Green in behalf of some Friend who is Prisener in England whome you may do more towards Inlarging than any won
Els they call for the Leter & I can add no more but that I wish
for the comfort of a leter from you & am under all circumstances your

                                        affectionate Sister

                        JANE MECOM

I began this at the Govenr but was fetched home to the funeral
of my Gransons Brothers wife who died in the same house
with us
I Inclose the memerandom about the man

"All the season Blooming"

[Here first printed from the manuscript in the American Philosophical Society. The Prince to whom Jane Mecom referred was the first son of Louis XVI and Marie Antoinette, Louis Joseph Xavier François, born October 1781, died June 1789. Franklin's "Granson" Benjamin Franklin Bache had won prizes at his school in Geneva. "Sturdy Bill" was William Bache, formerly called the Infant Hercules, in Philadelphia. The dead brother of Jonathan Williams Sr. has not been identified, but he was not John, who appears elsewhere in the notes to this volume. Elizabeth Williams had been married to Joshua Eaton on April 24, 1781. Boston Registry Records, xxx (Marriages 1752-1809), 448.]

DEAR BROTHER   Warwick 25 June 1782

I wrot you a few Days ago, & at Governer Greenes Request Inclosed a memerandom concerning a Prisoner I also Informed you of the Irreparable Lose I have mett with in the Death of my Dear Grand Daughter Greene with whome I had Lived in as Perfect composeure & Tranquility as Human-Nature will admit of, She was affectionate & Respectfull to me, an affectionate & Prudent wife, & an Indulgent mother, I am still at her Dieing Request that I would not Leve her children as long as I live & the Request also of her bereved Husband with Them in the Famely, He is kind & affectionat to me but something constantly Passes that keeps alive my sorrow tho I have Plenty of all Nesesarys & the same Beautiful Prospect arownd me & all the season Blooming I so much mis her sosiety that it spreads a gloom over all.

Cousen Williams has made me a visit He came Partly on Busness as far as Provedence & Partly to Recrute His Spirits affter the long Sickness & Death of His Brother who Died much about the same time my Child did, He has lost three grandchildren by His son John, has won by His Daughter Bettsey (who married a Mr Eaton) He seems much Pleasd with, as we all are with our litle wons, they are Realy Pleasant diverting things I seem as if I could not soport Life without mine tho they cause many sorrowfull Reflections, there Father desiers His Duty to you.

[215]

I have wrot many leters to you since I recved won I never atempt to give any acount of Publick affairs   I sopose you constantly recive all from good hands   I should neverthe less be gratified to to recive some from you   I give you Joy of the birth of the Prince & as sinsearly of the Progres yr Granson makes in His Larning & the Honours conferd on Him for it, I hope you will Live to see him a worthy & Usefull man; I long to hear of Sturdy Bill, & the Rest of the Famely which I sopose is Increasd since I heard from them which is more than two years, I think I have wrote twice to them since, I beleve some of my leters to you miscarry, but I think they cannot to them as I wrot by Post.

I am Informed yr Health is so ferm & yr Spirits so good that I am not out of hopes of seeing you again in your Native Place if the War should ceace as some Imagin it will soon God grant it may for the the Ravages of war are Horrible we have been Lately surprised with a considerable fleets apearing as tho t[hey] Intended to Reposes Rhoad island but they Passd by affter 3 or four Days Alarm, In won of my Leters I wrot my thanks for the Present you sent me throw Cousen Jonathan williamss hands many of the Articles came seasonable for my own Use the Rest I sould & Put the monny to Intrest. I hope I shall be so Lucky as hear this gits saif to yr hand cousen williams tells me it will go by a very good opertunity if it should let me hear from you soon & Refresh the hart of yr

Ever affectionat Sister

JANE MECOM

"I thought he must be Cleaver"

[First printed, and hitherto only, in the *Pennsylvania Magazine of History and Biography*, LXXII (1948), 270-272, from the manuscript in the Historical Society of Pennsylvania; and here printed, with some corrections, from that manuscript. Prudence Wright's son had told Jane Mecom of her brother's severe attack of the stone in the late summer of 1782; and of the impudent and demanding conduct of John Thayer in Paris. It was he whom Jane Mecom in this letter called "that, I had almost Sade worthles Litle Anemil Thare." The great-grandchild she had with her in Cambridge was Sarah Greene. Elihu Greene never got him "a nother wife."]

DEAR BROTHER   Cambridge Decr 26—1782

I wrot to you two months ago From Warwick, which cousen Williams has yet to carry, After wards I concluded to come Hither & spend the Winter as most agreable by being more Retiered, & Less Exposed to Doers opening on me which in cold wether Increeces my cough & is very Tedious to me, but on my Arival at Boston I had the maloncholy acount of a Distressing fitt of Illness you have had tho something beter when the mesenger came Away, I am Freequently Reflecting on the Paine you Enduered & the Danger of the Freequent Returns of the disorder you are Liable to; & fearing they may be too hard for you, may God who has hitherto given you so much Health Prevent it, & Restore you to Perfect Health again, if that may not be I hope you will be Endowed with all the submition nesesary on so Tryng an ocation.

It was Mrs Writes son who tould me of your sickness & of what mortified me very much besides the condition & behavour of that, I had almost Sade worthles Litle Anemil Thare, I sin-searly ask your Pardon for Introduscing him to you, & have no other Excuse to make but to Tell you He took me In by being the first that Informed me of a Book that contain all your Philosophical & Political Papers, & Runing on so Pritily on won thing & another contained in them that I thought he must be Cleaver, Tell me you forgive me this & I will take more care for the future by the way I have never been able to come at a sight of the Book yet, tho I am Tould Dr Cooper has it, & have sent times without Number after it & have been Put off with some Frivolus Excuse; I would gladly bye won if it were to be Purchased but cant find that it is, I wish my Brother would do me the favour to send me won & I may be so Lucky as to Recive it, I would be a grat Amusement to me & that is the most I have to seek after at Present. My Son Collas & Daughter who is all the Child I have Left & Jenny mecom (won of my son

Benjamin's Children) do all in there Power to make me comfortable & I go some times to Boston where I am kindly Entertained by Cousen Williams & famely and see a few other Friends. I have won of my Deceasd Grand Daughters children with me & Expect to Return with it in the spring as there I Live very Pleasantly all the warm wether & can do a number of things nesesary for Him & the Children Exept He should git Him a nother wife which I beleve there is no grat Likelihood of   He is so sensable it is Imposable to make up his Lose, she was Indeed an Extroydenary wife. Mr Williams will be able to Ansure you any questions you shall think fitt to Ask concerning me which might have been Tedious for you to have Read had I thought of any thing more to write, my Children Joyn in Love an duty with your Affectionat Sister

JANE MECOM

Jane Mecom to Richard Bache

[Here first printed from the manuscript in the New York Public Library. The present of money mentioned by Jane Mecom in her letter of April 29, 1783, to Franklin had come to her through Richard Bache, in part in the form of a draft on John Hancock. Sarah Duffield, daughter of Edward Duffield, and Mrs. Samuel Meredith were friends of the Baches whom Jane Mecom had met in Philadelphia.]

SIR   Cambridge Aprin 11—1783

yours of Decr 4th came to my hand about a Fortnight ago your Draughts were Deuly Paid, Mr Hancocks on sight; I thank you for yr care in the Afare, my Brother was Allways a Good & kind Benifacter to me but I had not had a Line from Him for three years Past till since I recd yours, I have receved won I sopose by way of Philadelphia as it came by Post, but the won you mention to have forwarded I have never Recived.

The complaint of forgitfullnes I think Lys on my side as I have wrot twice to you or my Neice since I had a Line from Ither till now, the Neglegt of corispondence betwen us is much Regretted by me for I Long to hear all about you, & Each of

[218]

the children, & sinsearly Rejoyce with you on hearing of Bennys Proficiency in Larning which cousen Jonathan Williams had Informed me of some time ago; may you all Live Long to be a Blessing to Each other, for my own part I have had such an Admonition this winter of the suddennes by which I might be calld out of this world which was suckceaded by a sevear fitt of sicknes that has taught me to be continuealy looking to the Decisive Hour when I shall have no farther concern in this world. I had porposed [*on next page*: proposed] to send this by Post but the Gentileman who is the Barer [*interlined*: Mr Samuel Bradford] was many years a near Nabour to me in Boston for whome I have a grat Respect, & is near being married to Cousen Williamss youngest Daughter, should be glad you would take Notice of Him as such, my Neice will have opertunity on His Return to send me the Long Promised & long Expected favour about the children, to which I beg she will add something concerning all our Agreable Acquaintaince we had when I was there, tell Sally Duffeild I had some Expectation she would have favoured me with a Line as I had wrot to her, But may I not Hope for still somthing beter now the Glorious News of Peace is Arived that I shall see some of you, Mrs Meridith said she would certainly come to New England when Peace was concluded; If such a thing should be, I hope they or any other of my Acquaintance would take Pains to Inquier me out & come to see me; I am Grown such a Vagrant I cant opine the Place I may be In as I have all won Four Homes, my Daughter Collas's hear, Mr Williams's in Boston, Governer Greenes & my Grandson Elihue Greene's in Warwick in Rhoad island State. Each of them would Recive Pleasure in Entertaining any of mine or my Brothers Friends from Philadelphia my most Respectfull Compliments to all such as alow me to call them by that Title, & sinsear love to your wife & the children from your Affectionat & obliged Aunt

JANE MECOM

"Sit down & spend the Evening with your Friends"

[Printed in part in Duane, *Letters to Benjamin Franklin*, pp. 123-126, and here printed for the first time in full from the manuscript in the American Philosophical Society. Franklin's letter to which this is an answer is missing, so that it can only be assumed that the "Grat Bounty" for which Jane Mecom was grateful was his promise to her of an annual income, perhaps in the amount of £50 a year such as he was later to leave her in his will. The answer of Nehemiah to "Tobias, & Sanbalet" (Tobiah and Sanballat) is in Nehemiah 6:3. "Corrl Johonett" was Lieutenant Colonel Gabriel Johonnot, son-in-law of Franklin's friend the Reverend Samuel Cooper in Boston. A son of Johonnot had been at school in Geneva with Benjamin Franklin Bache. Jonathan Williams Sr. had been in France in the early months of 1783 and in London from April, as letters to Franklin in the American Philosophical Society indicate. A letter from Williams in Boston of December 20 of that year shows that he had been "Looking Round," as Jane Mecom had done, for a house in which Franklin might settle on his return from France. There was an estate in Cambridge, Williams said, owned by Andrew Cabot, which might be suitable. Franklin in a letter of April 17, 1782, to Catharine Greene had recommended the Comte de Ségur to the "civilities and friendship" of the Greenes. Though Jane Mecom did not give the date of the letter she had received from her brother, and it is missing, it was evidently written by William Temple Franklin, who had served as secretary of the American commission that signed the treaty of peace with England.]

Boston April 29, 1783

DEAR BROTHER

I have at Length recved a Leter from you in your own Hand writing, after a Total Silence of three years, in which Time Part of an old song would some times Intrude it self into my mind,

Does He love & yet forsake me

for

can he forgit me

will he niglegt me. this was but momentary at other times I concluded it was Reasonable to Expect it & that you might with grate proprity After my Teazing you so often send me the Ansure that Nehemiah did to Tobias, & Sanbalet, who Endevered to obstruct His Rebulding The Temple of Jerusalem, I am doing a grate work; why should the work ceace whilest I Leave it & come *Down* to you.

[220]

And a Grate work Indeed you have Done God be Praised I hope now you, your self, will think you have done anouf for the Publick, and will now Put in Execution what you have sometimes wished to be premitted to do; sit down & spend the Evening with your Friends. I am Looking Round me at cambridge for a Comodious Seett for you, not with any grat Hopes of your coming there I confes (but wishes) knowing you are Accomedated so much to your mind at Philadelphia, and have your children there. I should However Expect a Share of your corispondence when you have Leasure; & Beleve me my Dear Brother, your writing to me gives me so much Pleasure that the grate, the very grat, Present you have sent me is but a secondary Joy, I have been very sick this winter at my Daughters, keept my chamber six weeks but had a suficency for my suply of every thing that could be a comfort to me of my own before I received any Intimation of the Grat Bounty from your Hand which your Leter has conveyed to me, for I have not been Lavish of what I before Posesed, knoing sicknes & misfourtins might happen & certainly old Age but I shall now be so Rich that I may Indulg in a small degree a Propencity to help some Poor cretures who have not the Blesings I Injoy.

My Good Fortune came to me all to gather to comfort me in my weak state, for as I had been so unlucky as not to recve the Leter you sent me throw yor son Bache's hands tho he Informes me he forwarded it Emediatly His Leter with a Drauft for twenty five Guneys came to my Hand Just before yours which I have recved & cannot find Expreshon suitable to acknowlidg my Gratitude, How am I by my Dear Brother Enabled to live at Ease in my old Age (after a Life of Care Labour & Anxiety) without which I must have been miserable.

The other Bills are not Paid yet & Corrl Johonett is Absent & there is some Demur about it but I sopose it may turn out Right by & by His cousen Promises to call on me Prehap He will before I close this Leter, I have waited a fortnight and cannot git the bill Accepted nor a sight of the Gentileman tho He has Promised many times He will come & talk with me, I am Informed since I came to Town that Mr Williams had recved the other.——

I yester day recved a Leter from Mrs Bache   She Informs me she Expects you Home this Sumer that She & her children are all well her Husband Gone to New York.

I was quite in a weak State when I came to Boston but find myself gro stronger Every Day   Porpose to go to the State of Rhoad Island in about a Fortnight to Spend the Summer   I think if you come to America & come this way you will not Fail to call on me & our Good Friend Greene   She Desiered me Long ago to tell you how Happy She was in the Acquaintance of some Gentleman you Recomended to them, how Exactly He ansures yor Discription, but I then forgot it & cant now Remember the Name. I heard from there Lately they are all well have an Increec of Grand chilldren which makes them very Happy.

I percive Mr Williams is Highly Pleased with His Entertainment in France writs about going to England & not Returning in Less than a year However that may be I shall chirish some Hopes that you will come with Him tho on second tho[ught] I think it will be two valeuable a Treasure among our famelyes to venture in won Botome but I Shall depend on that Provedence which has hitherto Been your Preserver Protecter & Defender and am as Ever your affectionat and

obliged Sister

JANE MECOM

My Love to W T F
whose Hand writing in your
Leter & His name in the Signing
the Trety as a Secratery
gives me Pleasure

Jane Mecom to Sarah Bache

[Here first printed from a copy in the Yale University Library. The third of Jane Greene's children, Jane, had died on April 27, 1783, but her great-grandmother had not yet heard of it.]

Boston, 18th May, 1783

MY DEAR NIECE. The distresses of so terrible a war make every feeling heart rejoice at so glorious a peace: but to you and to me, whose father and brother, has been such a happy instrument, it must be doubly pleasing, that he has not only done so well, but lived to see his work completed, and that we have a prospect of seeing him in his own native place again, superior to all his enemies; this is joy I want words to express: And how great will his be, when he comes to see his posterity so much increased, and such a promising future prospect: May he live to enjoy the fruition. I thank you for the description you have given me of the dear little creatures: I long to have them in my arms. I wrote to Mr Bache, as soon as the business was completed, by Mr Bradford, and suppose he received my letter, as we have received letters from him since he arrived in Philadelphia. You kindly inquire after my daughter Collas. I suppose you know she is all I have left of my twelve children; and she is not healthy; and her husband ill; sickness keeps her low, the body and mind are so connected, that if one suffers the other will suffer with it. He has been taken and cast away so often since the commencement of the war, that I believe the merchants are afraid of employing him; for he has been out of business a long time. I have been with them all winter at Cambridge, and am returning there this day, but shall go to Rhode Island state in about a week, to spend the summer, where I have spent some happy years; but the scene is much altered by the death of a most desirable grand-daughter, who left three sweet children to my care. Her husband is a very good man, but nothing can repair my loss.

Remember me affectionately to your husband and all the children, and most respectfully to all I was acquainted with.

Your affectionate Aunt

JANE MECOM

[223]

"If a Boston Man should come to be Pope!"

[Printed first, and hitherto only, in the *Collections of the Massachusetts Historical Society*, Series 6, IV, 260-261, from the manuscript in the Society; and here printed again from the manuscript. John Thayer had become a Roman Catholic on May 25 of that year. In a letter to Jonathan Williams Sr. of April 13, 1785, Franklin said that Thayer had "converted himself lately at Rome, and is now preparing a return home for the purpose of converting his countrymen. Our ancestors from Catholic first became Church-of-England men, and then refined into Presbyterians. To change now from Presbyterianism to Popery seems to me refining backwards, from white sugar to brown."]

DEAR SISTER,   Passy, Sept. 13. 1783

I received your kind Letter of April 29. and am happy that the little Supplies I sent you, have contributed to make your Life more comfortable. I shall by this Opportunity order some more Money into the Hands of Cousin Williams, to be dispos'd of in assisting you as you may have Occasion.

Your Project of taking a House for us to spend the Remainder of our Days in, is a pleasing one; but it is a Project of the Heart rather than of the Head. You forget, as I sometimes do, that we are grown old, and that before we can have furnish'd our House, & put things in order, we shall probably be call'd away from it, to a Home more lasting, and I hope more agreable than any this World can afford us.

Tell my Cousin Colas, that the Parson she recommended to me is gone to Rome, and it is reported has chang'd his Presbyterianism for the Catholic Religion. I hope he got something to boot, because that would be a sort of Proof that they allow'd our Religion to be, so much at least, better than theirs.—It would be pleasant, if a Boston Man should come to be Pope! Stranger Things have happened.

Cousin Williams went back for Boston from London about the Beginning of June, so that probably he is with you before this time. He laid out, by my Desire, the Money he receiv'd for you, in Goods, which you will receive of him. When you have sold them, perhaps it may be adviseable to put the Money at Interest, that it may produce you a little Income.

My two Grandsons are now both with me and present their Duty. I am ever, my dear Sister,

Your affectionate Brother

B FRANKLIN

"To settle in the House at Boston"

[Here first printed from the manuscript in the American Philosophical Society. The signature and the final words of farewell were cut off, presumably by some early autograph collector. The house in Boston which Jane Mecom was to consider her own was that which had formerly belonged to Elizabeth Douse and from which since 1763 Jane Mecom had been receiving the rent.]

DEAR SISTER, Passy, June 17. 1784.

It is long since I have had the Pleasure of hearing from you, but am glad to hear by Cousin Williams that you were well the Beginning of this Year, and about to settle in the House at Boston, which you may consider as your own, and I hope you will be happy in it.

I continue, Thanks to God, in very good Health, being at present only troubled with the Stone; which sometimes gives me a little Pain, & prevents my going in a Carriage where there are Pavements, but does not otherwise make me very unhappy; as I can take the Exercise of Walking, eat, drink, sleep, read, write and enjoy the Conversation of my Friends as usual.—Give my Love to your Daughter, and believe [*signature missing*]

"In your House at the North End"

[Printed first in Duane, *Letters to Benjamin Franklin*, pp. 130-132, and here printed from the manuscript in the American Philosophical Society. At the time of this letter Jane Mecom had been living in the Unity Street house about six months. A letter from Jonathan Williams Sr., dated December 29, 1783, and in the American Philosophical Society, informed Franklin that his sister expected to move into the

[225]

house the following week. The house, later numbered 19 Unity Street and not destroyed till 1939, is described, with some inaccuracies in respect to Jane Mecom's ownership and occupation of it, in Frank Chouteau Brown, "The Clough-Langdon House, 21 Unity Street, Boston," *Old-Time New England*, XXXVII (1947), 79-85. There is a photograph of the houses at 19 and 21 Unity Street, as they appeared in the early years of the twentieth century, in Annie Haven Thwing, *The Crooked & Narrow Streets of the Town of Boston*, rev. ed., 1930, facing p. 76.]

DEAR BROTHER   Boston July 4—1784

I often Recolect the Advice you wonce Gave won of my Sons to do the right thing with Spirit & not to spend time in makeing Excuses for not Doing it & I ought to have profited by it, but I have so long Delayed writing to you that I am hardly capable of makeing any Excuse at all, & now have no time to Atempt it. I have Removed From Cambridge with my Son in Law Collas & his wife & Live in your House at the North End & Mr Collas being Absent sildom see any won to Inform us How the world goes, am now at Cousen Williams where I am Informed a Ship is to sail this Day with a Gentileman in it who goes Directly to you, I cant Remember Ither His Name or office. by which you will see what a confused state my mind is in for I Just Heard it below, I am often Afflected with grat Dizenes & Expect or fear if I live much Longer to be in such Circumstances as Dean Swift was, If it Pleases God to hear my Prayer Death will be much Preferable, but who am I to Prescribe to the Allmighty the Anguish of mind I have undergone on your acount since I heard of the Greveous malady you are Exercised with has made me consider which which of the two cases I should Prefer & I think yours bad as it is, dont think by this that I dont feal all for you that the Intimate knolige of such cases, all the Tendernes & Affection that is Due to won who has been as a Father, Husband, & all ways the best of Brothers deserves, but your Retaining your Intlectual Faculties & such Fortitude to bare up under it must be Preferable to a Senslis Stupidetie

but O that After you have Spent your whol Life in the service of the Publick & have Atained so Glorious A conclution as I thought as would now Premit you to come home & Spend (as you Used to say) the Evening with your Friends in Ease & Quiett, that now such a dreadfull maledy should Atact you; my Hart is Reddy to burst with Greaf at the thought.

how many Hours have I Laid a wake on nights thinking what Excruciating Pains you might then be Incountering while I a Poor Useles, & wrothless worm was Premitted to be at Ease; oh that it was In my Power to mitigate or Aleviate the Anguish I know you must Endure—
I have been Flattered all the Spring & Sumer that you were coming home, I know your wisdom will Direct to Emprove all circumstances that will be most comodeious for the desiered End but I fear if you take Ship for Philadelphia. I shall never see you, traveling will be so Incomodous to you that when you are got home you will not Prevail with your self to see New England but If you come hear first you can go mostly if not Altogather by water as you know & it may not Be so trying to you. God grant I may see you again hear but if not that we may Spend an happy Eternity to gather In His Presence

Mr Williams has tould me he has Informed you Perticularly about my Affairs but I did not think that would Jestifie me in not writing my self but I have now nither Leters nor Papers nor time to say any thing more than that I am your most obliged & affectionat

                                              Sister

JANE MECOM

If wind or wither should detain the ship I will writ again at Present Pray forgive the very bad Spelling & Every other defect & dont let it mortifie you that such a Scraw came from your Sister

Mr williams says my Love to the Docter mine to your Grandsons

"*The House is Pleasant for Light and Air*"

[Here first printed from the manuscript in the American Philosophical Society. To simplify this letter's tangled account of the transactions involved: Jane Mecom had preferred not to accept the millinery goods mentioned by Franklin in his letter of September 13, 1783, and brought to her from London by Jonathan Williams Sr., but instead to take the value in money and leave it with Williams at interest; and the money Franklin had sent her in the form of a draft on Samuel Cooper arrived after Cooper's death on December 23, 1783, with resulting delay in payment. There is no letter from Franklin to his sister in which he said there are some things "Proper to convers with a Friend about that is not Proper to write," but it will be noted that in his replies to her most tragic stories about her family he never mentioned the actual details. The young gentleman whose father was a "Bankrupt and a vagabond" has not been identified. "Portt Rosway" to which the luckless Collas had gone "Down" was Port Roseway, "down east" from Boston and near Cape Negro, Nova Scotia. A "chase" (chaise) was a two-wheeled vehicle with a seat for two persons and a top; the top distinguished it from what was called a "chair."]

DEAR BROTHER   Boston August 16th 1784

It is my Duty as well as Inclination to Inform you much oftner than I have done of my situation and Afairs, I acknolidg I have Suffered very Trifling circumstances to cause me to Neglect it for the Time; you are the only Person in the world I wish to know all my Transactions an the motives to them as such a Friend as my Dear Brother would subject me to the Least Inconvenancy but you Long ago convinced me that there is many things Proper to convers with a Friend about that is not Proper to write.

you will undoubtedly think it Strange I have not Sooner Informed about the goods you Expected cousen Williams brought me from England, and I have all along Intended it; but was Flatered with the Expectaion of your coming Home & it was Likely you were on your Pasage; and I commonly find my Self in a fraim so unsuitable to write to you that I am too Apt to Neglect it., After Mr williams was gone I recd your Leter Informing me of the bill you had sent me, I then Aplied to Mrs williams & recved a Note of hand for it Jointly with her Son.

and when Mr Williams Returned I was at Rhoad Island and recved a Leter from Him Informing me that you had Desiered Him (by Leter a few days before he sailed for Home) to Lay out that money in goods for me, that He wrot you in Ansure that He soposed milenary would be as suitable as any, that he had Plenty of such Goods on board, which I might have, He accordingly wrot me He had a trunk of Gauzes & I beleve some other things, which I might have if I chose it, or the money, or I might Lett it Remain in His hands on Intrest; the Later Prosal I Prefered as I found my Self not in a capacity for Traiding, and if I had those goods were such a glutt they would not fetch the Sterling cost, and I did not think my Self obliged to take them as he had no Reference to me when He purchased them, I must have been Beholden to Him to have sould them for me which was what He found he could not do for Himself.

As to the Last Bill you sent me the Death of our Dear & Ever to be Lamented Dr Cooper has caused the Payment to be Postponed tho I am Tould it is saif that it shall be Paid but not till a year after His death as that is acording to Law, and I Dont find they are likely to alow any Intrest on it but I think that among Debts of Honour this stands Higest as it was money Paid out of your Pocket for which you had no consideration but to oblige a Friend, they do not Apear very Generous as the Executor wants Mr Williams to take the young Gentlemans fathers obligation for the money who is a Bankrupt and a vagabond but I Leve all to Mr williams who I hope will be Able to do us Justice

Dear Brother thus far I had wrote Intending to finish & send it when I had opertunity I have now recd your kind leter of June 17 which I thank you for & am glad you Aprove of my comeing into the house, Apearences are so much against me you must think me very ungratfull and I am shure it is Foreign from my Hart   I think there is not an Hour when I am a waik that I dont think on you with gratitude, it gives me Pain to see you Put an Emphasis on the words *this year*   I think Some of my Leters must have been Lost or you must have had some from

[229]

me Late in the Last year but Indeed I am very forgetfull
Grown, I have had a grat deal of Sicknes my self and Luckily
Imploid the critical minute to Remove to Boston and almost as
Soon as we got hear my Daughter was taken sick and keept her
chamber & allmost her bed for three months was very weak and
Poorly a long time affter and is far from being well now. Such
circumstances has keept my mind always Discomposed but still
hopeing to feel a more suitable disposition to morrow & to morrow. I did write to you about Six weeks ago but it was in a grat
hurry on a sunday bewen meetings as the Ship was Just going
to Sail but for my Life I cant Remember who it went by.

It gives me some comfort to hear you Injoy your Self so well
under that Grevous Disorder I feared it was wors with you but
I know your Admireable Patience dictates your Pen and makes
you use the Softest terms your case will admit of O I know too
much of the Anguish you must Suffer not to feal a constant Anxiety for you and think your case hard—very hard oh that there
was any hopes of Releaf but from cutting which I sopose at your
Age you have no thoughts of Submiting to may God continu
your Patience & not premit the Pains to Increace.

Mr Collas was in no Busines for a long time He thought if he
could git into Boston to Live he shuld be more likely to obtain
some which he did in about a month after we got hear & went
Down to Portt Rosway & has been coasting there Ever since
carring Lumber.
the House is Pleasant for Light and Air haveing a large opening back & forward (as nobody has bulded near it since you saw
it) and is very convenant for our Small Famely which consists
of my son & Daughter and Jenny Mecom won of my son Benjamin's Daughters and my self for some months past but three
of us. it is far from the few Relations & Acquaintance I have in
Town but I Remember your sentamments are that walking is a
most Healthfull Exercise and I practice it when I am able
many times when I am offered a chase but am so weak I make but
a Poor figure in the Street.

You dont say a word of coming home now are we never to see you more your Friends there & hear will be cuttin out work for you to keep you there if you Dont Force your self away my Daughter & Grandaughter send there Duty & be Asured

I am as Ever with the gratest Reason your

Gratefull and Affectionat Sister

JANE MECOM

"By the Marquis La Fayette"

[Here first printed from the manuscript in the American Philosophical Society. Lafayette had returned to America for a visit of six months to his friends from Virginia to Boston, and sailed homeward from New York on December 21, 1784. In this letter Jane Mecom for the second time compared the disorder from which she suffered with that of Jonathan Swift, which ended in total insanity. Acting on Jane Mecom's suggestion about the work of "Samuel Stnnett," Franklin on March 18, 1785, wrote to Richard Price asking him to make "a List of a few good Books, to the Value of about Twenty-five Pounds, such as are most proper to inculcate Principles of sound Religion and just Government." A newly erected township in Massachusetts had chosen the name of Franklin and had asked him for a donation for a bell for the church. Franklin had advised them to accept "Books instead of a Bell, Sense being preferable to Sound. . . . Besides your own Works, I would only mention, on the Recommendation of my sister, 'Stennet's *Discourses on Personal Religion*,' which may be one Book of the Number, if you know and approve of it." Samuel Stennett (1728-1795) was a Baptist minister in London.]

DEAR BROTHER   Boston Octr 21—1784

I propose to Send this by the Marquis La Fayette He is much Hond and Caressd among us.

I wish I was capeble of filling it with a Subject worthy your Atention, but I can only write what throw your Affection for me will be Pleasing, I am now Pritily settled have had two Rooms New Papered an Painted, have Procurd some conveniances for my own Chamber (for you know I Lost allmost every thing when the Town was Ravged) that if I should be confined

[231]

to it I might be comfortable for I cant say I ever feel Perfectly well; and the similarity of my Disorder with Dean Swifts makes me often very Apprehensive; I however Recreate my self in the best maner I can, I walk abroad often, viset my friends oftener than they do me hopeing they will Pay the debt in time of need. I Read as much as I Dare, but find it sometimes Affect my Head, I Injoy all the Agreable conversation I can come at Properly, but I find Litle, very Litle, Equal to that I have a Right to by Nature but am deprived of by Provedence which however does all things well an I submit, as old Jacob when He found tho he had been deprived of the comfort and company of his beloved Joseph for so Long a time sinces it was for such Porposes to save much People alive.—haveing this comforting hope which you yr self mention in won of your Leters that we shall meet in a more Joyous State. and a more Dureable habitation, never more to be Separated, tho we may be keept at this Distance the short Remainder of this mortal Life.

I observe in won of your Leters to cousen Williams your Intention to Present to Franklin Town a number of Books as a Foundation for a Parish Library hopeing the Franklins will Prefer Sense to Sound, I cant doubt but such a Library will consist of some Authers on Divine Subjects I therefor hope you will not think it too Presuming in me to Propose won, Viz Discourses on Personal Religion in two Volumes by Samuel Stnnett D D Printed in London by R Hett in 1769   I borrowed them and Read them with a grat deal of Pleasure and I think you yourself would if you could find time tho there may be many things in them not altogether Agreable to your Sentiments, which I sopose may be the case with Every Volume you Read on any Subject.

Mr Collas is now at home Preparing for sailing again to the French Westindies   His wife is in a beter State of Health than when I Last wrot you

She Joyns in Duty and Love to the best of Benifactors with your Affectionat Sister

JANE MECOM

[232]

Remember me Affectionatly to
Temple I hope he is as good
to you as Ever, & to Benny
Bache if with you.
Our Friend madam Greene
all way Inquiers after you
and desiers to be Remembred

"I know you give it with Pleasure"

[Printed first, and hitherto only, in the *Pennsylvania Magazine of History and Biography*, XXXVI (1912), 119-120, from the manuscript in the Historical Society of Pennsylvania; and here printed again from the manuscript. It appears that Samuel Bradford, son-in-law of Jonathan Williams Sr., was using the money Jane Mecom had received for the goods from London, and was paying her interest. Thomas Hubbart, whose first wife Judith Ray had died in 1775, was married to Anna Bigelow of Weston, Massachusetts, on August 5, 1784. Boston Registry Records, XXX (Marriages 1752-1809), 322. Captain Samuel Partridge had been one of the Overseers of the Poor in Boston in January 1779. Winsor, *Memorial History of Boston*, IV, 651.]

Boston May 26—1785

DEAR BROTHER

I recved you kind Leter Dated Octr 16 about a fourtnight ago, by way of Philadelphia, with grat Pleasure as it gave me to understand your Malady does not Increace upon you, but you always Represent your Afflictions as Light as Posable to your Sister because you know she constantly Greves for you, but I think I can Discover you to be in Pain even while you thus write. your Tendernes for me In that Respect as in all other Vertues far Exedes mine, for to my Regret I Reflect that my Last Leter to you contained two many complaints of my Ill State of Health and Natureal Decays, which I sopose you had not Recved, but God has been beter to me than my fears for tho it has Indeed been a Severe Winter I have had Less Indisposition than in Ither of the two Preceding Winters   I am however Dayly Looking forward to that State wich you wonce gave me a hint was more Proper for my contemplation than seeking a

[233]

New Place of Aboad In this world, however as it need not Impede our Journey to that beter country I am strongly Inclined to justifie my Project; as you have Profesed an Inclination to spend yr Last Days in your Ntive Place and I thought you had been so Long Used to Grandure in yr Apartments & Furniture you had by this time got a Surfitt of them and would Relish a Plain Simple Acommodation of Just convenancess which would take but litle time to suply yr self with, & you had I hoped anumber of years before you Pleas God you Live to the Age of your Ancestors.

but this scheme was before I heard of your Distresing calamity now alas I fear Every year & Every Day is a Burthen to you Exept you recive som Amusement by the wonderfull Philosophical Discoveries lately made in France.

I have some times fear'd as your old Friends in America have Died of so fast you would be so Atached to that country as not to wish to Return if your case would Premit.

you have heaped so many Blessings upon me I am at a Lose how to Express my Gratitude. I have a grat Deal of time to contemplate my happy state in aboundance of Perticulars and thought my self Richly Provided for in all things nesesary for my comfort, the Premision you now send me to Draw on you for fivety Pounds sterling gratly Increases the Store; I accept with a gratfull hart for I know you give it with Pleasure, and have Acording Drawn the Bills in favour of Jonathan williams or order I am alowd six present which they say was as much as could be got Mr Bradford has it & Pays me Intrest for it as I did not Emediatly want it.

I have Put a New Pump in to the well had it Emptied & cleaned to the Botom had a New platform & sink & all things it wanted but I had money anouf by me to do it.

would you think it Capt Patridge that married Bettsey Hubard is Gone to be Overseeer of the Almes House I have been to see them since they got there she apears chearfull & I beleve is tolarable contented Tommy Hubard is married to a Rich widdow in the country who he was a long time strugling to obtain & has conquered at Last

I have not heard from our friends at Road Island a long time I have thoughts of Taking a Journy thare our friend Caty Greene Desiers me allways to Remember her to you when I write.

my son Collas is now gone to the Eastward to bring a New vesel He is going to the west Indies in   She is a Poor weakly wooman hardly Ever well

Jenny Mecom is still with us strong & harty so there is won in the Famely free from complaints.

we have had grat Bustling hear about the choice of Govener and I hear are Like to have none this year, but I dont Doubt you will see all the Papers so shall only add that with the most sincear Gratitude & Prayers for your Ease an comfort

I remain your Affectionat Sister

JANE MECOM

my Daughter & Grandaughter
Desier there Duty, my Love to Temple
& Benny if with you

"Go home, and go to Bed"

[The first paragraph of this letter was printed in Sparks, *Works*, x, 213, as "to a sister in America." The whole letter was printed first in Smyth, *Writings*, IX, 363-364, with slight inaccuracies. It is here printed from the letter sent, now in the Henry E. Huntington Library. There is a copy in another hand, and apparently of a later date, in the American Philosophical Society. Thomas Truxtun, as he spelled his name, had been an active privateersman during the Revolution, and was later captain and commodore in the United States Navy. The ship in which he brought Franklin home was the Philadelphia-built *London Packet*, 300 tons, then on her maiden voyage which had included Charleston, South Carolina, and London before she arrived at Cowes. She carried a miscellaneous cargo, but according to her owners had "elegant and convenient accommodations for passengers." The best account of the homeward voyage is Charles F. Jenkins, "Franklin Returns from France—1785," *Proceedings of the American Philosophical Society*, 92, 417-432.]

St. Germain, 12 Miles from
Paris, July 13. 85.

DEAR SISTER

I left Passy, yesterday Afternoon, and am here in my Way to Havre de Grace a Seaport, in order to embark for America. I make Use of one of the King's Litters carried by Mules, who walk steadily and easily, so that I bear the Motion very well. I am to be taken on board a Philadelphia Ship on the Coast of England (Capt. Truxton) the beginning of next Month. Not having written to you, since that which contain'd a Bill for you on Mr Vernon, and as I may not have another Opportunity before my Arrival in Philadelphia, (if it pleases God I do arrive) I write these Particulars to go by way of England, that you may be less uneasy about me. I did my last public Act in this Country just before I set out, which was signing a Treaty of Amity and Commerce with Prussia. I have continu'd to work till late in the Day; tis time I should go home, and go to Bed.

My Love to your Daughter and to Cousins Williams, & believe me ever, my dear Sister,

Your affectionate Brother

Mrs Mecom   B FRANKLIN

[*In the margin*]

Tho' going to my own Country, I leave this with Regret, having receiv'd so much Kindness in it, from all Ranks of People

Temple and Benjamin are with me, and send their dutiful Respects.

[*Address*]

To
Mrs Jane Mecom
to the Care of Jona Williams
Esq Mercht
to be sent to the
New Engd Coffee House
No 61 threadneedle Street to go per first Ship

"After a pleasant Passage"

[Here first printed from the manuscript in the American Philosophical Society. Franklin had landed in Philadelphia on September 14. In the tumult of his reception the earliest letters he found time to write were this to his sister and one to John Jay, secretary of foreign affairs for the Continental Congress, to whom it was Franklin's duty to report. On the twentieth he wrote to the William Greenes and to George Washington. The "5 Weeks & 6 Days from Land to Land" is either a slip or else must mean from the last sighting of land in the Channel to the first in America. The *London Packet* sailed from Cowes on July 28, and Franklin and his party did not leave it for six weeks and six days.]

Philada Sept. 19. 1785.

DEAR SISTER

I arrived here last Wednesday with my two Grandsons & Cousin Jonathan Williams all well, Thanks to God, after a pleasant Passage of 5 Weeks & 6 Days from Land to Land. I wrote a few Lines to you just before my Departure from France. I am continually surrounded by congratulating Friends, which prevents my adding more than that I am ever

Your affectionate Brother

B. FRANKLIN

Mrs. Mecom
My Love to your Children, and
Love to Cousin Williams and Family
in all which my Grandsons join.

"Saif to his Desiered Porte"

[Printed in part in Duane, *Letters to Benjamin Franklin*, pp. 132-133, and here first printed in full from the manuscript in the American Philosophical Society. Franklin in a letter of April 13-14 to Jonathan Williams Sr. had sent his sister a draft on William Vernon of Newport, to whose son William Henry Vernon in Paris Franklin had lent money. See Franklin's letter to William Vernon, October 14, 1785, first printed in Carl Van Doren, *Benjamin Franklin's Autobiographical Writings*, pp. 658-662.]

Boston Sept 23—1785

Blessed be God who has brought my Dear Brother Saif to his Desiered Porte, that has Ansured my Dayly Prayrs for his comfort & Ease, that you have had so good a Pasage, & but won Days Illnes from the malidy, that Atends you. I never can be thankfull Enough for these perticulars; nor for His continual mercies to me which are all a long beyond my conception as well as Deserts. I Long so much to see you that I should Immediatly seek for some won that would Accompany me & take a Litle care of me but my Daughter is in a Poor State of Health and gone Into the country to try to git a litle beter and I am in a Straight betwen two, but the comfortable Reflection that you are at home among all yr Dear chilldren & no more Seas to crose will be constantly Pleasing to me till I am Premited to Injoy the happines of seeing & conversing with you.

The Day I recd yrs of Apr in which you sent me the Generous Present of a Bill on Mr Vernon of Newport I was setting out on a Visit to that State, & while there I recd a Leter from Mrs Bache Informing me She Expected you the Next month which causd me not to writ you About it till now, He Paid it all but five Dolars which H absolutly Refused saying it was the Proper Exchange & I was Glad to git that for he made some cavel about Paying it at all saying his son Never wrot to Him & he had forbid him Drawing on Him three years ago, our friend Catheren Greene is the same kind good Natuered creature she Ever was (& so Indeed is the Governor & all the famely) she bids me Never forgit to Remember her to you when I write—

You will forgive all omitions & Deffects as I fear the Post will be gone before I can git it there & can only Add God Bless you all to Gather forever

Prays yr Affectionat Sister

JANE MECOM

[238]

"*I hope in the Spring to be able to visit Boston*"

[Here first printed from the manuscript in the American Philosophical Society.]

Philada Oct. 1. 1785

DEAR SISTER,

I received your kind Letter. I should be happy to see you here, but cannot think of allowing you take such a Journey for that purpose, as I hope in the Spring to be able to visit Boston.

I am sorry you did not receive the whole of Vernon's Bill; but we must think it well that you got anything, since the Son drew on the Father without Permission; and the Letter I formerly receiv'd from the Father, requested only of me to give the Son Advice, and said nothing of lending him Money. I did both. But I am afraid I disoblig'd the Son more by the Advice, than I oblig'd by the Money: tho' at the Time he was in great Need of both. And the Father hardly thinks himself oblig'd to me for either.

My Love to Cousin Williams, to our Friend Mrs Greene, and to your Children; and believe me ever,

Your affectionate Brother

All here send their Love.   B FRANKLIN

"*Domestic Chit Chat like comon folks*"

[Printed first, and hitherto only, in Duane, *Letters to Benjamin Franklin*, pp. 133-134; and here printed from the manuscript in the American Philosophical Society. Franklin had on his return to Philadelphia at once been nominated for a seat in the Supreme Executive Council of Pennsylvania, and his sister had heard of the nomination though the election was not to be held till October 11. On that day he was elected to the Council and he was elected President on the 18th. The two grandsons who had accompanied him home were William Temple Franklin and Benjamin Franklin Bache.]

Boston Octr 1—1785

DEAR BROTHER

I cant Expres to you How much Joy I feal at knowing you are at home & so much more at Ease than I expected in Regard to your boddyle state, but I Perceive by the News papers you are not to be suffered to Rest as long you are Alive, I was in hopes you would have Resolutely Rersisted all Solicitatons to Burden yr Self any more with the concerns of the Publick, & Flattered my self if I were with you I should Injoy a litle familiar Domestic Chit Chat like comon folks, but now I Imagine all such Attempts would be Intrusion, and I may as well content my self at this Distance with the hopes of recveing wonce in a while a kind Leter from you, & beleving you are happy with your other connections.

you mention yr writing to me Just before yr Departure from France I have not recd such a won the Last I recd from you was Dated Apr 12 which I mend to you Last Post, I am greved Ever since I sent it that I did not mention how much I felt my self affected with the Affectionat mention cousen Jonathan williams made of me in his Leter to his Father but I thought he would Emediatly folow his Leter & I should have the Pleasur of telling him my self, I Rejoice too at the Arival of yr two grandsons who I am shure must be very happy in being deservedly caressed by all there friends & old Acquaintance

my Daughter is still in the country but she Informs me she is beter, my Love to Mr & Mrs Bache and all the children from yr Affectionat Sister

JANE MECOM

"*K*indnes of hart by Deads Express"

[Printed first, and hitherto only, in Duane, *Letters to Benjamin Franklin*, pp. 135-136. Duane printed

"I know your judgment as well as practice is,
Kindness of heart by deeds express"

as two lines of verse, without authority from the manuscript in the American Philosophical Society, from which the letter is now printed. A few sentences from the present letter were printed in Sparks, *Works*, x, 326n. Jane Mecom's "kindnes of hart by Deads Express" was a reference to the line "Kindness of heart by words express" in her Uncle Benjamin Franklin's verses sent her from England by her brother in his letter of September 16, 1758.]

DEAR BROTHER   Boston Oct 19—1785

I Long much to See you and as my Niece had Just before
you Arived Informd me it was Imposable for you to come
hear I had thoughts of going to you, but would not Determine
till I should know if it would be Agreeable to you, yr kind Leter
of Octr 1. Lets me know yr mind & I am Satisfyd, and will hope
too that I shall See you hear in the Spring, as it was before what
I utterly dispard off yet thoughts of your Injoying so much Ease
as to hope it, will chear many a gloomy Hour I should other
ways had throw the winter.

I am apt to be two communicative, I had beter have suprressd
the Information I gave you of Mr Vernon Ingratitude tho I
then thought it would be best for you to know the man, you
come at two much of such Painfull knolidge, and I fear it apears
to you I am of the Number of Ingrats I did not tell you how
Thankfully I Recd the Benefitt, But be Asured my Dear Brother
that there is not a day Passes that my hart does not overflow
with Gratitude to you, and Adoration of the Supreme Benefactor of all mankind who Puts in your Power not only to make me
as happy as humanity can Expect to be, but Enables you to Dif-
fuse your Benifitts I had Allmost said to the whol Univerce

I know your Judgment as well as Practice is kindnes of hart
by Deads Express, but it is my opinion words should not be Excluded (tho I sometimes Neglect them) Espesially when there
is no opertunity to Perform Deeds.

I think it was not till the very Day you Arived that Mr Williams got that Bill you sent me on Dr Cooper Transferd to Him
I Expect He Either has or will write you the Perticulars.

Affter my Love to my two Nephews give me Leave to beg
the Favour of won of them by yr Premition to give me a Catalogue of the Books you Designe for Franklin Town, my Reason for this Request is I have a grat deal of time on my hands,
I Love Reading, it is a Present Amusement tho my memory is
so bad that I cannot Retain it as many others do; now I am sure
that will be a collection worth Reading, & I dont doubt I can

[241]

Borrow of won & a nother of my Acquaintance from time to time such as I have a mind to Read.

my Daughter is Returnd from the Country much mended in her health, she with my grand daughter Jenny mecom Deserer there duty

Remember my Love to Mr & Mrs Bache & all the children

Your Affectionat Sister

JANE MECOM

[*Postscript on cover*] I wrote Mrs Bache by a Vesel some time ago

"*Presents to Friends in France*"

[Here first printed from the manuscript in the American Philosophical Society. "Cousin Jonathan," Jonathan Williams Jr., who had accompanied Franklin from France, had lost all his money in shipping ventures, and now thought of soap-making as a possible new business.]

DEAR SISTER,   Philada Oct. 27. 1785

I was just going to write to you for Information whether the Bill I drew on Dr Cooper before his Death, had ever been paid; and the Pen was in my hand, when I receiv'd your kind Letter of the 19th Instant, acquainting me that Cousin Williams had receiv'd the Money, of which I am very glad,—on your Account.

This will be delivered by our Cousin Jonathan, whom I very much esteem for his many valuable Qualities. He was very desirous in France of knowing how to make Crown Soap, and I promis'd him a Copy of the Receipt you were once so good as to write for me: But in my Absence it is lost with many other of my Papers.—You will oblige me by writing it over again for me, but more by making a Parcel for me of 40 or 50 pounds weight, which I want for Presents to Friends in France who very much admir'd it. Jonathan will be glad to assist you (for the Instruction's sake) in the working Part. I wish it to be of the greenish Sort that is close and solid and hard like the Specimen I send; and not that which is white & curdled and crumbly.

I do not complain of any suppos'd Ingratitude in Vernon; I can excuse his being out of humour with his Son's Drawing on him, who stays in Paris spending his Time & Substance unprofitably, contrary to his Father's Will. I wish you had mention'd the exact Sum he paid, that I might have judg'd whether he was right or wrong in paying five Dollars short of what you demanded. I take him to be a very honest good Man, and believe he will still do what is right if I can show him that he was wrong. Cousin Jonathan will calculate it for us.

You shall have a Copy of the Catalogue of Books as soon as I can find it; but you will see it sooner in the Hands of Cousin Williams, to whom the Books were consigned. Those you recommended of Dr Stennet are among them.

I am glad to hear that your Daughter's Health is better. My Love to her and your Grand daughter, in which this Family joins with

Your affectionate Brother

B FRANKLIN

When you have a little Leisure write
me an Account of all the Relations
we have left in New England
Oct. 29. I inclose the Catalogue

"I never had a Tast for High Life"

[Printed first, and hitherto only, in Duane, *Letters to Benjamin Franklin*, pp. 137-138, with about half the text omitted; here first printed in full from the manuscript in the American Philosophical Society. The reference to "Popes mind" is to Pope's *An Essay on Man*, IV, 80. Samuel Bradford had married a daughter of Jonathan Williams Sr. The bearer of this letter to Philadelphia, and of other letters, was "Mr Wouters," not otherwise identified. The sickness of Jonathan Williams Sr. was described by his son Jonathan Jr. in a letter to Franklin of September 6, 1789, as the result largely of the elder Williams' addiction to a mystical philosophy which he had derived from Jakob Boehme in the year 1772. This letter is in the American Philosophical Society. The accounts of Franklin and Williams for 1764 to 1773 show that in

[243]

March 1773 Williams paid £5 12s. for "Behmens Works" ordered from London through Franklin.]

DEAR BROTHER   Boston Novr 7—1785

You must Indulge me in writing often to you since I cannot see you, this is the third since yr Last to me I should not have wrot again so soon for fear of being troblesom but on seeing Mr williams He Desiered me to make an Apology to you for his not writing, Said he had been Giulty of a Criminal Neglect, that he had not the Less Gratitude for all yr Favours or Veneration for your character, Says He has Atempted Several times to write you to congratulate you on yr Arival but his Afflictions have Presd on Him so hard he could not compose his mind to write; and Indeed He is in a Deplorable Situation, Distress and Anguish in His Countenance, no Apetite, to his food, Emaciated to amazing degree; and so feble he can hardly walk, He says he shall not Live to see you & I am of the mind he will not if he has not speedy Releaf, he says there is no cure for a Distresd mind, his wife tells me he Poisons Himself working on Nights trying Experiments with Poisonous Drugs but this is what she must not be soposd to know, I think it is Likely you know from his Son Jonathan the Situation of his Famely, and some Diffeculties he is under which are Atended with such Agrevations as he is not Able to bare. His wife soports her self Exeding well under all.

as to my self I Live very much to my Likeing, I never had a Tast for High Life, for Large companys, & Entertainments, I am of Popes mind that Health, Peace, and Competance, come as near to Happynes as is Atainable in this Life, and I am in a good measure In possession of all three at Present, if they are at Times a Litle Infringd ocationaly or by Accedent, I Vew it as the common Lot of all and am not much Disturbed.

our Friend Cathrine Greene Expresd such Lively Joy at the News of yr Arival that her children tould Her it had thron her in to Histericks but she says she is not subject to that Disorder She tells me you have Honord them with a Leter

I wrot the Above some time ago since which Mr Williams is

something beter gos abroad a Litle & at times more chearfull but as I have this Day an opertunity to send it by a Gentleman who has conections with Mr Bache going directly there I send it, it may not be Amiss to you. no won Els need see my Leters

I dined with this Gentleman at Mr Bradfords & Ventured to Invite Him to come & Drink Tea with us which he Readily accepted, & very Politely offred to carrie your Leter, we Live all ways Cleen and Look Decent and I wanted he should tell you he saw me at home.

my Daughter has Returnd from the country much mended in her Health her Husband is Expected Every Day from the west indies has a prospect of doing beter than comon if he gits in saif.

She with my Grandaughter Jenny Mecom Remember there Duty to you. Remember Love to all yrs from yr Affectionat Sister

JANE MECOM

"It would be cleaver to have thirteen Stars"

[Printed first, and hitherto only, in Duane, *Letters to Benjamin Franklin*, pp. 138-140, without the name of "Mr Olever of Chelsey"; here printed entire from the manuscript in the American Philosophical Society. "Cousen Jonathan," that is, Jonathan Williams Jr., had brought his aunt the catalogue of the books presented to the town of Franklin, and was now learning with her to make crown soap. "Mr Olever" was Nathaniel Oliver. His son Daniel graduated from Dartmouth in 1785, and in 1787 became pastor of the Second Congregational Church of Beverly, Massachusetts. Nathaniel Oliver's son Nathan, under arrest with Samuel Cleansey, James Thompson, and John Atkinson, had been convicted in the County Court of Quarter Sessions, Philadelphia, of "a riot and assault and battery," but their fines had been remitted on November 5, according to *Colonial Records of Pennsylvania*, XIV, 571. See Franklin's reply to this letter, dated January 1, 1786. Young Nathan Oliver (whose name is given as Nathaniel in Boston Registry Records, XXIV, Births, 1700-1800, 311) was a half-brother of the Rev. Daniel Oliver, and son of his father's second wife Sarah, daughter of Captain Thomas Hill. The "Grandmother on his mothers side" with whom Jane Mecom had been long acquainted seems to have been Captain Hill's wife Hannah Cushing, married on July 13, 1727, exactly two weeks before Jane Franklin and Edward Mecom were married.]

DEAR BROTHER
Boston Novr 30. 1785

I rcd yrs by Cousen Jonathan Williams with the Catalogue for which I thank you and shall with Pleasure comply with all you desier, the Leaches are sett up for the soap we make it next week, Cousen Jonathan is very Alert in Assisting and I am Pleasd that it will not Totally Die. I have no stamp and I fancy if any should be made for America it would be cleaver to have thirteen Stars, for the Crown Soap now vended among us is as contemptible as the British Head that now wears won, dirty Stinking Stuff.

I yesterday recd your kind Leter you wrot me while you were on the Rhoad in France, your constant Atention to my comfort and satisfaction affects me much, that thare could be such an Easey carrige for you by Land how happy. I wish we had such in America, you were keept at work till the Last minute and Glorious work have you Performed; may God still Prosper & soport you.

I have began the Acount of our Relations and shall send it in my Next, Cousen Jonathan & I have not yet had time to gather without other company to cast up that mater abou Mr Vernons Bill, but we shall take that time while we are makeing soap.

There is in your Gaol a young man son to Mr Olever of Chelsey who is Dead who is condemnd for an Assault, he has Neither friends or Relations there His Father Died Poor but he has a Brother who has workd him self with the help of Charity throw Dartmouth College and is now studing Devinity, I have ben many years Acquainted with his Grandmother on his mothers side a worthy woman but in Low circumstances & now near Expiering with the Palsey I sopose on the strength of that acquaintance He thought he might make Aplication to me, he says his Brother writs him he is Perfectly Innocent of the Crime lade to his charge, that it was commited by a nother person blonging to the same Vesel who is runaway,

They think you can do Every thing & I know you will do Every thing that is Proper & convenant for you to do but I very much fear the Impropriety of my giveing you the Troble of so much as Reading this Acount of the matter but they Plead your Humanity & I was forcd to Promis I would mention it to you.

If the Lad writs the Truth & there can be a way found out that will Ansure the Penalty of the Law by Binding him to serve some won at Sea, which he has been Used to, that he may not suffer throw a winter in a Prison & your Speaking about the Affair will Prevent it I wish it but I know nothing of the Lad he may Deserve a Halter for all I know notwithstanding his being a Branch of a Good famely, you can know the Truth of the mater Prehaps if you Inquier but I fear I have made two free with you on the Acount forgive me & tell me so if I have.

My Daughter Joins me in most Dutyfull and and Affectionat Regards

JANE MECOM

"I ought to let you know the Truth"

[Here first printed from the manuscript in the American Philosophical Society. Jane Mecom appears to be saying that the soap she now sent to Franklin was made at the house of Catharine Greene, but she actually meant that she had made there the soap of a particular green which he had asked for in his letter of October 27. Peter Collas on October 12, 1779, had written that he was sending Franklin 27 cakes of crown soap made by Jane Mecom at Governor Greene's. The Collas letter is in the American Philosophical Society.]

DEAR BROTHER   Boston Decr 29—1785

I send with this a Box of soap containing Sixty Pounds it is good & soled but not so high a green colar as the sample you sent I thought it best to make it acording to Ruil as cousen Jonathan was to Inspect it and the Extraordenary Green colar of that was Produced by a circumstance which I should not be willing to Put in Practice if I had opertunity fearing it might not be wholsom if any of it should be Used as medison, I made it at our Friend Greenes in a Brass ketle [*interlined*: by the way it must all ways be brass or copper] & some circumstance which I have forgot causd an Intermition of I beleve a week

betwen the first & second Boiling considerable of the Soap
Sticking to the kittle & was clean   I did not have it washd but
turnd it down to keep it from dirt and when I came to use it it
was grown Green round where the Soap Stuck & not considering
it as I have done since & thinking the salt Lye might settle it I
proceded to finishe it, I know I Deserve your censure for this and
feel Ashamed to confess it but I know you Pry in to all Apearances and I ought to let you know the Truth I have also a conjecture but not a certinty that by some mistake in the weights
I put in a Larger Proportion of wax than I ought, this I intend
to try if I Live till Spring & let you know, I have Left the Exact
Recipt in cousen Jonathands hands to take a coppy & shall send
it to you, I hope you continue as well as when you come & do
not over Fatigue your self with Biusnes. Love to all from yr
Affectionat Sister   JANE MECOM

P S as you Love to know the meaning of all Apearances I must
tell you the Reason of my sending some Irreglar Peices of Soap
in the Box, the mold to cool it in is made Exactly twelve Inches
in width and twelve inshes in Depth but much Longer than I
had Soap to fill we therefore fixd a board to shorten it without
taking the proper Dementions and did not take the care I might
have done in cuting up so that I had not Even cakes anouf to
make the weight I had a mind to send neither are they Regular
as they ought to be if they were for Sale which shuld be Exactly
Eaght ouzs when cut up and many of those were ten & I have
a gage on purpose to Regulate them singly, but I thought it of
no consequenc now, and the Rouf Peeces will Ansure for your
self and Famely   J M

"The Name of the Street you live in"

[Printed first, and hitherto only, in Goodman, *A Benjamin Franklin
Reader*, pp. 771-772; here printed from the manuscript in the American
Philosophical Society. Franklin had been accustomed to send his letters
to Jane Mecom in care of Jonathan Williams Sr. "Mr. Mifflin" was
Thomas Mifflin, who in 1788 succeeded Franklin as President of the
Supreme Executive Council of Pennsylvania.]

Philada Jan. 1. 1786

MY DEAR SISTER,

Our good God has brought us old Folks, the last Survivors of 17 Brothers & Sisters, to the Beginning of a new Year. The Measure of Health & Strength we enjoy at so advanc'd an Age, now near Fourscore, is a great Blessing. Let us be chearful & thankful.

I received in their time your kind Letters of Nov 7. & 30. I am sorry our Cousin W. troubles himself with chemical Experiments for which he does not seem to have had the proper previous Instruction, to prevent their being dangerous to his Health. You do not explain to me what the Difficulties are that distrest his Mind, and which I wish to know. I am glad to hear he is better, that your Daughter is mended, & your Son-in-law has good Prospects.

Young Oliver's Fine was remitted before my Arrival, but he lay in Gaol for his Fees. He is now, as I hear, discharged, thro' the Good Offices of Mr Mifflin.

Send me the Name of the Street you live in, that I may direct my Letters so as not to give Cousin W. any Trouble. My Love to him & his Family, and to yours, from your affectionate Brother

B FRANKLIN

This Family joins in Love &c

"I have two favours to Ask of you now"

[Printed first, and hitherto only, in Duane, *Letters to Benjamin Franklin*, pp. 140-142, without the enclosures. Here printed, with the enclosures, from the manuscripts in the American Philosophical Society. *The Life of the Late Earl of Chesterfield: or, The Man of the World*, printed in London and reprinted in Philadelphia for John Sparhawk in 1775, is the most likely source for the "Ansure" of Chesterfield "to his sons widow on such an Ocation." It is on page 386: "Upon my word, madam, you interest yourself in the state of my existence more than I do myself; for it is worth the care of neither of us. I ordered my *valet de chambre*, according to your orders, to inform you of my safe arrival here; to which I can add nothing, being neither better nor worse." "Mrs killcup" was Lois Rogers (Britton) Kilcup, widow of Dudson

Kilcup who had been one of the witnesses of John Franklin's will in January 1756. This "Mrs church" has not been further identified. It is clear that Jane Mecom knew Franklin's *Petition of the Letter* Z slyly referred to Ralph Izard, who "when he," she says without benefit of antecedent, "was at Rhoad Island," in 1780, "talked very freely about Dr. Franklin."]

DEAR BROTHER   Boston 6 Janr 1786

I want much to know how you are and have been since you have been at home but fear to be two offten Inquisitive Least I should Provoke you to Return me such an Ansure as chesterfeild did to his sons widow on such an Ocation [*crossed out*: which would brake my hart I remember you wonce bad me not be fussy] [*interlined*: forgive I wont think it Posable]

I have alredy wrot you concerning the soap in a Leter to go with the Box, I now send the Recipt, the catalogue of Relations, and all concerning the money I recved of Mr Vernon, it will be a Large Paquet but I thought it best to send it by the Post. Let me know whither you Aprovd or disaprovd of my writing to Mr Vernon, I want (now you are so near) to have the Privilege of your correction, and Instruction, in Every thing that can come to your knolidge, I know I am troblesom to you in some things Pirticularly about that Poor young Lad in jail I fear my maner of writing was Rude to you, & Inhuman of him, but I am glad to hear he is cleard and on his way home.

by the Recomdation of a cople of old women Like my Self, Mrs killcup, & Mrs church, I was soliseted to beg your asistance to a Poor woman whose Husband was killd in Hopkinss Fleet, was a 2d Lieutenant, his Name was Philip Gaudin has much Due to her the Agents she says is at Philadelphia   I Evaded it as much as I could but I don't know but she will come again when she has got all her Vouchers Reddy, all that are in troble & know I am your Sister seem to think I can do somthing for them so that you must give me some directions how to Proceed and say Hither to shalt thou go and no farther or I shall always be in Pain on such Application and think you will be Afraid to Recive a Leter from me for fear of being Teasd.

I have two favours to Ask of you now your New Alphabet of

the English Language, and the Petition of the Letter Z it would be a Feast to General Greenes wife if I may be Premitted to Let her see it, when he was at Rhoad Island he talkd very freely of Dr Franklin & she tould him if he talkd so along the country as he went to Philadelphia the People would stone him for they all Adored you but I heard he was not discouridged, I forgot to tell you in my Last that Mr williams was Bravely again Eats & Drinks and was chearfull & I hop continus so but I have not see him this three weeks.

I rejoyce in Every Honourable mention that is made of you but I can not find in my Hart to be Pleasd at your Accepting the Goverment of the State and Therefore have not congratulated you on it, I fear it will Fatigue you two much

Enough of all conscious you will say and therefore

I shall only add yr Affectionat Sister

JANE MECOM

ENCLOSURE I: "RECIPT" FOR MAKING CROWN SOAP

[Here first printed from an incomplete and damaged manuscript in the American Philosophical Society.]

it must be taken of yr mould which [*word torn off*] is to be Redy Repared with some small [?] tises in the sides clos to the botom [?] to Let of any Ley first you cant avoid puting in with the curd there is also to be taked in a cours Lining [?] Smooth [?] which when the sides of the mould are taken off will Peal off with out any wast of the wax the time for cooling will be acording to the Quantity, it ought to be cut as soon as throw cool Least it grow two hard, & not before because it will then twist & be more apt to crack, the Gages for cutting up must be in size I think about Six Inches Long & three Broad & in thikness about three quarters of an Insh I have not the Gage by me threfore cannot be Positive but when they are first cut up the wey about half a Pound they are Stampd Emediatly Every slab of it is cut or the surfice will Dry & not take the Impreshon so well, I think you must Remember

[251]

the Large Slabs are cut with a strong Brass wier (for Iron is Equally Prenicous to this as to the Dye) and the small cakes [with?] strong thrid or silk & as it is all most Imposable to cut them Perfictly of a size we have a small Gage Just fitt for won cake that we Pare any that needs it

N B the stamp as also the wier is touchd with a Litle Sweet oyl now & then as it needs it, the wax must not have been coulered before hand with any thing to make it Green: if the Plank the moulds are made with are not very thick they will soon warp & be unfitt for use, no other wood is as suitable as Pine

ENCLOSURE 2: WILLIAM VERNON'S OBLIGATION

[Here first printed from the manuscripts in the American Philosophical Society.]

the Demand was 840 Livres which is equal to £48 Pounds Lawfull Money at the Exchange of 17.10 for a Pound Lawfull Money

155 Dollars at 6/ amounts to .... £46., 10.
Balance due 1. 10
                                                    ——————
                                                    48. 0

the very Individual cash Mr Vernon Paid me was crowns and half crowns* to the amount of won hundred and fivety five Dolars the crowns you know Passes hear for Six & Eight pence, the Dolars for Six Shillings I will Enclose you a coppy of what I wrot him after I recd it but had no Ansure   J M

[*Marginal note*] * I told this to cousen Jonathan Least that might make some Diffrence

                    a coppy of a Leter I wrote from
                    Warwick to Mr Vernon at Newport
Sir
I have receivd by the hand of Colle ward a Hundred and fifty five Dolars on the Bill you Accepted from Dr Franklin. I was Informed before I came from Boston there was a New Regulation concerning the Exchange from France,* but that

it did not take Place till since that Bill was Drawn as my Brother mentiond in his Leter to me it was a 160 Dolars which I am certain he would not have done had not your son Receivd that sum from him I Look upon it as a Debt of Honour, & from the character I had Receivd of the Gentleman on whom it was Drawn I Expected to be Honourable Paid

you Sir are Sensible if you had occasion to have sent a Bill to France the Purchase would have cost you Six Pr Ct above Par. When you consider these circumstances I am convinced you will think it but Reasonable to make up the full Sum, which if you should Determine to do you may have an opportunity by madam Greene, who is now in Newport whose Return I shall wait hear for

your Humble Servant

I had no Ansure

[*In the margin*] *Cusen Jonathan says it ought to be & he Pays since he came hear as he has stated it in the bill

"It should not be made publick"

[The third and fifth paragraphs of this letter were printed in Sparks, *Familiar Letters*, pp. 203-204n., as "to a relation." The whole letter is here first printed from the manuscript in the American Philosophical Society. The petition of Elizabeth Gaudin, of whom Jane Mecom had written on January 6, to the Continental Congress and the inconclusive report on the matter are in the *Naval Records of the American Revolution* (Washington, 1906), pp. 211-212. A letter-press copy of Franklin's letter to Mrs. Gaudin is in the Library of Congress, but the copy he sent to his sister is missing; as is also, unfortunately, the "Account of our Relations in New-England" which he acknowledged. Ezek Hopkins of Rhode Island was commander in chief of the Continental Navy from December 1775 to January 1777.]

Philada Jan. 24. 1786.

My dear Sister,

I have received your Letter of the 6th Inst. with the Receipt for making Crown Soap, which is very clearly written, and I thank you for it, as well as for the Account of our Relations in New-England, who are more numerous than I imagin'd, tho' I think you have omitted some; (unless they are all dead) I mean a Family at Providence, their Name I forget, but the Mother was a Daughter of our Brother Samuel, or a Granddaughter.

As to my Health which you enquire after, it is much the same as it has been for some Years past. The Pains caus'd sometimes by the Stone do not augment, my appetite continues good, and my Temper generally chearful; my Strength & Activity diminishing indeed but by slow degrees. [*Words erased*] I don't know what the Answer was which Chesterfield gave to his Son's Widow.

Your Letter to Mr Vernon seems to me very proper and well-written, and I think he was wrong in detaining the Five Dollars. But when we consider that he was under no legal Obligation to pay a debt contracted by his Son, we may be glad that we have recover'd so much of it; and that when it is so common to pay the Interest of an old Debt in ill Language, he has paid you only in Silence. It is a Family I have formerly been in Friendship with, and I would not have you trouble them with any farther Demands.

I have receiv'd a Letter from the Widow you mention as having had a Husband kill'd in Hopkins's Fleet, but she has sent me no Vouchers on which I might found an Application in her Favour, and I am afraid she has no other Proof of the Fact but a *strong Persuasion*, as she tells me, "he was in the Fleet *as sure as I am now alive*, and lost his Life in their Cause." and afterwards says, "I have waited near Eight Years in hopes that he was taken and would return, but now my hopes are all fled;—that he fell a Victim in their Cause I *have not the least doubt.*" It is strange that in eight Years she had not been able to learn whether he had been kill'd or not; and as the Congress long since appointed commissioners to examine and settle the Claims of Persons or the Representatives of Persons who had served in their Ships or Armies, which Commissioners are doubtless provided with Muster Rolls of the several Corps, I wonder at her not having apply'd directly to them.—But there are People in the World, I have met with many such, who love to have a kind of Pocket Complaint, always at hand, with which they endeavour to procure Compassion, by exhibiting it every where and to every body but those whose proper Business it would be to redress it: These they avoid, lest their darling Complaint being examined should be found to have no Foundation. I have written an Answer to her Letter, which I enclose.—If you should have any future Applications of this sort made to you to be handed to me, I think you may avoid giving your self any trouble with them, by acquainting the People, that I was absent all the War, must be unacquainted with the Facts, am now at a distance from Congress, have at present no Connection with that Body; and that the Application is more proper to be made to the Delegates from their own State than to me.

My new Alphabet is in a printed Book of my Pieces, which I will send you the first Opportunity I have by Water. The Petition of Z is inclos'd. It should not be made publick.

I do not wonder at your blaming me for accepting the Government. We have all of us Wisdom enough to judge what others ought to do, or not to do in the Management of their Affairs; and 'tis possible I might blame you as much if you were to accept the Offer of a young Husband. My example may teach you not to be too confident in your own Prudence; as it teaches me not to be surpriz'd at such an Event should it really happen.

We all join in Love, &c. and I am ever

Your affectionate Brother,

B FRANKLIN

ENCLOSURE: *The Petition of Z*

[This *Petition* was first printed by Sparks, *Works*, VI, 304-305, without the marginal notes, whether because Sparks printed from another copy or because he did not wish to offend the descendants of Ralph Izard of South Carolina. It is here first printed with the notes, from the manuscript in the American Philosophical Society. Since the original *Tatler* ran to only 271 numbers, the "No 1778" was Franklin's close-mouthed jest and an indication of the year 1778 when Izard was most annoying to the American Commissioners in Paris, and when this skit may have been written. Though Izard had in fact abused Franklin more than Arthur Lee, Franklin in his satire offers no defense of himself and shows no sign of personal resentment.]

BENJAMIN FRANKLIN AND JANE MECOM

FROM THE TATLER N 1778

TO THE WORSHIPFUL ISAAC BICKERSTAFF, ESQ;

CENSOR-GENERAL

THE PETITION OF THE LETTER Z COMMONLY

CALLED EZZARD, ZED, OR IZARD,

MOST HUMBLY SHEWETH,

He was always talking of his Family and of his being a Man of Fortune.

That your Petitioner is of as high extraction, and has as good an Estate as any other Letter of the Alphabet.

And complaining of his being treated, not with due Respect

That there is therefore no reason why he should be treated as he is with Disrespect and Indignity.

At the tail of the Commission, of Ministers

That he is not only plac'd at the Tail of the Alphabet, when he had as much Right as any other to be at the Head; but is, by the Injustice of his enemies totally excluded from the Word WISE, and his Place injuriously filled by a little, hissing, crooked, serpentine, venemous Letter called s, when it must be evident to your Worship, and to all the World, that Double U, I, S. E do not spell or sound *Wize*, but *Wice*.

He was not of the Commission for France, A Lee being preferr'd to him, which made him very angry; and the Character here given of S, is just what he in his Passion gave Lee.

Your Petitioner therefore prays that the Alphabet may by your Censorial Authority be reformed, and that in Consideration of his *Long-Suffering* & *Patience* he may be placed at the Head of it; that S may be turned out of the Word Wise, and the Petitioner employ'd instead of him;

The most impatient Man alive

And your Petitioner (as in Duty bound) shall ever pray, &c.

Z

Mr Bickerstaff having examined the Allegations of the above Petition, judges and determines, that Z be admonished to be content with his Station, forbear Reflections upon his Brother

Letters, & remember his own small Usefulness, and the little Occasion there is for him in the Republick of Letters, since S, whom he so despises, can so well serve instead of him.

"That New & more Beautifull Edition"

[Here first printed from the manuscript in the American Philosophical Society. In the Boston *Directory* for 1789 Henry Roby, glazier, is listed in Fish Street, and in that for 1796, at "head of Lewis's wharf house Unity Street." Jedidiah Parker is listed, with no occupation given, as living in Unity Street in the *Directory* for 1796. The "Daughter to our Brother Samuel" was Elizabeth, who married William Compton in 1732, and had five daughters and a son. The *Providence Gazette* for July 3, 1773, recorded the death of Elizabeth Compton, wife of William Compton; and for August 29, 1786, the death of William Compton, who had for many years been town sergeant. *Vital Records of Rhode Island*, XIII, 290. The "Grandson of our Sister Harris's whose Name is Fullar who I hear is a Genius" was Joseph Fuller, son of Jacob Fuller and Ann Harris, and grandson of Ann (or Anne) Franklin Harris, sister of Jane Mecom and Benjamin Franklin. Joseph Fuller was captain of a Rhode Island militia regiment in the Revolution and was called Deacon Joseph Fuller at the time of his death in Providence on April 7, 1822, aged seventy-six. W. H. Fuller, *Genealogy of Some Descendants of Captain Matthew Fuller, John Fuller of Newton, John Fuller of Lynn, John Fuller of Ipswich, Robert Fuller of Dorchester and Dedham* (1914), pp. 177, 231-232. Jane Mecom's grandson, Josiah Flagg, then twenty-five, had written to Franklin on January 24 of this year, from Petersburg, Virginia, saying he desired a clerkship in Philadelphia: the letter is in the American Philosophical Society. "I will Desier cousen Jonathan to send you what I wrot to him about it" means that Jane Mecom would ask Jonathan Williams Jr. to send Franklin a copy of the letter she had written to Josiah Flagg about his "Audacity."]

MY DEAR BROTHER   Boston febr. 21.—1786

your kind Leter wrote on Newyears Day came to my hand on the first of febr and I shuld have Ansured it sooner but I had some uncommon hinderances no otherweiys Disagreable. we have Accustomed our selves so Litle to call the streets by there names that we who Live in them do not know it, my Next dore Neighbour Mr Roby calls it Clow Street, the Register for 1784 calls it Eliott Street, but another Neighbour Mr Parker who was Brought up in it says the Records of his Deedes call it Unity

Street, which I beleve must be Right. the other Information you Desier I inclose I was writing this when cousen Jonathan came in an brought me your Agreable Packet, I did not know Mrs Gauden had wrote to you for tho she gave me a more Plausible Story than she appears to have given you I advised her not to write till she could git all nesesary Vouchers, Poor wooman I beleve she had none, & is much in the condition you discribe.

The Name of the Famely you mention as Living at Provedence was Compton, the woman was Daughter to our Brother Samuel, She has been Dead some years, he had a Famely of children what Number I know not, won Daughter I heard was comfortably married I forgot her Name.

the first time I was at Provedence after I came from Philadelphia I went to the House saw the then Present Wife and two Daughters, I Left my Name and that I shuld be at mr Welcom[e] Arnolds but have Nither seen or heard any thing of the Famely since, and I did forgit to mention them. I forgot also a Grandson of our Sister Harris's whos Name is Fullar who I hear is a Genius & Lives at Provedence, I think his Occupation is a Shop Joiner I never saw him, there are Divers more of that Famely but I Dont know where.

I am happy to know your Disorder does not augment and that your Appetite continues Good and that you are chearfull, that helps us a long among many Litle Annoyances which we cannot Expect to be totaly freed from till we Atain to the Injoyment of that New & more Beautifull Edition we hope for in a Future State.

I am Proud that you commend what I wrot to Mr Vernon I never had the Least Intention to say any more about it but to give you the Information you desiered.

I ask your Pardon if I appeard to Blam you for accepting the Goverment I knew you must have had Wise & Good Reasons for your Conduct but I feard the Consequence of so close Atention as Apered to me to be Nesesary in this Difficult Situation of Affairs. may God give you help & Prosperity

My son Collas is come home well, & my Dayghter beter in Health, they with my Grandayghter Jenny mecom Remember there Duty to you & Joyne in Love to yr children & Grandchildren with your Affectionat Sister

JANE MECOM

febry 26   cousen Jonathan has Just now Informed me that my Grandson Josiah Flagg has Aplied to you to Put him in to Busness, tho he is my Grandson & I wish him well settled to somthing he can git his Liveing by I am Angry with him for his Audacity in writing to you on such an Acount, he is a Poor unfortunate youth by haveing had a fall in his childhood [*interlined*: made him Lame in won knee] that desinables him for most sorts of Busnes & has too Proud a Spirit to conform to the occupation he was Taught, & what his capasety is for Any other I am not qualified to Inform you tho I am his Grandmother, he has been at so Grat a Distance from me Ever since the war commencd, but in ansure to all my Inquieries I have allways heard he behaved Honestly & uprightly & he has Apeared so when he has been to see me but has had so few advantages that it must be the highest Impropriety in him to Adres you on such an ocation

I can write no more for fear I Loose this opertunity of sending it I will Desier cousen Jonathan to send you what I wrot to him about it

J M

"*You may possibly teach me a better Method*"

[Printed first in Bigelow, *Works*, IX, 311-312, from the letter-press copy in the Library of Congress, from which the letter is here printed more accurately than in Bigelow, or in Smyth, *Writings*, IX, 506-508. Franklin had sent 26 (not 22) cakes of the soap to Ferdinand Grand with a letter of March 20 of that year, naming the friends in Paris among whom they were to be distributed. Smyth, *Writings*, IX, 497-498.]

Philada April 8. 1786

DEAR SISTER,

I received your kind Letter of the 21st of February. I have also received the Box of Soap, the Substance of which appears to be very good, but its Consistence had probably been affected by the Frost, for unless very tenderly and cautiously handled, the Cakes would crumble into little Pieces between one's fingers. However having an Opportunity of sending some to my Friends, in France, who much admir'd what I had of you formerly, I with some difficulty took out 22 Cakes, which I wrapt separately in spongy Paper, hoping that as they dry'd they might consolidate, and the infinite Number of little Cracks that appear'd in them be closed, and the Parts again united, and so I sent them away in a small Box. But having since dry'd a Cake very gradually, I fear I shall be disappointed in that Expectation, for it seems as crumbly as before, and comes to pieces in the Water, so that I am sorry that I sent any of it away, till I had consulted you upon it, who probably must have met with the like Accident before, and might know of some Remedy. Business having prevented my Writing, Sally has been making an Experiment. She put 3 or 4 pound of the Crumbs, about the Size of Chestnuts into a little Kettle with some Water, and over a slow Fire melted them together, and when the whole was uniformly fluid, laded it out into little Paper Pans of the Size of the Cakes. These grew stiff when cold, but were rather soft and shrunk greatly in drying. Being now dry, they are exceedingly hard, close-grain'd and solid, and appear to have all the Qualities of excellent Crown Soap, only in drying they are twisted and warp'd out of Shape; wherefore I have not continu'd the Process, but resolved to send you this particular Account, thinking you may possibly teach me a better Method.

Capt. All is just arriv'd here, who has given me the Pleasure of hearing that you were very well a few Weeks since: he says he does not remember you to have ever look'd better, or to be more active. I continue much as I have been for some time past, and am always   Your affectionate Brother

                                              B FRANKLIN

Draw upon me for the Expence
of the Soap, and your Bill shall
be paid on Sight.

[260]

Josiah Flagg to Jane Mecom

[Here first printed from the manuscript in the American Philosophical Society. Josiah Flagg had come from Virginia to Philadelphia, after letters to Franklin dated January 24 and February 18 and now in the American Philosophical Society, to visit his uncle and had been hospitably received. He had come by water, in the company of a Captain Robinson who had introduced the youth to Franklin: probably Isaiah Robinson, of Philadelphia, who had carried letters between Deborah Franklin and her husband and had commanded the armed vessel *Andrea Doria* during the war. Josiah, asking his grandmother not to give away the secret that he had "spun out three Years under the patronage of St Crispin" (that is, worked as a shoemaker), caused her to accuse him of "Ridiculous Vanety" in her letter of May 3, and of the want of "Verasity" mentioned in her letter of July 21. On May 3, sending Josiah's letter of April 17 to Franklin, she asked him to return it, but this seems to have been overlooked and the letter remained among the Franklin Papers.]

Hon'd Grandma.   Philadelphia April 17. 1786

I have the pleasure to inform you of my Safe arrival in this City from Virginia after a passage of fourteen Days, which in good weather is accomplish'd in three prior to my Intention of Visiting this place, I wrote my Uncle Franklin, and he was kind enough to Honour me with a favourable Answer. I was Introduc'd to him by Capt. Robinson a Citizen of Phila who came passenger with me, and was received in a very cordial and Affectionate manner. I expect to be employ'd in writing for him three or four months, and if you would use your Influence with him in a Recommendation of me, it may perhaps be attended with favourable Consequences. I endeavour to behave as well as my slender Education and Knowledge of the World will admit,—No mans Abilities are so remarkably shining, as not to stand in need of the praises of a Friend, a patron, and even a proper Opportunity to Recommend them to the Notice of the World.

If you will be kind enough to point out to his Excellcy my good Intentions, and the Character which I have ever sustaind Unblemish'd, it may have a pleasing Effect.—I was Candid with him in telling of my indigent Circumstances, but I never told him I spun out three Years under the patronage of St Crispin and I humbly beg you'd omit that in your Letter to him.

Dear Grandma now is the time for me to appear to the best Advantage, and your kind Assistance will Confer a peculiar favour on your ever Dutiful

Grandson
JOSIAH FLAGG

Please to give my Love to Uncle and Aunt Collas and Cousin Jenny

"My Dear good Gentileman"

[Here first printed from the manuscript in the American Philosophical Society. A "chease of Thirty wight" was a cheese of thirty pounds weight.]

DEAR BROTHER   Boston Apr 22, 1786

Yours of the 8th Inst found me at the Soap copper Indevouring to gratifie you as I had Promised with some Soap Green as well as good, and have Accordingly added more wax than the Proportion which is a third, I have now Put 12 lb Wax to 20 lb of Tallow the Produce I shall send you by the first Vesel, but I am much mortified at your Disopointment of the other, (I had not the Least Aprehention of such a thing I never saw a Like Instance nor Even knew the Frost to have such Influence on it Exept it was Exposed singly when very Green) it was Exellent Good & the Peeces I reserved fror my self Remane so haveing had them in a warm Dry Room,

Prehaps an Accedent some what similar I have Expearanced this winter may comfort you concerning what you sent away, we Bought a chease of Thirty wight that had stood in the Frost till it was so crumbly we could not cut a bit as big as a dolar that would hold together but keeping it in a warm celar somewhat Damp some time after I could cut a considerable slice, who knows but a warm Damp Vesel may have the same Effect on the Soap; for the Recovery of what you have Left, I at first thought it might Ansure to make a fine clear small ley to Desolve it in & carry it thro the second Proces as when first made, but on second thots I should Prefer my Nieces Menagement as more certain, with this Difference to Use as litle water as Posable to make it Uniformly Fluid, & Cool it all in a body in a Draw (with a cloath in side) or git a Litle Trough made on Purpose with a few holes in the Botom & the sides to Let Down when it is cold, leting it stand in a boddy as long as it will bare without being too hard to cut up—and then make your Gage as much larger then the size as you Percive the others to have shrunk and after cutting to keep them in a close Pile covered with a cloath till Dry Anouf to be out of danger of warping, Observe it must not be Desolved in Iron but Brass or Copper,

I am obligd to Capt All for giveing you such a Favourable Ida of yr sister, the truth is when I am in Agreable company it Raises my Spirits & might then have some Influence on my Activity & for the Gratest Part of my time when I am sitting at home I am apt to Imagine as Samson did when He Lost his Hare, that I can Arise & Shake my Self & Go forth as at other times but on Tryal Like him I am wofully Disopointed & find my Feet cripling & my Breath Short, but I am still chearful for that is my Natural Temper and am as you Advise me thankfull that I Escape many Grevious clamities Incedent to old, Age & that my Dear Brother Does not grow wors of his.

And now my Dear good Gentileman how could you mention my Drawing on you for the cost of a Litle Soap when all I Injoy is of yr Bounty I could not help crying when I Read it the Pleasure I Injoy in the hops of Gratifieing you is a full compensation, I hope the Litle I have now made will be more sucksesfull, Remember my Love to Mr & Mrs Bache & all the young Famely

from your Affectionat sister

JANE MECOM

I know there is few words spelt
Right & it is miserable bloted but
my Dear Brother will Excuse it as
I have not time to correct it.

[263]

"My Proposal of a new Alphabet"

[First printed in Bigelow, *Works*, IX, 313, from the letter-press copy in the Library of Congress, and here printed from the letter actually sent, now in the Yale University Library. Franklin's "Proposal of a new Alphabet" had appeared as *A Scheme for a new Alphabet and reformed mode of Spelling* in Vaughan's collection of 1779. The grandson who presented his duty to Jane Mecom was Josiah Flagg.]

Philada April 25. 1786

DEAR SISTER,

I wrote you a long letter lately about the Soap, which I suppos'd to have become crumbly by means of Frost; and acquainting you that we had made some of the Crumbs solid again, by re-melting them with Water. I farther requested your Advice whether to re-melt it all, & in what manner. That you may better understand the Case, I send you herewith some of the crumbly Soap, and a Piece of that which we consolidated by re-melting the Crumbs. But since I wrote that Letter I find that a few of the Cakes which appear'd ready to fall to pieces, being set separately on their Edges upon a Shelf in a Closet to dry gradually, seem now to have become very firm; and I have therefore this day taken all out of the Box, and set them to dry in the same slow manner, perhaps they may all grow firm, and make the re-melting unnecessary.

I send you also with this, one of the Books in which is printed my Proposal of a new Alphabet, which you desired to see. I am, ever, your affectionate Brother

B FRANKLIN

Your Grandson presents his Duty

Mrs Mecom

"The most honourable of all our Employments"

[Printed first, and hitherto only, in the *New England Historical and Genealogical Register*, XXVII (1873), 249, from a manuscript formerly in the possession of Josiah Flagg and his descendants and now in the New England Historic Genealogical Society. There is also a letter-press copy in the Library of Congress. The letter is here printed from the original as sent.]

DEAR SISTER,   Philada May 2. 1786.

I wrote to you lately by a Vessel, and sent you two Volumes of my Papers that they have printed in London. In one of them you will find the new Alphabet you desired.

Your Grandson Flagg is now with me. I give him some present Employment in Writing for me. He presents his Duty.

Temple is busy establishing his Farm, that which was formerly his Father's near Ancocus. He seems seriously intent upon a Country Life, which I much approve, as being the most independent, the most useful & therefore the most honourable of all our Employments. The rest of us are well and join in Love to you and yours. I should write to Cousin Jonathan, but that I am told he is coming here. My Love to that Family, and believe me ever

                            Your affectionate Brother

                                        B FRANKLIN

"I have wrote too sevre to Poor Josiah"

[Here first printed from the manuscript in the American Philosophical Society. The letter Jane Mecom had written before this to Josiah Flagg is missing. The "character" of her grandson she had sent Franklin "some time ago" was in her postscript of February 26 to her letter of the 21st.]

MY DEAR BROTHER   Boston 3d May 1786

I had thought to send some more soap by this Vesel but I have it not yet quit reddy I however would not miss writing as my Grandson has Informed me he is with you; I am sorry you are as it were forced to bare the Burden of soporting my whol Famely, but I quiet my self with concidering on yr acount, that it is more blessed to give than to recive tho I think my self aboundantly Blessd as the Latter.

I think it was Disrespectfull in him to me not to ask my advice but as he has now desiered my Recomendation I will Inclose you his Leter to me wherin you will see the man as he is, & I can Add nothing to it as it contains all I beleve about him.

he has as I think Thrust himself Rudely under your Protection I however thank you for your Notice of him & hope he will so Behave as to obtain yr future Aprobation I know your Wisdom and Goodnes will Incline you to watch over and Admonish, or Reprove Him, as you find occasion, and if you can make him Ashamed of that Ridiculous Vanety he so much Indulges, an convert him from it, you may by that means save a soul from Death and hide a multitude of Sins.

I dont wish him to know I sent you his Leter and if you have a convenant opertunity Pleas to send it back again.

all my famely Joyn in the most
Dutifull & Affectionat Respects to you
and yours with your Sister

JANE MECOM

I beleve I have wrote too sevre to Poor Josiah & as he is among all Strangers & so much his Superours it may Depres his Spirits & I Realy think him a good young man in the main   I know no fault he has but his Vanety, you will know whither he wants Encourigement & your Goodnes will Adminester it in the Properest way I should be sorry to have him take a Disgust at his old Grandmother & I must send these or none as the Vesel is Just going

[*In the margin*] you kno I have sent you his charecter some time ago

"Your Profile Done more to your Likenes"

[Printed first, and hitherto only, in Duane, *Letters to Benjamin Franklin*, pp. 142-144, and now printed from the manuscript in the American Philosophical Society. The original is not dated, and the conjectured date "Between May & July 1786?" is in another hand. The date is certainly May of that year, for it acknowledges the receipt of the books Franklin had sent on April 25, and it is referred to by Franklin in his letter of June 3. The "young Niece in particular that made me such a Present" was Elizabeth Franklin Bache, then eight years old. The "Profile" from the Benjamin Vaughan collection which Jane Mecom thought so good a likeness of her brother is reproduced in this volume. It seems impossible to identify the particular Cutting who carried this letter.]

DEAR BROTHER   [Between May & July 1786 ?]

I sincerely thank you for your valuable Present of the Books, which are the more so for haveing in it your Profile Done more to your Likenes than any I have heartofore seen. my Daughter & I sat down to Study the Alphabet Imagining we should soon Larn it so as to write you in that way, as the leters being formd in Italics I sopose you mean to have the writing and Printing as near alike as Posable and it must be a more Acute Pen than mine that can Imitate it, I however could Read it Perfectly, Prety soon as I wrote it every word the third Day in my own way; but to Learn the Pronunceation it will be nesesary to have a master to sett the Example. I am glad you have beter hopes of the Soap but Prehaps you have been too Precipitate in spreding it as you found it begin to unite it might have been more sure to have continued some time longer in the same situation and it would have been a good way to have Piled it some times together across Each other as masons Lay there Bricks that Prevents Its warping, I have some more Redy to send by the first Vesel that goes & then shall writ to my Grandson, I thank you for Imploying Him, writing he apears to me to be well Qualified for, & with your Premition he may in the mean time Learn many Valeuable things by being near you and makeing Observations; and I beg my Dear Brother you will as far as you can without Interfering with your other Affairs Inspect his conduct, his Disposion, and his capasety, & Reprove, Advise, an Direct him, in what you see to be most Proper for him; which if he does not observe he need not Expect Prosperity any way. he is to be shure as Destitute of friends capeble of Asisting him almost as any won. I hope he will do well my Love to him.

I am Pleasd with Temples Inclining to setle near you can he Realy be happy in a Country Life that's charming I feard he would Incline to go back again to England, but you cant go to see him there if it is His Fathers Farm that Mr & Mrs Bache & all of us went to see when I was there it Is so far from the Water. Remember me Affectionatly to him I all ways Loved him.

[267]

I want to hear somthing about my Nephue Benjamin how he goes on since he came home and all about all the Litle wons my young Niece in Perticular* that made me such a Present it is very much Admiered as well as her writing by so young a Person, I Design to writ to her mamah when I send the soap

the crums of soap you sent me Retain the coular and smell well & I dont know but you will prefer it to send to France If it Units as I wish but I will send this by the first Vesel, cousen Jonathan is hear has Indevoured to see Mr Vaughan but had not when I heard from him Last Remember me to yr Famely

yr affectionate Sister

JANE MECOM

* Sett Josiah to write me those Perticulars.
favoured by
Cutting Esq.

"The Hansomest cakes to send to France"

[Here first printed from the manuscript in the American Philosophical Society. John Vaughan had seen Franklin in Philadelphia. The grandson Jane Mecom mentioned was Josiah Flagg. There is a draft of a part of this letter, with a few variants, on the back of Franklin's letter of April 25 of that year. "I mention these things that you may see that I do Injoy Life hear, but Truly my Dear Brother I am willing to Depart out of it when ever my Grat Benifacter has no farther Use for me. for tho but litle of that apears to me now I know the most Insignificant creature on Eirth may be made some Use of In the Scale of beings, may Touch some Spring, or Verge to some wheal unpercived by us; may I not Live to hear of the Departure of so Benificial an Agent as my Dear Brother." The letter was sent in care of Captain Cob or Cobb (not further identified) with the box of soap which was to be left with the Philadelphia merchants Hughes and Anthony. The Philadelphia Directory for 1785 gives their address as the Chestnut Street wharf.]

DEAR BROTHER   Boston May 29th 1786

with this I send you a Box with four Dozn crown soap which I hope will Ansure yr Expectation but it does not Perfectly Pleas me yet, but I find my self so often disopointed when I am over Anxious that I am discoureged from trying any more at this time.

I had Put in more wax than the Proportion to make it Greener & by that means made it so Britle that after I had Boxd it up I found it crack so much that it would not do to send, & haveing melting it over with a litle water as Mrs Bache did I found as you may Percive by hers that it Discolourd it; I made a New weak lye and carried throw the second Proces & it came out as you see good soap, but not so good a coulour, I send two the best I could save of the first, I beleve my Brother John Perfectly understood the Exact proportion that would do best. I hope the first has Ansured you Expectation in Drying, I do not Paper it singly that you may Pick out the Hansomest cakes to send to France,

I have seen Mr Vaughan an he gives me the satisfaction to hear you have not been so Ill since you got home as to keep house on that Acount (for which I Bless God) tho he does not give me any Incouragement that you will be Able to come to Boston, the Spring is gone & I have no hopes now, but who knows but we may Live to Another Spring you not being worce & prehaps Eased of the care of Goverment may Bless yr friends this way with a Visit, I Love to hope the Best; in the mean time Premit me to write you with Freedom & without cerremony, as to the spelling Part I am quite Incouragd Since I am but won of the Thousands, & thousands, that write on to old Age and cant Learn, I hope you understand me and I know you will allways Put the best construction on the sence If you have a Litle Leazure it will oblige me very much to hear from you somthing about my Grandson where he Lives, how he be-haves, what company he keeps, & what you think of him, he is the son of a Dear worthy Child, his Sister was Remarkably Dutyfull & affectionat to me, & I wish him well but should never have consented to his throwing himself upon you

Therefore he has Acted as those who are colld the wise of this world are apt to do to Indevour to make himself a friend of won

who is Able to help him, & if he so behaves as to be worthy yr
Notice I shall not be sorry he did not ask my Advice.

I have this Spring been new planking the yard made New gate,
& new Cedar Dores, & am Painting the Front of the House to
make it look Decent that I may not be Ashamed when any
Boddy Inquiers for Dr Franklins Sister in the Neibourhood.

I tell you these things that you may see I do Injoy Life hear,
but Truly my Dear Brother I am willing to Depart out of it
when ever my Grat Benifactor has no farther Use for me, for
tho but Litle of that Apears to me now, I know the most Insignificant creature on Earth may be made some Use of in the
Scale of Beings, may Touch some Spring, or Verge to some
wheel unpercived by us.

but oh may I not Live to hear of the
Departure of My Dear Brother

yrs Affectionatly

JANE MECOM

There is a good deal of Phylosephy in the working of crown
soap that I cant comprehend the coular was taken out of wonside
of this Green cake by laying on a Damp won and by Drying will
not Recover it

Per Captn Cob   with a Box at Hews and Antonys

Jane Mecom to Sarah Bache

[Here first printed from a copy, in another hand, in the Yale University Library. The Misses Clifton were three sisters, "all very handsome . . . the children of a wealthy English apothecary." *The Autobiography of Benjamin Rush*, 1949, edited by G. W. Corner, p. 295.
There is a letter from Anna Maria Clifton to Franklin, March 4, 1777,
in the American Philosophical Society. She was the last survivor of the
three sisters, and died April 13, 1790, in her seventieth year. All three
of them were close friends of the Franklins and Baches. When the
Baches left Philadelphia before the advance of the British, Sarah Bache
sent her most valuable possessions to "Miss Clifton," including Franklin's "little black trunk." See Sarah Bache's letter to her father, March
29, 1780, in the American Philosophical Society.]

Boston, May 29, 1786

DEAR NIECE—You may perhaps consider it unnecessary for me to keep a Dr and Cr account between us about writing: I will therefore give that up, and take this opportunity to tell you what pleasure I have had in hearing particulars about your family from Mr Vaughan, who, after speaking respectfully of Mr & Mrs Bache, spoke highly of your son Benjamin. He tells me how much pleasure the little ones give my brother: I rejoice at this with you all. He did not seem so ready to give me a particular description of my nephew Will: he said he was not acquainted with him; and I told him what a little Hillman, who was at school with him some time, said of him, that he was a funny fellow, and would play some pranks, that would make the master laugh, though he was angry with him. Mr Vaughan said he believed he pretty much answered that description. Tell them all I love them, and my niece Miss Betsey in particular: tell her the pin-cushion she sent me is much admired: but I question if it may ever be said of it what I can tell you of the pocket-book you worked for your grand-mother Franklin, when you were but five years old. It was done in cross-stitch and was very beautiful. When my mother died I gave it to cousin Kesia Coffin, who admired it, and always used it when she went abroad, which was a great deal: and, when it got soiled, she cleaned it and new bound it. The last time I saw her, which was since the peace, she had it in her pocket; but it had been so much worn that she had it lined with a piece of fine scarlet broad-cloth, and darned it down on that, and made it up so that it looked still quite bright and handsome. Tell Betsey hers shall be kept as long as I live.

Do write and tell me all about Mr Duffield's family: I can never hear any thing of them: of all the rest I knew I can hear from some one or another. I believe I forgot to ask of Capt. All, but he had been so long absent from there that I was not particular, as otherwise I would have been. Don't you keep up your acquaintance with the Misses Clifton: I hear they are still living there. My respects to them, and Capt. All, and every acquaint-

[271]

ance to whom they will be acceptable. Does Temple live in the house with you? his grand-father informs me he inclines to settle in the country. If that is his taste, I don't doubt he will be very happy: but his happiness cannot be complete without a helpmate: if there is any such thing in agitation, tell me who it is. Where does my poor grandson live? for, 'though my brother has been so good as to permit him to be there and to employ him for the present, I know your house is too small and your family too large, to find room for him there, and I hope he is in no way troublesome to you.

If your father should be able to come to Boston, while I live, I shall expect to see you and Mr Bache with him, to whom remember me affectionately. My children and grand-daughter Jenny Mecom join in love to you with your affectionate Aunt

JANE MECOM

Mrs Sarah Bache

"*I am not fond of giving Advice*"

[An excerpt from this letter was printed in Sparks, *Familiar Letters*, 129n. The whole letter was first printed in Smyth, *Writings*, IX, 514-515, from the letter-press copy which Franklin kept and which is in the Library of Congress. The letter sent, now in the American Philosophical Society, is printed here. The Italian poet whom Franklin did not name, to his sister, was Ariosto, *Orlando Furioso*, Book XXXIV. In a letter of February 1, 1778, to the more learned James Hutton, Franklin had said he thought the poet was Ariosto and had told the same anecdote about advice. The "Episcopal Academy" was the Academy of the Protestant Episcopal Church founded in Philadelphia in 1785.]

Philada June 3. 1786

DEAR SISTER,

I have just receiv'd a kind Letter from you without Date, but it is that in which you mention learning the new Alphabet, &c.

Your Grandson behaves very well, and is constantly employ'd in writing for me, and will be so some time longer. As to my Reproving and Advising him, which you desire, he has not hitherto appeared to need it, which is lucky, as I am not fond of giving Advice, having seldom seen it taken. An Italian Poet in his Account of a Voyage to the Moon, tells us that

All things lost on Earth are treasur'd there.

On which somebody observ'd, There must then be in the Moon a great deal of *Good Advice.*

Ben, concerning whom you enquire, is at the University, and very diligent in his Studies. Will is at the Episcopal Academy, & learns well, the rest are all promising, your Niece particularly; and the whole Family, Thanks to God, enjoy at present very good Health.—We join in Love to you & yours. I am ever,

Your affectionate Brother,

Love to Cousin Williams   B FRANKLIN
& Family.

"Bad Spelling, or what is call'd so"

[First printed, without the opening paragraph, in Sparks, *Familiar Letters*, pp. 209-210, as "To a Friend"; and in Sparks, *Works*, x, 264-265, as "To Mrs. Jane Mecom." Printed by Smyth, *Writings*, IX, 522-523, with some details from the letter-press copy in the Library of Congress but in part straight from Sparks. Here printed from the letter which was sent and is now in the American Philosophical Society. Franklin's memory was at fault about the signing of the Declaration, which had been voted on July 4, 1776, but signed on August 2, and by some of the Signers, still later.]

DEAR SISTER,   Philada July 4. 1786

I receiv'd the second Box of Soap, which appears very firm and very good, I am much obliged by the Pains you have taken to humour me in that Matter.

You need not be concern'd in writing to me about your bad Spelling: for in my Opinion as our Alphabet now Stands, the bad Spelling, or what is call'd so, is generally the best, as conforming to the Sound of the Letters and of the Words. To give you an Instance, A Gentleman receiving a Letter in which were these Words, Not finding Brown at hom, I delivered your Meseg to his yf. The Gentleman finding it bad Spelling, and therefore not very intelligible, call'd his Lady to help him read it. Between them they pick'd out the meaning of all but the y f, which they could not understand. The Lady propos'd calling her Chambermaid; for Betty, says she, has the best Knack at reading bad Spelling of any one I know. Betty came, and was surpriz'd that neither Sir nor Madam could tell what y, f was; why, says she, y, f spells Wife, what else can it spell? And indeed it is a much better as well as shorter method of Spelling Wife, than by Doubleyou, i ef, e, which in reality spells Double-yifey.

Your Grandson is well and behaves well. The Family also is all well. There is much Rejoicing in Town to day, it being the Anniversary of the Declaration of Independence, which we sign'd this day Ten Years, and thereby hazarded Lives and Fortunes. God was pleas'd to put a favourable End to the Contest, much sooner than we had reason to expect. His name be praised. Adieu. Your aff. Brother   B FRANKLIN

"Thousands of Boyles Clarks and Newtons"

[Printed first, and hitherto only, in Duane, *Letters to Benjamin Franklin*, pp. 145-146; here from the manuscript in the American Philosophical Society. "Comencement Day" was at Harvard College. The "Clark" whom Jane listed with Newton and Robert Boyle was Samuel Clarke (1675-1729), one of Newton's early disciples.]

DEAR BROTHER   Boston July 21 1786

you have given me Grat Pleasure in the short acount you have wrot concerning my Granson, for *you* not to Percive that he wants Either Advice or Reproff is a good charecter, but I percive you have some Exeptions to the Lose of your Advice & I flater my self I am won.

I am glad you have recd the soap & Like it I wish to know whither the first United as I hoped

I percive you have keept the 4th July very Honourably as well as Joyfully, we also observed as Usal but we had so Lately celebrated the opening the Bridge on Charles River being a

New thing the other was not so much Noticed in our Papers, you will I hope Next Spring have the Pleasur of seeing it yr self, it is Realy a charming Place they have Leveled the Riseing Ground that Led to it & Nicely Paved it, that at some Distance as you Aproach to it it is a Beautiful Sight with a Litle Vilidg at the other End the Buldings all New the Prospect on Each Side is Delight full, I frequent go on the Hill for sake of the Prospect & the walk, & if I tell you I have wonce walkd over I sopose you wont allow it as grat a feeat as yr walking ten miles befor Breakfast, but I am strongly Inclined to Alow it my self, all circumstances considered, It is thought the Tol gatherers Recved yesterday being Comencement Day five Hundred Dolars, Prehaps it may only be an Extravagant Geus,

I beleve Josiah is quite a Proficient in your new mode of Spelling he has wrot me a Leter I beleve Perfectly Right I can Read it very well but Dare not atempt to wright it I have such a Poor Fackulty at making Leters; I think Sir & madam were deficient in Sagasity that they could not find out y f as well as Bety, but some times the Betys has the Brightst understanding.

Dr Price thinks Thousands of Boyles Clarks and Newtons have Probably been lost to the world, and lived and died in Ignorance and meanness, mearly for want of being Placed in favourable Situations, and Injoying Proper Advantages, very few we know is Able to beat thro all Impediments and Arive to any Grat Degre of superiority in Understanding

My Health is Tolarable, the Rest of the Famely as Usal, all Joyn in the most Affectionat Remembrance of you & yours with yr affectionit Sister

JANE MECOM

Jane Mecom to Josiah Flagg

[Printed first, and hitherto only, in the *New England Historical and Genealogical Register*, XXVII, 250-251, from the manuscript in the New England Historic Genealogical Society which had received it from descendants of Josiah Flagg; here printed again from the manuscript. It is evident that Jane Mecom had received other letters from Josiah since his letter of April 17, which could not have been called long. "Mr

Pratt the Lawyer" whose example Jane Mecom cited to her grandson was Benjamin Prat, a noted Boston lawyer, who went on crutches, according to John Adams, *Works*, x, 245, and for the last two years of his life was chief justice of New York. Neither he nor Josiah Flagg had actually lost a leg, only the use of one. Josiah's brother from whom his grandmother had lately heard was Elihu Greene, husband of Jane Flagg. Nathanael Greene had died in Georgia on June 19 of that year. Jane Mecom had probably read "Dr. Price's Dessertations on Provedence" in Richard Price's *Four Dissertations*: i. *On Providence*. ii. *On Prayer*. iii. *On the Reasons for Expecting that Virtuous Men shall meet after Death in a State of Happiness*. iv. *On the Importance of Christianity, the Nature of Historical Evidence, and Miracles*. London, 1777.]

DEAR GRAND SON   Boston July 21st 86

I have recd yr Long leter & read it many times & never without Tears, by which you may see that I am not without Affectionat feelings [to]wards You, but I have allways made it my Pra[c]tice in my conduct towards my first children [to] Reprove & advise where it apeared to me to be Nesesary, and I Still Presist in the beleif of its being Proper & usefull, for which I could bring many Instances but there are two very striking in Scripture of the Utility of Giveing Advice without asking, won of Joseph to Pharoh, in Egept, the other of Jepthrow [Jethro] to His Son-in Law Moses in the Willdernes, and I hope what I wrot to you has not been of any Reale Prejudice to you; you may Asure your-self it Proceeded from a Sincear Desier of your best Good & shall always Rejoyce at what ever turns out to your comfort or Advantage.

I much Aprove of yr conduct in not makeing Acquaintance while you Remain in that Famely your Reasons are very judi-tious if you can but look on the Time you Spend in that Retiered maner as a Scool in which you are to Acquire Expearance & Judgment to goveren your future Life it will Pass with Less Reluctance, may you go on and hold out in the Principles you Apear now to Act from and God Bless you & Prosper you.

by no meenes suffer your self to Dispond & Perticularly on acount of the Lose of yr Leg, was Mr Pratt the Lawyer Ever Respected the Less by Sensable People for the Loss of His.

[276]

for the quieting your mind in that Respect I would Advise you to Read The first Sec. of Dr Price's Dessertations on Provedence, my Brothers Liberary will firnish you with it I dont doubt if not try to borrow it, it will be a usefull Subject for your Reflection in your Laesure Hours, He thinks Every Persen Injoys more happynes than Adversity therefore take your share and be content.

I acknolidg what I wrot concerning Verasity had such an apearance as you sopose, but cou[ld] not convenantly Alter the Terms at that time   I own I had no other cause than the Request yo[u] then made me which besides its not being agreable to my Judgment was then out of my Power to comply with for I had allreddy wrot concerning it, but now all is well & I hope you will Try for the Future if you can *honestly* write Affectionat as well as Dutifull Grandson.

the two Leters I have recd from you since the Long won I am much Pleasd with & Perticularly that in yr Uncles new mode of spelling I shall Like to have you cultivate that method of writing to me in Perticular as I can Read it Perfectly but am not proficient anouf to atempt to write it.

yr Aunt & Jenny Mecom boath write to you now & so I thought they did when I Last wrot which was the Reason I made no mention of them in mine.

Remember me Affectionatly to Mr & Mrs Bache & all the Children & to Jenny's sister Smith, I am & Ever was yr affectionate Grandmother

JANE MECOM

I Lately heard from your Brother & the children
they were well but have Recived a Severe Strook of
    Provedence in
the Death of His Brother Genll Greene.

"Accept at least my Thanks"

[Here first printed from the letter-press copy in the Library of Congress. The letter was taken to Boston by John Williams, whose nephew Jonathan Williams Jr. was still there on a visit to his father. The pamphlet

Franklin sent was pretty certainly his *Maritime Observations*, which was separately reprinted that year from Volume II of the *Transactions* of the American Philosophical Society.]

Philada July 30. 1786.

DEAR SISTER,

Tho' I wrote to you very lately, I cannot let this Opportunity by Mr Williams slip, without a Line to acquaint you that I continue well. I had the Pleasure of hearing a few Days since that you were so when Mr Vaughan left Boston, but he brought no Letters. We have long expected Cousin Jonathan, but he does not appear. If he is still there, give him the Pamphlet you will receive with this. If gone, keep it for yourself. In my last I inform'd you that I had receiv'd the Soap, and that it was very solid and firm, not showing the least Disposition to crack, and seems otherwise very good. Since you will not let me pay you for it, accept at least my Thanks, which indeed you have merited by your Readiness to oblige me, even if you had allow'd me to reimburse you. My Love to your Children, and believe me ever

Your affectionate Brother

B FRANKLIN

Love to Cousin Williams
and Family
Mrs Mecom

"A Leter from you wonce a month"

[First printed, without the final paragraph, in Duane, *Letters to Benjamin Franklin*, pp. 146-148; here printed from the manuscript in the American Philosophical Society. Blackberry jelly was one of the remedies Franklin had tried as a possible solvent for the bladder stone with which he was afflicted.]

Boston August 25 1786

DEAR BROTHER

I Realy think my self highly favoured in Reciveing a Leter from you wonce a month as I have for three Past, it is Indeed a Short Spase of time to what I used to Suffer in Anxiety, your last in Perticular Seems to Express more Positively the good

State of your Health which maks me hope there is truth in what is taken from a Philadelphia Paper concerning the Efficacy of Black-berry Jelly, and that my Dear Brother is the Subject there mentiond O if it Is; how Shall I Enough Bless and Prais that mercifull compassionate Being who has Directed to such a medicine for your Releif.

I did not Design Mr Vaughn should have gone without a Leter to you but my Notice of his going was too short, I however sent as soon after as I could & I hope you have recd it, with some to my Grand Son whos being there I am happy to hear is Agreable to you & the Famely.

the Book I recd and sent it to cousen Jonathan who tells me he has a nother & will Return it to me for my Son Collas, to whom it may be of Grat Service, I Read it my self before I sent it and found a grat deal of Pleasure in it as I do in all you write as far as my capasety Enables me to under stand it, and farther too for I keep your books of Philosophy, and Politics, by me (tho I have Read them throw several times) and when I am dull I take won up & Read, and it seems as tho I were conversing with you, or hearing you to some who can understand and I find a Pleasure in that.

Our North Church folks are Repareing there Steeple, and it was thought the Electricil wier was too small to conduct a Large Strook of Lightning, I felt uneasey about it & got Mr Collas to Inquire about it & he tells me they have made it three times as big as it was before.

I will accept your thanks for the soap and thank you for recveing so kindly, it has not altogether Pleasd me yet. that Art I all ways meant to Instruct Josiah Flagg in when he shuld be in a Sittuation to Observe it, I have keept a Recite by me for that Porpose, & now He is with you you will in some discorce with him some time if you think on it Inform him somthing about the Nature of the working of such Ingredents togather which may help him more Easely to comprehend the Instructions he may after Recive, & it may be of some service to him some time or other.

I am in tolarable Health but my Daughter is sick all most all the hott wether Looses her Apitite & is Exeding weak She seems however now to be groing a litle beter. She Desiers her Duty. my Respectful complements to all to whome it may be Agreable & love to the children

from your Affectionat Sister

per favour of Mr Williams   JANE MECOM

"Three Medals"

[Here first printed from the letter-press copy in the Library of Congress. The medal struck in 1782 "to commemorate our two important Victories," Saratoga and Yorktown, and that struck in 1784 by "a private Friend," who was Augustin Dupré, are reproduced and described in *Benjamin Franklin and his Circle*, a catalogue of an exhibition held at the Metropolitan Museum of Art in New York in May-September 1936 and published that year by the Museum. The Lodge of the Nine Sisters (*Neuf Soeurs*), the Freemasons of Paris, struck two medals each bearing a bust of Franklin: one engraved by Pingret to commemorate Franklin's initiation as a Master Mason of the Lodge in 1778, and the other engraved by Bernier and issued to commemorate the peace in 1783. W. T. R. Marvin, *The Medals of the Masonic Fraternity* (Boston, 1880), p. 40. Dupré struck in 1786 another medal of Franklin. William S. Appleton, *Augustin Dupré and his Work for America* (Cambridge, Massachusetts, 1890), pp. 4-6. Josiah Flagg, returning to Boston with this letter to Jane Mecom, took with him a certificate which has hitherto been printed only in the *New England Historical and Genealogical Society*, XXVII (1873), 249. It is here printed from the manuscript signed by Franklin now in the Harvard School of Business Administration, Howard Corning's office.

"This is to certify whom it may concern, that Josiah Flagg has lived with me near Five Months, being employ'd as a Clerk and Accountant, and has behav'd with great Ability, Diligence and Fidelity, so as to give me perfect Satisfactions. Philadelphia, Sept 4. 1786.

B. FRANKLIN

"This Testimony is given unask'd."]

Philada Sept. 4. 1786

DEAR SISTER,

Your Grandson being about to return home, I cannot let him depart without a Line to you, tho' having written lately I have little to say. I receiv'd your kind letter of July 21. I rejoice with you at the Success of your Bridge. It was I think a noble & hardy Enterprise. This Family joins in Love to you and yours with

Your affectionate Brother

B FRANKLIN

Mrs Mecom

P.S. I send you herewith three Medals, One that I struck to commemorate our two important Victories, and in honour of France for the Assistance she afforded us: The other two struck as Compliments to your Brother, One by the Lodge of the Nine Sisters, of which he was President, the other by a private Friend.

"Usefull to Every Indevidual of mankind"

[Printed first, and hitherto only, in Duane, *Letters to Benjamin Franklin*, pp. 148-149; and here printed from the manuscript in the American Philosophical Society. Dr. John Morgan of Philadelphia was then on a visit to Boston and had seen Jane Mecom.]

DEAR BROTHER   Boston Sepr 13—1786

My Grandson Arived hear on Saturday night well & very gratfull for the kindness you shewd him, has brought me yr favours of the 3. medals & chany covers, for which I thank you, your Device in the first is very Striking, the others are very Pretty; multitudes that have a disposition to shew you Respect, has no other means than an Honest Acknolidgement of yr Vertues and Servises, it is your Due, for he who is allways studing to be usefull to Every Indevidual of mankind is Intitled to all the Respect in there Power to shew.

I am glad you are so perfectly Recovered of the Gout. I hope Mr & Mrs Bache's Health is also confermed. Dr morgan tells me the Fevour & Ague is more freequent there than it formerly was. I hope yr whol Famely will have beter health in future. Excuse me to Mrs Bache. I will writ to her next opertunity, Remember me to Temple & all the Rest of the Good creatures,

[281]

my Daughters is still very sick, but allways Desiers her Duty to you.

Your Affectionat Sister

JANE MECOM

"We are apt to forget that we are grown old"

[First printed by Bigelow, *Works*, IX, 341-342, from the letter-press copy in the Library of Congress; here printed from the original, now in the American Philosophical Society. The "Cousin" of this letter was John Williams.]

MY DEAR SISTER,   Philada Sept. 21. 1786

I received your kind Letter of the 25th past by our Cousin Williams, who besides informs me of your Welfare, which gives me great Pleasure.

Your Grandson having finished all the Business I had to employ him in, set out for Boston a few Days before Cousin Williams arrived. I suppose he may be with you before this time.

I had begun to build two good Houses next the Street instead of three old Ones, which I pulled down. But my Neighbors disputing my Bounds, I have been obliged to postpone till that Dispute is settled by Law. In the mean time, the Workmen & Materials being ready, I have ordered an Addition to the House I live in, it being too small for our growing Family. There are a good many Hands employ'd, and I hope to see it cover'd in before Winter. I propose to have in it a long Room for my Library and Instruments, with two good Bedchambers and two Garrets. The Library is to be even with the Floor of my best old Chamber: & the Story under it will for the present be employ'd only to hold Wood, but may be made into Rooms hereafter. This Addition is on the Side next the River.—I hardly know how to justify building a Library at an Age that will so soon oblige me to quit it; but we are apt to forget that we are grown old, and Building is an Amusement.

I think you will do well to instruct your Grandson in the Art of making that Soap. It may be of use to him, and 'tis pity it should be lost.

Some knowing Ones here in Matters of Weather predict a hard Winter. Permit me to have the Pleasure of helping to keep you warm. Lay in a good Stock of Firewood, and draw upon me for the Amount. Your Bill shall be paid upon Sight, by

Your affectionate Brother

B FRANKLIN

The Family join in Love
to you and yours—

"Many Ingenious contrivances for others"

[Printed first, and hitherto only, in Duane, *Letters to Benjamin Franklin*, pp. 149-150; here printed from the manuscript in the American Philosophical Society. The "Poor Distracted State" of Massachusetts was then involved in what has come to be called Shays's Rebellion. Josiah Flagg never learned the art of making crown soap, but remained in Lancaster, where he married Dolly Thurston on June 7, 1809, and had six children. From 1801 to 1835, except for the year 1825, he was town clerk of Lancaster, and he died February 11, 1840, aged seventy-nine. *The Birth, Marriage and Death Register . . . of Lancaster, Massachusetts* (1890), edited by Henry S. Nourse, 1890, pp. 130, 181.]

DEAR BROTHER   Boston Oct 12—1786

I am sorry you are Pesterd with Law disputes in your old Age but as that is the case it is well you have Plenty of Ground to Inlarge your Present Dwelling it will not only be an Amusement but in all Probelilety a sample of many Ingenious contrivances for others to Profit by in Future. I Imagin Part of your Plan will be to have a Front Dore, Entry & Stare case, to go all the way up to your Lodging Rooms & Garretts; besides a Pasage from the mane Hous as I sopose thro won of your best chamber closets which will be saifer in case of Fier. I shall Expect Mrs Bache to Inform me how it is Decorated when Finished if I live so long which it is Proble Enouf I may not. It is a Favourable circumstance that you can sometimes forgit you are grown old otherwise it might chick you in many Usefull

Discoveries you are makeing for yr fellow men, I wish our Poor Distracted State would atend to the many good Lesons which have been frequently Publishd for there Instruction, but we seem to want Wisdom to Giued, & honesty to comply with our Duty, & so keep allways in a Flame.

I have wrot you since my Grandson was hear he went to Lancaster & I have not heard from him since I porpose to Learn him the Art of makeing the Crown Soap if I can git an opertunity my Daugter is no beter & I am as usal allways yr thankfull & affectionat Sister

JANE MECOM

My love to yr
children & Grandchildren

"A man that made yr stickado"

[Here first printed from the manuscript in the American Philosophical Society. The original is undated and unsigned, and the conjectured date is in another hand. The letter was evidently written after Jane Mecom received Franklin's letter of September 21 about firewood, which she did not mention in her letter of October 12. Though Thomas Foot is here said to have made Franklin a sticcado, a kind of xylophone, on Franklin's last visit to Boston, which was in 1763, nothing further is known of the instrument. Foot, who had been "burst," that is, ruptured, seems later to have improved his fortunes, for the Boston *Directory* of 1796 indicates that he then had a shop of his own, as a cabinet maker, in Creek Square.]

[Between Oct. 12 & Nov. 5. 1786?]

My Dear Brother often minds me that he would Prevent my haveing a Anxous thought and Indeed you do it Efectualy; my Situation in Life has Taught me all Ways to live Frugaly and in that way I am contented,

and tho you are at all times makeing such Ample Provision for me I do not think it Right to be Profuse; but have allways keept it in my Power to make my self comfortable and have done so, besides supling my grandaughter Jenny Mecom with most of her cloathing as she is very Atentive to me, but as the old saying is I cut my coat according to my cloath, I do not

furnish her with Gu Gaus but keep her Decent I never have bought her any thing beter than a caleco Gownd, and I bye some litle nesesarys in the Famely now & then as I Pleas, But when my Son collas has where with all he Provides for the Famely very comfortably in all nesesary Articles He suplied us last year with twelve cords of wood which Lasted us till warm wether as we keept but won Fire Exept on some Extroidenary ocations but he has been so unsucksesfull as to be now Eight months out of Busnes & has Spent what he had Acquiered before, that I beleve he does not know now how to git won cord without Runing in debpt, (he is now Prepareing to go to Verginey as a sort of a Factor to some Gentilemen who Put Stock into his hands to sell for them & make Returns, I hope he will make out.) I was not Anxous however for I knew I could but
       am
Ask for some of the Princeple of which I recve the Intrest & Suply all I want & wery Probably shuld have suficent for the Remander of my Life left but your goodnes in ofering the wood makes it needles to Ask. wood is now fourteen Shillings a Cord & it will cost three Shillings a cord to Saw it & bring in and I now will venter to tell you I wish for a Load or 2 Extroidenary to bestow on a Poor Famely who are worthy objects of charity, but if you think this is too boldly presing on your Beneficance like Puting my hand in to yr Pocett to Suply others wants as well as my own I will not think it hard to be Deniged, I will tell you the Famely & the circumstances, you may Remember a man that made yr stickado when you were last in Boston, & his wife who had been my Son Edwards Widdow, He has had the misfourtune to be Burst; that he is not able to do the harder Part of his ocupation which you may Remember is a Shop Joyner or more Properly cabenett maker, but going out of Town in the Seage he lost all his Tools they were some how thrown over board & could not be Recovered, they lived in the country some years she keeping Scool & he Jobing about till her helth grew very Inferm, & they grew very Poor, they were advised to come back to Boston I sopose for fear they should become a charge to the Town. heer he works Jurniwork

[285]

and litle maters in other mens Shops as he is able, and she has done Every kind of thing that she was able to git a liveing (& she is Ingenious and Industrious) till she grew so Decriped & Inferm that for some years she has been allmost Inteirly Deprived of the use of her Lims, & they Live mostly on the charity of Friends among whome I have not been alltogather neglegent of contributing my mite, but I think ought to be but a mite without yr Premishon on whos Bounty I Live.

[*Unsigned*]

"*You have Never Deniged any Request I made*"

[Here first printed from the manuscript in the American Philosophical Society.]

DEAR BROTHER   Boston Nov 5—1786

I have acording to your very Affectionate Desire taken in ten cord of wood for which I shall Draw a bill on you as you Directed, I Dont know as yet in whose Faver, Mr. Collas Layd in four cord before he went away so that we shall have Plenty should your Prognosticator's hapen to be in the Right,

I dont know but I deserve to be cencered of those unreasonable Persons to whom if you give an Inch they will take an Ell, for you only Desiered the Pleasure of helping to keep me warm but I Remembred another Expresion you wrot to cousen Jonathan Last winter that you would not have me Pinch, & you see now I have Effectuly garded against it, I also did take the Liberty to send a small Portion to the Poor Famely I mentiond, for you are so good you have Never Deniged any Request I made you, if you think I have Presumed too far you will only Laugh at it a litle, but you must give me a caution not to make so free with you another time.

My Por Daughter who has often Expresd a desire to be like you in Every thing now finds she would willingly be Excused from Pertaking the same Infirmities since she has not your Philosephy to bare it She has got I think the Gout to a grat degree but she however acknolidges it is Easeyer borne than the disorder in her stomack which is Removed, I hope it may soon go off. Remember my Love to Mr and Mrs Bache & all the Children, and Accept yr Self the most Gratfull thanks from your Affectionat Sister

JANE MECOM

Remember my love to cousen Jonathan
My Daughter Desiers you would
Accept her thanks as She will
Pertake of the Benifit with me

"You have not mentioned this Family"

[Here first printed from the letter-press copy in the Library of Congress. Anthony Stickney of Chester, New Hampshire, had written to Franklin on July 22 of that year. The letter is in the American Philosophical Society.]

DEAR SISTER, Philada Dec. 3. 1786

I have to acknowledge the Receipt of two or three kind Letters from you since I wrote to you. I have been much busied in Building. I hope you receiv'd the Barrel of Flour I sent you. I approve of the friendly Disposition you made of some of your Wood. I wish you a comfortable Winter. It begins to set in here, but my Buildings are now covered so as to fear no Damage from the Weather. We are all well and send our Loves & Duties. I have lately receiv'd a Letter from a Person who subscribes himself Stickney, says he is a Grandson of my Sister Davenport, and has a son named Benjn Franklin, to whom he desires to give a good Education, but cannot well afford it. You have not mentioned this Family in the List you sent me. Do you know any thing of them? I am ever, my dear Sister

Your affectionate Brother

Mrs Mecom B FRANKLIN

[*In the margin*] Your Bill for the Wood has not yet appeared. If you find it difficult to sell such a Bill, let me know the Sum and I will send one for you to receive the Money in Boston.

"The care of some good Neibours"

[Printed first, and hitherto only, in Duane, *Letters to Benjamin Franklin*, pp. 151-152, with the third paragraph omitted; here printed entire from the manuscript in the American Philosophical Society. The "Friends from London" who had come to Philadelphia were Mrs. Mary (Polly) Hewson and her children. Jonathan Williams lived in Ann (now North) Street, about a mile away from Jane Mecom's house.]

MY DEAR BROTHER   Boston Decr 17—1786

Mr Bradford has Just informd me of his going to Philadelphia to morrow morning. I would not let him go without a Line as I have not yet had opertunity to thank you for the charming Barrill of Flower you sent me. he is to take the Bill you Premited me to Draw,

I some times Seem to feel guilty at being so Expencive to you, but why should I; when I know it gives you Pleasure to make Every won happy: & I constantly feal the Blesing, your Predictons concerning a hard winter are begining to be Verified in a formidable maner. the Snow has been so Deep & we no man in the House that we might have been Buried Alive were it not for the care of some good Neibours who began to Dig us out before we were up in the morning, & cousen Williams came Puffing, & Sweating, as soon as it was Posable to see how we were & if we wanted any thing, but thank God we had no want of any thing Nesesary if we had been Shutt up a fortnight. Except milk—

My Daughters Gout, or Rhumitism or what Ever it is, has not Left her yet; but She can Just hobble about the chamber, She desi[res] her Duty to you.

I want much to know if you were so Luckey as to git yr New Apartments covered in before the hard wether, I think it could not be before you had the Agreable Addition to your Famely of some of your Friends from London, but we cannot Easely feel our Selves croweded with the company of those we Love, I think you feel your Self happy in the circle about you, &

cousen Jonathan too I sopose injoys it, my Love to him & thanks for his kind atention to me & my most Respectfull Complements to Mrs Hewston & tell her I hope She will Like America.

I had Intended to have wrote to my Niece but cannot at this time but Remember my Love to Mr & Mrs Bache & all the Dear Children

from yr Ever obliged & Affectionat Sister

JANE MECOM

"Very Bold in writing to you"

[Printed first, and hitherto only, in Duane, *Letters to Benjamin Franklin*, pp. 152-154, and here printed from the manuscript in the American Philosophical Society. Jane Mecom's story of the Stickney descendants of Sarah Franklin Davenport came from Mrs. Jonathan Williams Sr. and Mrs. "Rodgers" (Rogers), an aunt of the Anthony Stickney who had written to Franklin. The reference to Franklin's "hansom Present" to the father of his correspondent may have reminded Franklin of a letter he had written to Captain Anthony Stickney of "Newbury Port" twenty-three years before. The letter, copied by Benjamin Franklin Stickney in April 1833 and sent to Jared Sparks, is now in the Harvard University Library.

"Philada June 16   1764

"Loving Kindsman,

I received yours of the 16th May, and am glad to hear that you and your Family are well, and that your wife is safely delivered of another Daughter, which I hope will prove a Blessing to you both. I got home without any farther incident, but have not yet recovered fully the former Strength of my Arm. Your Brother Josiah Davenport is still at Pittsburgh, near 400 Miles west of this Place, where he has the Care of the Provincial Store, that was establish'd there during the Peace, for the Indian Trade; and since the War broke out again, there has been no good opertunity of bringing off the Goods, so he is oblig'd to remain with them. His wife and children are here; she seems to be in a bad State of Health, but the Children are well. My wife and Daughter thank you for your good wishes, and return theirs for you & yours.—Present my best Respects to Mr & Mrs Lowell, and my Love to your Wife and Children. Remember me too, to your Brother Davenport & his Family.

"Your affectionate Uncle

B Franklin"

The letter to Captain Stickney is here first printed. The Rev. John Lowell, married to Elizabeth Cutt, was in 1764 minister of the third congregation of Newburyport. *Sibley's Harvard Graduates*, VI, 496.]

DEAR BROTHER   Boston Janr 6—1787

yours of Decr 3 was brouaght me by Col Sergeant with aboundance of complesanse he Informed me how very well & chearfuly you were to a Prodegy he said. you have I hope before now recd the Bill by Mr Bradford, at the same time are Informed that I recd yr kind Present of the Barril of Flower with my thanks. I Rejoyce to know you got yr Building Covered before the winter sett in, it has been severe anouf with us but thanks to God and my Dear Brother I have not wanted any comfortable thing. but the Lose of Such a multitude of Lives in the storms is Terrable & surpases all I Ever Remember in a Season.

Our Sister Davenport had a Daughter Dorcas who married to a Mr Stickney & lived at Newbury he was a chare maker by traid but never loved work, but that is not the thing, thay had been so long Dead & I had no Remembrance of there Leaveing any Children & had never seen any of them that I sopose I did not think of the Famely when I wrot the List, when I recd your Leter our Streets were unpasable by any means for old folks but a few Days after I Sent to Mrs Williams to Inquier what She knew about them, & had for Ansure all she knew of the man who wrot to you, was that he was a good for nothing Impudent Lazey Felow Just like his Father, I thought however as he had an Aunt in the Town I would know somthing farther before I ansured your Leter. I therefore Got a Carrage & went to her & Inquierd about the Famely, She Tould me that when her Sister was married her Husbands mother & Grandfather were Liveing on a Litle Estate they had in Newbury where he also carried his Wife after trying to live by Shopkeeping in this Town, but haveing so litle means of soport they became exdding Poor, in which time she says you went to see them & made them a hansom Present (I sopose at the time you Put out yr Shoulder at Portesmouth) His Grand-

father Lived to be above 90 year old but He and his Daughter
Dieing Left the house to our cousen but they could not feed
long upon that, he Therefore took a Prudent Step sould it &
bought a good Farm at Derry, & went to Live on it where his
wife helpd to work on it & thay got to Live Extradinery well,
but she Mrs Rodgers thinks shortned her Days by too hard
Labour, & her husband Died soon Affter her & left the Farm
to this man & a sister who are all the children they left & who
live to gather on it & do very well, She says he has a Good
charecter as a Sober Honest man but does not Increce his Estate
as won tould her he Entertaind too many Strangers in hopes
of Entertaing Angels unawares, She says she saw Him about a
year & half a go & he tould her he had such a son that he Named
for you, that he gave him all the Education he was able, but
she thinks him very Bold in writing to you She is shure she
shuld not have don it, as to the Boy I omited to Inquire Perticularly about him as the carrage waited for me Put it out of my
mind   we have had a short spell of moderate wether I am as
well in Health as useal my Daughter growing beter slowly She
Joyns me in Duty & love to you & yours with your Affectionat
Sister

                                        JANE MECOM

"You must build an Academy"

[Printed first and hitherto only in Duane, *Letters to Benjamin Franklin*, pp. 155-156; here printed from the manuscript in the American
Philosophical Society. Morgan Stillman was a son of Samuel Stillman
and a nephew of Dr. John Morgan. The "sisters Grandson" was Anthony Stickney. The "Grate-Grandson" who might have claims on
Franklin was Franklin Greene, of whom Jane Mecom had written to
her brother on December 29, 1780, that she and the child's parents had
"left out the Benjamin that he might not be called ben."]

DEAR BROTHER   Boston March 9 1787
    I Embrace this opertunity by my Neibour Mr Morgan Still-
man, who is by his Uncle Dr Morgans Invitation Going to Settle in yr City, as he is a young Gentleman who bares a good

charecter hear it may be of Service to him, for you to have heard it, if he should chance to be Spoken of in your company.

I know it will be a Pleasure to you to know that I have had as good health as I could Expect this most Intolarable hard Winter, your Prediction has held Invariable thus far, & as it began in October I dont see why it mayn't hold till may for any apearance yet to the contrary, I have wanted nothing for my comfort but Air an Exercise which it has been Imposable for me to take; as the Feet of Every Woman, as well as the hand of Every man, has been Seald up, it is trew I do walk, some times in the House but I don't think of it offten anouf.

you can never want Exercise for body or mind & I sopose this winter you have Deverted yor Self with Inspecting yr Building, I want to hear all about it; but more Perticularly concerning your Health, it seemes a long time since I heard from you, but I had the Pleasure in a Dream Last night to hear you Play a delightfull Tune on the Harpsecord

when I wrot you concerning our sisters Grandson I mistook the Places of his abode he Lives at Chester, in the county of Rockingham, State of Newhamshire. he has been to see me the first time tho he is forty yrs old   Says how happy he should be to have the honour of a Leter from you, which I beleve would Elevate the Poor man to a high Degree, he sade he was Advised to write you concerning his son. I tould him if you were to take such Notice of all who had been named In Respect to you you must build an Academy for there Reception, that I had a Grate-Grandson Prehaps would clame Admitance when it was well Established tho I had not yet Preposed it

Remember my Love to yr children & Granchildn

from yr Ever Affectionate Sister

JANE MECOM

Dear Brother Pardon the
Blots & Blunders I cant
make a Pen my self & have no
won near me who can

"Like a young man of Twenty-five"

[Printed first, and hitherto only, in Duane, *Letters to Benjamin Frank-lin*, pp. 157-159, and here printed from the manuscript in the American Philosophical Society. William Pierce of Georgia, a delegate to the Federal Convention at Philadelphia, where he met Franklin at about the time this letter of Jane Mecom's was written, himself wrote in his Notes on the delegates that the sage possessed an "activity of mind equal to a youth of twenty-five years of age." The "Pamphlit" to which she here referred as by "your Author" seems to have been Samuel Romilly's *Observations on "Thoughts on Executive Justice"* (London, 1786), an anonymous pamphlet to which was added Franklin's letter to Benjamin Vaughan of March 14, 1785, called by Romilly *A Letter from a Gentleman abroad to his Friend in England*. "Tommy Hubard" was Thomas Hubbart, whose wife was Catharine Ray Greene's sister Judith. Their daughter Deborah married "Mr. Gouch" (actually William Gooch). Her "Uncle Tuttle" was Tuthill Hubbart, a stepchild of John Franklin. Hubbart was sixty-seven when this letter was written, and lived till 1808—when, however, his numerous nieces and nephews inherited his considerable fortune. The "Corll Sargeant" who carried the letter was probably Winthrop Sargent, appointed by the Continental Congress the following October to be secretary of the Territory Northwest of the River Ohio. His military rank was only brevet-major at the time, and if he was called Colonel Sargent it was a courtesy title.]

DEAR BROTHER   Boston May 22d 1787

Corll Sargeant has Obligingly calld on me to let me know he is going to Philadelphia & will take Pleasure in conveying a Leter to you, I gladly Embrace the opertunity as I wanted to tell you how much Pleasure I Injoy in the constant and lively mention made of you it the News papers, which makes you Apear to me Like a young man of Twenty-five, Just Sitting out for the other Eighty years full of grate designs for the Benifitt mankind, and your own Nation in Perticular, which I hope with the Asistance of such a Nmber of wise men as you are connected with in the Convention you will Gloriously Accomplish, and put a Stop to the nesesity of Dragooning, & Haltering, they are odious means; I had Rather hear of the Swords being beat into Plow-shares, & the Halters used for Cart Roops, if by that means we may be brought to live Peaceably with won a nother, but I cannot Join in opinion with your Auther who thinks it not Right to Put a man to Death for Any crime   I fear we should have a much worse Socity, tho we should Adopt His Scheme of a Prison built in a horrable Place, with Groaning Hinges, & Melancholy keepers, in such a Confinement would there be no Proliblity of its groing fimilier & Indiferent to them, & I do not concive of there being such an Entertaining Tale as to Impress the minds of children so as to have any Lasting Effectt.   or that won of Thousand would be Reformed by it) it has been said Dr Franklin was the Auther of the Pamphlit but I think not.

I think I have not wrote you since I recived the Explanation of the medal I thank you for it, I should be much gratified with the Explaination of the other two. I sopose them to contain Encomiams on yr self but it is yr sister that asks it.

The Dreadfull clamity This Town has suffered by Fier has Included a Daughter of Tommy Hubards who married Mr Gouch, I think the worthyest of the Famely, they had there House burnt Down & lost aboundance of there cloathing & nesesaries her Uncle Tuttle is very Rich but Prehaps he thinks he may live to want all Him self I beleve He is not more than Seventy.

but some others has been charitiable notwithstanding the Dificulty of the Times, Aunt Patrage too is very Poor—in Sprit.

I will now tell you somthing that will Pleas you our worthy cousen Jonathan Williams has the Honourary Degree of master of Artes confered on him by the Corporation of our Colage, Dor Lathrop of of them tould me of it, you will see it after Comencement.

Remember my Love to yr Children & Grand children from yr Affectionat Sister

JANE MECOM

per favour of
Col: Sargeant

"We can dine a Company of 24 Persons"

[First printed in Bigelow, *Works*, IX, 392-393, from a letter-press copy in the Library of Congress, and now more correctly printed from that copy. On May 16 the delegates to the Federal Convention had dined with Franklin in his new dining room. Nine delegates from other states are known to have been in Philadelphia that day, besides the eight Pennsylvania delegates including Franklin, but it is not known how many of them were actually at dinner with him. A brief description of the room and house on that occasion may be found in Carl Van Doren, *The Great Rehearsal* (1948), p. 12.]

DEAR SISTER,   Philada May 30. 1787.

In your Letter of March 9. you mention that you want to know all about my Buildings. To the East End of my Dwelling House, I have made an Addition of 16 Feet and an half wide and 33 feet long, that is the whole Length of the old House, so that the Front and Back of the old and new Building range even, and the Row of Windows, Eaves & Roof are continu'd so as to appear but one Building. By this Addition I have gain'd a large Cellar for Wood, a Drawing Room or Dining Room on the same Level with our old Dining Room, in which new Room we can dine a Company of 24 Persons, it being 16 feet wide and 30½ long; and it has 2 Windows at each End, the North and South, which will make it an airy Summer Room; and for Winter there is a good Chimney in the Middle, made handsome with marble Slabs. Over this Room is my Library of the same Dimensions, with like Windows at each End, and lin'd with Books to the Cieling. Over this are 2 lodging Rooms: and over all a fine Garret. The Way into the Lower Room is out of the Entry passing by the Foot of the Stairs. Into the Library I go thro' one of the Closets of the old Drawing Room or bed Chamber. And into the two new Rooms above, thro' a Passage cut off from the Nursery. All these Rooms are now finished and inhabited very much to the Convenience of the Family who were before too much crowded.

The two new Houses next the Street, are three Stories high, beside the Garrets, and an arch'd Passage is left in the middle between them to come thro' down to my Dwelling, wide enough for a Carriage; so that I have the old Passage Lot left free to buld another House. The two Houses are 24 feet front each, and 45 deep.

We are all well, and join in Love to you and yours. I am ever
Your affectionate Brother

B FRANKLIN

"Indeed a Lowly Dweling"

[Printed first, and hitherto only, in Duane, *Letters to Benjamin Franklin*, pp. 159-160; here printed from the manuscript in the American Philosophical Society.]

MY DEAR BROTHER   Boston August 16 1787

I cant Express to you the Pleasure it gives me on reading yr Description of yr Building. I Rejoice that you have got thorough so much to your Satisfaction, that God has blesd you in that Respect is mater of thankfullnes as all the blesings God Afords us are, for none can Ascribe merit to them selves, yet as the Riteous has the Promis of this Life and that which is to come; if we may Judge of the fittnes of things we may Surely Expect won who has Imployd His whol Life to Defuse Happines to all the world has a Right to live in a comodious House, and that all about Him should combine to Promot His Happines. our Grat Benefactor delights to Bless those that trust in Him, which I am sure you do, and you conferm me in that Judgment as you say you beg the continuance of his favours but shuld submit to his will should a Reverse be determinied, in that disposition of mind you are happier than you could be in all that the world could give without it. Let us my Dear Brother goo beging and we Shall certainly be Reciveing, all that is best for us till we come to the full Injoiment in our Fathers Habitation.

It was Indeed a Lowly Dweling we were brought up in but we were fed Plentifully, made comfortable with Fire and cloathing, had sildom any contention among us, but all was Harmony: Especially betwen the Heads—and they were Universally Respected, & the most of the Famely in good Reputation, this is still happier liveing than multituds Injoy.

Blessed be God that you & *I* by your means have the Addition of more Pleasing apearance in our Dwellings.

I wrot you by Coll Sergant which I sopose you have recived when you have Leasure you will let me know, I depend on cousen John Williams to convey this by some Philadelphia Gentleman whose name he had forgot, my Friend & Neibour Dr Lathrope wishes for an opertunity I shall let him know of this

Present my love to yr children and Grandchildren & beleve Ever your Gratfull as well Affectionat Sister

JANE MECOM

"Water to a dry Pump"

[First printed in a short-lived New York newspaper, *The Evening Signal*, edited by Park Benjamin and Rufus W. Griswold, on October 23, 1839, from a manuscript not now known to exist; and here printed by the courtesy of the New-York Historical Society from the file of the *Signal* in the Society's possession. Sparks, *Works*, x, 444-446, printed the letter from the newspaper but followed his own style in spelling and punctuation. Smith, *Writings*, ix, 612-614, made use of the letter-press copy in the Library of Congress, of which only pages 1 and 4 of the original have been preserved, but for the remainder took his text from Sparks, even to the sentence "It is a discourse well written," which is not in the letter-press copy and in the *Signal* reads " 'Tis a Discourse well written." John Lathrop on August 30, 1787, had sent Franklin a copy of *A Discourse, before the Humane Society in Boston: Delivered on the second Tuesday of June, 1787. By John Lathrop, D.D. Boston: Printed by E. Russell, 1787.* Writing in the third person, Lathrop had referred to Jane Mecom as "a near neighbor, a particular friend, and a worthy member of the society of christians with which he is connected." In the *Evening Signal* this "Original Letter of Benjamin Franklin to his Sister," as the head reads, is preceded by an editorial note: "We have much pleasure in laying before our readers the following letter from the celebrated Benjamin Franklin, which is now for the first time published. Of its genuineness there is no doubt, and any one who may be incredulous on this point, can examine the original autograph letter at this office. The internal evidence will, however, we believe, be considered sufficient to stamp its truth. The memorandum on the letter is 'concerning the War.' " The *Signal* text seems to have been printed with close fidelity to the letter which Franklin sent, in which he presumably added the commendation of Lathrop's *Discourse* after the letter-press copy had been taken. An excerpt from this letter had been printed in the *Boston Gazette* for March 3, 1794, just before Jane Mecom's death. This may mean that the whole letter had got out of her hands and so found its roundabout way to the editors of the *Signal*.]

DEAR SISTER,   Philada. Sept. 20, 1787

I received your kind Letter of the 16th past, which gave me the great Pleasure of learning that you were well. I thought I had before acknowledg'd the Receipt of yours per Colonel Serjeant.

The Convention finish'd the 17th Instant. I attended the Business of it 5 Hours in every Day from the Beginning, which is something more than four Months. You may judge from thence that my Health continues; some tell me I look better, and they suppose the daily Exercise of going & returning from the Statehouse has done me good. You will see the Constitution we have propos'd in the Papers. The Forming of it so as to accommodate all the different Interests and Views was a difficult Task; and perhaps after all it may not be receiv'd with the same unanimity in the different States that the Convention have given the Example of in delivering it out for their Consideration. We have however done our best, and it must take its Chance.

I agree with you perfectly in your Disapprobation of War. Abstracted from the Inhumanity of it, I think it is wrong in Point of Human Prudence, for whatever Advantage one Nation would obtain from another, whether it be Part of their Territory, the Liberty of Commerce with them, free passage on their Rivers, &c. &c. it would be much cheaper to purchase such Advantage with ready Money than to pay the Expence of acquiring it by War. An Army is a devouring Monster, and when you have rais'd it, you have, in order to subsist it, not only the fair Charges of Pay, Clothing, Provision, Arms & Ammunition, with numberless other contingent & just Charges to answer and satisfy, but you have all the additional Knavish Charges of the numerous Tribe of Contractors, to defray, with those of every other Dealer who furnishes the Articles wanted for your Army, and takes advantage of that want to demand exorbitant Prices. It seems to me, that if Statesmen had a little more Arithmetick, or were more accustomed to Calculation, Wars would be much less frequent. I am confident that Canada might have been purchased from France for a tenth Part of the Money England spent in the Conquest of it. And if instead of fighting with us for the Power of Taxing us, she had kept us in good Humour by allowing us to dispose of our own Money, and now and then giving us a little of hers, by way of Donation to Colleges, or Hospitals, or for cutting Canals, or fortifying Ports, she might easily have drawn from us much more by our accasional voluntary Grants and Contributions, than ever she could by Taxes. Sensible People will give a Bucket or two of Water to a dry Pump, that they may afterwards get from it all they have occasion for. Her Ministry were deficient in that little Point of Common Sense;—And so they spent 100 Millions of her Money, and after all lost what they contended for.

I lament the loss your Town has suffered this year by Fire. I sometimes think Men do not act like reasonable Creatures, when they build for themselves combustible Dwellings in which they are every Day oblig'd to use Fire. In my new Buildings I have taken a few Precautions, not generally Us'd; to wit, none of the Wooden Work of one Room communicates with the Wooden Work of any other Room; and all the Floors, and even the Steps of the Stairs, are plaistered close to the Boards, besides the plaistering on the Laths under the Joists. There are also trap Doors to go out upon the Roofs that one may go out and wet the Shingles in case of a neighboring Fire. But indeed I think the Stair Cases should be Stone, and the Floors tiled as in Paris, and the Roofs either tiled or Slated.

I am much oblig'd to your Friend & Neighbor Mr Lathrop for his kind Present, and purpose writing to him. 'Tis a Discourse well written.

I sent you lately a Barrel of Flour, and I blame myself for not sooner desiring you to lay in your Winter's Wood, and drawing upon me for it as last Year. But I have been so busy. To avoid such Neglect in future, I now make the Direction general, that you draw on me every Year for the same purpose.

Adieu, my dear Sister, and believe me ever

Your affectionate Brother

B FRANKLIN

"The nearer the bone the sweeter the meat"

[Printed first, from a manuscript now missing, in Sparks, *Works*, x, 325-327, from which it is here reprinted. Franklin misquoted Pope's *An Essay on Man*, IV, 205, where the line reads "Stuck o'er with titles, and hung round with strings."]

DEAR SISTER, Philadelphia, 4 November, 1787.

I received a kind letter from you lately, which gave me the pleasure of being informed that you were well. I am glad you have made the provision against the winter, which I mentioned to you. Your bill is honored. It is impossible for me always to guess what you may want, and I hope, therefore, that you will never be shy in letting me know wherein I can help to make your life more comfortable.

It was my intention to decline serving another year as President, that I might be at liberty to take a trip to Boston in the spring; but I submit to the unanimous voice of my country, which has again placed me in the chair. I have now been upwards of fifty years employed in public offices. When I informed your good friend Dr. Cooper, that I was ordered to France, being then seventy years old, and observed, that the public, having as it were eaten my flesh, seemed now resolved to pick my bones, he replied that he approved their taste, for that the nearer the bone the sweeter the meat. I must own, that it is no small pleasure to me, and I suppose it will give my sister pleasure, that, after such a long trial of me, I should be elected a third time by my fellow citizens, without a dissenting vote but my own, to fill the most honorable post in their power to bestow. This universal and unbounded confidence of a whole people flatters my vanity much more than a peerage could do.

"Hung o'er with ribands and stuck round with strings," may give nominal, but not real honors.

This family are all well, as I also am, thanks to God. We join in best wishes for you and yours. And I am ever, my dear sister, your affectionate brother,

B. FRANKLIN

"Quarilsome spirits against the constetution"

[Printed first in Duane, *Letters to Benjamin Franklin*, pp. 162-163; here printed from the manuscript in the American Philosophical Society. In the current turmoil in Rhode Island politics John Collins was governor. His sister, "old maddam Greene mother in-law to my Grandson," was actually stepmother to Elihu Greene. The opposition to the ratification of the Constitution in Massachusetts was defeated by a vote of 187 to 169 on February 16, 1788. Catharine Greene's letter to Franklin of November 8, 1787, is in Roelker, *Benjamin Franklin and Catharine Ray Greene*, pp. 130-131.]

DEAR BROTHER   Boston Nov 9—1787

I wrot you Lately which Mr Wouters took the care of & I sopose you have recd but as he [is] now going him self & offers to take a Leter I will not omit writing tho it will as Useal be a boran Performance and to Inclose my Friend Mrs Greenes, her Affection for you is really so grate that she seemes at a lose to Express it, the Leters from us two old women Proceeding from such a cause, will be a Variety & amuse you a litle under the Fatigue of Publick Business. She is the same good harted creature she Ever was & with some otheer Females in there State are afflicted with the Horrid Iniquity of the Publick Proceedings   old maddam Greene mother in-law to my Grandson is sister to Governor Collins but she says if she had an Apron full of Voits to dispose of she would throw them all in Against her Brother,

you Percive we have some quarilsome spirits against the constetution but it does not apear to be those of Superior Judgment. my gratest comfort is God Reigns we are in His hands. we are as well as Usall & Joyn in Love & Duty to you & yrs with your

Affectionat Sister

Mr Wouters has been hear several   JANE MECOM
Times & is very Agreable.
I have heard nothing of a barrill of Flower but what you mention Since that yo sent me a year ago. I fear it is lost if you cannot Recolect who you sent it by.

Jane Collas to Benjamin Franklin

[Here first printed from the manuscript in the American Philosophical Society. If the letter is evidence of a fluttering affectation in Jane Collas, it is evidence also that she felt herself dominated by her "Monoplizeing Mamma" and resentful of Catharine Greene's greedy adoration. Franklin, replying in a letter of April 12, 1788, which is printed in Smyth, *Writings*, IX, 642-643, took no notice of his niece's references to her mother and her friend from Warwick, and made only the mildest comment on John Thayer's extraordinary behavior in obtaining letters of introduction to him. "He gave me but little Trouble," Franklin said, "and I had the Pleasure of doing him some good; tho' he is rather an insignificant Body, and has turned to the Papists, who do not much value the Acquisition, and I suppose we may easily bear the Loss." In this Franklin had the authority of no less a Papist than the Papal Nuncio in Paris, who on July 1, 1784, had called on Franklin. The Nuncio, Franklin noted in his journal of that day, "spoke lightly of their new Bostonian convert Thayer's conversion; that he had advised him not to go to America, but settle in France. That he wanted to go to convert his countrymen; but he knew nothing yet of his new religion himself." Carl Van Doren, *Benjamin Franklin's Autobiographical Writings*, p. 607. Thayer in fact got on badly with other Roman Catholic priests in America, to which he returned in 1790, and he ended his days in Limerick, where he had considerable success in promoting emigration from Catholic Ireland to Boston and other parts of the United States.]

MY DEAR AND HONORD UNCLE   Boston, Nov. 11. 1787

I can hold out no longer. Madam Grean has been permited to write you without one objection from my Monoplizeing Mamma; and if Love can Apologize for troubling you with one Female letter, why not for another? no one breathing can plead a greater Share than myself, and I have more then wonce, shed tears on being denied the pleasure of telling you that I love and reverence you even to Adoration, and should I ever have the happiness of seeing you tho I would not bite a bit off you as Mrs Gr - - n seems to long for, I would shove in among the croud, and if possable, touch the hem of your Garment; and trust to your benevolence for forgiveness, and notice of the intruder, the least share of which would make me happier then all the honers of the United World without it.—I hope to slide this unpercieved into the Hand of the obliging Mr Wouters and do not you blame me my dear Uncle for disobedance to a parent, as we are only to obay them *in the Lord*, which I take to be Conscientiously, and my Consciance has long accused me for that which appeard to me disrespectfull not to testify my joy on your return to us by a letter of Congratulation.—Heaven is my witness how greatfull I am for so great, so unexpected, a Mercy.

Another thing which has laid very heavey on my Heart, and for which I ought long ago to Apologized was lending my helping hand to that bold intruder Mr Thayer, who I understand was much trouble and Expence to you, he teazed me for months, for a letter of recommendation to you, which I all along refused, and beg'd to be excused from writing atall, telling him I had never presumed to trouble you with my scrawls, but he would not let me rest till he forced from me a few lines of intreduction, I gave it him unsealed in about a weak he returnd with it and beg'd I would make some allteration, ask'd for pen and paper to write the Ideas he would wish me to convey.—I could not help laughing in his Face tho: I complied with his request. Mamma was then with me on a Visit at Cambridge and after I had perused what he had wrote for me to Coppy, I told him I should not certainly write a line more then I had wrote, but as I had no reason to doubt, the truth of what he had writen I would oblig him by signing my Name and beg the favor of Mamma to do the same which would put an end I hoped to all further trouble, Mamma laughed very hartily at the drolery and the poor fellow with all his Assurance look'd greatly mortified, I pity'd and spared him to plead his cause with Mamma which he did so Effectively as to get a letter of recommendation from her, tho she never saw him before, but I never wrote any other than the first I gave him, which could not be call'd a recommendation, and if you recived such a one from me he must have wrote it himself.—I now beg pardon for that, and and my presant intruding so long on your patience which after thus easing my Heart of its burthen I never will again attempt without some incoragement from you.

[303]

My tender regards waits on Mrs Beach I should be happy in her rememberance of one who often thinks of her, and hers, with tenderst affection.

Now my dear Uncle may we flatter ourselves with the hope of seeing you in the spring   I rejoyce all our friends with my strong faith that you will come, and the foundation I have for it, that God may preserve your health and enable you to make the Harts of hundreds glad by such a visit is the fervent prayer of her who begs leave to subscribe herself

with the greatst respect your Dutifall

and ever Affectionate Neice

JANE COLLAS

Boston   Novr 11th 87

"*Proportion my Assistance to your Wants*"

[Printed first in Bigelow, *Works*, IX, 445-447, from the letter-press copy in the Library of Congress. Bigelow modernized the text, and Smyth, *Writings*, IX, 623-624, who made use of the manuscript, was not altogether accurate. The letter is here printed more correctly from the Library of Congress copy. The letters in square brackets are missing on a defective margin, but the context leaves no doubt what they are.]

DEAR SISTER,   Philada Dec. 11. 1787.

Since I wrote to you last, your Son Collas has been here from N. Carolina, where he kept a Store; but it has not answered his Expectations. He wanted to take up Goods on Credit here, but could not obtain any unless I would recommend it to our Merchants to give it, which I could not do without making myself liable, and that I did not incline to do, having no Opinion either of the Honesty & Punctuality of the People with whom he proposed to traffic, or of his Skill & Acuteness in Merchandizing. I write this merely to apologize for any seeming unkindness on my part in not so promoting his Views.

You always tell me that you live comfortably; but I sometimes suspect that you may be too unwilling to acquaint me with any of your Difficulties, from an Apprehension of giving me Pain. I wish you would let me know precisely your Situation that I may better proportion my Assistance to your Wants. Have you any Money at Interest, and what does it produce? Or do you do some kind of Business for a Living? If you have hazarded any of your Stock in the above mentioned trading Project, I am afraid you will have but slender Returns. Lest you should be strait[ened] during the present Winter, I send you on a Corner of this Sheet a Bill of Exchange on o[ur] Cousin Tuthill Hubbart for Fifty Dollars, which you can cut off and present to him for Payment.

The Barrel of Flour I formerly mention'd to you as sent, was not then sent, thro' the Forgetfulness or Neglect of the Mercht who promised to send it. But I am told it is now gone, and I hope will arrive safe.

I received your late Letter with one fro[m] my dear Friend Mrs Greene, and one from [my] good Niece your Daughter; all which I h[ave] at present mislaid, and therefore cannot now answer them particularly, but shall as soon as I find them.

My Love to all our Relations & Friends, and believe me ever

Your affectionate Brother

B FRANKLIN

"The shameless Impudence of the wretch"

[Printed first, and hitherto only, in Duane, *Letters to Benjamin Franklin*, pp. 162-166, without the final sentence; here printed entire from the manuscript in the American Philosophical Society. This letter contains the most consecutive account of Peter Collas to be found in Jane Mecom's letters. The original manuscript breaks off abruptly, and it is not known how much is missing.]

MY DEAR BROTHER   Boston Janr 8—1788

I never mean to Decive you by Any thing I write but your Penetrating Eye Discovers the smallest simtom & the Remotest consequences I do indeed Live comfortable, (but can not Indulge such a childish disposition as to be Runing to you with every complaint when I know it will give you Pain.) I have a good clean House to Live in my Grandaughter constantly to atend me to do whatever I desier in my own way & in my own time, I go to bed Early lye warm & comfortable Rise Early to a good Fire have my Brakfast directly and Eate it with a good Apetite and then Read or work or what Els I Pleas, we live frugaly Bake all our own Bread, brew small bear, lay in a litle cyder, Pork, Buter, &c. & suply our selves with Plenty of other nesesary Provision Dayly at the Dore we make no Entertainments, but some Times an Intimate Acquaintance will come in and Pertake with us the Diner we have Provided for our selves & a Dish of Tea in the After Noon, & if a Friend sitts and chats a litle in the Evening we Eate our Hasty Puding (our comon super) after they are gone;

It is trew I have some Trobles but my Dear Brother Does all in His Power to Aleviat them by Praventing Even a wish, that when I Look Round me on all my Acquaintance I do not see won I have Reason to think Happier than I am and would not change my Neighbour with my Self where will you Find one in a more comfortable State as I see Every won has ther Trobles I sopose them to be such as fitts them best & shakeing off them might be only changing for the wors.

about a year after you left me at Philadelphia I went to Rhoad Island and lived with my Granddaughter Greene till she had Borne four children, very happily, but she Died, her Husband Invited me to continue with Him but I chose to come to Cambridg to my Daughter, it happened to be at a time when it was soposed he [*interlined*: her husband] had got much by Privetearing but in a short time after I got there I found He had Hiered money on Intrest to Live on, which was then Near Expended, I all the while let them have money for nesesaries and it was acounted as Pay for my board, but there was no Prospect of beter doings he going Dayly to Boston to seek for Busnes and finding none I asked why He did not git a House & Remove ther He said he could not, I sopose for the same Reason that he could not git cridit at Philadelphia. I then got this

House cleard as soon as Posable & concluded to come & live in it   He by writen Agreement to Give me my Board for the Rent

we came in the midle of winter and about April by some means or other He made out to go a sort of a Traiding Trip to Novescoci staid there a grat while & came back with litle I should first have tould you that when we were about to move His Landlord declared we should [not?] carrie away any thing till he was Paid His Rent which was 2 year behind, he tould me of it but all the Ansure I gave him I was no Expence to them   Afterwards Collas came and askd me to be bound for Him   I tould him I would not but I would lend Him a consolodated note I had out of our Treasurie of fourteen Pounds some shillings which with twelve Dolars he had of me before he settled the Afair so that we were premited to come away, after the Novescoci Afair He Staid at home a long time at last got to be master of a Vesel belonging to frenchman who was shut up for Debt most of the Time He was Gone as soon as he Returnd & they settled there Voige the French man went off & Collas was out of Busnes again. after a long time He got another Vesel for the West Indies from such Owners as I hoped would keep Him in ImPloy but he staid much longer than was Expected & never wrot a line to His owner the whol Voige he said there was no need of it for He was consigned to another there who did write the consequence was he was Dismisd Emediatly & never Earnd a peney for Nine months him self & a boy by that time all he had Earnd was Gone my Debpt still Increceing besides many others I thought it Absolutly nesesary to Secure there nesesary furniture Least it should be Atached by some other creditor & got him to make it over to me. He then Run in Debt, to all who would trust him & Patchd up this Traiding Voige, was to sell all & return in two months with the Produce of all there Efects he stayd seven made no remitances sent his wife in the time a bill of fivety Dolars which if it was Right she should receve She was cheated off he thinking she had recd it came home to help Eate it & brought another small bill but not a farthing Returns for any of the Ad-venturers how could they Expect it he said the Goods were not sould most he had sould was on credit and he could not git the Pay, & he had left all in the Hands of a nother Person who had Provd Him self a Vilan if he himself was Honest

this being his case I trembled at Every knock at the Dore least it should be some officer with demands on him. I at lenth tould him he had no Right to live without Labour any more than another man he was strong & Able & if he could not git to be master of a vesel he must go mate. He should not chose to do that Nither. I tould him the Expences of the Famely when he was at home were Doble to what they were when he was absent & that if I continued to spend as I now did I should have not for my own soport he acknoliged it all & went back to the same Place. but the shameless Impudence of the wretch to go to Philadelphia and make such aplication to you was beyond my conception

"A Fall on the Stone Steps"

[Here first printed from the letter-press copy in the Library of Congress. In spite of excuses to his sister, Franklin had written a few letters in his own hand between January 21 and April 8 of that year. "Aunt Pope" was Bethshua Folger Pope, an elder sister of Franklin's mother.]

DEAR SISTER,   Philada. April 12. 1788.

A whole severe Winter has now past without our hearing from one another how we have passed it. I hope you have done it comfortably. In the beginning of January I had a Fall on the Stone Steps leading into our Garden, which sprain'd my Wrist and right Arm up to the Shoulder. This disabled me long as to writing, it being but lately that I have recovered Strength enough in it to hold a Pen longer than to write my Name. I have been and continue pretty well in other respects, Thanks be to God for the same, and all his other Mercies.

The Bearer being an Inhabitant of Boston, & offering kindly his Services, I embrace the Opportunity of renewing our Correspondence with the Spring and hope soon to receive a Line from you, acquainting me with your Welfare. His name is Pope, and he tells me his Family is originally from Salem, where I remember we formerly had an Aunt Pope. I heard her spoken of when I was a Child, but do not recollect having ever seen her. Do you know whether she left any Children? for if she did the Bearer is probably our Relation. I am as ever

Your affectionate Brother

B FRANKLIN

[*In the margin*] This Family is all well, and present their Dutiful Respects.

"*Imagining & foreboding*"

[Here first printed from a copy of a copy, now in the Harvard University Library. A copy had been found among the papers of John Bromfield, in Bromfield's hand, and this copy was copied for Sparks by Eliza S. Quincy, May 13, 1850. Saying "I shall take care to make it as small a one to you, as possible," Franklin no doubt had in mind the provision of his will, signed on July 17 of that year, which left Jane Mecom his Unity Street house in Boston and an annuity of £50. Oliver Smith was a noted Boston apothecary, who lived in Milk Street, kept his shop in Cornhill, and in 1784 had taken a leading part in restoring and beautifying the Common, damaged during the Revolution. N. B. Shurtleff, *A Topographical and Historical Description of Boston*, pp. 325-326.]

DEAR SISTER.   Philadelphia. May 31. 1788.

I received your letter of the 5th inst. by Mr. Hilliard, in which you mentioned your sufferings last winter by imagining & foreboding that some Sickness or misfortune had befallen me. It may not be amiss to allow ourselves beforehand the enjoyment of some expected pleasure, the expectation being often the greatest part of it, but it is not so well to afflict ourselves with apprehensions of misfortunes that may never arise. Death, however is sure to come to us all, and mine cannot now be far off, being in my 83d year; but that may be to me no misfortune, and I shall take care to make it as small a one to you, as possible. This family is all well, and join in love to you and yours.

Inclosed is a letter to Mr Oliver Smith, who on your present-
ing it will pay you twenty dollars, which please to accept from
your loving brother

B. FRANKLIN.

"*I cannot bare my Brothers Displeasure*"

[Here first printed from the manuscript in the American Philosophical
Society. The letter of May 31 from Franklin, which his sister first
thought of as written in anger and then was not sure it was, had been
brought to Boston by Timothy Hilliard, minister in Cambridge, who
had gone to Philadelphia with a letter of introduction from Jane
Mecom's pastor John Lathrop. Franklin, writing to Lathrop on May
31, said: "I am glad my dear sister has so good and kind a neighbor. I
sometimes suspect she may be backward in acquainting me with circumstances in which I might be more useful to her. If any such should occur
to your observation, your mentioning them to me will be a favor I shall
be thankful for." The letter concerning Peter Collas which had not been
shown to his wife was that from Franklin of December 11, 1787.]

Boston June 25 1788

DEAR BROTHER

I have recd your Leter by Mr Hilliard and I see you are
Angry with me and I cannot bare my Brothers Displeasure, I
am Anxous for your Life it is true, but also for your Sufferings
hear as I had Reason from my own Expearance of a fall from
the Same Place, the Efects of which I felt for some years, but
is it posable my Dear Brother can think my concern for Him
is mearly for my own Soport, can he not see that I am Sensable
he has alreddy done for me beyond all posable Expectation
from me & does he not know that my gratfull hart has no grater
Pleasure than she feals in hearing of his Health and Vertues,
I think he does, but I know all I have opertunity to convers
with on the Subject See it.

I See I have given you Just cause of offence in not shewing
my Daughter your Leter concerning her Husband but she was
in such a State of boddy & mind at that time I could not; (and
what I have wrot about it I have forgot) I therfor when
she was Affected at seeing me Shed Tears on Reading your
Leter Determined to shew it to her & she says she is sincearly

glad he did not git any goods there as it must have Increeed his Difeculties & that she had not any suspicion of his makeing such an Atempt.

I have now got over the Restrant I had in writing to you as she comonly sees my leters, & hope for the continuance of yours to me & tho I nither fear Death as a misfortune to me I wish to Live long anouf to receve from you a conviction by your Returning to your former Stile of writing to me that you have forgiven my offence whatsoever it is, for it would be Terable to me to Emagin I had lost my Dear Brothers Affection while I remane in this Life.

I shall send your order on Mr Smith & dont Doubt of Recveing it & thank you for it with the same Gratitude & sincerity I have ever done for yr numerous & Amaizingly grat and undeserved Benifits and am as Ever yr Affectionat Sister

JANE MECOM

I am glad you have wrote to Dr Lathrop he has been hear & shewd me yr Leter I thank you for the Affectionat concern you there Expres for me.

July 1st   I have recd the money from Mr Smith

I wrote the above the Day After I receved yours but on Reading it several times since I bigin to Doubt whither you were Angry or no, if you were not Pray dont let this make you so, but Impute all to a weaknes of mind depraved by *my* Old Age which was never very strong, I am not Positive that you Recved the Long Leter I wrote you by Post in which I acknolaged the Recept of the fivety Dolars I only took it for Granted Pray let me know in your Next

my Love to all

J M

"We dispared of her Life"

[Here first printed from the manuscript in the American Philosophical Society. Jenny Mecom, whose life had been "dispared of," was still alive in 1859 at the age of ninety-four. Duane, *Letters to Benjamin Franklin*,

p. 4. The New York *Directory* for 1786 shows that Cox & Berry, referred to by Jane Mecom, had already become Berry & Rogers, merchants, Hanover Square. The "Neibour Mrs. Walker" who had sent Jane Mecom a "Billit" was the widow of Thomas Walker, a Montreal merchant whom Franklin and the other commissioners of the Continental Congress had met on their mission to Canada in 1776. Mrs. Walker had traveled with Franklin as far as Albany on the way home. Her request was written out in a letter to Jane Mecom which is in the American Philosophical Society, undated, and in the *Calendar of the Benjamin Franklin Papers*, IV, 224, conjecturally, and wrongly, assigned to circa June 1776. The request said that when Charles Carroll and Daniel Chase, Franklin's colleagues on the commission, left the Walker house in Montreal they took with them some small articles of plate and two plated saucepans. (Jane Mecom thought that Mrs. Walker ought to have "mend"—that is, mentioned—"the Perticulars of Plate" in more detail.) These had never been returned, and Franklin was requested to obtain them and forward them to Mrs. Mecom's address. Jane Mecom's present letter to her brother had been entrusted to Sarah Franklin Davenport's grandson in New York, as the superscription indicates.]

DEAR BROTHER   Boston Sept 5th—1788

It seemes long to me since I heard from you, & I have Suffered a Sore tryal since I wrot to you, in the sicknes of my Grandauter Jenny who is my constant Atendant and comfort, for Six weeks my Exercise of boddy & mind was so sevear I had scarse time to think of any thing Els for Eight & forty hours we dispared of her Life her Phisicion said Afterwards tho he had long Practice he had never a Patient with all the Simptomes of Death on them as she had that Recovered, but thank God she is again about House & we have hopes of a Perfect Recovery.

I my Self held out bravely & we had the Asistance of a number of kind friends & Providence so ordered it that there was nothing thought nesesary for her Relief or comfort but what it was in our Power to Procure & administer Imediatly, O my God I never did Distrust thy Kind Providence & thou art continuealy conferming me in that Dependance upon Thee.

Cousen Rodgers Informd me of this opertunity His Son

who now Lives at New york is going to Philadelphia in about a month   Prehaps I may write by him, but if I Should not as I doubt not but he will call on you I would now Inform you that He is a Reputable young man was brought up a merchant has been a Number of years a Princeple in Partnership with Cox & Berry, & has Acquiered somthing conciderable, has married in England a Reputable young Lady with a Prity Litle Fourtin has all ways been good to his Parents His mother you know was Sister Davinports Daughter.

My Neibour Mrs Walker has made a Request to me which I could not Refuse & shall Inclose you her Billit I think she ought to have mend the Perticulars of Plate but Prehaps she did not know, she is Left very Destitute Exept she can Recover her thirds of there Estate at Canedy & she says she does not know how to git there. they were forcd to sell most of there Plate and Furniture to Live on,

my Daughter & my Self continue in beter Helth than Usal Prehaps the Extroidenary Exercise has been servicable to us.

I am as Ever, my Dear Brother

your Affectionat Sister

JANE MECOM

Recd Under Cover and Forwarded by
     Your most Hum Serv
New York Sep 15 1788 John Rogers

"The Finest children in Philadelphia"

[Printed first, and hitherto only, in Duane, *Letters to Benjamin Franklin*, pp. 169-171. Here printed, with some corrections, from the manuscript in the American Philosophical Society. Franklin's missing letter of September 16 seems to have announced the birth of Sarah Bache, born on the 12th of that month. She was her mother's eighth and last child. The third, named Sarah, had died in infancy. The "serts of yr son Williams the Governors Knolton" were former servants (named Knowlton) of Governor William Franklin, and were now employed by John Rogers, grandson of Sarah Franklin Davenport.]

Boston Sept 26—1788

DEAR BROTHER

I recved yours of the 16th by cousen John Williams wherin you so Early give orders for the cash for my wood, but I had Drawn on you for it some Days before & had got it in I felt ashamed that I apeared in such a hurry but there was a talk of Letting the Small-Pox spread in the Town & that wood would be Dearer & that then was the best time ad that you had said I was allways too Difident & would be Pleasd with my Doing as I did so I sopose it will be of no consequence that I had it not to Recive of the other Person. & have now to thank you for yr never ceasing bounty.

When I see you did not mention Perticulars concerning the Exeptions to your Health, I feared they weree Larger than Useal, and I now understand you have had a severe Ill turn; I can with sinserity say as our Friend Catey said when she heard of yr fall I should have been Glad to have born Part of the Pain to have Eased my Dear Brother they tell me you are much beter may God Continue you so, I Rejoyce with you & the other happy Parents in the Increace of yr Famely it is said Mr Bache is Remarkable for haveing the Finest children in Philadelphia, how much Pleashure must they give you when you have Ease to Enjoy it, I long to have Every won to Kiss & Play with that I see Pass the Street that Look clean & healthy. you did not give me the Name, I think this is the Seventh Mrs Bache may make up my Number Twelve tho she did not begin so young. My Love to them all God Bless them says there Affectionate Aunt, & your Affectionat and Gratfull Sister

JANE MECOM

Does nurs Ashmead yet Live
& nurs her if she does
Remember me Respectfuly to her.

This cousen Rogers of ours who is to take the care of this to New york has got som serts of yr son williams the Governers Knolton, & his wife, & Daughter Ever since the Governer dismisd them & finds them such faithfull servants & they give

[314]

them such high Wages he says they will make them selves a Litle fortune I know it will Pleas you & Temple to hear it it does me I Asure you.

"Some chuse to Embelish the Language"

[Printed first, and hitherto only, in Duane, *Letters to Benjamin Franklin*, pp. 171-173; here printed from the manuscript in the American Philosophical Society. "Mr Cushing" was Thomas Cushing Jr., son of Franklin's old friend who had died the preceding February. The missing words indicated by dots in the fourth paragraph are on a corner torn from a page. The "Accadimy" mentioned was presumably Franklin College at Lancaster, Pennsylvania, to which Franklin contributed £200. The first mass was said in Boston by the Abbé de la Poterie in the chapel in School Street on November 2, nine days before Jane Mecom reported this contemporary gossip. The "French man Mr Nancreene" was presumably the "Mr. De Nancrede" who during 1788 advertised, in the *Boston Gazette & Country Journal*, his "Evening School in the French language (Conversation, etc.)." By "the Paquitt william Daaggett" was meant the packet (mail) boat commanded by the master of that name. The story of the Frenchman and the poker had been told by Franklin in the *Pennsylvania Chronicle*, March 23, 1767, in a letter To the Printer reprinted from the London *Gazetteer* of January 15, 1766. Pretending to be an Englishman, Franklin had there commented on an alleged rumor in London that the British government intended to make the Americans pay for all the stamps they ought to have used while the Stamp Act was in force; "and that since they are highly favour'd by the Repeal, they cannot with any Face of Decency refuse to make good the Charges we have been at on their Account. The whole Proceeding would put one in Mind of the Frenchman that used to accost English and other Strangers on the Pont-Neuf, with many Compliments, and a red hot Iron in his Hand; *Pray Monsieur Anglois*, says he, *Do me the Favour to let me have the Honour of thrusting this hot Iron into your Backside?* Zoons, what does the Fellow mean! Begone with your Iron or I'll break your Head! *Nay Monsieur*, replies he, *if you do not chuse it, I do not insist upon it. But at least, you will in Justice have the Goodness to pay me something for the heating of my Iron."* The story had been revived in an "Anecdote" published in the *Massachusetts Centinel* of Boston on November 1, 1788, ten days before Jane Mecom reported it to her brother. "Dr. Franklin," the *Centinel* said, "as agent for the province of Pennsylvania, being in England at the time the parliament passed the stamp act for America, was frequently applied to by the ministry for his opinion respecting the operation of the same, and assured them the people of America would never submit to it. The act was nevertheless passed, and the event shewed he had been right. After the news of the destruction of the stamped paper had arrived in England, the ministry again sent for the Doctor, to consult with him, and concluded with this proposition: That if the Americans would engage to pay for the damage, done in the destruction of the stamped paper, &c. the parliament would then repeal the act. To this the Doctor answered, that it put him in mind of a Frenchman, who having heated a poker red hot, ran into the street, and addressing an Englishman, he met there, 'Hah, monsieur, voulez vous give me de plaisir et de satisfaction, and lete me runi dis poker only one foote up your backside.' 'D - - n your soul,' replies the Englishman—'Welle, den, only so far,' says the Frenchman,' pointing to about six inches of the poker.' 'No, No,' replies the Englishman—'d - - your soul; what do you mean?'—'Well, den,' says the Frenchman, 'will you have de justice to paye me for de trouble and expense of heating the poker?'—'No, d - - n me if I do,' answered the Englishman, and walked off."]

Boston Nov 11—1788

My Dear Brother

I am uneasey when I do not hear from you often but all I have heard Lately I think give me Reason to fear yr Health is Declining & that you Suffer a Depreshon on yr Spirits, and I know you must Feal gratly to have it Perciveable by bystanders, o that I could mitigate yr Pains or greafs, but in steed of beeing able to do that, I & mine have allways been a grat cause of care & troble to you tho Blessed be God you have never discovered any thing but the Pleasure of doing good, & Heaven has Blessd you in the deed, tho you Suffer what is the Lott of all men in a grater or Lessor Degree Pains & Sickness, the consciousnes of the Rectitude of the motives of all yr Actions Boath for Priviat and Publick Benifitt will Soport your Hope for a more Blessed State to all Eternity where my Dear Brother we shall meet, tho may it be yet many years before you are calld off this Stage in Favour to the Inhabitants, who will gratly mis you when Ever that time comes you dont know how it Refreshes me when I hear you are chearfull, Mr Cushing has not been to see me as I understood by Mr Williams you Desired Him, & prehaps that is the Reason because he left you Ill with the Goute, I hope it soon left you & you have Recovered yr Former cheerfullnes

I fear you have not Recved two Leters a wrot you since the

Boston No. 21 – 1788

My Dear Brother—

I did not reve the Leter you [d Aug 31] you
wrote me when John williams was at Philad.ᵃ
till the Day befor yester Day, I then heard of
its being Advertizd on the List in the News
-paper by won who come out of the country
but had I rec.ᵈ it Emediatly as it happened I
Sopose things would have remand Feuġt y they
are, for I had Drawn the Bill & Got in
"the wood a Day or two before He come
Home he knowing that I have heard nothing
more about it, I have already wrot you con-
-cerning it But Perhyps you do not git all I
write.

your greevious fit of Sickness has
distres'd me but alas I can do nothing to Aleviate
it all I can do is to wish and Pray for your
Returning Health & that you may at all
times have the Spirit of God comforting &
Sustaining you, that will be a Sopport when
flesh & hart Fails.

I and my Famely are as useal Togging
on in the old Frack Remember me
Affectionatly to all that Love and comfort
you & Long may you feal the Influence of
Such Blessings Prays yo.ʳ Sister

Jane mecom

Jane Mecom to Benjamin Franklin, November 21, 1788

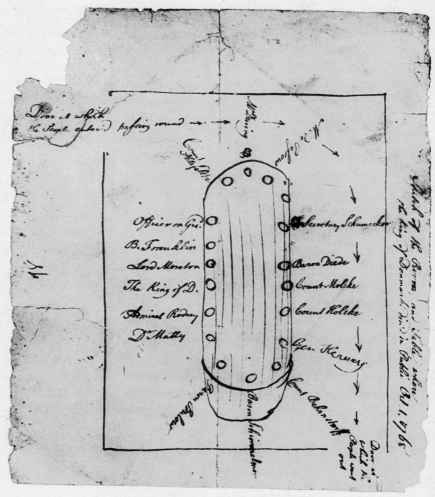

"Form of Table K of Denmark"

date of your Last by cousen John williams dated Sept 16 throw
the hands of Mr John Rodgers of New york won containd a
Billet from Mrs Walker Desiering me to Inform you of Several
thing which I thought best to send in her own words, tho I feard
it was somthing Presuming in me as well as her I was unwilling
to Refuse her as she is a widdow and distitute. in the other I
congratulated you on the Increece of yr Famely & the Health
& Happines they Injoy, I hope it continues, & to let you know
I had Drawn a Bill on you for my wood before John williams
came Home & so had no ocation to take it of him, if those Leters
came to your hand be so good as to let me know it when it is
convenant for you.

I sopose you see our News papers where you see how fond
our People are to say something of Dor Franklin I beleve
mostly to do him Honour but some chuse to Embelish the
Language to there own fancy the Storey of the French man with
the Pocker was a good story when you tould it but it apears to
me there was none of your D - - n . . . . . . you Souls in it.

What we had in the Last . . . . . . of yr Present to the . . . . . .
Accadimy was truly Honourable . . . . . . Like your self & Re-
joices the hart of every good Person O that our all Bountifull
Benifactor would give you Ease as well as such Noblenes of
mind.

we have at Length got a Mase house which the Roman
catholicks asembled Last Sabath, the Preist has married a Buti-
full young Garl the only child of her mother a widdow to
French man Mr Nancreene who some say has a wife in Philadelphia the Poor Garl did not understand a word the Preist
said but Nancreene told her He would cut his Throt if She did
not comply

Excuse my writing you such Stuff I sopose it is but litle more
than you have to bare with in all my Leters tho writen from a
hart full of sincear Gratitude of your Affectionate Sister

JANE MECOM

I write this to go by the Paquitt william Daaggett

[317]

"A Soport when flesh & hart Fails"

[Here first printed from the manuscript in the American Philosophical Society. Franklin's letter of August 31, now missing, had been advertised by the Boston post office as uncalled for, but Jane Mecom had not seen the notice and did not know of it till she was told by some "won who came out of the country."]

MY DEAR BROTHER   Boston Nov. 21—1788

I did not recve the Leter Dated Aug 31 you wrote me when John williams was at Philadela till the Day befor yester Day, I then heard of its being Advertizd on the List in the Newspaper by won who came out of the country but had I recd it Emediatly as it happened I sopose things would have remand Jeust as they are, for I had Drawn the Bill & Got in the wood a Day or two before He came Home he knowing that I have heard nothing more about it. I have alreddy wrot you concerning it But Prehaps you do not git all I write.

your Grevious fit of Sicknes has distresd me but alas I can do nothing to Aleviate it all I can do is to wish and Pray for your Returning Health & that you may at all times have the Spirit of God comforting & Sustaining You, that will be a Soport when flesh & hart Fails.

I and my Famely are as Useal Jogging on in the old Track Remember me Affectionatly to all that Love and comfort you & Long may you feal the Influence of such Blessings Prays yr Sister

JANE MECOM

by Capt. Young

"My way of telling the story"

[Printed in part in W. T. Franklin's edition of his grandfather's *Private Correspondence*, pp. 115-116, and first in full, from a manuscript now missing, in Sparks, *Works*, x, 366-367, from which it is here reprinted. That Franklin wrote almost no letters through July, August, September, and the first three weeks of October can be accounted for by the fact that, at least from August on, he was writing the third, and longest, part of his Memoirs, or *Autobiography*, about which on October 24 he wrote to both Louis Le Veillard in Paris and Benjamin Vaughan in London that the narrative had now been brought down to 1756 or Franklin's fiftieth year.]

MY DEAR SISTER,   Philadelphia, 26 November, 1788

I received your kind letter of the 11th instant. The two former ones you mention, I had answered, though it seems the answer had not reached you. If it has finally miscarried, I will look for the letters, and answer them again.

I am sorry you should suffer so much uneasiness with tears and apprehensions about my health. There are in life real evils enough, and it is a folly to afflict ourselves with imaginary ones; and it is time enough when the real ones arrive. I see by the papers that to-morrow is your thanksgiving day. The flour will arrive too late for your plum puddings, for I find it went from hence but a few days since. I hope, however, it will be with you before the winter shuts up your harbour.

I never see any Boston newspapers. You mention there being often something in them to do me honor. I am obliged to them. On the other hand, some of our papers here are endeavouring to disgrace me. I take no notice. My friends defend me. I have long been accustomed to receive more blame, as well as more praise, than I have deserved. It is the lot of every public man, and I leave one account to balance the other.

As you observe, there was no swearing in the story of the poker, when I told it. The late new dresser of it was, probably, the same, or perhaps akin to him, who, in relating a dispute that happened between Queen Anne and the Archbishop of Canterbury, concerning a vacant mitre, which the Queen was for bestowing on a person the Archbishop thought unworthy, made both the Queen and the Archbishop swear three or four thumping oaths in every sentence of the discussion, and the Archbishop at last gained his point. One present at this tale, being surprised, said, "But did the Queen and the Archbishop swear so at one another?" "O no, no," says the relator; "that is only *my way* of telling the story."

This family is all well at present, and join in love to you and yours, with your affectionate brother,

B. FRANKLIN

"Teaching Children to read"

[Printed first, and hitherto only, in Carl Van Doren, *Benjamin Franklin's Autobiographical Writings*, p. 768, and here printed again from the manuscript in the American Philosophical Society. The books in question had been printed in 1788 by Benjamin Franklin Bache in his new printing house under his grandfather's eye. They were actually reprints of four English books by Anna Letitia Barbauld: *Mrs. Barbauld's Lessons for Children, from Two to Four Years Old, Mrs. Barbauld's Lessons for Children of Four Years Old, Mrs. Barbauld's Lessons for Children from Four to Five Years Old, Mrs. Barbauld's Lessons for Children of Five Years Old*. Each of them, the title-page read, *With alterations, suited to the American climate*. Since Jane Mecom's letter of January 10, 1789, is missing, it is not quite sure what her difficulties had been with the books, which were evidently sent to her for her benefit as well as Benjamin Bache's. Franklin seemed to think that Jonathan Williams Sr., to whom the books had been consigned for Jane Mecom, was remiss. A letter from Jonathan Williams Jr. to Franklin, dated September 6, 1789, and in the American Philosophical Society, helps clear the matter up. "I have attended to the affairs about the Books sent for the use of aunt mecom, and found in the first place that one of the Bundles containing the whole of the 3d Volume had been stolen, the Thief finding only good books instead of banknotes left them in the cellar of an old uninhabited House, there they were found & published (advertised) by a constable in order to discover the owner, before they were missed by our family. The number was reduced by being scattered & damaged, what remained were given to a Bookbinder at 1/3 for binding, so that at my return I found the 1. 2. & 4th Volume in sheets as at first, and about 60 of the 3d Volume bound in marble. I have ordered all the remainder to be bound in the same manner & on the same conditions, which I am told are the customary ones: I then propose to agree with a Bookseller at a certain price, as high as I can, in this way: He to give a note of hand payable at a given time for the Amount, but conditioned that if any of the Books remain unsold when the note becomes due, they shall be received again at price cost. I think it will be well to try this experiment before they are sent back, especially as I believe that when the Books are better known they will be in fresh demand as to make our Booksellers apply to Benjamin for more. This is a Business which I do not very well understand but I will do the best I can. I find it vain to attempt an absolute sale, & by making the conditions of return I may perhaps get them off at a higher price: The few that have sold went for 4/ this Curr(enc)y per Dozen."]

DEAR SISTER   Philada. Feb. 22. 1789

I received yours of Jan. 10. expressing the Difficulties you meet with in Disposing of the Childrens Books. It was not my Intention you should have any Trouble with them, as you will see by the enclos'd Copy of my Letter to Coz. Williams. By his sending them to you, it seems as if there was some Misunderstanding between you, or that he is tired of rendring you Services.—If you do not find some Bookseller who will buy them of you in the Lump, I think you had better pack them up, and send them back again. It is reported here, that they had like to have been sold to pay Freight and Charges, which if true, implies that Cousin Williams refus'd to meddle with them, and he has not answered my Letter, which confirms my Suspicion of there being some Miff. As they are not like to produce any thing for you, you may draw on me for forty Dollars, and your Bill shall be duly honour'd.—As to the Books themselves, how much soever your People may despise them, they are really valuable for the purpose of teaching Children to read. The largeness and plainness of the Character, and the little Sentences of common occurrence which they can understand when they read, make them delight in reading them, so as to forward their Progress exceedingly. Our little Richard not yet 5 Years old, has by their Means outstript his Brother Lewis in Reading, who is near nine. I am ever your loving Brother

B FRANKLIN

The Copy of my Letter to Cousin Williams may be a Curiosity to you, as it is not written but taken from the Original by a Press.

"Poor Laco"

[Printed first, and hitherto only, in Duane, *Letters to Benjamin Franklin*, pp. 174-175; here printed from the manuscript in the American

Philosophical Society. "Laco" was the pseudonym used by Stephen Higginson in a series of articles in the *Massachusetts Centinel* in February-March of that year. They bitterly attacked the character of John Hancock, who was candidate for governor and was elected.]

MY DEAR BROTHER   Boston Apr 2d—1789

we have had a Long cold winter since I receved yr Last & I have heard nothing Emediatly from you since, but I got so composed by yr chearfull maner of writing then, & the Information you gave me of your beter Health that I have Lived on it all winter; & have not Indulgd a Disponding thought, I still hope it has been well with you, I wrot you wonce to Inform you I recved all you sent me, & all I could about the Books which I sopose mr Williams has also Informed you, all who see them Admire the Tipe, the Paper & method of Printing, as well as the maner of Instruction; but whatever is the cause of the Bookbinders not Incuridging them I know not but think they will take affter a litle while.

I do not Pretend to writ about Politics tho I Love to hear them & you must have seen the Squabling we have had all winter about Election we have had Poor Laco chalkd on the fences as hangd & Damd but his wisdom keeps Him Secreet.

My own Famely has been as Usal some times sick & some times well & I have keept my self all winter at Home & not Exposed my self to the cold. fare well Dear Brother may God Bless you & all yr chilldren Prays your affectionat Sister

JANE MECOM

I have a Litle viseter hear from Rhoad Island Sally Greene my Daughter Flaggs Granddaughter she begs me to put her Name in the Leter for she says you dont know you have got a Grat Grand Nice   I had a Leter from our friend Catey Greene by her she all ways Inquiers after her Good *Old* Friend which is a Term you will like in some sense.

"Something to wean us from this World"

[Printed first, and hitherto only, in the *New England Historical and Genealogical Register*, XXVII (1873), 250, from a fragment copied from the original by Josiah Flagg and now in the New England Historic Genealogical Society.]

Philadelphia July 1 1789.

As to the Pain I suffer, about which you make yourself so unhappy, it is, when compared with the long Life I have enjoyed of Health & Ease, but a Trifle.

And it is right that we should meet with Something to wean us from this World and make us willing, when called, to leave it:

Otherwise the parting would indeed be grievous I am ever

Your affect Brother B. F.

"At the back of the north Church"

[Here first printed from the manuscript in the American Philosophical Society. It appears that Franklin's letters sent in care of Jonathan Williams Sr. were more likely to be delivered than those addressed merely to Unity Street. What Jane Mecom here calls the "north Church" was the Episcopal Christ Church which faced Salem Street with its back toward Unity Street; and is not to be confused with the Congregational Second Church, or Old North, which after the destruction of its meeting house by the British for firewood during the occupation had been merged with the congregation of the New Brick Church in Hanover Street, under the pastorate of John Lathrop and with the name Second Church. The *Massachusetts Centinel* for July 22, 1789, had a death notice which read: "In this town, Mrs. Susannah Hubbart." No notice has been found of the death of a Mrs. "Larrabe," but she is presumed to have been related to the Abigail Larrabee who was a member of the Second Church and who appears in the Boston *Directory* for 1796 as "huckster, Unity Street." The "Grat Grand Daughter" mentioned in the postscript was Sarah Flagg Greene's daughter Sarah, and the "Grand Daughter" was Benjamin Mecom's daughter Jane.]

DEAR BROTHER   Boston July 23—1789

I recd yrs Dated 1st of the month on the 19 was much Rejoycd to see yr hand writing & that you Retain such Fortitude under your severe Afflection you can hear of few that in your circumstances would be able to make such comparisons, but many who would Rather say I have mett with such & such Dificulties & been trobled all my Life I think it is now time I should Live at Ease this is comon where People meete with nothing Extrodnary.

I beleve cousen Jonathan did not Desire to sett things in a wrong light nor did he say yr Illnes was the cause of yr not writing [*interlined*: it was an inferanc of my own] but as they were writing to him from his Fathers & I knew him to have such grat Rever’nce & affection for you that he would certainly know, I therefore Desiered him to let me know he tould me he thought yr Disorder Increecd & leaft you fewer Intervals than before & that he began to think it would happy for you to have gone thro the operation in Europe as you were Blessd with such an Exelent constitution which sett you twenty years younger than comon People.

Cousen Williams came Emediatly Down to me with the Leter as he allways does & finding you had sent so many that I had not Recd he went in the morning to the office & they made a shift to finde two but that Dated may is not to be found they say they did not know there was such a Person in town & that they had Advertizd them, but this is not the first time they have served me so by several, they are too Lazey to Look, for my Grandaughter has asked at the office many times in this space of time; I have formerly been tould there were Leters there for me & when I sent there was none, send a second time by some won who would stand by them & force them to Look & got them, I have sent a second time after your may Leter but without succes.

there misconduct has Led you in to a grat mistake concerning cousen Williams there never was a Person more Assiduous in there Indevours to oblige than he has all ways been to me, we never had a word with Each other that had the Least Apearance of Miff & he says he can Lay his hand on his Haert & Say it has allways been the gratest Pleasure to him to have it in his

Power to Render me any Service & it has allways apeared so to me. with Regard to the Books he says it was not an Hour after he know of such a consignment to Him before he sent & fecthed them to his House & I am satisfied has done all he could to Dispose of them Properly, he shewed me yr Leter as soon as he recd it but the Books were never sent Except a small Parcel I sent I sent for to try my own Ingenuity but found it Deficent.

our People some of them at Least have the good sense to Percive all the good Properties in them that you mention but there few that have the good Reading of there children so much at Heart as to think it nesesary for them to Inspect it them selves, yet I beleve no won who has Ever seen them that can dispise them, but the Book selers & Printers have so many hundreds of an Inferer sort on hand which they sell for all most nothing with the Prity Picturs, & I think there is a nother cause they are Jealous of a young Printer who so far surpases them in the Art & accuracy of his Profeshion & are not willing to Incuridge him by Disposeing of his work.

Mr Williams says he was to blame in not writing at the Time but that he was very unwell & his mind so discomposed with troble he could not sett about writing to you, He is Realy Greved that you should have such a suspicion of him, the taking coppies of Leters as you do is a grat convenancy as well as curiousity, I have no conception how it can be done so Exactly & not deface the origenal.

Sucky Hubart was buried the night before Last & we have a Neibour now lies Dead the Last of the old sett of Inhabatants of this street Mrs Larrabe there has been won or too Deaths in Every house in the street since we came to Live hear ours only Exempt, we have no Reason to Expect it will Remain so Long. our Friend Mrs Greene Recved yr Leter she calls it a Dear good Leter & says she will bring it when she comes to see me in the fall.

I beleve I wrot you Mr Collas came home in the fall he had not been able to Procure traid or a Vesel to his mind was with-

out Biusnes to his mind & after he had been home about a fortnight he Entered a board a Brig as mate workd constantly &
Dilegently till She was Reddy to sail & went in her to the west
Indies & South Carolino he was not able to leave his wife more
than twenty Dolars when he went a way which was but small
to suply the Famely and his wife with what nesearys she wanted
for her own Person, all but that has lane wholly on me Ever
since (till about a fourtnight ago he sent her a small suply from
carolina) this being the case I was carefull to Live very frugaly
& have not ben much straitned till the very Instant her mony
came, but I had unavoidably contracted a large Debpt for my
Grandaughters Sicknes a year ago which I have not been able
to Pay She was Extreemly sick I had very nearly lost her
& it is a valuable Life to me the Docter was Exeding atentive
for two months & she Recovered but has never been so strong
& hardey since, on this acount & to Indulg my self in a few litle
things I will thankfull accept the Forty Dolars as I see no
Proble Prospect of Paying this Dept without it & Debpt is a
Burden I cannot bare I owe no won Els a Farthing Exept a
litle back Rates for my Pue at meteing which I have not been
askd for it, I shall have more Intrest Due the Last of next
month & Mr williams Pays me his Punctaly but I comonly have
it apropreated in my mind to some Perticular uses, that with
your ocational Bounty Enables me to live comfortable, and
credibly & I know it would Greve you if I did not as wel as
have Just cause to be Angrey & think I had misconducted, & I
should be Ashamed of my self for Every won knows that my
Brother is a Never failing sours of Good to his Ever Gratfull
Sister   JANE MECOM

my Grat Grand Daughter is ten years old she
Desiers her Duty may be Remembred to you as
does my Daughter & Grand Daughter. if my Dear
Brother would add to his Super scriptions of
his Leters at the back
of the north Church I
might git them the Redier

"The Word Excellency does not belong to me"

[This letter, except for a few words of the opening sentence, was first published by Sparks, *Familiar Letters*, pp. 216-217. It was printed by Smyth, *Writings*, x, 33-34, from the defective letter-press copy in the Library of Congress. It is here printed, more correctly, from the letter sent, which is now in the American Philosophical Society. Franklin, having ceased to be President of Pennsylvania, was no longer to be called His Excellency.]

DEAR SISTER,   Philada Augt 3. 1789

I have receiv'd your kind Letter of the 23d past, and am glad to learn that you have at length got some of those I so long since wrote to you. I think your Post Office is very badly managed. I expect your Bill, & shall pay it when it appears.—I would have you put the Books into Cousin Jonathan's Hands who will dispose of them for you if he can, or return them hither. I am very much pleas'd to hear that you have had no Misunderstanding with his good Father. Indeed if there had been any such, I should have concluded that it was your Fault: for I think our Family were always subject to being a little Miffy.—By the way, is our Relationship in Nantucket quite worn out?—I have met with none from thence of late Years who were dispos'd to be acquainted with me, except Capt. Timothy Fulger. They are wonderfully shy. But I admire their honest plainness of Speech. About a Year ago I invited two of them to dine with me. Their Answer was that they would—if they could not do better. I suppose they did better, for I never saw them afterwards; and so had no Opportunity of showing my Miff, if I had one.—Give my Love to Cousin Williams's and thank them from me for all the Kindnesses to you, which I have always been acquainted with by you, and take as if done to myself. I am sorry to learn from his Son, that his Health is not so firm as formerly. A Journey hither by Land might do him good, and I should be happy to see him.—I shall make the Addition you desire to my Superscriptions, desiring in Return that you would make a Substraction from yours. The Word Excellency does not belong to me, and Dr will be sufficient to distinguish me from my Grandson. This Family joins in Love to you and yours, with

Your affectionate Brother

B FRANKLIN

"Your Reproof of my Miffy temper"

[An excerpt from this letter, the passage "I was a Litle suspicious . . . another time," was printed, though considerably altered, in Sparks, *Works*, x, 395n.; and the whole letter, except for the fourth and fifth paragraphs, is in Duane, *Letters to Benjamin Franklin*, pp. 175-178. It is here printed from the manuscript in the American Philosophical Society. Of the "Nantucket Relations" mentioned in the letter, Abisha Folger ("Fougre" in Jane Mecom's spelling) was a grandson of Abiah Folger Franklin's brother Eleazer; for thirty years he represented his town in the Massachusetts Assembly, and may have boarded with his Cousin Mecom during the legislative sessions in Boston. He had several brothers and several sons, one of whom was Captain Timothy Folger, mentioned elsewhere in notes in this volume. The "Jenkinss" in question were Seth and Thomas Jenkins, of the Folger kin, who left Nantucket for Providence, and later were leaders in the Association of Proprietors who after the Revolution founded the town of Hudson on the Hudson (North) River as an inland port then available to vessels of any existing draught. Seth Jenkins was mayor from 1785 to 1793, and then Thomas till his death in 1808. *Columbia County at the End of the Century* (Hudson, New York, 1900), I, 297-300, 407; II, Appendix paged separately, 19-20. Kezia Folger Coffin, who "Took to the wrong side" during the Revolution, was one of the outstanding Nantucket women of her time. She was a great-granddaughter of Eleazer Folger, married to John Coffin in October 1740. In April 1779 a raiding party of seven (or eight) small boats manned by loyalist refugees from New York landed on the island and carried off rebel property, including goods valued, the loyalists said, at "£10,666, 13s, 4p lawful money," from the Jenkins warehouse. Thomas Jenkins set the value of his lost spermaceti oil, whale bone, iron, coffee, and tobacco, at "Twenty five thousand Guineas at least." He charged his cousin Kezia Coffin with assisting the loyalists in their raid. He probably made the charge in the hope of recovering payment for his property from Kezia Coffin, a wealthy woman, and others involved with her, but found that his charges against the others might amount to treason, and so withdrew his complaint in March 1780. Jane Mecom's version of the complicated story is tolerably accurate. The best account of it, on the whole, is in Alexander Starbuck, *The History of Nantucket* (1924), pp. 205-229.

R. A. Douglas-Lithgow, *Nantucket A History* (1914), pp. 227-228, says that Kezia Coffin's life and character were drawn upon for the heroine of J. C. Hart's novel *Miriam Coffin; or, The Whale Fisherman* (1834), the earliest American novel about whaling; and that she died on May 29, 1798, of a fall downstairs. The "Neibour Jemmy Leach" was James Leach, son of James Leach and Sarah Coffin, who was of the Nantucket connection. Jemmy Leach was then twenty-seven, and presumably lived with his father in Bennet Street. *New England Historic and Genealogical Register*, XIX, 255.]

MY DEAR BROTHER   Boston August 29—1789

O that I could with Truth begin with the old fashioned stile I hope this will find you well, but that I dispare of Except I could confine all to your Intellets which thank God Apear as sound as Ever, which must suply you with a Source of Entertainment beyond what comon mortals can Expearance, I have Even my self in times Past Lost the snse of Paine for some time by the Injoyment of good Company.

yrs of Aug 3 by cousen Jonathan was very Pleasing the knoing you had recd mine so soon & was Pleasd with the contents gave me grat satisfaction & the sight of Him whom I Love like a child was a grat Addition, He is Truely a worthy man.

you Introduce your Reproof of my Miffy temper so Politely, won cant a Void wishing to have conquered it as you have if you Ever had any, that disagreable Temper.

I have Drawn as you Premited Recd the money and Paid of my Docr Bill, I added the thirty Dolars for the wood which you give me orders constantly to Draw thinking it would be Less Troble to you & fearing cousen Jonathan may not have the succes he wishes & Endevours about the Books & shall Take in the wood next week.

I have also Recved the Leter you sent by our Neibour Jemmy Leach.

I was a Litle suspicious wither Exellency was acording to Ruel in Adress to my Brother at this time but I never write any my self & of Late Because He Lives nearer than cousen Willims have sent them to Dr Lathorps who is very obliging to me, &

I thought must know what was Right & gave no Directions about it, but shall another time. He de[siers] allways to be Respectfully Remembered to you when I write.—I beleve there are a few of our Nantucket Relations who have still an Affection for us, but the war time which made such Havock every where Devided & scatered them about, those I was most Intimate with were Abisha Fougre; His Brothers, & Sons, Timothy won, the Jenkinss & Kezia Coffin, who was many years Like a Sister to me & a grat friend to my children. She sent me two very Affectionat Leters when the Town was shut up Inviting me to come to Her & She would Sustain me that was her word, & had I Recd them before I left the Town I should certainly have gone, but a Wise & Good Providence ordered it otherways. She Took to the wrong side & Exerted Her Self by Every method she could devise Right or rong to Accomplish her Designs, & Favour the Britons, went in to Large Traid with them, & for them, & by mis-management & not suckceding in her Indevours has sunk Every Farthing they were Ever Posesed of & have been in Jail boath Her Husband at nantucket & her self at Halifax. She was allways thought to be an Artfull wooman, but there are such Extrordinary Stories tould of her as is hard to be leved.

the two Jenkins' Seth & Thomas stood in the same Relation to us & alwaye very Friendly & Afectionat to me they were at Pheladelphia when I was there you spok something for them at Congres) they were men of considerable Property & had a grat quantity of Oyl in there stores when a Vesel Belonging to the Tories went Down & Robd them of all, it was Proved that Kezia Pointed it out to Them, the owners Prosecuted her & she was Brought up to Boston to stand tryal, but I think there was no final condemnation at Court, she says they could not find Evedence. they say the Evedence was so strong that had they suffered them to come in to court it would have hangd her & so they supresd it not being willing it should Proceed so far they settled at Provedence a few years whose Famelies I used to stop at when I went backwards & forwards & the were very kind to me. sent there sons to carrie me from there to my grandsons therteen miles in ther [chais?] & Every other obliging thing in there Power, but Afterwards they settled a Township on North River I forgot the Name there is a City & Thomas Jenkins is the Mayer. I have not seen Ither of them since. I dont know if they come to Boston if they do they do not know where to find me, & tho the Foulgers some of them sail out of this Place I Beleve it is the same case with them for I have not see a Nantucket Person since I Lived hear, I have a Next Dore Neibour who Lived there wonce & I now & then hear somthing of them by Him

I know I have wrote & speld this worse than I do sometimes but I hope you will find it out   Remember my Love to yr children & Grandchildren tell my Niece Bettey that I sent her Pocket Book to Mrs Coffins Daughter & I dont doubt she had it but she was at Halafax.

I am yr Affectionat & Gratfull Sister

JANE MECOM

"That you may Injoy grater Tranquility"

[Here first printed from the manuscript in the American Philosophical Society. The "Dutch Dr" was Jan Ingenhousz, Franklin's friend and correspondent in Europe, who had invested money in America through John Williams.]

Boston Sept 10—1789

DEAR BROTHER

I would not let this opertunity by cousen John williams Pass without leting you know I am as well as usal tho I have nothing Els to write haveing wrot by Post about ten Days Past & Informd you of my Desposing of the Bill & all other circumstances, I have never heard any thing from Him about the acount that was in the Dutch Dr Favour & by yr maner of writg I soposed you did not much Expect it but I thout it might be well to tell you now he is going there. I dont know if I tould you that Coll Ingorsol is Dead his first wife was our Sister

[331]

Sarahs Eldest Daughter he has Left two Daughters won in England.

I only my constant wishes for the mitigation of yr Pains that you may Injoy grater Tranquility & a firm Asureance of Eternal Happines, Remember me Affectionatly to yr Famely yr affectiont sister

JANE MECOM

"Sometimes better, sometimes worse"

[First printed in Bigelow, *Works*, x, 149-150, from the letter-press copy in the Library of Congress. Here printed from the letter sent, of which only the signature is in Franklin's hand, now in the Yale University Library. The letter was addressed to Unity Street and carried by John Williams.]

DEAR SISTER, Philada Octr 19—1789

I received your kind Letter of September the 10th by Cousin John Williams. I have also received & paid your Bill, and am pleased that you added to it on Account of your Wood; As to my Health it continues as usual, sometimes better, sometimes worse; & with respect to the Happiness hereafter which you mention I have no Doubts about it, confiding as I do in the Goodness of that Being who thro' so long a Life has conducted me with so many Instances of it.—This Family joins in best Wishes of Happiness to you & your's with

Your affectionate Brother

B FRANKLIN

Mrs Mecom

"Chearfull & as merry"

[Here first printed from the manuscript in the American Philosophical Society. The sermon which Jane Mecom sent was, it is supposed, *A Sermon, on sacred musick, preached at a singing lecture in Braintree, on the 21st of May, 1788, from Ephesians v. 19. . . . By Ezra Weld, v. d. m. pastor of the second society in said town.* Springfield: Printed by Ezra Waldo Weld. 1789. (Title from Charles Evans, *American Bibli-*

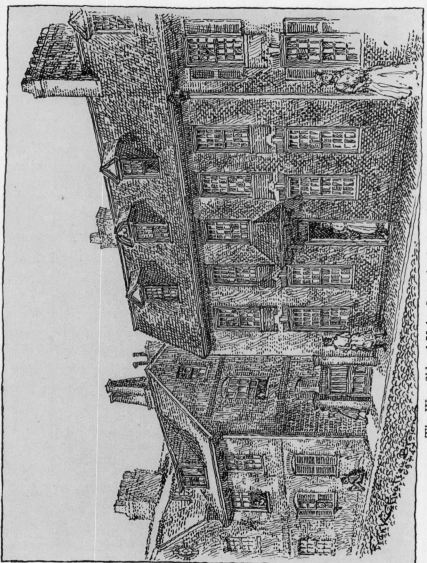

The West Side of Unity Street in the late eighteenth century

Christ Church

ography, Vol. 7.) "My Niece Mrs Williams," the wife of Jonathan Williams Sr., died the following March. Major Samuel Shaw, aide to Major General Henry Knox during the Revolution, sailed on the first American vessel sent to Canton, in 1784-1785, and served as the first American consul in China from 1786 to his death at sea in 1794. The "bit of Paper" enclosed, with the question about Baron Trenck, is in another hand, presumably that of the unidentified acquaintance who applied through Jane Mecom to her brother for the desired information.]

MY DEAR BROTHER   Boston Nov 24—1789

your kind Letter of Octr 19 Informs me your Health is not wors & I am Dubly Pleasd with hearing by cousen John williams that you are as chearfull & as merry & seem as well as Ever at times & that you say yr Pains in comon are not so Exquesat as Formerly, your fierm Rielience on Gods Goodness must keep you chearfull & Enable you [to?] Bare much, I felt happy to hear you had not been Exercised with the Universal Sicknes & hopes your not going abroad might secure you from it, it would be Dubly greveous to you as Coughing Shocks Every Part of the boddy I have had it Prety severly & am not quite got over it. I think cousen Jonathan Tould me before he went away He had wrote you all about the Litle Books that Parcel calld Himns were Returnd to me & shall wait your Directions, & I have a Near Neibour Capt Obediah Ritch who makes very Raped Trips to yr Place I think he has made four in the cours of this sumer & fall he will be a handy Person to send them by if you chuse to have them sent some other time as he is now going in a few Dayes, I have a strong Inclination to send you a Sermon on Sacred musick tho my Friend Dr Lathrop & his wife tell me the Dr has been ust to Read composition on the subject so much beter it may not apear to him as I Expect, it Pleasd me & I know you will give it a Reading & tell me if it is not a Pritty Discorse from a country minester who has Every circumstance to Depres him.

I am Desiered by an Acquantance to beg the favour of yr opinyon of what this bit of Paper contains my Niece Mrs Williams is very sick but I am tould is Rather beter yester day. Since I wrot thus far Capt Ritch has calld & tould me he has a Barrill Flower on Board for me thank you Dear Brother you are allways mindfull of all Posable wants I my have & suply them before I can feel them.

Our good old friend Mrs Greene has been to see me to our Grat mortification she has some how mislade your Leter she thought she Brought it but finds her Self mistaken.

This Goes by Major Shaw marchant of the New Ship going to the East Indies   He is a Border of Cousen williamss   Remember my Love to Children & granchildren in which my Famely Joyns as in all Dutyfull Respect from yr Affectionat Sister

JANE MECOM

My Daughter Desiers to be
Perticularly Remembred to you

[*The bit of paper*]

> Whether the General
> Circumstances
> mentioned in the
> History of *Baron Trenck*
> are Founded on Fact

"*I think my self very Lucky*"

[Here first printed from the manuscript in the American Philosophical Society.]

DEAR BROTHER   Boston Novr 25—1789

I think my self very Lucky that you happened to Light on my Nibour to send the Flower by for tho you have been Equaly good at all times in sending it we have all ways found it very dificult to find it when it came. this is a courtious obliging man is a Near Nebour came & tould me he had it on Board & sent it up to me without any troble,

I send the Leter also by Him for tho I was tould Major Shaw was going to Philadelphia I hear since he goes no farther than Newyork, yours Affectionatly

JANE MECOM

favor'd by Capt Rich

"*I am told it is fine*"

[Here first printed from a copy, in another hand, in the Library of Congress. "Our little Girl" was Deborah Bache, then eight years old.]

Mrs Mecom   Phil. Nov. 30. 1789
DR SISTER

I wrote you by Cousin Jn Wms which I hope you have recd. I have since sent you a Barrel of Flour for your Winter Puddings. I am told it is fine & wish it may prove so. This Family is in good Health & joins in love to you. Our love to Cousin Williams & Family

I am ever

yr affec. Brother

B. FRANKLIN

P.S. Our little Girl has had the small Pox very favorably by Inoculation & is perfectly recover'd.

Mrs Jane Mecom

"*It is* founded *on Falsehood*"

[The second and third paragraphs of this letter were first printed in William Temple Franklin's edition of his grandfather's *Private Correspondence*, 1 (1817), 125 (later called Volume II of W. T. Franklin, *Memoirs of the Life and Writings of Benjamin Franklin, LL. D.*); and so reprinted by subsequent editors. It is here first printed entire from the manuscript in the American Philosophical Society. The cod's "Sounds" for which Franklin asked were the fish's swimming bladders. The famous, and fabulous, autobiography of Baron Trenck appeared in German (*Des Friedrichs Freyherrn von der Trenck Merkwürdige Lebensgeshichte*) in 1786-1787 and in French (*La Vie de Frédéric*

Baron de Trenck) in 1789. Translated from German into English by Thomas Holcroft in 1788-1789, *The Life of Baron Frederic Trenck* was for years extremely popular, and it was published in Philadelphia in 1789. The English edition contained the misinformation about Franklin that had been omitted from the French. "From the year 1774 to 1777," Trenck said, "I chiefly spent my time in journeying through England and France. I was intimate with Dr. Franklin, the American minister; also, with the Counts St. Germain and Vergennes, who made me advantageous proposals to go to America; but I was prevented accepting them by my affection for my wife and children." (Here quoted from the Dublin edition, 1789, II, 72.) What Franklin had formerly written on music "in one of my printed Letters" was the letter "To Mr. P. F. Newport, New England" in Franklin's *Experiments and Observations on Electricity* (London, 1769), pp. 473-478. This letter was written while Franklin was in England, at some time between 1757 and 1762.]

DEAR SISTER,   Philada Decr 17—1789

I received your kind Letters of the 24th & 25th past,—I am glad the Flower has got to hand so soon. As this Capt. is so well disposed towards us, tho' I did not know him, before, I shall for the future endeavour to look out for him, when I have any thing to send you. And as I imagine it might be some Pleasure to you, if you knew of any thing agreeable to me, that you could send me, I now acquaint you, that I have lately wished to regale on Cod's Tongues and Sounds; and if you could now and then send me a small Keg of them, containing about two Quarts, they would be very acceptable & pleasing to your affectionate Brother.

You tell me you are desired by an Acquaintance to ask my Opinion whether the general Circumstances mentioned in the History of Baron Trenck are founded in Fact; to which I can only answer, that of the greatest Part of those Circumstances, the Scene being laid in Germany, I must consequently be very ignorant; but of what he says, as having past in France, between the Ministers of that Country, himself & me, I can speak positively, that it is *founded* on Falsehood, and that the Fact can only serve to *con*found it, as I never saw him in that Country, nor ever knew or heard of him, any where 'till I met with the mentioned History in Print, in the German Language, in which he ventured to relate it as a Fact, that I had with those Ministers solicited him to enter into the American Service.—A Translation of that Book into French has since been printed, but the Translator has omitted that pretended Fact, probably from an Apprehension that its being, in that Country, known not to be true, might hurt the Credit & Sale of the Translation.

I thank you for the Sermon on sacred Music; I have read it with Pleasure—I think it a very ingenious Composition. You will say this is natural enough, if you read what I have formerly written on the same Subject in one of my printed Letters, wherein you will find a perfect Agreement of Sentiment, respecting the complex Music, of late, in my Opinion, too much in vogue, it being only pleasing to learned Ears, who can be delighted with the Difficulty of Execution, instead of simple Harmony and Melody.

The Loss of my Letter to Mrs. Greene is not very great, as I could send you one of our Press Copies, if you were desirous of seeing it.

This Family joins in best Wishes to you & yours, with

Your affectionate Brother

[*signature missing*]

"*This Day my Dear Brother compleats his 84th year*"

[Printed first, and hitherto only, in Duane, *Letters to Benjamin Franklin*, pp. 179-180. Here printed from the manuscript in the American Philosophical Society.]

Boston Janr 17—1790

This Day my Dear Brother compleats his 84th year you can not as old Jacob say few and Evel have they been, Exept those wherin you have Endured such Grevious Torments Laterly, yours have been filld with Enumerable Good works, Benifits to your felow creaturs, & Thankfulnes to God; that notwithstanding the Distressing circumstance before mentioned, yours must

[337]

be Esteemed a Glorious Life, Grat Increece of Glory & Happines I hope Await you, may God mitigate your Pain & continue yr Patience yet many years for who that Know & Love you can Bare the thoughts of Serviving you in this Gloomy world.

I Esteem it very Fortunet that cousin John willims is Returning to Philadelphia again & will take a Keg of souns & Toungs by Land as there is no vesel Likly to go till march I have Tasted them & think them very Good shall as long as they are Aceptable send you fresh & fresh as I have opertunity.

I am as you sopose six years younger than you Are being Born on the 27th March 1712 but to Apearance in Every wons sight as much older.

we have Hitherto a very moderat Winter but I do not Atempt to go abroad my Breath but Just Serves me to go about the House without Grate Pain & as I am comfortable at Home I strive to be content.

Remember my Love to your children

from yr Affectionat Sister

JANE MECOM

"*I am as Ever your Affectionat Sister*"

[This last surviving letter from Jane Mecom to her brother is here first printed from the manuscript in the American Philosophical Society. Since Franklin's letter of January 29 is missing, it is not clear what "the Performance of my Nephey William" was.]

DEAR BROTHER   Boston febr 6—1790

The winter has been so moderate that my Neibour Capt Rich is going to take a Trip to Philadelphia a month sooner than he Expected. I would not Neglect the opertunity to Inform you I have been & am as well as Useal, that I wrot by cousen John Williams the 17th of Janr & sent a Keg of Toung, which I hope you have recd & find agreable I do not send any by Capt Rich because there is none to be had but the verry same & it may be by Next trip I may be able to Procure some Newly come in.

I hope to hear when Cousen williams Returns that you have not been worse & that you still keep up your Spirits

I am as Ever your Affectionat Sister

JANE MECOM

I had Just finshed my Leter to go by my Neibour to morrow when Mr John williams sent me yours of Janr 29 I was very Sure there was Danger of yr being disgusted with the quantity I sent but was over ruldd but determined not to send more at a time for the future than you mentioned, I hope how you have been able to Regale on them more than wonce as I beleve they are so throwly Preserved they will Reman sweet all the cool wether. I Bless God for all the Intervales of Ease you have & am your

Affectionat Sister

J M

I am Pleasd with the Performance of my Nephey William it Looks to me to be Accuratly Done must have taken a grat Deal of time & is worth Preserveing haveing Just Recved it I have not had the Pleasure of Shewing it to beter Judges.

[*Apparently in Jane Collas's handwriting*] Mrs Collas desires her duty to you and love to Mrs Bach

"Quite free from pain"

[Printed first, from a manuscript now missing, in Sparks, *Works*, x, 425-426, from which it is here reprinted. In the three weeks free from pain of which Franklin spoke he had written his famous letter about his religious beliefs to Ezra Stiles, on March 9, and on March 23 the spirited and witty parody *On the Slave-Trade* which was published in *The Federal Gazette* in Philadelphia on March 25. Since the manuscript is missing, it is not clear what Franklin meant by "the crooked lines"; but the last thirteen lines of the original manuscript of his Memoirs, as he always called his *Autobiography*, slant upward toward the right as if he might have been writing them too in bed. After this letter to Jane Mecom, Franklin is known to have written only one other, that to Thomas Jefferson of April 8. He died on April 17. His sister Lydia,

[339]

married in 1731 to Robert Scott, died in 1758; but the present investigation has found nothing about her daughter, even the date of her death.]

MY DEAR SISTER,   Philadelphia, 24 March, 1790.

I received your kind letter by your good neighbour, Captain Rich. The information it contained, that you continue well, gave me, as usual, great pleasure. As to myself, I have been quite free from pain for near three weeks past; and therefore not being obliged to take any laudanum, my appetite has returned, and I have recovered some part of my strength. Thus I continue to live on, while all the friends of my youth have left me, and gone to join the majority. I have, however, the pleasure of continued friendship and conversation with their children and grandchildren. I do not repine at my malady, though a severe one, when I consider how well I am provided with every convenience to palliate it, and to make me comfortable under it; and how many more horrible evils the human body is subject to; and what a long life of health I have been blessed with, free from them all.

You have done well not to send me any more fish at present. These continue good, and give me pleasure.

Do you know anything of our sister Scott's daughter; whether she is still living, and where? This family join in love to you and yours, and to cousins Williams, with your affectionate brother,

B. FRANKLIN.

P.S. It is early in the morning, and I write in bed. The awkward position has occasioned the crooked lines.

Richard Bache to Jane Mecom

[Printed first in the *New England Historical and Genealogical Register*, XXVII (1873), 252-253; here printed from the manuscript formerly in the possession of Josiah Flagg and now in the New England Historic Genealogical Society. The name of the friend through whom the letter was sent does not appear, as it was sent under a separate cover. Jane Mecom endorsed it: "to go into the Litle Trunk."]

DEAR & HOND MADAM   Philadelphia April 19th 1790

My duty calls upon me to make you acquainted with an event which I know will be a sore affliction to your affectionate Breast. And lest the news should reach you & be communicated to you in an abrupt manner & that your tender feelings might still be more wounded, I have thought it best to inclose these few lines to a friend, who I hope will first prepare you for the shock— Amidst the affliction of a distressed Family, I am hardly connected enough to offer any consolation,—my condolence at present must suffice—and my dear Madam I do most sincerely condole with you on the loss of so excellent a friend & Brother— I have not time at present to add more, than that he died on Saturday last at 10 o'Clock at Night, he had not been long very ill, & therefore we had hardly an opportunity of informing you of it; besides we had been in daily expectation of his getting better, but nature was at last worn out—I beg of you to look upon me as your Sincere Friend, & as one who will be very happy in rendering you any Services in his Power—I am

Dear Madam

Your affectionate Kinsman

RICH. BACHE

Mrs Mecom

Jane Mecom to Sarah Bache

[Here first printed from a corrected copy, in an unidentified hand, in the Yale University Library. "Mr. Peters" was probably the Reverend Richard Peters, rector of Christ Church, Philadelphia, at the time of Jane Mecom's first visit there in the winter of 1769-1770. "Miss Bache" was Sarah Bache's daughter Elizabeth. "Mr. Hubbard" was probably Tuthill Hubbart. By "cousin John Will" Jane Mecom meant John Williams. "Jonathan and his family" were Jonathan Williams Jr. and his wife Mariamne Alexander, to whom he had been married in France in 1779. "Mr. Bohlen" has not been identified. The "two lines of a song" are really one line, "But now they are wither'd and wede all away," from an old Scottish lyric by Alison Cockburn written by her for the older tune *The Flowers of the Forest*. Richard Peters may have sung "waned" for the Scots "wede," or Jane Mecom may have misheard him.]

[341]

Boston, September 6, 1790

DEAR NIECE—It is a cordial to my heart to receive such affectionate notice from my dear brother's child. He while living was to me every enjoyment. Whatever other pleasures were, as they mostly took their rise from him, they passed like little streams from a beautiful fountain. They remind me of two lines of a song Mr Peters used to sing at your house

"But now they are withered & waned all away"

To make society agreeable there must be a similarity of circumstances and sentiments, as well as age. I have no such near me; my dear brother supplied all. Every line from him was a pleasure. If I asked questions, he did not think proper to inform me on, he would sometimes give me a gentle reproof. At other times he entirely passed it over: that I knew was always fittest for the occasion, and all was pleasure.

"But now they are withered and waned all away."

It is, however, very agreeable to me, to see there is hardly a newspaper comes out in this town without honorable mention of him, and indeed it is a fund that cannot be exhausted.

The letter you promised should follow Mr Bohlen in a few days, I think, never came to hand. If what came by Hubbard was all you intended for me, you omitted the gratifying some of my requests; but, perhaps, that is best, and I am content. I shall be highly pleased with Miss Bache's picture: the pincushion she was so good as to send me is much admired.

I hope my nephew will succeed in his undertaking of a daily paper; but it seems to me a vast one. May he inherit all his grand-father's virtues, and then he will be likely to succeed to his honours. I hope he will remember his old aunt, with a present of some of his papers, when convenient by a vessel.

I miss my friendly neighbour Rich: he goes longer voyages now.

When I sit down to write to you, I think I will try to correct my writing and spelling; but, I am grown so infirm and so indolent, the task is too arduous. If you can find out what I mean, you must accept it as it is; if not, let me know, and I will get my daughter to write for me.

I have not seen Mr Hubbard; but, when he brought down the letters, we were sitting down to dinner; he came in, but he would not dine with us, as he was engaged. I invited him and expected he would come often, but he has not: I begin to fear he will not call for my letters.

I ought to have let Mr Bache know by cousin John Will I had received the bills, but was unwell and could write no more then. I hope you see Jonathan and his family, as they greatly loved your dear Father. Pray, remember me to them, and if there are any others to whom it will be acceptable from your affectionate aunt

JANE MECOM

Mrs Sarah Bache

Jane Mecom to Sarah Bache

[Here first printed from the manuscript in the Historical Society of Pennsylvania. Benjamin Franklin Bache had begun the publication of his *General Advertiser* on October 1 of that year. The name was changed to *Aurora General Advertiser* on November 8, 1794. Jane Mecom's reference to the "mis youse of a Tempting Aple" remains a tantalizing mystery. The "cousen williams" (not to be confused with "cousen John Williams") who "was going to see His children" was Jonathan Williams Sr. His son Jonathan with his wife had settled in Philadelphia, where he began a successful career as jurist and scientist and, on the appointment of Thomas Jefferson in 1801, first superintendent of West Point. There is a copy of this letter in the Yale University Library.]

MY DEAR MRS BACHE Boston Decr 2d—1790

I have wrot twice to you & wonce to Mr Bache besides the Short Line I sent by John Williams & have never Heard whether you Recved them it is Trew they were of Litle consequence to any won but my self but that I am not willing to forego the Last was by cousen williams who was going to see His children which I thought so fine an opertunity I wrot a good deal but it seems He has Proved that the Aple that Eve Eate was not the only mischevious won the Earth was to bare, I sopose he has tould you as He wrote me that with the mis youse of a Tempting Aple my Leter to you was Distroyd, I have forgot what it containd but should be very glad to know in a Line by Post if Mr Bache recd that I wrote to Him and also beg the Favouer of Him to write me a Proper form of Adress to my Brothers Executers when I shall have ocation next month & how I Shall Direct to them for I have not a Soul to confer with on such an ocation,—

I hear my Dear Brothers will is Printed. I wish you would send me won of them when you send me Miss Betseys Picter I have not Given up that yet, I Expected to Recve it by cousen John Williams as He came by water, He has sent me won of my Nepheu Benjamins Daly Papers it Apears to me very Respectable if his Wensdays Paper fills Equaly it may soon create for him an Estate in the clouds as his Venerable Grandfather usd to say of His Newspaper Debpts, my Daughter Joyns me in Affectionat Respects to you Mr Bache & children

with yr Affectionat Aunt

JANE MECOM

Jane Mecom: Conveyance

[Here first printed from the manuscript, in a legal hand, in the Historical Society of Pennsylvania. Franklin had bequeathed his sister fifty pounds a year in his original will of July 17, 1788, and then had increased the annuity to sixty pounds in the codicil of June 23, 1789. The Boston *Directory* for 1789 gives the address of "Gardner Joseph, Esq; justice" as Bennet Street, which was in Jane Mecom's neighborhood. Gamaliel Larrabee was presumably related to the Abigail Larrabee who is listed as "huckster, Unity Street" in the Boston *Directory* for 1796.]

Whereas by the last Will and Testament of my late Brother Benjamin Franklin deceased, an Annuity of Sixty Pounds Sterling, is devised to me during my natural Life, payable out of the Interest or Dividends annually arising from twelve Shares of Bank Stock, which he held at the time of his death in the Bank

[344]

of North America, established at Philadelphia, as by his last
Will & Testament more fully appears And Whereas a subscription will shortly take place, for the purpose of establishing a
Bank under the authority of the United States of No America;
to be entitled the "Bank of the United States"—and it appears
to be the wish of Richard Bache & Sarah his Wife, to whom the
said Bank Stock is bequeathed (chargeable as aforesaid) to
transfer the said twelve Shares of Bank Stock in the Bank of
No America to the bank of the United States—I do hereby
consent & agree that the said twelve shares in the Bank of No
America as aforesaid, be sold or disposed of, and the amount
thereof vested in the Stock of the Bank of the United States, as
soon as the subscription to that Bank shall be opened, so as that
the said Stock be liable to and chargeable with the payment of
the said Annuity of Sixty Pounds Sterling, in like manner, as if
it had remained as Stock in the Bank of North America. Witness
my hand and Seal at Boston this twenty third day of June in
the year of our Lord one thousand seven hundred & ninety
one—

Signed Sealed & Deliv-
ered in presence of
Joseph Gardner
Gamaliel Larrabee   JANE MECOM

Commonwealth ⎱ Suffolk ss.   Boston June 23. 1791
of Massachusetts ⎰

Jane Mecom the subscriber of the above written Instrument
acknowledged the same to be her voluntary Act & Deed. Before Joseph Gardner Just Peace

Jane Mecom to Henry Hill

[Here first printed from the manuscript, in another hand, but signed
by Jane Mecom, in the Historical Society of Pennsylvania. Though
the letter itself is addressed to Henry Hill, it was intended for the other
executors as well: John Jay, Francis Hopkinson, and Edward Duffield.

[345]

Franklin in his will had left fifty pounds to be equally divided "among the children, grandchildren, and great grandchildren of my sister, *Jane Mecom*, that may be living at the time of my decease." In this letter Jane Mecom named five in New England and one in Perth Amboy or South Amboy, New Jersey. The remaining ten were presumably children or grandchildren of Benjamin Mecom living in Philadelphia.]

HONRD GENTLEMEN   Boston August 6 1791

I feel myself guilty of a very disrespectfull Neglect in not writing to the Gentlemen The Excecutors of my dear, Venerable, Brothers Will for so long a time.

Gentlemen whom I know he had an Affection for, and whom he confided in to comply with His desires in disposeing the Effects his Benevolence had bestowed in his Will.

The only Apology I can make is a consciousness of the insufficency of my capacity to address you in a proper manner, and my Kinsman Bache very affectionately offer'd me every Service he could do me, and I accepted his kind offer, (flattering my-Self it would allso be some easement to you) to the the Neglect of my duty and good Manners.

I ought infallible to have consulted you Gentlemen on my Signing the Transfer from one Bank to another   I am not other ways Apprehensive I have done Amiss but Shall be Strengthen'd by your approbation if your Honours Should favor me with it, and continue to receive my Legacy through his Hands if most agreeable to you.

The July payment 1791 is now due.

There is another Small Article that falls to my Posterity which I now take the Liberty to apply to you for, tho: my Daughter Seems to be the properst person to receive it.

It is the Legacy of Fifty pound sterling to be devided between the whole number, which were sixteen, liveing at my dear Brothers Death. If it could be done without difficulty, or Impropreity, I Should desire only such a part as belongs to my daughter Jane Collas, my Grand Daughter Jane Mecom, My Grandson Josiah Flagg of Lancister, and two great Grand Childran Sarah and Frank[lin] Greene, liveing at Road Island, from whom we have a power to be sent this way. My Daughter and myself will will give a full discharge for that Sum and ingage to deliver it.—All the others are there at Philadelphia accept one at Amboy, Mrs Elizabeth Mecoms Daughter Abiah Mecom.

If your Honors will favor me with an answer by Post you will very much oblig your

Humble Servt

JANE MECOM

Jane Mecom to Henry Hill

[Here first printed from the manuscript in the Library Company of Philadelphia. The letter is in another hand but is signed by Jane Mecom. Sarah Bache, to whom her father had left in his will "the king of France's picture, set with four hundred and eight diamonds," had sold all of them except "those immediately connected with the picture," which Franklin had directed to "be preserved with the same," and had gone with her husband on a tour of Europe.]

HOND SIR   Boston August 2d 1792

Mr Bache when he was about to Embark for England, wrote me by his Wife that Mr Bache, had Settled matters in such a manner with Mr Hill, that my dear Aunts Annuity . . those were her words) would be as Regularly Sent her half-yearly, as if We ware here" I received it in July, and January. I thought he would have wrote me again but he did not.

You will please now to Send it by Post, or any other way you think most Convenient which will much oblige your

Humb Servt

JANE MECOM

Jane Mecom to Henry Hill

[Here first printed from the manuscript in the Historical Society of Pennsylvania. The letter is in another hand but is signed by Jane Mecom.]

[347]

Hond Sir

I have the Satisfaction to inform you I have received your polite letter per post, containing a Bill on the Bank for a hundred and thirty six dollars, it has not yet been presented, but will Soon by a friend who is kind enough to take a little care of me, for I have no Brother, Son, nor Nephew near me; I felt Sensibly Effected at Mr Bache and Wifes departure; and am greatly obliged to you Sir for the information concerning them; it is all I have had, tho: I dont doubt my Niece has wrote tho: they have not reach'd me.—I feel great pleasure in the expectation of their returning Sooner then at first expected.

I have an opportunity tomorrow of sending to Philadelphia a few Kegs of of pickled Lobsters   I am told they are very nice, hope they will prove So and beg your acceptance of one of them.

I shall direct them to be delivered to my Nephew Mr Bache who will deliver it to you from your much obliged friend and humble Servt:

Jane Mecom

Henry Hill Esqr

Boston July 29th—93

Jane Mecom: Copy of The Chiding

[Here first printed from a manuscript in the American Philosophical Society. It is in Jane Mecom's hand, with a note at the end about the "Grat Satisfaction" she had taken in reading it. There is no indication of the date when the copy was made, but it was presumably in her later life. The missing words have been effaced by folds in the paper, one in each sheet. The "Unkl" was of course her father's brother Benjamin, who followed Josiah to New England about 1715 when Jane was three.]

THE CHIDING

Shall Heirs of God Repine
For whome best meat & wine
Is till the Last Reserved.
Shall they a foital Dearth
Fear while they are on Earth
and say they shall be starved

2

Shall these that have the hand
that all things does comand
 for there security
Shall these because they han't
what they but seeme to want
 vex & rePine & cry

3

Shall those that have the Hart
that best of things Impart
 Live Hear in Discontent
tho they have such a measure
of Inestemable Treasure
 as never can be spent

4

Rouze up sad soul & Pore
upon thy wants no more
 Let Joy be on the wing
Lay by thy mournful Plaint
Thy sad & surly [*word missing*]
 And thou His Prais shall sing

5

Let others take there fill
of Earths unsavory swill
 Reserve thine Apetite
[*words missing*] Shore
Where thou canst wish no more
 Nor want no more Delight

6

Hear thou hast but short stay
at Inn upon thy way
 this is not thy Abode

Eye but thy Journeys End
Long to be with thy friend
   Cast Toys a way that Load

7

Let Joy sit on thy Brow
Down Hill art going now
   Next stage may give the flight
From all those Earthly things
Up to the King of Kings
   In uncreated Light

8

my soul still thither bend
Thy steps all this way tend
   Thy all to this Aply
When thow art wonce got there
Past want & woe & care
   Thou'rt Blest Eternaly

this is won of my Good old Unkl Franklins Poims & tho the Poitry is not so good & some of His I have taken Grat satisfaction in Reading it

J M

Jane Mecom: Last Will and Testament

[Here first printed from the Registry of the Probate Court of Suffolk County, Massachusetts. The silver porringer marked P F M had belonged to Peter Franklin Mecom. Abigail Woodman, a member of the Second Church, appears in the Boston *Directory* for 1789 as "staymaker & man-taylor, Creek Lane"; and in the *Directory* for 1796 as "toy-shop, Back Street." Elizabeth (Sayer) Lathrop was the Reverend John Lathrop's second wife. The "white medallion" bequeathed to her was presumably the Wedgwood "Head" which Franklin had sent to his sister with his letter of February 26, 1775. In bequeathing the Unity Street house to Benjamin Sumner and John Lathrop in trust for Jane Collas, her mother was evidently securing it from the unreliable hands of Peter Collas, if he was still living. Sumner, for whom the *Directory* of 1796 gave the address "Cold lane," was married to Mary, daughter of Jacob Greene of Coventry, Rhode Island, an elder brother of Jane Mecom's grandson-in-law Elihu Greene. Of the witnesses, Martha Rob appears in the *Directory* for 1796 as "retailer, Sun Court street"; John Lathrop Jr. was the son of Dr. John Lathrop and his first wife Mary Wheatley, and was later a lawyer and poet of some distinction; Achsah Lombard has not been certainly identified, but she was possibly related to Captain Ephraim Lombard who, according to the Boston *Directory* for 1796, lived in Back Street. Of the specified legacies to the grand-daughter Jane Mecom, the bed her grandmother commonly used was no doubt the best in the house; and the "small bell mettle skillet" was probably the same as the "old Bell mettal Skillet" which had been in the kitchen of the Hanover Street house and inventoried with the estate of Edward Mecom in 1765.]

In the name of GOD. Amen — I Jane Mecom of Boston in the County of Suffolk and Commonwealth of Massachusetts, Widow; being, although weak in body, yet of sound mind and memory; well knowing that the time must arise when I shall be called upon to resign this decaying frame to its parent dust, and my spirit to the GOD who gave it; do this seventeenth day of February in the year of Our Lord One thousand seven hundred and ninety four, ordain, make and publish this my Last will and testament, in manner following.

Imprimis I give and bequeath unto my Grandson Josiah Flagg my silver porringer marked P F M, and the sum of ten pounds Lawful money.

Item I give and bequeath unto my Great-Grand children, Franklin Greene, my gold sleeve buttons, and his sister, Sarah Greene, a mourning ring, which was given me at the funeral of my kinsman Josiah Williams.

Item In consideration of the extraordinary attention paid me by my Grand daughter Jane Mecom, exclusive of her common and necessary concerns in domestic affairs and the ordinary business of the family, I think proper to give and bequeath unto her several articles of household furniture, particularly, as follows—The Bed, Bedstead and Curtains which I commonly use; the three pair of homespun sheets lately made, and the bedding of every kind used with this bed both in Summer and winter; consisting of two blankets, a white Counter pane and two Calico

bed quilts, one of which is new;—The Chest of Drawers and table which usually stand in my Chamber, and six black walnut chairs with green bottoms; also two black chairs; my looking glass which I bought of Samuel Taylor, and which commonly hangs in my Chamber; a large brass kettle, a small bell mettle skillet, a small iron pot, a large trammel, a pair of large iron hand-irons, a shovel and pair of Tongs, a black walnut stand and Tea-board, two brass candlesticks, a small copper tea kettle and one half of my wearing apparel of every kind, which I desire may be divided by Mrs Elizabeth Lathrop and Miss Abigail Woodman and any other friend whom they may chuse to assist them in the business—and also the sum of Ten Pounds L M.
Item   I give and bequeath to the said Mrs Elizabeth Lathrop a white medallion of Dr Franklin—
Item   I give and bequeath unto the Reverend John Lathrop D D and Benjamin Sumner, Merchant both of Boston aforesaid, the brick dwelling house with all the land and appurtenances of the same, situate in Unity [lane *struck out*] street, and which was given me by my late brother Dr Franklin—To have and to hold the same to them, their executors, administrators and assigns, Upon this special trust and confidence, that they shall suffer and permit my daughter Jane Collas to have, use, occupy and fully to enjoy the income, rents, profits or other emoluments arising from or out of the said house, or to dwell in, inhabit and reside therein if she chuses, for and during the term of her natural life—And I do also give and bequeath unto the said John and Benjamin all and every part of my personal estate, not herein otherwise disposed of, upon this further trust and confidence, that the personal estate now bequeathed them, shall be by them held to the sole use and advantage of My said daughter Jane Collas for and during the term of her natural life: And in case the income, rents, occupying and emoluments of, or arising out of the house and land with their appurtenances, and the use, benefit and advantage of my personal estate, as above bequeathed in trust for her, should not be sufficient to support and maintain my said daughter comfortably, or, of an

increase of expence to her from sickness or any other unforeseen contingency, [then *struck out*], I do hereby authorise and empower the said Lathrop and Sumner to give to my said Daughter any such part of my personal estate as above bequeathed to them in trust [to her *struck out*] as they shall see fit and esteem adequate to the purpose; or if they judge it most expedient, I do further authorise and empower them to hire such sum or sums of money by pledging the said house as security for the money or monies so hired, as may in their opinions be necessary to her comfortable maintenance and support.

And my Will and intention further, is that after the decease of my daughter Jane Collas all my real estate, together with what may then remain of my personal estate shall be sold by my executors, and the proceeds of the sale of them divided and apportioned in the following manner, to wit—in two parts or divisions—One part shall be divided equally between my Grandson Josiah Flagg, and my great-grandchildren Franklin Greene and Sarah Greene, children of Elihu Greene of the State of Rhode-Island, and the other part shall be equally divided between the children of my son Benjamin Mecom deceased—

Item—I do hereby constitute and appoint the said John Lathrop D D and the said Benjamin Sumner, merchant Executors of this my Last will and testament.—

In witness whereof I have hereunto set my hand and seal on the day and in the year first above written

Signed, sealed, published and declared by the said Testatrix as and for her last will and testament, in our presence, who, at her request, in her presence and in presence of each other have subscribed our names as witnesses thereto. The words "then"—"to her," being first erased, and an addition of ten pounds made to Jane Mecom's legacy from the testatrix and the word "street" interlined over the erasure of the word "lane."

} JANE MECOM

MARTHA ROB
ACHSAH LOMBARD
JOHN LATHROP JR

Jane Mecom: Inventory and Appraisment

[Here first printed from the Registry of the Probate Court, Suffolk County, Massachusetts. A notation signed by Geo[rge] R[ichar]ds Minot, Judge of Probate, and dated July 22, 1794, says that John Lathrop and Benjamin Sumner "presented the aforegoing & made Oath the same is the whole estate of said deceased except the specific legacies given by the Will of the deceased & that had come to their knowledge & if more hereafter appear they will cause it to be added & account therefor." It seems impossible to identify any of these household goods with those listed in the inventory of Edward Mecom's estate in 1765 for want of precise descriptions in either case. The expression "the other Garrett" is not clear; no garret has been mentioned before it. Since the list of furniture in the Front Chamber did not include the bed Jane Mecom had left in her will to her granddaughter Jane Mecom, and yet there was another bed there, it may be supposed that the young woman was accustomed to sleep in the same room with her grandmother. The child's desk in Jane Mecom's own room presumably had some sentimental association. The Unity Street house was unmistakably much better furnished than that in which Jane Mecom had lived in Hanover Street in 1765.]

Inventory and Appraisment of the Estate of Mrs Jane Mecom late of Boston Widow Deceased (exclusive of what is given away by Will) taken this 4th day of June 1794, by us the Subscribers, viz.

In the	8 Leather bottom chairs 12/	4.16.	
Front	2 Stuffed back easy Chairs	2. 2.	
Parlour	1 Mahogany Scallop'd tea Table	1.10.	
	a pair brass Hand Irons Shovel & tongs ..	1. 4.	
	1 Square Mahogany Dining Table	2. 2.	
	1 pr butter boats 1 pr Candlesticks plated	3. .	
	1 doz teaspoons, Punch Ladle & 2 tablespoons 10wt	3. 6. 8	
	China, Glass and Delft Ware in Beaufett	.18.	
	a Scotch Carpet	1.10.	20. 8. 8
In the	a Mahogany Beausoir	2. .	
Front	Bed, Bedstead bedding & Curtains	6. .	
Chamber	a Looking Glass (broken)	. 9.	

	a Childs Desk	. 6.	
	2 ps Carpeting	. 9.	
	An arm'd cane backed Chair	. 3.	
	4 Table Cloths, 6 pr Sheets & Six Napkins	1.16.	
	4 Pictures, Toilet Table & Brushes	. 6.	
	a Mahogany Close Stool & frame	1. .	
	5 Volumes of Books	. 6.	12.15.
in the Back Chamber	a Chest of Drawers	.12.	
	a looking Glass	1.16.	
	Bed, bedstead & bedding	5. .	7. 8.
	an old Case of drawers	. 3.	
	a Table Stained	. 4. 6	
	a Bed, bedstead & bedding	3. .	
	a Smaller ditto	2.10.	5.16. 6
	Lumber in the other Garrett		1.
In the Kitchen	Brass, Copper and Tinn Ware	2. 9. 6	
	Glass and Cooking Ware	1. 4.	
	1 Smal Mahogany Table 9/ Round ditto 12/	1. 1.	
	a Tea Table 4/6, Box with Knives & forks	. 9. 6	
	Pine Table 2/3 Flat Irons 4/6	. 6. 6	
	Hand Irons 6 Warming pann 3/	. 9.	
	Iron Ware, Bake frame, pots & Kettles	1. .	6.19. 6

Personal   £/ 54. 8. 8

Real Estate
A Brick Mansion House Situate in Unity
Street North End of Boston ....   400. .

£454. 8. 8

Samuel Ruggles ⎫
Jacob Rowe   ⎬ Appraisers
Richard W. Cooper ⎭

Jane Mecom: Notes and Securities

[With the Inventory and Appraisment in the Registry of the Probate Court of Suffolk County, Massachusetts, is a document headed "A List of Notes & Securities belonging to the Estate of the late Jane Mecom of Boston," which is here first printed. The Boston *Directory* for 1789 lists a Henry Newman as "merchant, Long-acre" and a Margaret Newman as "five doors below the drawbridge," but nothing has been found to connect them with Jane Mecom or to explain why she had lent them, or others of that name, money in 1791 on what was presumably Henry Newman's note for which Margaret Newman was security. The note of Christopher and Elihu Greene seems to represent a loan to Jane Mecom's grandson-in-law in Coventry, Rhode Island, with his brother Christopher as co-signer. Samuel Taylor has not been positively identified or connected with Jane Mecom. The "dls cts" written above the amounts of the United States notes indicates that the dollar sign ($) had not in 1794 come into general use in Boston.]

A List of Notes & Securities belonging to the Estate of the late Jane Mecom of Boston

Margaret Newman's & Henry Newmans note dated Septr 24
1791, with two years Interest endorsed thereon for   £130.0.0
Elihu & Christopher Green's note of Feby 16. 1791 for   70.
with £13.6.9 Int. endorsed
Saml Taylors note dated
27 July 1790 for   90.
  Int. due 27 July 1794 4 yrs   21.12
              ————
             £111.12

Endorsed July 30. '90   13.1.8
  4 yrs Int   3.2.4
End Mar: 22.1792   15.
  2/3 yrs Int   2.2.   33.6   78.6.0
        ————   ——
              £278.6.0

One United States Note No 307
         dls cts
  6 pr Cent Int for   82.71
One do 3 pr Ct No. 306   62.95
One do defered Stock
   No 295   41.35

Jane Mecom: Administration of Estate

[Records in the Registry of Probate, Suffolk County, Massachusetts, not only show the course of the administration of Jane Mecom's estate but also throw a good deal of incidental light on her life and persons connected with her. On May 13, 1794, three days after the funeral, Martha Rob and John Lathrop Jr. appeared before George Richards Minot, Judge of Probate, and made oath that they had seen Jane Mecom sign her will; "and that she was then, to the best of their Discernment, of a sound disposing Mind and Memory," and that they "together with Achsah Lombard" had signed their names as witnesses. The will was presented for probate by Dr. John Lathrop and Benjamin Sumner, who that day gave bond, joined with "James White Stationer Samuel Sumner Mercht all of Boston," in the amount of £5000 for the faithful execution of the will, and were accepted as executors by the Judge. They were instructed to post notices of their appointment as executors, and to advertise it in *The Independent Chronicle*, then published in Boston by Thomas Adams and Isaac Larkin. The notice and advertisements called upon "all Persons having Demands upon the Estate" to "exhibit the same" and all "Persons indebted to the said Estate" to make payment. Benjamin Sumner on July 22 made oath that he had carried out these instructions. On May 13 Judge Minot appointed Samuel Ruggles, Jacob Rowe, and Richard W. Cooper to make an appraisal of the estate, which they had completed by July 22. Dr. John Lathrop was not active in the executorship, which was in the hands of Benjamin Sumner till his death in Coventry, Rhode Island, on January 31, 1811.

The document called "The Estate of the late Jane Mecom in Account with Benjamin Sumner" in the Registry of Probate gives the cost of Jane Mecom's "funeral Charges" as £7.3.10, paid on May 13. In August Sumner paid the bill of £3.9.5 presented by Hannah Milliquet, who was a milliner at 26 Cornhill, according to the Boston *Directory* for 1796. On July 27, 1795, there was a bill for £2.2 "for Medicine &c" from Dr. Isaac Rand, a distinguished physician who had been an admitted loyalist during the Revolution but had not been molested by his fellow citizens, who admired him for his skill and kindness. On August 20, 1795, Sumner paid £2.8.9 for "Tax on Pew in New Brick"—the church Jane Mecom had attended.

Jane Collas may have continued to live in the Unity Street house for a time, but on March 14, 1796 John Floyd paid £10 rent, during that year £12 more in two payments, and £4.10 in February 1797. In 1797 George Dommett paid £30 rent, and was himself paid £1.8 "for Cleaning Cellar &c." After his death his executors paid $12.92 for rent due on February 28, 1800. On January 14, 1800, "Mr Jacob" paid $23 "on Acct of rent" and the same amount again on March 3, 1801 (the year is not clear in the manuscript). Floyd was a shipwright, Dommett a merchant. "Mr Jacob" has not been identified. "The Statistics of the United States Direct Tax of 1798, as Assessed on Boston," lists the house as owned by Jane Collas with John Barton as "occupier" (Boston Registry Records, XXII, 143), but Barton is not mentioned as tenant or credited with the payment of any rent in Benjamin Sumner's accounts. The assessed value of the property was $1,000, about half what it sold for in 1802.

During 1795 Jane Collas had £60 from the estate, which then brought in no rent, and during 1796 £34, which was £12 more than the house earned. In 1797 the house earned £35, and Jane Collas drew £62.10. No rent is entered for 1798, but she got £12.12 from Sumner and £8.14 from Elihu and Christopher Greene paid on their note; and after the change that year from pounds to dollars, $30 on July 13. In 1799 she was boarding with Jane Mecom, her niece, and on August 22 the estate paid Jane Mecom $40 "on Acct of Jane Collas's board." Jane Collas herself was paid $100 that year. In 1800 she received $96; in 1801, only $5; in 1802, $60 on August 6. Then in October the estate paid Samuel Carpenter $75.83 "for the funeral Expences of the late Jane Collas." There was a charge of $2 for "Hack hire to the funeral." Dr. Isaac Rand was paid $29 for "Medicine & attendance," and Dr. Kast $16.50. This was Thomas Kast, a physician at 18 Hanover Street, according to the Boston *Directory* for 1803. On September 7, 1803, the estate paid Martha Rob $8.43 for "sundries"; and $92 to Jane Kinsman for "Nursing Washing &c." This was Jane Mecom the granddaughter, who had been married, at about thirty-five, to Simeon Kinsman, a shipmaster, forty-seven, on February 13, 1800. *The Kinsman Family. Genealogical Record of the Descendants of Robert Kinsman of Ipswich, Mass.*, Boston, 1876, p. 69. They had no children, and Captain Kinsman died in Boston in January, 1818. His widow was still living in 1859. Duane, *Letters to Benjamin Franklin*, p. 4.

Of the securities held by Jane Mecom at her death, Henry Newman's note, co-signed by Margaret Newman, was paid, interest and principal, on August 13, 1794. After various payments of interest and principal the balance due from Elihu and Christopher Greene was paid on December 15, 1802. On that same day a "dividend" of $27.72 was received from "S. Taylor's Estate" in payment of a debt that now amounted to $231.28. Presumably Samuel Taylor had died in debt and his estate had been pro-rated among his creditors.

On that same December 15 the house in Unity Street was sold, or at least paid for in cash, for a net of $1920.75 and "Sundry Articles furniture appraized" at $88.25. Before the sale of the house Sumner, as executor, had paid to Jane Collas or for other charges on the estate more than $200 above what it had earned. When on March 17, 1806, he made an accounting to the Probate Court he had paid out $1,528.26 and had taken in $3,206.95. This left a balance of $1,678.69, which by the terms of Jane Mecom's will was to be divided in two parts: one part to go to Josiah Flagg and the children of Elihu Greene (of whom only Franklin Greene was then living), and the other part to be equally divided among the children of Benjamin Mecom. There is no record among the probate papers of the final disposition.

On May 11, 1812, after Sumner's death, Nathan Whiting of East Greenwich, Rhode Island, the widowed Mary Sumner of Coventry in that state, and Samuel Sumner of Boston gave bond for the execution of what was left of Jane Mecom's estate. Nathan Whiting, administrator de bonis non (that is, de bonis non administratis), on June 25, 1815, presented his account to the Suffolk County Judge of Probate. Whiting had sold the remaining part of Jane Mecom's public securities for $139.49 (which was in addition to the $133.83 Sumner had formerly accounted for) and had paid out $22.75 in various charges. This left a balance of $116.74, which he prayed might be "carried to the Credit of the Estate of Benjamin Sumner, decd late Executor of the Will of Jane Mecom." This appears to have been allowed by Thomas Dawes, then Judge of Probate.

The house in Unity Street was sold in December 1802 to Noah L. Lincoln, passed through various hands, deteriorated, was altered in 1899 by the addition of a third story to replace the original gambrel-roofed attic, and in 1939 was destroyed. The site of the house, No. 19 Unity Street, and of No. 21 to the south is now enclosed in a small walled garden at the Unity Street end of the Paul Revere Mall extending from Unity Street to Hanover Street. On the south wall of the Mall a bronze plaque commemorates Benjamin Franklin and says that the house formerly standing at the head of the Mall was "occupied by his sisters" without mentioning either Elizabeth Douse or Jane Mecom by name.]

INDEX

A

Academy of the Protestant Episcopal Church, 272

Adams, Abigail (Mrs. John Adams), 164

Adams, John, 16, 138, 156, 172; takes crown soap to BF in France, 199-200

Adams, Samuel, 156

Adams, Thomas, 357

Address to the Protestant Dissenters of all Denominations, An, by Joseph Priestley, 145

Adventure, American schooner, brings news of Cornwallis's surrender, 212

Ahlefeldtz, Count, 104

Alexander, Marianne. *See* Williams, Marianne Alexander (Mrs. Jonathan Williams Jr.)

All, Isaac, Philadelphia shipmaster, 8, 118, 120; visits JM, 260, 263, 271

Alliance, 203-204

Alphabet, devised by BF, 250-51, 255, 264-65; JM has difficulties with, 267; BF comments on, 273-74, 277

Ancocus, Temple Franklin's farm at, 264, 267

André, John (Major), 177

Andrea Doria, American armed vessel, 261

Anne, Queen, and the Archbishop of Canterbury, BF's anecdote of, 319

Ann Street, Boston. *See* North Street, Boston

Antigua Gazette, The, 10, 48

Appeal to the Justice and Interest of the People of Great Britain, by Arthur Lee, 145

Ariosto, 273

Arnold, Welcome, of Providence, 258

Articles of Belief and Acts of Religion, by BF, 38

Ashbridge, Mr., 169

Ashmead, Mrs., nurse in the Bache household, 119-20, 187, 314

Asworth, Captain, 136

Atkinson, John, 245

Aurora General Advertiser, published by Benjamin Franklin Bache, 342-44

Autobiography, by BF, 5, 339

B

Babcock, Henry, 209-10

Babcock, Joshua (Dr.), 78, 209

Bache, Benjamin Franklin ("Kingbird"), grandson of BF, vi, 111, 113-14, 119, 127, 129; reminds BF of his son Francis, 133-35, 137, 159-61; goes to France with BF, 169, 177, 185-86; goes to Switzerland to school, 191, 193, 197, 200, 207, 208; JM desires news of, 210, 215-16, 219-20; rejoins BF in France, 225, 227, 233, 235; returns to America with BF, 237, 239-40, 241, 268; John Vaughan speaks highly of, 271, 273; prints Mrs. Barbauld's books, 320-21; publishes daily newspaper, 342-44

Bache, Deborah, granddaughter of BF, has smallpox by inoculation, 335

Bache, Elizabeth Franklin, granddaughter of BF, 201-2, 266; her gift of a pincushion, 268, 271, 273, 331, 341-42, 344

Bache, Franklin, great-grandson of BF, vi-viii

Bache, Louis (Lewis), grandson of BF, 201-2, 321

Bache, Richard, son-in-law of BF, 15, 24; marries Sally Franklin, 98-99; visits Boston, 106-7; JM's good opinion of, 108, 111; goes to England, 113-14, 118, 120; visits BF in England, 134-35; returns to Philadelphia, 135-37, 153, 155, 163, 169-70, 176-77; JM has no word from, 183-84, 187; has had no word from France, 194, 202, 204-5; letter to, 218-19, 221-23, 240, 242, 245, 263, 267, 271-72, 277, 281, 287, 289, 294, 297; informs JM of BF's death, 20, 341, 344-46; goes to Europe, 347-48

Bache, Richard Jr., grandson of BF, 321

Bache, Sarah, granddaughter of BF, 165, 188; death of, 313

Bache, Sarah, eight and last child of Sarah Franklin Bache and Richard Bache, 20, 313-14

Bache, Sarah (Sally) Franklin (Mrs. Richard Bache), daughter of BF, 15, 20, 24, 30, 74; accompanies BF to

[361]

G

Partridge, Samuel (Captain), 152, 233-34

Partridge, Rebecca, stepdaughter of Elizabeth Hubbart Partridge, 152, 154

Passon, M. de, 104

Paul Revere Mall, Boston, 359

Pennsylvania Academy, 164

Pennsylvania Chronicle, The, 12, 118, 315

Pennsylvania Gazette, The, 170

Pennsylvania Journal, The, 92

Penny Post, The, Philadelphia paper published by Benjamin Mecom, 12

Perkins, John, Boston physician, 51, 64-65, 69

Peters, Richard, rector of Christ Church, Philadelphia, 30, 341-42

Petition of the Letter Z, by BF, 249-50, 255-57

Pierce, William, of Georgia, 293

Political, Miscellaneous, and Philosophical Pieces, by BF, ed. by Benjamin Vaughan, 210-11, 213, 217, 264

Polly, servant, 136-37

Poor Richard's Almanac, published by BF, 10-11, 28

Pope, Alexander, quoted by JM, 83-84, 243-44, 300

Pope, Bethshua Folger, aunt of JM and BF, 308-9

Poterie, Abbé de la, 315

Prat, Benjamin, 276

Price, Richard (Dr.), 275-77

Priestley, Joseph, 145

Private Correspondence, of BF, London, 1817, v

Proctor (Prockter), Mr., 137

Providence Gazette, The, 257

Public Advertiser, The, 141

Putnam, James, 157

Q

Quincy, Josiah, Jr., 152-53

R

Rand, Isaac, Boston physician, 357-58

Rand, Love Hawk. *See* Loring, Love Hawk Rand (Mrs. Caleb Loring)

Rand, William, vii

Ray Catharine. *See* Greene, Catharine

Ray (Mrs. William Greene)

Ray, Judith. *See* Hubbart, Judith Ray (Mrs. Thomas Hubbart)

Read, Deborah. *See* Franklin, Deborah Read (Mrs. Benjamin Franklin)

Reilly, James, tenant of Unity Street house, 78

Religion, BF on, 38

Replay (Ripley?), ----, son of Mrs., 137

Replay (Ripley?), Mrs., 137

Rich, Obadiah, Boston shipmaster, neighbor of JM, 25, 333-36, 338, 340, 342

Rob, Martha, 354, 357-58

Robinson, Colonel, 162

Robinson, Isaiah, Philadelphia shipmaster, 261

Roby, Henry, glazier, neighbor of JM, 25, 257

Roebuck, British ship, 167-68

Rodney, George Brydges, Admiral in the British Navy, 104-5

Roger, Captain, 137

Rogers, John, Jr., grandnephew of JM and BF, 312-15, 317

Rogers, John, Sr., nephew-in-law of JM and BF, 312-13

Rogers, Lois. *See* Kilcup, Lois Rogers (Mrs. Dudson Kilcup)

Rogers, Mary Davenport (Mrs. John Rogers Sr.) niece of JM and BF, 289-91, 313

Rogers, Mrs. John, Jr., 313

Romilly, Samuel, 293

Ross, Elizabeth (Betsey). *See* Mecom, Elizabeth (Betsey) Ross (Mrs. Benjamin Mecom)

Ross, Joanna, 59

Ross, John, brother-in-law of Benjamin Mecom, 59

Ross, John, of Elizabeth, father-in-law of Benjamin Mecom, 59

Ross, Mary. *See* Baldwin, Mary Ross (Mrs. Matthias Baldwin)

Rowe, Jacob, 335

Royall, Abigail Tailer (Mrs. Jacob Royall), 17-18, 153-54, 160

Royall, Jacob, Boston merchant, 17

Ruggles, Samuel, 355

Rules for reducing a Great Empire to a Small one, by BF, 141-43

S

Y